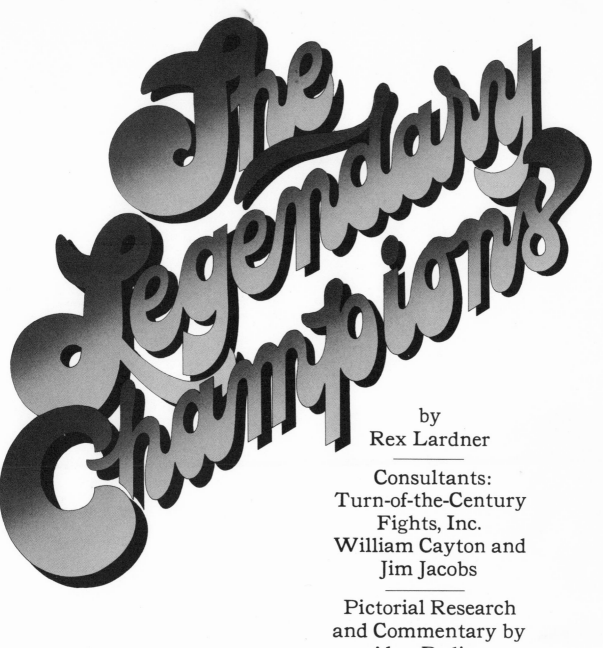

The Legendary Champions

by
Rex Lardner

Consultants:
Turn-of-the-Century
Fights, Inc.
William Cayton and
Jim Jacobs

Pictorial Research
and Commentary by
Alan Bodian

American Heritage Press

A Division of McGraw-Hill Book Company
New York   St. Louis   San Francisco   Düsseldorf
London   Mexico   Sydney   Toronto

For Martha, Rex, Mike, Lon

American Heritage Press makes grateful
acknowledgment to the following persons for
their generous help in providing pictorial
material from their collections: Alfred
Di Lauro, Mark Dittrick, Peter Heller,
Jim Jacobs, Justin Kerr, Willard Manus.

The quotation on page 110 from *The Roar of
the Crowd* by James J. Corbett, G. P. Putnam's
Sons. Copyright 1924 by James J. Corbett,
copyright renewed 1953 by Mrs. James J.
Corbett.

Book design by Ira Teichberg

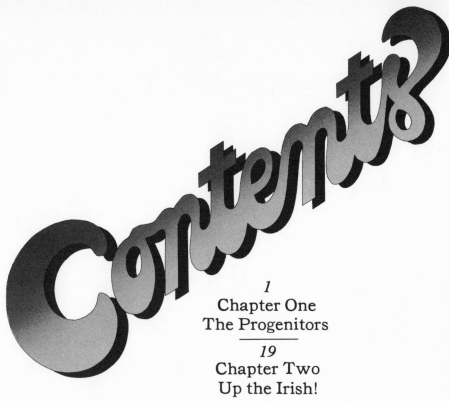

Contents

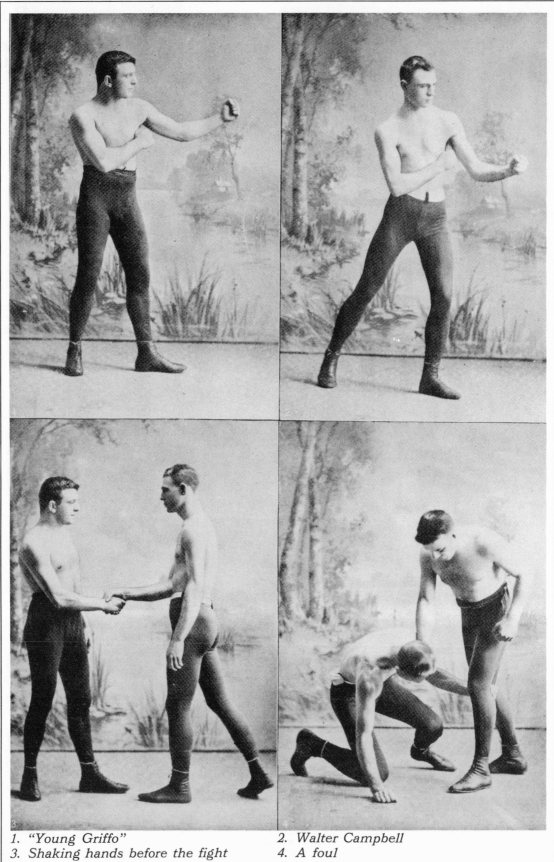

1. "Young Griffo"
2. Walter Campbell
3. Shaking hands before the fight
4. A foul

5. Left hand lead and guard   6. Same reversed
7. Duck and counter low   8. Same reversed

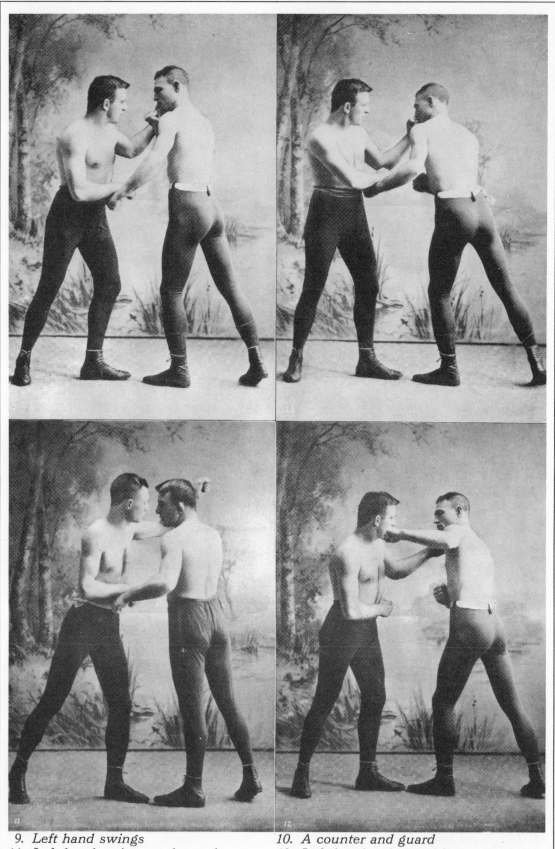

9. *Left hand swings*
10. *A counter and guard*
11. *Left hand swings and guards*
12. *Left hand swings without guards*

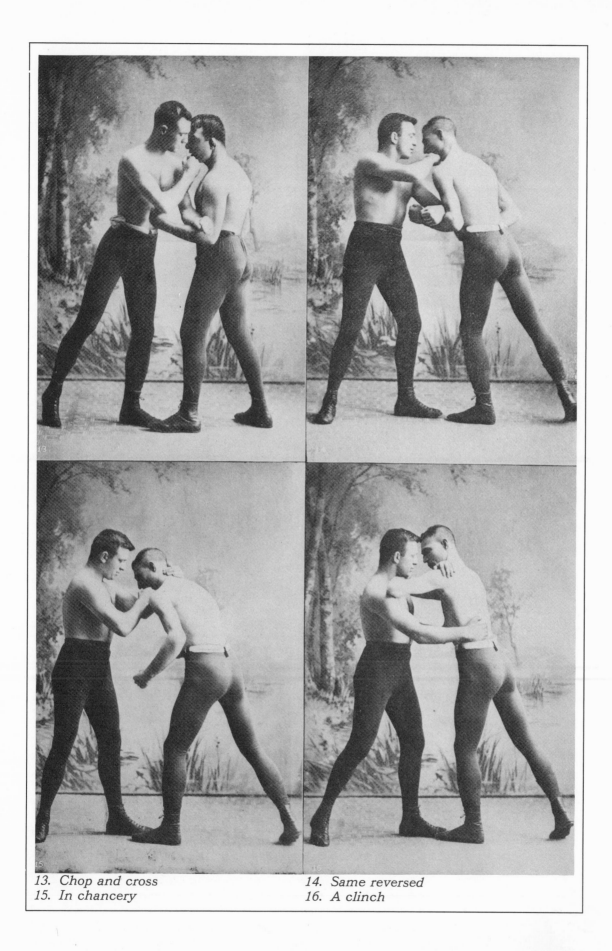

13. Chop and cross   14. Same reversed
15. In chancery   16. A clinch

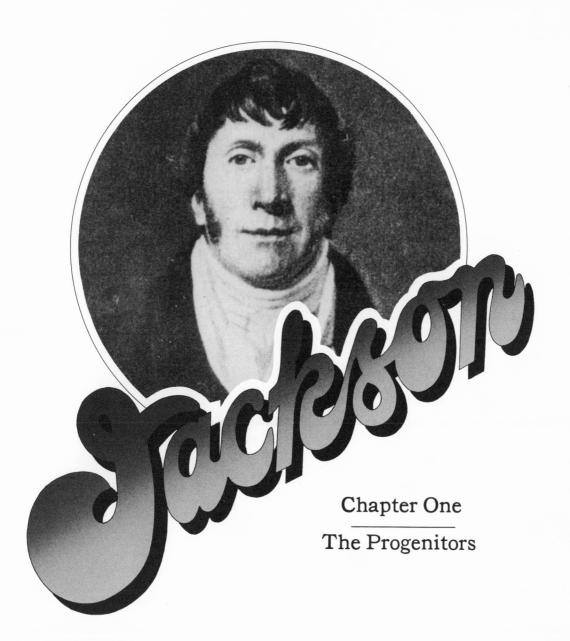

Jackson

Chapter One

The Progenitors

John Sholto Douglas, the eighth Marquis of Queensberry, who was to revolutionize the sport of prizefighting, was a slight, dapper man with heavy eyebrows, a high, aristocratic forehead and a prominent aquiline nose. The last was a target, one supposes, for many a stiff left jab and right cross—for Douglas was an ardent amateur boxer in his youth.

In his later years the Marquis became quite irascible, disowning his son, the poet Lord Alfred Douglas, threatening Oscar Wilde with violence and causing disturbances at his club, on the street and in theatres. Frank Harris, a literary light of the time and a biographer of Wilde, would write that the Marquis had "a combative face" and "hot grey eyes." But boxing fans are likely to forgive him all that.

The Marquis's lineage was impeccable. He was a direct descendant of the Black Douglas, who served Robert I, "the Bruce," of Scotland valiantly during the Border Wars of the fourteenth century. He was related collaterally to numerous other Scottish warriors and chieftains named Douglas—the Grim, the Hardy, the Gross.

One of his ancestors, Charles Douglas, the fourth Marquis, had taken up boxing in the late eighteenth century in the fashionable company of Lord Byron and other aristocratic devotees of "the Fancy" or "the Sweet Science," as boxing was then called. They regularly attended Gentleman John Jackson's Boxing Academy in London, sparring with one another. A few noblemen even ventured to exchange blows with Jackson, who had won the English championship in 1795 in the presence of the Prince of Wales. With Byron and the Dukes of York and Clarence, sons of King George III (who was slowly going mad from the ministrations of his physicians), Charles Douglas had helped found the Pugilistic Club in London. There, over goblets of sack and port, the merits of Jem Belcher, "the Napoleon of the Ring," and Tom Cannon, "the Great Gun of Windsor," could be argued. Wagers could be made. Young aristocrats could learn the art of self-defense from less well born instructors.

In no sport was there ever a closer link between the high born and the low.

In 1859, at the age of fourteen, John Sholto Douglas inherited several castles and other properties—altogether a fortune estimated at £780,000. At nineteen he entered Magdalene College in Cambridge. There Douglas, an athletic prodigy, met another athletic student named John Graham Chambers, who soon began to share the Marquis's enthusiasm for boxing. In 1866 the pair—both in their early twenties—founded the Amateur Athletic Club, to encourage young men to box. They also drew up fourteen stipulations for the sport. These were to affect not only amateur boxers but professional prizefighters as well, infusing an element of humanity and stability into the sport. The stipulations have come down to us as the Marquis of Queensberry rules.

The regulations laid down by the Marquis were probably the most important and significant ever devised to change the face and spirit of a professional sport.

Professional prizefighting in England up to 1866—and for some time thereafter—could be a cruel sport. It was not that the London Prize Ring rules, adopted in 1838 and revised in 1853, permitted physical carnage; it was just that the umpires (as referees were called) largely ignored the brutality, and the spectators seemed to relish it as part of the entertainment. Holding-and-hitting and ear-pulling were blinked at. Wrestling was permitted, and a favorite tactic was to hurl one's opponent off his feet with a hip lock or by tripping him, and then land on him heavily—as though by an oversight—so that a knee or elbow could stove in a rib or flatten his nose.

Before the London Prize Ring rules were adopted, of course, prizefighting in England had been even more brutal. In 1743 Jack Broughton, called the father of the English school of boxing, had drawn up a set of regulations that forbade a contestant's hitting his opponent when he was down or seizing him by the breeches or by any part below the waist. Nor could he kick. But even this set of rules gave some latitude to a determined competitor. Many fighters of that era shaved their heads so their opponents could not grab a handful of hair with one hand and punch them in the face with the other. This was the tactic used by Gentleman Jackson in 1795 to defeat the shorter, slighter Daniel Mendoza for the English championship. Mendoza's long dark locks presented Jackson with an advantage—permitted by the umpire over Mendoza's protests—that he could not afford to ignore.

In Broughton's time and for long years thereafter, a round ended when a man went down, and he was considered to be down whether he was flat on his back or if only one hand or knee was touching the ground. Hitting or kicking him at that point was considered a foul—unless it was in self-defense. (On rare occasions a fighter would swing at his opponent with a knee on the ground.) Both fighters enjoyed a half-minute respite. If the downed fighter was groggy or unconscious, his cornermen used this time to drag him to his corner and by various means, including feeding him brandy, bring him to. A bottleholder was present to guard the beverage from foul play. Since no stools were allowed in the ring, the fighter's second knelt down and the principal rested on his knee—whence the phrase "to give a knee to," meaning granting assistance when it is called for. If a fighter was so battered that he could not, after half a minute had expired, come to scratch—a line drawn in the center of the ring—his opponent was awarded the decision. Sometimes the cornerman and the bottleholder were able to restore their man to consciousness fifteen or twenty times, allowing him to stagger up to scratch each time.

The longest bareknuckle fight—between Jack Smith and James Kelly in Melbourne, Australia, in 1856—lasted for six hours and fifteen minutes. In 1825 Jack Jones and Patsy Tunney fought the greatest number of rounds: 276. In 1846 Young Norley (George Hall) gained a measure of fame by fighting 110 out of 160 rounds with a broken arm.

Some canny fighters, assailed by weariness or pusillanimity, would drop after a single light punch, ending the round and availing themselves of the half-minute respite. If a fighter went down without being hit, the umpire usually awarded his opponent the decision. Broughton advocated the use of gloves ("mufflers") for sparring and for giving instruction, and he used them in his London Academy. He did not advocate them, however, for professional use.

The outcome of bareknuckle bouts was often determined by the endurance of a fighter rather than by power or skill in punching. Blows were blocked with the forearm rather than the hand, and the accepted defensive position was with the arms crossed in front of the body at about nose height or lower, so that a blow could be warded off in either direction. This position of course limited a fighter's ability to strike anything but straight-ahead blows, but it was useful for delivering the legal chopper—that is, a blow struck with the bottom part of the fist, the way one would pound a table.

The rules composed by Broughton, who was buried in Westminster Abbey for his services to the sport, were superseded by the London Prize Ring rules. These suggested that there be water in the bottleholder's bottle, as opposed to revitalizing spirits, and expanded the list of fouls that could result in disqualification: no butting, no gouging, no tearing of the flesh with the fingernails, no biting, no hitting one's opponent while on one's knees, and so on.

The London Prize Ring rules were not revolutionary; the Marquis's rules were. Their principal stipulations were: Rounds were to be of three minutes' duration, with a minute of rest in between; no wrestling was allowed; if a man was knocked down he had ten seconds to get up or he was counted out; and gloves were to be worn in professional fights.

The latter was as important a rule as any of the others in affecting the sport. For the human fist—however suitable for saluting, making a threat, or knocking on a door—was not constructed to strike repeated blows against hard objects without some kind of protection. The skin of the knuckles is thin and readily bleeds; if a blow is struck improperly, the fingers can be sprained or the knuckles can break. Even if a blow is struck properly by a person without the "fighter's fist," these misfortunes can occur. (Sometimes fighters presented the top of the head—notoriously hard—to an opponent in the hope that he would break a knuckle, a finger, or his hands on it.) And even if the fingers do not break, after many blows the knuckles become extremely sensitive. Before the use of mufflers by prizefighters, the hands took a terrible beating. One advantage of the chopper was that it did not hurt the hand as much when used repeatedly, since the bottom of the clenched hand is much less tender than the knuckles. Wrestling holds were resorted to mainly because the fighter could not stand the pain in his hands or wanted to give them time to recuperate. In 1824, Tom Spring beat Jack Langan for the English championship, but his hands were so damaged he was unable to fight ever again. Despite the use of brine to toughen the hands—a ritual of most bareknuckle fighters—the winner was sometimes in worse shape than the loser because of the damage his hands suffered. In ancient times this danger had been clearly recognized.

The sport of boxing came to England via the Roman occupation, the Romans in turn having borrowed the idea from the Greeks. The first mention of boxing in literature is in the twenty-third book of the *Iliad*. In recalling the epic battle between Epeius and Euryalus, Homer recited to a rapt audience:

"A girdle first he [Tydeus's son] cast about him [Euryalus], and thereafter gave him well-cut thongs of the hide of an ox of the field. So the twain, when they had girded themselves, stepped into the midst of the place of gathering, and lifting their mighty hands on high one against the other, fell to, and their hands clashed together in heavy blows. Dread then was the grinding of their teeth, and the sweat flowed on every side from off their limbs. But upon him goodly Epeius rushed as he peered for an opening, and smote him on the cheek, nor after that, methinks, did he [Euryalus] long stand upright, for even there did his glorious limbs sink beneath him. And as when beneath the ripple of the North Wind a fish leapeth up on the tangle-strewn sand of a shallow and the black wave hideth it, even so up leapt Euryalus when he was smitten. But great-souled Epeius took him in his hands and set him on his feet, and his dear comrades thronged about him and led him through the place of gathering with trailing feet, spitting out clotted blood and letting his head hang to one side; and they brought him out wandering in his wits and set him down in the midst of their company and themselves went and fetched the two-handled cup."

That is, Euryalus went down from what was probably a hook to the cheek and bounced back up again, but the crowd felt the bout was over and gave the loser a shot to ease his pains. Note that both fighters wore a primitive form of gloves.

Boxing became an Olympic sport in the thirty-third Olympiad, about 880 B.C., and boxing champions, like the winners of other Olympic events—the race in armor, the chariot race, the pentathlon, the long jump with weights, the pancratium, wrestling and flute playing—were accorded immense honors. A herald proclaimed the victor's name, his heritage and his country. He was awarded a garland of wild olives. His name was canonized on the Greek calendar. Poets like Simonides, Pindar and Euripides were engaged by the state to sing paeans to his skill, endurance and courage. Sculptors like Phidias and Praxiteles carved statues of him. If he was an Athenian he received a sum of money and free meals for life; if he was a Spartan he was accorded the privilege of marching in the forefront of the troops in battle. Since the Games had as much religious as athletic significance, it might be considered that Olympic victors, by defeating all opponents, had been granted commissions as demigods on the field of battle. When they returned home they were rendered tumultuous greetings by all the citizens, who believed their cities or towns had won the favor of the gods.

But victory did not come easily. Training was arduous. Athletes had to swear they had undergone a strict ten-month regimen of preparation before arriving at Olympia. There for a month they practiced under the strict scrutiny of instructors and officials. At the training table they fed on a diet of cheese and water, thought to purify them.

The pancratium (from the Greek *pan,* meaning "all," and *kratos,* meaning "strength") was the roughest of the Olympic events. It consisted of wrestling and boxing, and nearly everything but biting and hitting below the belt was allowed—even strangling. Wearing nothing on their hands (and with nothing on their bodies but a coat of oil and dust), pancratists kicked, boxed with the open hand (fists were not allowed), pulled hair, dislocated joints and broke bones with wrestling holds. However, killing one's opponent disqualified the winner. One pancratist who killed his opponent in the final by what was considered to be foul means was disqualified and disgraced, and his opponent was awarded the laurel wreath posthumously.

Boxers, by contrast, wore thongs around their hands and wrists, and the rules of behavior were quite strict. A fight continued until one boxer was knocked out or gave up. If a boxer killed his opponent, unless it was deemed accidental, he was disqualified. One great athlete named Theagenes, the son of a priest of Hercules, was convicted of a boxing foul and disqualified, but his fellow townsmen thought so highly of him that they erected a statue of him anyway. One night a sullen rival who felt Theagenes had no right to such immortality pushed over the statue, and it fell on him and killed him. One can imagine the awe Theagenes' townsmen felt when they saw what the gods in their anger had wrought.

From the use that the Greek boxers and pancratists made of ear guards in practice, and from the statues of boxers and pancratists that clearly show what the Greeks called "pancratist's ear" (what we would call a cauliflower or, in pugilistic argot, a tin ear) but no smashed noses, it would seem that the Greeks threw blows in a kind of windmill fashion, as opposed to the modern

It was the Romans who originally brought boxing to Britain.

classic way of hitting straight from the shoulder. In the more civilized way of fighting, the nose takes as much punishment from jabs and right crosses as the ears do. Homer refers to Grecian punches as "falling blows." In Greek comedy, too, humorous reference is made to mashed ears rather than mashed noses.

The Greeks greatly admired courage in their Olympic boxers. Two of the most renowned were Glaucus of Arthedon and Diagoras of Rhodes, but the most courageous must have been a certain Eurydemus. He took a tremendous smash in the mouth from his opponent and swallowed his teeth rather than let his opponent know he had hurt him. The ploy worked. His opponent, discouraged that his fiercest blow had failed to shake Eurydemus, virtually gave up the battle.

Diagoras of Rhodes was one of the Olympic champion boxers whose fierce grace in the ring was celebrated by the Greek lyric poet Pindar. Pindar's eulogy went, in part, like this:

Today the lyre and flute and song
Roused by Diagoras, I move
Hymning fair Rhode from Venus
    sprung,
The sun's own nymph and watery
    love:

With her the giant boxer's praise
    to sound,
The champion's noblest hire,
By Alpheus' stream Castalia's
    fountain crown'd;
And Damagete his old and upright
    Sire,
Pride of the beautous Isle whose
    Argive host
By Asia's beaked shore three
    Sovereign Cities boast.

Of course, this is not quite like the staccato electronic, "A right, another right, the champion is staggering, he's against the ropes, he's hurt—listen to that crowd—a left to the head, the champ can't get out of the corner, a *hard* left hook to the head, another left, a left that misses, the champ is desperately trying to cover up, the champion is DOWN! A straight right that snapped

his head back. Now picking up the count—three . . . four. . . . The champ is trying to get to one knee, his hand on the ropes . . . six. . . ." But it well served in those less harried days to memorialize and honor the feats of the greatest and most revered athletes of the time.

When the glory of Greece faded and that of Rome grew, circuses in vast amphitheatres became one of the most useful ways for Roman emperors and the wealthier nobles to win the enthusiasm of the populace. Part of the entertainment, exciting to spectators partly because it afforded them the chance to make wagers, was the spectacle of fights between gladiators—prisoners of war and captured criminals. Some fought with swords, others with net and trident. But some, borrowing an idea from the Greeks, fought without weapons. That is, without conventional weapons. To make the bouts more interesting—for both nobles and the populace had low thresholds of boredom at the time—the Romans added pointed metal studs to the cestus (thongs that bound the hands and wrists of the combatants) to form a kind of hand and finger protector with built-in brass knuckles. The cestus could cut and bruise and deliver a hard knock; and used by an expert, it could deal a deadly blow.

The Emperor Caligula, one of the most conscientious impresarios of circuses, imported the best Campanian and African fighters for the bouts. Some of the fiercest came from Lusitania, a section of North Africa, where the prizes for local champions were not olive wreaths or immortalization in verse but virgins. Both the Emperor Augustus and the Emperor Marcus Aurelius were especially fond of boxing bouts. The Emperor Commodus actually engaged in gladiatorial contests, but he was intelligent enough not to fight a boxer armed with cestus; instead he fired arrows at exotic animals from a platform.

When the Romans conquered England in A.D. 43 (they remained there until A.D. 410), they brought with them an enthusiasm for gladiatorial bouts with the cestus, and they staged their own provincial circuses in that then-barbaric land. Thus combat with the fists was introduced into the country, and admiration for this form of self-defense apparently remained with the English, though the first written mention of boxing in England did not come until the end of the seventeenth century.

During the reign of George I (1714–27), the first Hanoverian king, the gazettes contained references to fighting with the bare fists for purses. In 1719 James Figg, a powerful six-footer, became the first acknowledged English heavyweight champion. He opened an academy in London at which not only the Sweet Science but cudgeling and the use of the backsword were taught to the English "bloods"—wealthy, enthusiastic sportsmen—and also to commoners who had the wherewithal to afford Figg's instruction. William Hogarth, the satiric artist, an admirer and friend of Figg's, painted the champion's portrait (with decorous wig) and also drew up an advertising card for his academy.

George Taylor, who succeeded Figg as champion (by Figg's appointment rather than by beating anybody), was trounced by Jack Broughton, a fine defensive fighter as well as a powerful hitter. Broughton found a patron in the Duke of Cumberland, the first of many of the nobility to sponsor (and wager heavily on) fighters, but he lost the Duke's imprimatur in 1750 when he was defeated by Jack Slack, a Norwich butcher whose specialty was hitting his opponents on the back of the neck—what we would call today a rabbit punch. (The blow, today illegal, paralyzes certain nerves in the upper spine, putting a fighter out of commission for a while.) The Duke thereupon adopted Slack as his protégé but grew chilly toward him when he learned that Slack, whose other interest was a boxing academy in Bristol, was not only throwing fights right and left but was arranging for others to be thrown. The Duke became disenchanted with both Slack and the Fancy after Slack lost to Bill "the Nailer" Stevens, whose patron was the Duke of York. His pockets considerably lightened, Cumberland stormed off, making threatening noises, and arranged to have legislation passed in

Parliament to bar boxing entirely in England.

Thereafter, although prizefighting continued, the championship lay in a confused state until 1791, when the Duke of Hamilton, the patron of Benjamin "Big Ben" Brain, arranged for a bout between his protégé and Tom Johnson, the then-reigning champion. Bothered by a broken nose and a broken finger, Johnson ceded the championship to Big Ben after eighteen rounds. Brain, finding no worthy challengers, retired, and the first era of British prizefighting came to a close.

The second era began with the rapid rise of Daniel Mendoza, the first Jewish boxer to win the heavyweight championship. The son of East End parents who were artisans and reportedly were descended from Spanish nobility, Mendoza was small by heavyweight standards. But he was agile, courageous and a careful student of the art. Though he eventually lost the title to Gentleman Jackson in 1795, he did much to revolutionize the philosophy of British boxing, which had been to stand toe-to-toe and slug it out until one's knuckles could take the punishment no longer, whereupon wrestling holds were resorted to. Mendoza's great punch was the straight left, and after his defeat by Jackson he traveled all over England demonstrating this punch and the various means of self-defense he had developed. Jackson, for his part, introduced the science of footwork and advocated the careful measurement of distance before launching a blow. But perhaps his greatest contributions to English prizefighting were his polish and his all-around athletic ability, which made him readily acceptable in royal, noble and even literary circles.

With Jackson as a kind of statuesque representative of man's nobility and virility, boxing in England entered its Golden Era. Both the high born and the low became enthusiastic spectators, prizefighting being one of the few sports which the inhabitants of the most class-conscious of countries could enjoy in common. Patrons of the sport as well as the sport itself became known as the Fancy.

The nobility and the gentry, with

their leisure time, their estates, their servants and their happy freedom from restrictive legislation, could indulge in such recreations as hawking, hunting, shooting pheasants and grouse, steeplechasing and engaging in vast regattas. The poor could also hunt, but it was termed poaching and was severely punished. So was the ownership of a greyhound or a hawk or a falcon by anyone who did not own property. For the most part, the sports of the poor were unsophisticated ones: catching a greased pig, running blindfolded or in a three-legged race, climbing a greased pole for a leg of mutton, playing skittles (something like lawn bowling), ratting (watching a dog run down rats), throwing rocks at a cat and mob football, in which entire villages played against one another, with as much attention paid to knocking heads as to kicking the ball. In debtors' prison, there was always fives, a kind of handball which, curiously enough, eventually evolved into "real" tennis, the most aristocratic of games, played by royalty and the nobility.

All classes, however, could fish, bet on cockfights and attend bull-baiting and bear-baiting competitions and hangings. But the great human leveler in the Regency period was prizefighting. It had the approval not only of Prinny (as the Prince Regent was called), his brothers and others of the nobility but also of the great artists and writers of the time. The British prime minister, Sir Hugh Walpole, Jonathan Swift and Alexander Pope regularly attended bouts at Figg's London Academy. George Cruickshank and Jean Louis André Théodore Géricault, the great French artist, sketched and etched and painted fights. Galsworthy came to be a fight fan and wrote a poem about an aged fighter. Dickens was a regular spectator at fights. A Staffordshire pottery mug artistically commemorates one of the fierce fights between Mendoza and Dick Humphries, known as "the Gentleman Fighter." Lord Byron, who once said, "I would rather be Brummel than Napoleon," and who probably would rather have been Gentleman Jackson than either, collected clippings and newspaper sketches of the great fights which were later incorporated

into a giant and historically valuable illustrated screen. The Prince of Wales was an aficionado and won a good many wagers on fights, even sponsoring a fighter, Tom Tring. Tring, alas, was battered senseless by Ben Brain and was abandoned by his royal sponsor.

The Duke of York, at one time commander in chief of His Majesty's forces warding off Napoleon in Holland, was such an ardent supporter of the Fancy that fighters began calling their fists "Duke of Yorks," which eventually became shortened to "dukes," a synonym we still retain: "He's handy with his dukes." A "duke man" is a pickpocket's helper, and to be accepted by the lords of the criminal hierarchy is to be "duked in," from the handshake that signifies approval. Thus do sports influence language.

The well born seemed attracted to the low born who had won fame in the ring with their courage and their ability to batter their opponents into senselessness. Noblemen dined and drank at the sporting houses run by prizefighters and ex-prizefighters. Eminent, venerable names were numbered among the clientele: The Marquises of Tweeddale and Worcester; Lords Chetwynd, Sefton, Wilton and Yarmouth; the Dukes of Clarence and Beaufort. At George IV's coronation in 1820 a special honor guard of boxers was present, all dressed decorously (and probably painfully) and all under the supervision of Gentleman John Jackson. Little wonder that such prestigious support of prizefighting led magistrates and lawmen to cheer at bouts instead of daring to halt them.

A few fighters with enterprise and ambition became more than pub owners when their careers were over. There was Gentleman Jackson, of course, admired by the mighty. The most remarkable advance was made by John Gully, the son of a butcher in Bristol. Thrust into debtors' prison as a young man, he was visited by a hometown friend, Henry Pearce, the much-respected English heavyweight champion. To amuse the bedraggled inmates, they sparred a few rounds. Gully held his own so well with "the Game Chicken" that the news spread to the city and beyond. Colonel Harry Mellish visited the prison and told Gully he would pay his debts if Gully would consent to fight Pearce for the championship. Gully consented, as anyone would. He lost the fight after an hour and seventeen minutes, but his showing was so impressive that on his retirement Pearce appointed him champion.

Gully successfully defended his title several times, then decided he wished to retire—he had other ambitions beside being a boxer. The Duke of York, a fan of his, pleaded with him to reconsider, but Gully remained obdurate. With his winnings he bought a stable of horses and won a fortune on the turf. Twice his entries won the English Derby. Subsequently he became a large landholder and was elected to Parliament.

William Hazlitt, the great English essayist and critic, was intrigued enough by the Fancy to write about the fight between Tom Hickman, "the Gasman," and Bill Neate, "the Bristol Bull," in Newberry in 1822. Neate was taller and heavier, but apparently the Gasman was nastier, for Hazlitt criticizes his attitude before describing the fight itself.

"Modesty should accompany the FANCY as its shadow. The best men were always the best behaved. Jem Belcher, [and] the Game Chicken (before whom the Gasman could not have lived) were civil, silent men. So is Cribb, so is Tom Belcher, the most elegant of sparrers, and not a man for everyone to take by the nose. . . . A boxer was bound to beat his man, but not to thrust his fist, either actually or by implication, in everyone's face. Even the highwayman, in the way of trade, may blow out your brains, but if he uses foul language at the same time, I should say he was no gentleman. A boxer, I would infer, need not be a blackguard or a coxcomb, more than another. Perhaps I press this point too much on a fallen man—Mr. Thomas Hickman has by this time learnt that first of all lessons, 'That man was made to mourn.' He has lost nothing by the late fight for his presumption; and that every man may do as well without! . . . Few but those who had bet on him wished Gas to win. With my own prepossessions on the subject, the result

of the 11th of December appeared to me as fine a piece of poetical justice as I have ever witnessed. The difference of weight between the two combatants (14 stone to 12) was nothing to sporting men. Great, heavy, clumsy, long-armed Bill Neate kicked the beam in the scale of the Gas-man's vanity. The amateurs were frightened of his [Hickman's] big words, and thought they would make up for the difference of six feet and five feet nine. Truly the FANCY are not men of imagination. They judge of what has been, and cannot conceive of anything that is to be. The Gas-man has won hitherto; therefore he must beat a man half as big again as himself—and that to a certainty. . . ."

This is Hazlitt's blow-by-blow account of the end of the fight:

". . . About the twelfth it seemed as if it must have been over: Hickman generally stood with his back to me; but in the scuffle he had changed position, and Neate just then made a tremendous lunge at him, and hit him full in the face. It was doubtful whether he would fall backwards or forwards; he hung suspended for a second or two, and then fell back, throwing his hands in the air, and with his face lifted up to the sky. I never saw any thing more terrific than his aspect just before he fell. All traces of life, of natural expression were gone from him. His face was like a human skull, a death's head, spouting blood. The eyes were filled with blood, the nose streamed with blood, the mouth gaped blood. He was not like an actual man, but like a preternatural, spectral appearance, or like one of the figures in Dante's *Inferno*. Yet he fought on after this for several rounds, still striking the first desperate blow, and Neate standing on the defensive, and using the same cautious guard to the last, as if he had still all his work to do; and it was not till the Gas-man was so stunned in the seventeenth or eighteenth round, that his senses forsook him, that he could not come to time, that the battle was declared over. . . . I asked Cribb if he did not think it was a good one? He said, *Pretty well!*" The carrier-pigeons now mounted into the air, and one of them flew with the news of her husband's victory to the bosom of Mrs. Neate. Alas, for Mrs. Hickman! ..."

The greatest chronicler of English prizefighting in the Regency era and beyond was not Hazlitt but Pierce Egan. Egan, a man of many parts, lent a color, vitality and sometimes even poetry to his writing that has led many to consider him the greatest boxing writer of all time. His vocabulary to our ears is quaint: a fighter who took punishment without retreating a step was an "insatiable glutton"; fighting was "milling"; a pedestrian who walked long distances to see fights was a "foot-toddler"; a fighter abounding with energy was a "prime bottom fighter."

Describing one lively round in the Tom Oliver–Ned Painter match in 1814, Egan wrote rapturously: "Such a complete determined *milling* round is not to be met with in the Annals of Pugilism, and there was more execution done in it than in many fights of an hour's length. It was enough to *finish* any two men. By a correct stop-watch, it continued FOUR MINUTES AND A HALF AND TWELVE SECONDS!"

Oliver won the fight, but Egan gave each of the protagonists his literary due: "They were both *punished* in the extreme, and Painter was quite blind, and his nose beat flat upon his face. Oliver's body was terribly beaten, his head much disfigured, and one of his eyes nearly closed."

He could be caustic, too, as befits a fight critic. In a rematch between the pair six years later, which lasted fifty-five minutes, not many blows were struck. Egan commented, "The *punishment* that both combatants dealt was so truly light for such heavy men that they were up at an early hour the next morning to breakfast." He doubted, however, if the bout was "a X"—a "cross fight," or a fight which one combatant had agreed to lose—because of his faith in the integrity of Ned Painter. (A "double X" was a fight in which the fellow who had consented to lose had a change of heart, to the surprise of his opponent. Sometimes it was a most dangerous practice.)

In the Golden Era of boxing, the common folk—the tinman, the potter, the collier, the cobbler, the hosier, the tenant farmer, the tar, the stevedore, the waterman, the pipemaker, the brewer, the butcher and the coachman—had a merry time on the days before a great fight. The health of the contestants was drunk to in many a pub, and then the journey, generally a long one, began toward the site of the bout. Some foot-toddlers started days in advance. Later hackneys would start out, bearing the more affluent milling coves (fighters wishing to spectate) and flash coves (men with splendid knowledge of the respective skills of the contestants, bettors all). Accompanying them were sporting girls, known as Cyprians, all well supplied with "blue ruin," the term for gin. Sometimes the flash coves never reached the battleground. Blue ruin ruined them.

It was also a gay time for the Corinthians—noble or wealthy or royal followers of the Fancy—who, in their clubs or castles, toasted the fighters or King George or Prinny or the Duke of York and speculated about the fight. On the day of the fight, heads busting, the Corinthians would rush to the site in fast traps or on horseback, trying to arrive early so they could mull over odds and place sizable wagers on their favorites. Here it was that the flash cove could converse with a prince, and the pickpocket with a literary giant.

There were many extraordinary English fighters in the bareknuckle era besides Hickman, Neate, Oliver and Painter. Jem Ward, called "the Black Diamond" although he was white, was a splendid fighter. But he was gullible and like putty in the hands of crooked advisors, and he "sold" fights to win bets for his friends. If he was found to have bet on his opponent, the smart money put their faith in his opponent, too. In 1822 he was so brazen about dumping a fight that he was expelled from the Pugilistic Club in London. He persevered at his trade, however, and twice beat Phil Sampson, a major contender. When champion Tom Spring retired, Tom Cannon claimed the title. Ward challenged him and took both the title and a thousand-pound side bet in a fast ten minutes. He promptly lost the title to the Irishman Simon Byrne, in a match that is sometimes called "the Leicester Hoax." The Fancy were so appalled at Byrne's easy triumph and the vast amounts of money that changed hands that Ward was again repudiated. But Byrne was so uppity in his glory that Ward's popularity was restored—he became a kind of English White Hope—and a return was arranged between the pair. In 1831 Ward defeated Byrne at Warwick after a grueling hour and seventeen minutes.

James Burke, "the Deaf 'Un," was the son of a Thames waterman and grew up along the boisterous riverfront. Orphaned early, he was taken in hand by a tavern owner who encouraged him to box and steered him into matches with experienced men, whom he surprisingly beat. Among others, Burke defeated Young Girdler, Sambo the Black and Jack Carter—the last by offering his head to Carter, who broke his arm on it. When Jem Ward retired in 1832, Burke became the acknowledged champion. Simon Byrne, the Irish champion, was quick to challenge. After a bout of three hours and sixteen minutes—the longest heavyweight championship fight on record—Burke scored a knockout. Byrne died as a result of the blows he received, and as a consequence of the ensuing uproar, Burke traveled to America, where his adventures surpassed anything he underwent in England.

Tom Sayers, a small, gutsy man, was probably the most beloved of English boxers in the middle of the nineteenth century. The son of a Brighton shoemaker, he was apprenticed to a bricklayer and fought his companions as time allowed. When he was twenty-two he decided to box professionally, even though he weighed less than 150 pounds and stood only five feet seven inches tall. Although police kept stopping his fights, his rise was rapid. Small even for a middleweight, Sayers developed a remarkable habit of pecking away at his opponents' eyes with a marksmanship never equaled. In this manner he was able to beat the much larger Henry Poulson in 109 rounds, and in a title match in 1857, score a TKO over William Perry, "the Tipton Slasher."

Jem Mace, "the Swaffham Gypsy," was called the father of scientific boxing. As a teenager in the environs of Norfolk he used to play a fiddle in the manner of a cellist for the few coppers the music would bring. He got into the business of boxing after a drunken fisherman busted his fiddle while he was playing outside a Yarmouth tavern. Annoyed, young Mace knocked the fisherman out. A passerby who enjoyed the show handed Mace a sovereign and advised him to take up the Fancy professionally. Fiddleless, Mace trained briefly, beat Slasher Tom Slack and Posh Price and then won the heavyweight title from Sam Hurst in 1861. He lost it to Tom King, an ex-tar, reclaimed it after King's retirement and defended it against Irishmen, Americans and Englishmen. Mace then traveled to America for a few fights and eventually went to Sydney, Australia. There he set up a most respectable boxing school. He greatly influenced Australia's progress as a fistic power and was indirectly responsible for the rise of such Antipodean stalwarts as Peter Jackson, Bob Fitzsimmons and Frank Slavin.

———————

Stand-up boxing would seem to be ideally suited to the Anglo-Saxon temperament. A thug of the old days in southern India might strangle you with his *ruhma,* while one of today's Indians might disable you with *varmannie—* something like jujitsu. A Frenchman would tend to kick you with *la savate.* Some Latin-Americans prefer to settle their differences with knives. There is a South American tribe, the Chavales, that specializes in breaking arms. A Korean would disable you with karate (or a dozen special forms of it), a Japanese with judo or jujitsu or aikido, a Russian with *sambo—*a rougher form of judo. There are other areas of the world where a sharp kick in the knee, the use of the tightly closed fingers thrust as a knife, the use of the thumbs as eye-gouging instruments and even the unsuspected smash of a buttock are means of self-defense.

But from the Anglo-Saxon viewpoint, and especially the spectators' viewpoint, boxing is the ideal one-on-one combat sport. The contestants are erect, bare-chested, their actions limited to a great extent by formal rules, and you can see the feints, the parries, the slipped blows, the measuring of a blow, the counter-punches, the fast combinations, the blows that miss and the blows that hurt. If blood flows, it can clearly be observed. Bruises, swellings, cuts and other damage to one fighter or the other are clearly visible, arousing anticipation or dismay on the part of the spectator and giving the round-by-round bettor a chance to think about the odds he will give or take. The imminence of a knock-out is often obvious—the greatest excitement a fight has to offer. But the threat of an unexpected knockout, especially among the heavyweights, is always present, lending another kind of excitement to the bout.

In the early 1800's, an English essayist rhapsodized about the courage that fighters show: ". . . To see two men smashed to the ground, smeared with gore, stunned, senseless, the breath beaten out of their bodies; and then, be-fore you recover from the shock, to see them rise up with new strength and courage, stand ready to inflict or receive mortal offence, and rush upon each other 'like two clouds over the Caspian' —this is the most astonishing thing of all: this is the high heroic state of man! . . ."

There is a spirit of chivalry about the sport, a spirit that existed even in the English bareknuckle days. You did not kick a man when he was down. You did not hit below the belt. Fighters could be fierce as tigers within the ring, and after having tried to destroy one another, emerge the best of friends. One recalls the scene in Edgar Rice Burroughs' "The Mucker," where his antihero and a friend were attacked by a group of savage natives. The mucker, out of desperation, was landing a few shots below the belt. His friend took time out to upbraid him for the tactic, and the mucker promptly raised his blows. It was a step, one assumes, toward his later regeneration. Burroughs, an American, thought like an Englishman.

Pierce Egan, the greatest chronicler of early English fighting, enriched the language with his perceptive style. Because boxers flailing at each other suggested the action of windmills, the term "milling" was born.

When nonprofessionals get into informal fights (as in a pub or saloon), there is satisfaction in striking a good, clean Anglo-Saxon blow in the face; more than in grappling on the ground, surely. As an extension of this, in the American cinema, the clean blow to the villain's jaw—generally a noisy roundhouse right—is an eminently satisfactory way of determining ownership of grazing land or solving a murder case.

In the reign of King George I, a French traveler in England had this to say about the curious proclivity of the English to fight, not with poniards or daggers, but with their fists:

"Anything that looks like fighting is delicious to an Englishman. If two little boys quarrel in the street the passengers stop, make a ring around them in a moment that they may then come to fisticuffs. Each pulls off his neckcloth and waistcoat and gives them to hold to the standers-by. During the fight the ring of bystanders encourage the combatants with great delight of heart and never part them while they fight according to the rules; and those bystanders are not only other boys, porters and rabble, but all sorts of men of position. . . . These combats are less frequent among grown men than children, but they are not rare. If a coachman has a dispute about his fare with a gentleman that has hired him, the coachman consents with all his heart; the gentleman pulls off his sword and lays it in some shop with his cane, gloves and cravat, and boxes in the same manner that I have described above. I once saw the Duke of Grafton at fisticuffs in the open streets with such a fellow whom he lambed most horribly. In France we punish such rascals with our cane and sometimes the flat of our sword, but in England this is never practised; they neither use sword nor stick against a man that is unarmed."

And in his *Boxiana,* Pierce Egan wrote admiringly of a feat of Dr. Samuel Johnson—"that truly great Colossus of Literature"—which shows another side of this sesquipedalian, dyspeptic gentleman. "The learned Doctor himself," Egan wrote, "was another *striking* proof of pugilism being a national trait, by having a regular set-to with an athletic brewer's servant, who had insulted him in Fleet-Street, and gave the fellow a complete milling in a few minutes."

It is interesting to note that the lone Frenchman whose name appears on the lists of fighters for bareknuckle purses between 1750 and 1830 was Monsieur Petit, credited as the first Frenchman to take up boxing. He was six feet six inches tall—a monstrous height for those days—and weighed 220 pounds. He met the British champion, Jack Slack, "the Knight of the Cleaver," and was beaten in twenty-five minutes. The most famous Italian importation was Tito Alberto di Carni, known as "the Venetian Gondolier," a ferocious fighter discovered and backed by the Earl of Bath in 1733. The Earl's high hopes of aggrandizing a fortune in bets were dashed when Figg, fourteen years after winning the championship, worked himself into shape and soundly thrashed Carni, who thereupon returned to Venice.

Among the English nobles and gentry of the late nineteenth century, the blow with the clenched fist seemed to be an excellent way of settling personal disputes. The Marquis of Queensberry himself, as Frank Harris recalls, came charging and swinging at a dignified gentleman named Haseltine at the Pelican Club one afternoon and was sent backwards and head over heels with a straight right. After picking himself up, the Marquis sat at a table for hours, presumably brooding. Like so many of the nobles of his time, the Marquis was extremely comfortable in the company of prizefighters. When he visited Oscar Wilde in his home to threaten him with bodily harm, he was escorted by a large bruiser. The Marquis demanded that Wilde stop paying court to the Marquis' son, Lord Alfred Douglas. Wilde's answer was, "I don't know what the Marquis of Queensberry rules are, but the Oscar Wilde rules are to shoot on sight." Wilde, who could look tough despite being a poet and sporting long locks, stood up abruptly, and the Marquis left. On another occasion the Marquis appeared at the opening of Wilde's play *The Importance of*

Being Earnest. He was in the company of several prizefighters and bore with him a huge basket of turnips and carrots. Presumably they were to be hurled at the actors onstage or saved for Wilde himself should he acknowledge cries of "Author!" However, a cordon of bobbies effectively kept the Marquis and his friends out of the theatre.

Another one-punch imbroglio involved Harris himself. After being insulted in the Café Royal by Lord Alfred, a poet of distinction but hot-tempered, Harris let fly with a roundhouse left, dropping Lord Alfred and ending the fight. Lord Alfred later complained in print that Harris outweighed him by quite a few pounds, but said nothing (Harris relates) of "his advantage of twenty-five years of youth."

━━━━━━━

Prizefighting, alas, fell into gradual decline after the accession of the Prince of Wales to the throne in 1820. As George IV he had affairs of state to ponder over and was preoccupied with how to murder his wife Caroline (so it was rumored). At the same time, Gentleman Jackson, becoming older and less energetic, devoted less and less time to his informal regulation of the Fancy. Promoters and swindlers, seeing a good thing, began replacing noblemen as patrons of fighters. An era of corruption commenced. Audiences soon began to consist less of boxing fans than pickpockets, thieves and ruffians. The practice of "playing for dark" (throwing the fight) became prevalent. Police, with antiboxing laws supporting them, became more belligerent, the clergy became more vocal in their condemnation of the sport, and the press became more outraged that laws against prizefighting were not more rigidly enforced. The utmost secrecy had to be maintained for carrying out fights—where and when and who and the means of transportation—and the interest of the boxing public collapsed.

Curiously, a fight between the American champion, John C. Heenan, and the British champion, Tom Sayers, in 1860 was the catalyst that brought down the hammer most heavily on the sport. The first international fight for the world heavyweight title, the bout got immense play in both the English and American press—which made the police that much more eager to stop it. Heenan had to move from village to village in England as he trained in the final weeks. He kept a bulldog, famous for its victories in the pits, to scare off strangers. On the day of the fight Heenan, wearing a beard that made him resemble Rasputin, met Sayers at London Bridge station; then they entrained for Farnborough, along with cars filled with spectators. Thackeray, Dickens, members of Parliament, newspaper artists like Tom Nast (later to lampoon Boss Tweed out of office), representatives from *The Police Gazette* and *Leslie's Weekly,* army and navy officers and Lord Palmerston were in attendance.

In the thirty-seventh round of the battle, Sayers showed signs of fatigue. Earlier he had broken his right arm, and being much smaller than Heenan, was taking a thorough pasting, although he managed, as was his wont, to peck at Heenan's eyes with his remaining good hand. Aware that he would soon be sightless, Heenan sprang at him energetically, knocked him backwards and tried to strangle him while his back lay across the ropes. The crowd, most of whom had bet on the Englishman, went wild. Some fans clambered inside the ring and some ruffians, or possibly Sayers supporters, cut the ropes. Sayers's seconds attacked Heenan, who fended them off and made his escape, chased by an angry, shouting mob. Each country later claimed its representative had won the bout, but it was officially declared a draw and two winners' belts were awarded. However, the uncontrolled fury of the mob resulted in renewed vigilance by the police, and it became very difficult to promote and stage a fight in England for years thereafter.

The sport might have died out entirely had it not been for the great sensibility and relative humanity of the Marquis of Queensberry rules, and for the new life infused into the sport—however reprehensible the desperadoes at its outer edges, however farcical some of its contests—by the lively people across the sea. ■

Although this is an ancient Italian mosaic, the sport might well be boxing.

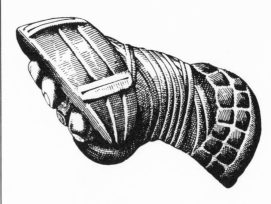

Roman gladiators bound the cestus, above, around hand and wrist to fight.

Although the Etruscans left no written history, some of their customs are evident in their art. These scenes from Etruscan vases clearly show that fighting was part of their culture.

This magnificent Roman gladiator, his hands and wrists bound, is ready to enter the arena. One can almost hear the roar of the crowd awaiting his performance.

"Gentleman Jackson" was a favorite of English royalty in the 1700's.

In 1719 James Figg became the first heavyweight champion of Britain.

Jack Broughton, the third heavyweight champion, and James Figg (left). For the rules he drew up, Broughton was called the father of the English school of boxing.

In Britain's golden era, both the high-born and the low came together to watch "the Fancy," as boxing was then known. Some of England's best artists depicted the spectacle of two men demonstrating "the Sweet Science."

In 1824 Tom Spring defeated Jack Langan for the heavyweight title. More than 30,000 spectators, including literary folk and royalty, enthusiastically jammed the Worcester race course in England, where the seventy-seven-round match was held.

Gentleman Jackson's fashionable boxing academy on London's Bond Street was a meeting place for fight enthusiasts. Lord Byron, a dedicated fan, was a frequent visitor.

Above, Daniel Mendoza and Richard Humphries in 1788. Mendoza, the first Jewish heavyweight champion of the world, weighed only 160 pounds.

Molyneaux

Chapter Two

Up the Irish!

While Britain was toasting her doughty champions in rum, gin and sack and while many of her nobles were lining their purses with gold or coming close to ruin by trying to predict the outcomes of bareknuckle bouts, America—for all her lusty encroachments on Eastern forests, skirmishes with savages and political infighting—lagged far behind the mother country in the development of, and enthusiasm for, the sport of boxing for prize money and acclaim.

To be sure, Americans fought. They fought in saloons over party principles, religion, the favors of hostesses and national origin. They fought over business on the decks of barges, riverboats, flatboats and canalboats. They fought for their lives in such bandit-ridden areas as the Natchez Trail, San Francisco's Barbary Coast and New York City's murderous Five Points and Bowery. They fought, for economic reasons, as butcher boys, longshoremen and runners soliciting trade for immigrant boarding houses (where there was intense competition for the privilege of fleecing greenhorns); as truckmen, cabmen and hostlers. They were more apt, however, to use the tools of their trade than the naked fist. Rivermen afloat used boathooks and belaying pins. The axeman used his axe or hobnailed boots. Coopers used hammers; the woodsman, his double-edged, razor-sharp bowie knife; the mule skinner, his whip; the Irish canal diggers, their pickhandles and shovels. And if the contestants fought weaponless, they relied more on wrestling holds, kicking and gouging than on the clenched fist, paying little attention to the rules laid down by Broughton in 1743. In saloons they improvised weapons—the leg of a chair, the chair itself or the jagged neck of a bottle smashed in haste.

British tars from Bristol and Liverpool, visiting American ports like Boston, New York, Charleston and Philadelphia, were happy to introduce native sailors to the superiority of British stand-up boxing. In fights on the waterfront and in waterfront saloons, the recourse of the hapless American was to fight a little bit dirtier than his British cousin, and he more than held his own. Once in a while, two battlers, hailed by their mates as champions of this or that flotilla or this or that 'tween deck, would be matched clandestinely before a few dozen appreciative spectators in the back room of a saloon (formal fighting before an audience was banned in every state). If any semblance of rules was followed, the British tar, his fist ever ready for a knockdown blow, usually won.

When an American sailor or lubber did show some knack with his mauleys and a stoicism toward bruises, he was quite likely to journey to England, where his skills might be appreciated. It never occurred to an American impresario in the country's formative years that there was money to be made and fame to be achieved through such entertainment. Harness racing, dogfights and turkey shoots were much more to the American sportsman's liking. That the cry of "Find a White Hope!" did not arise when the New York admirers of Tom Molyneaux, a black man, claimed the American championship for him at the beginning of the nineteenth century shows how casually the nation took the sport.

If it had not been for the enterprise and zeal of what might be called the American nobility—the wealthy plantation owners in the South—the nation's prizefighting would have gotten off to an even slower start than it did.

Some of these sporting gentlemen had visited England as youths as a necessary part of their education and had witnessed the damage a scientific fighter could inflict on an opponent with his fists, and the excitement that was aroused in a spectator when the fighter of his choice began to pummel his opponent mercilessly. Some of them even took lessons in this exotic form of self-defense in boxing academies. When they returned home they retained their enthusiasm for the sport. The young men boxed among themselves, and slaveowners of all ages began to look around for likely bucks who could be trained into becoming reasonably skilled boxers. It shortly became a matter of pride and prestige to own a fine fighting slave. The slave so designated, indeed, was likely to serve as his master's bodyguard on trips to nearby cities, dressed in silk and cotton finery, black boots and a tall black hat. It was possibly the most enviable position a slave could attain.

The plantation owner, seated on the veranda of his stately pillared mansion in the still of evening, would sip applejack or bourbon and be tempted to brag to a guest on the fighting prowess of a particular slave he owned. If the plantation owner's guest had a slave with a similar propensity for fighting, a mild argument might ensue: "Ain't a buck in the Carolinas can make a match for my Jim." And since boxing, no less than horse racing, cockfighting or a terrier pursuing rats, demands the placement of money as a testament of faith in one's judgment, wagers would be made. The wagers—especially if the owners were "high up to pickin' cotton," as the Georgia phrase describing inebriety went—could be huge: thousands of dollars or entire plantations.

There being no arenas for the bouts, they were generally held at crossroads of easy access to spectators, who would back one or the other of the contestants. The slave who lost a large sum of money for his master would likely be demoted to field hand and stripped of his fine clothing and would no longer be allowed to eat his meals at the big house. A number of these bouts ended in the death of the losing contestant, since biting and strangling were usually allowed. The winning slave reaped great rewards: good food to keep up his strength, more cast-off finery to wear, the admiration of his fellow slaves, the attention of other plantation owners. Sometimes, if the wager was large enough, his master would offer the slave his freedom should he win. This was the case with Tom Molyneaux, who, some might argue, was the first American heavyweight champion.

Molyneaux, of middle height but stocky, was the property of a Virginia plantation owner named Algernon Molyneaux, who used him mainly as a bodyguard. The son and grandson of fighting slaves, Tom had won a few bouts for his master. Then, one sultry evening, with the cicadas chirping a counterpoint to the susurrus of conversation and the clink of glasses on the veranda, Algernon offered a gigantic wager on Tom. It was duly accepted by his guest, and the place and date were set. Because the bet was so large, Tom's owner, to get the last ounce of effort from him, promised to free him if he won. The fate of Tom's opponent is not recorded; but the winner has become a kind of American sporting legend, with even the British acknowledging his greatness as a ringman.

Tom made his way north, arriving in New York City in 1802, where he found work as a porter in the Old Catherine Market at the south end of Manhattan. In his leisure time he fought the best black fighters in the district in informal street bouts. Sometimes he won small sums of money and sometimes select pieces of fish. After a while he was referred to as the champion of America—as indeed he may have been, though he never fought under a formal set of rules, nor did he fight a white man in this country.

However, his aggressiveness and skill did attract the attention of a British skipper who knew boxing. The skipper told Molyneaux he was too good to be fighting in Manhattan and suggested he travel to England and challenge England's best. Lured by the prospect of winning large sums of money and the chance to test himself against British competition, Molyneaux worked his way across the Atlantic as a deckhand on a square-rigger, landing finally in Liverpool. With no end of difficulty in understanding directions, he found his way to London, specifically to a cozy tavern called the Horse and Dolphin, owned by perhaps the only other black American in the entire city, Bill Richmond.

Richmond's story is no less exotic than Molyneaux's. Born in 1763, Richmond was the son of a Georgia slave and had come into the hands of a Reverend John Carlton, a Southerner who came north and settled on Staten Island. Working as a field hand on the cleric's farm, Richmond became wirily strong and polished his fighting skills in the rough-and-tumble contests that were part of growing up.

In 1777, during the occupation of Staten Island by the British, he happened to be carrying out his master's business in a tavern in Stapleton when he was jeered at and set upon by three lobsterbacks, as British soldiers were called by the Revolutionists. The quickness with which the young Negro dispatched them caught the attention of General Earl Percy, in command of the British garrison. Like many of his contemporaries, the general was an avid follower of the Fancy. He accounted that Richmond must be extremely skilled with "the raw 'uns" since one of the trio he whipped was Sergeant Joseph Burns, who had fought professionally in England under the sobriquet of "the Birmingham Blacksmith." Percy sent a squad to get Richmond, who was apprehended in the act of trying to flee from his master, and was brought to Percy's headquarters.

Unable to believe that someone so young could defeat three of His Majesty's dragoons, the general summoned Burns, and a bout was immediately arranged. A ring was set up, both men stripped to the waist, and as the general and his officers marveled, Richmond gave Burns such a walloping that the Englishman quit after three rounds—that is, knockdowns. The general thereupon appropriated Richmond as part of the spoils of war. When he returned to Northumberland, the northernmost county in England, he brought Richmond back with him. There at Alnwick, Percy's sprawling castle afloat on waves of carefully nurtured green carpet, the black man was given boxing lessons, learning to jab and hit straight punches and block blows in the English style.

When the general thought Richmond ready he arranged for his first professional bout. Though only five feet six inches tall and never more than a middleweight, Richmond disposed of his first opponent, a heavyweight, with ease. Next he defeated a string of experienced boxers, including Dockey Moore, a Sheffield knife grinder, and Frank Meyers, "the York Bully." His only loss was to George Maddox. Then, to the surprise of most of England, Richmond, now extremely popular with the Fancy and having acquired the nickname of "the Black Terror," cut up and defeated Jack "Tom Tough" Holmes. Holmes's finest achievement was having milled for an hour and a half with the great Tom Cribb before being battered to sleep.

Richmond's victories had won numerous wagers for the general and had boosted his own confidence, so now he dispatched, with the general's approval, his formal challenge to Cribb. Cribb finally accepted the challenge of the former slave, who was now forty-two years old. But partly because the opportunity to fight Cribb had been so long in coming and partly because Richmond had become the pet of snuff-taking London swells with corseted hips and pale faces, he was woefully out of shape. This was perhaps all that saved Cribb, for despite his wind being short and his reflexes shaky, Richmond stayed with him for a desperate hour and a half before succumbing.

In despair over losing his chance to beat the durable Cribb, Richmond virtually retired from the ring and opened his tavern. It immediately became a favorite of the Fancy, with Lord Byron a frequent visitor who reveled in listening to accounts of his host's battles.

When the apparition that was Molyneaux appeared at his door, Richmond noted his size—now two hundred pounds bulked on a frame five feet eight inches tall, with arms of superlative length—fed him, and the next day began training him as he himself had been taught. Molyneaux progressed rapidly, and finally Richmond launched him on one of the most spectacular careers in nineteenth-century boxing.

Through the good offices of some of the toffs who patronized the Horse and Dolphin, a fight was lined up for the American. This was with Jack Burrows, who bore the unprepossessing title of "the Bristol Unknown"—although any adult male from Bristol, the fount of bareknuckle boxing, was bound to be handy with his mauleys. Burrows, a protégé of Cribb's, was soundly whipped despite his vast experience. Molyneaux, now called "the Moor," proceeded to beat a number of heavyweights, including Tom Tough. Then, prompted by Richmond, he delivered a blow that shook all England: He claimed the British heavyweight title. His reasoning was that Cribb, who had won the title from Jem Belcher in 1809, had promptly retired. Molyneaux had defeated all other possible contenders; therefore he was the champion. Some of the Fancy laughed up their lace sleeves. Others bedamned the Nigger for his insolence. Cribb was urged to emerge from retirement and punish the pretentious American ex-slave. But Cribb, a victim of high living, was dubious about returning to the ring. Indeed, he might not have, had Molyneaux not made a powerful enemy.

This was Captain Robert Barclay, a gentleman and a Scottish officer who was without peer as a trainer of boxers.

A fine athlete, he regularly attended Gentleman Jackson's gymnasium on Bond Street, where he enjoyed sparring with other members. On one occasion, while pitted against a much smaller man, the captain got careless, walked into a left hook and was floored. Embarrassed, Barclay lost his temper and waded into his opponent, muttons awhirl, cornered him and was about to give him the coup de grâce when Gentleman Jackson hastened over and cried reprovingly, "For shame, Captain, for shame!" Barclay dropped his hands and allowed his opponent to stagger off to the dressing room. When Gentleman Jackson spoke, one listened.

The captain was tricky. He kept a pair of gloves in the gymnasium from

A section from Lord Byron's Screen showing Tom Cribb and Tom Molyneaux.

24

which the padding had been removed. Thus his hands received protection but the impact of his punches was not cushioned, the gloves could cut, and because they were light, the captain's arms did not get tired. On one occasion he graciously asked Molyneaux to visit the gymnasium and spar a bit. The captain was late, and while he was waiting, the Moor, all unknowing, borrowed the doctored gloves to punch the heavy bag. Then, when the amateur arrived, Molyneaux proceeded to give him a sound and painful drubbing with his own gloves. It was the bitter memory of this that prompted the captain to try to convince Cribb that for the honor of England, he should take his title back. And the captain promised he would work Cribb into splendid shape for the bout.

Though the captain's theories on training and diet seem quaint now, he was then considered the country's best authority on the subject. He thought meat the best training food. Vegetables, no; too difficult to digest. Milk, no; it was supposed to curdle in the stomach. Butter, cheese and soup were forbidden. However, if the fighter's taste turned to raw egg yolks, that was fine. And he could eat as much meat as he wished. Stale bread was recommended. He drank strong ale to add to his strength.

Pierce Egan recorded the captain's physical training program for fighters in *Boxiana:*

"The patient is purged with strong medicines; he is sweated by walking under a load of clothes, and by lying between feather-beds. His limbs are roughly rubbed. . . . He must rise at five in the morning, run half a mile at top speed uphill, and walk six miles at a moderate pace coming in about seven to breakfast. . . . After breakfast he must walk six miles at a moderate pace, and at twelve lie down in bed without his clothes for half an hour. On getting up, he must walk four miles. . . . Immediately after dinner, he must resume his exercise, by running half a mile at the top of his speed, and walking six miles at a moderate pace. He takes no more exercise for that day. . . ."

One would think not.

On December 10, 1810, the first championship fight between a white man and a black was held at Copthall Common, near East Grinstead, in Essex. Broughton's rules prevailed. Gentleman Jackson, the referee, pitched the ring himself as twenty-five thousand spectators stood uncomfortably in a chilly, driving rain, tensely waiting for the principals to clash.

Molyneaux was the aggressor from the beginning, the canny Cribb relying on the patient, defensive style which had served him so well. The Moor drew first blood in the second round and in the ninth knocked Cribb to the turf with a jolting right to the head. Molyneaux continued to punish his man for the next dozen rounds, with Cribb's superb condition the only factor that enabled him to return round after round to toe the mark.

In the twenty-third round Cribb landed his best blow, a solid smack directly in Molyneaux's left eye, which so enraged the black man that he threw a left hook to Cribb's body, seized him around the waist, lifted him high and flung him to the ground. There the champion of England lay, flat as a mackerel, and after he was dragged to his corner, no amount of pinching, prodding, shaking, dousing, face-slapping and shrieking by his handlers could restore him to consciousness. Three times Gentleman Jackson called "Time!," according to the rules; Cribb was unable to come to scratch.

But meanwhile, one of Cribb's cornermen, alert to the emergency, accosted Molyneaux on the other side of the ring and accused him of using foul tactics—specifically, of holding a bullet in each hand to give more weight to his blows. Molyneaux was bewildered by the accusation, and Richmond protested vehemently. Gentleman Jackson, who took no handler's word, strode over to Molyneaux and examined his hands; they contained no metal. This did not satisfy the second, who kept making a fuss. The crowd roared its approval of the delay; the majority had bet on Cribb. Meanwhile, Molyneaux, who was not enjoying the luxury of being unconscious, was getting soaked by the rain and was shivering in the cold. He began to sneeze and felt chills running down his back.

And now, with the long delay, Cribb's other cornerman had been able to restore the superbly conditioned man to consciousness. He finally came to scratch at Jackson's next call of "Time!" Now he faced a cold, weakened, psychologically debilitated opponent. Neither man fought with a great deal of spirit—Cribb because of the punishment he had taken, Molyneaux from an onset of the ague—but Molyneaux was the more listless of the two, and he succumbed from exhaustion in the fortieth round.

Thus for some the honor of England had been saved. Others recognized that Molyneaux, for all his objectionable antecedents, had been the better fighter on that day.

Molyneaux did take on Cribb once more, the following year. In this bout, held under clear skies at Thistleton Gap in Leicester, Molyneaux entered the ring overweight and poorly trained. Cribb broke the Moor's jaw in the eleventh round to end the bout. Molyneaux fought a few times after that, but the 1810 swindle had apparently taken something out of him. He paid little attention to conditioning and never again attained the heights he had reached against Cribb. He died of tuberculosis, a champion robbed of his crown.

━━━━━━━━━━

During the time that black warriors were fighting one another at Southern crossroads, little interest was being shown in boxing in the North, except in the waterfront areas. Not until 1816, in New York City, did Jacob Hyer and Tom Beasley fight what was reportedly the first battle between white men under bareknuckle rules. That same year Hyer's son Tom was born. Tom Hyer was later to make a considerable impression on the prizefight world.

In subsequent decades, until the inundation of the Irish, American boxing was dominated by invading Englishmen. In 1818, William Fuller, an English boxer and actor, came to America to perform in *Tom and Jerry*, a play written by the versatile Pierce Egan. At the conclusion of its run Fuller stayed over to give lessons in the manly science, "whereby gentlemen," Egan reported in *Boxiana*, "after a few lessons are enabled to chastise those who may offer violence and protect themselves against the attack of the ruffian." Fuller eventually opened a school in Charleston which attracted numbers of rich young bloods, the scions of plantation owners. Fuller had been beaten by Molyneaux, so he could hardly lay claim to the English championship. But distance lends credibility, and such was the unlettered state of American boxing that even though he merely gave exhibitions in threatres, no one challenged him when he pronounced himself champion of America.

Among others who visited these shores were some of England's most eminent fighters. The list includes Deaf Burke and Ben Caunt; and, sometime later, Joe Goss, Tom Allen and Jem Mace. Of them all, Burke probably furnished American prizefighting in the first half of the nineteenth century with its greatest melodrama. In this he had the help of an Irishman named Samuel O'Rourke.

After Burke, while he was British champion, had had the misfortune to kill Irish challenger Simon Byrne, he went into disconsolate retirement, whereupon O'Rourke, the Irish title-holder, challenged him. Burke refused the challenge when O'Rourke insisted that the fight be held in Ireland; the decision was a wise one, for feeling about Byrne's death ran high.

Running out of opponents in Ireland, O'Rourke set sail for America, settling temporarily in New York. There he let it be known that the Deaf 'Un was afraid of him. Burke, meanwhile, unable to engage in a major fight because of ill feeling against him in England, also voyaged to America in search of opponents. Aware of O'Rourke's unjustified claims, he was determined to close his mouth for him. But when he landed in New York in February, 1834, he learned that O'Rourke had fled south.

It was a smart move on O'Rourke's part. After giving some exhibitions in that more boxing-oriented section of the country, he set up a tavern in New Orleans that featured boxing. It immediately became the favorite hangout of longshoremen and sailors as well as gamblers and a variety of thugs and hoodlums. Bubbling with confidence while surrounded by this entourage, O'Rourke let it be known through the newspapers that he, as "world champion," would fight anyone who dared face him for a side bet of a thousand dollars.

While O'Rourke was the peacock of New Orleans, Burke was having a hard go of it, fighting exhibitions for small money. Then he was apprised of O'Rourke's offer. Determined to destroy him, Burke raised part of the side-bet money and undertook the long sea voyage to New Orleans.

O'Rourke, aware that he had the backing of his tough friends, consented to the bout. The ring was set up at a juncture of bayou roads near the sludgy Mississippi outside of New Orleans. The unruly crowd was composed, according to the New Orleans *Item,* of "fashionable Creoles, French gamblers, half-breeds, Yankee sharps, Irish toughs, and smugglers and picaroons from the Barataria swamps and lakes." O'Rourke was well represented by armed thugs. Burke came with a small contingent of his own. Pistols, bowie knives and clubs flashed into sight from time to time.

In addition to the inner ropes of the 24-foot ring, outer ropes were strung in a square pattern several yards beyond to keep the crowd from swarming in too close. But the outer ropes were cut the moment "Time!" was called, and shouting desperadoes soon surrounded the fighters. Most hollered insults at Burke and encouragement to O'Rourke. Burke sent his opponent to the ground with a cross-buttock throw, ending the first round. After the second had begun, one of O'Rourke's cornermen, Mickey Carson, sprang into the ring behind Burke and shoved him into O'Rourke's arms. O'Rourke promptly flung Burke to the ground and fell on top of him. Arising, Burke angrily threatened Carson with calamity if he repeated the act. Undaunted, Carson drew his bowie knife and threatened to disembowel Burke if he came close.

As the third round started, Burke struck two fine blows, closing O'Rourke's right eye. The sight enraged Carson, who crept up on Burke from behind with his drawn bowie knife. Burke quickly turned and smashed him in the face, knocking him onto his back. Snarling, roaring and screaming vengeance, O'Rourke's company of thugs cut the inner ropes and surrounded Burke. He flailed at a few of them, aided by a second, Jim Phelan. Then, seeing that murder was imminent, Phelan shouted, "Run for your life, Jem!" to Burke. Burke managed to plough his way through the crowd and headed for the nearby woods. One of his backers, John Caldwell, who owned a threatre in New Orleans, was standing by a horse saddled for just such an emergency. Caldwell rammed a bowie knife into Burke's hand. Burke clambered aboard the animal and the horse galloped off, with Burke, his torso muddied and bloody, leaning over clutching its neck. During his wild ride he panicked coachmen, horses and Creole ladies but did not slow down even when he came to the city. Across Canal Street and down Camp Street he rode, hair flying, body a kind of mottled gray, until he came to Caldwell's theatre. Dismounting, he darted through the stage entrance and burst onstage, startling the great Junius Brutus Booth and his players, who were rehearsing *Hamlet.* Burke was hustled into Booth's dressing room until the police could arrive. Then he was spirited onto a steamer headed up the Mississippi. He debarked at St. Louis and returned to New York. After winning a fight with Paddy O'Connell on Hart's Island he went back to England, where he lost his title to William Thompson and dropped from sight. O'Rourke, for his part, had a fittingly bad end. He left New Orleans to become a lumberjack, then a gambler, then a smuggler. He was found murdered one morning in Canada.

The next notable Englishman to arrive on the American shore was "Big Ben" Caunt, conqueror of Nick Ward, Jem's brother, for the British championship. Big Ben helped popularize the sport in this country by giving exhibitions. Much admired for his size and skill, Caunt was surprised, while touring

27

through Michigan, to be challenged by an unknown named Charles Freeman. Indeed, Freeman's backers were ready to put a thousand dollars up as a side bet. Delighted at the prospect of what seemed easy money, Caunt returned to New York, the site of the projected bout, as soon as he was able. Thus he was somewhat aghast to see, on their first meeting, that Freeman stood six feet ten inches high and weighed three hundred pounds, almost all of which was rock-hard muscle. Instead of risking his neck in the ring, Caunt suddenly turned impresario and promised Freeman a fortune if he would return to England with him.

Freeman was agreeable, and the two gave sparring exhibitions all over the British Isles. Freeman ("the American Giant" now) was extremely agile for his size and filled the spectators with awe. His competence in the ring discouraged all contestants until Bill Perry consented to meet him. A happy-go-lucky fellow, especially when in his cups, Perry once spied a Try Your Strength machine at a Handsworth racetrack—a metal-and-wood clown with a kind of target in his belt—and aggressively approached it. The proprietor, recognizing a leading contender, pleaded with him to go away, but Perry was unheeding. Tossing the proprietor a penny, he hit the machine such an uppercut that it splattered to smithereens in a shower of wood and metal. The delighted crowd chipped in to pay the owner for a new one.

In the fight against the American, however, Perry was far from aggressive. When Freeman moved forward to launch his blows, his opponent frequently sank to the turf to avoid punishment. After seventy rounds and with darkness coming on, it was decided to put off the bout until the following day. Then, at the request of Perry, who apparently had not fallen down fast enough nor often enough and carried numerous hurts, it was postponed for two weeks. When battle was rejoined Perry again made use of his stratagem. At the end of thirty-seven more rounds, the referee disqualified him and declared Freeman the winner. It was Freeman's only official fight. He contracted tuberculosis and died in 1845. According to accounts, if Freeman had fought the British champion, an American might have been champion of Britain in the 1840's.

Even when American boxing did get under sail, beginning in the 1850's, it was far from being the respected sport that cockfighting, horse racing and sculling were—though none of these, to be sure, was without its occasional X or double X. But boxing, by its very nature, lent itself more to corruption and intimidation than any other sport. To begin with, it was illegal, and fans and principals were subject to arrest. This meant that crowds were generally composed, for the most part, of the lower, more raffish elements of society. An estimated one-fifth of many audiences was composed of pickpockets who, taking advantage of bursts of excitement in a match, plied their trade with great insolence. Also, fighters had their claques and cliques—heavy bettors and loyal supporters—who often played a large part in determining the result of the fight, either by distracting a fighter or harassing him physically. Often weapons were brandished in the audience to frighten one of the fighters. Referees were likewise intimidated by spectators, hesitating to call fouls against an offender or to remonstrate with the audience lest they be trampled to death or cut to pieces in the ensuing riot.

It has been axiomatic in American boxing that the most desperate and poverty-stricken races have produced proportionately the greatest number of boxers. Irish immigrants and their sons at the middle and end of the nineteenth century furnished American boxing with a spirit, a drive and a drama without which the sport probably could not have survived.

The downtrodden Irish! They were rendered illiterate by an official act of British Parliament. Their desperate needs in times of famine were largely ignored by the British Government. Under the tenant system, after the British Parliament's Act of Union, English landlords were able to place twenty tenants on a plot of land that had previously supported a single farmer and his family. If a crop failed, the result was disaster. If a crop prospered, rents were raised. Potatoes, planted in spring, were the farmer's staple, because they required no cultivation. And while they burgeoned underground the farmer went to England to search for some kind of job while his wife and children begged on street corners. In fall he returned to harvest the potatoes and try to survive the winter.

America had been the salvation of many migrating Irishmen and their families before the Revolution. The letters they sent back to their relatives were most optimistic about the lot of the Irish in America, and entire villages would turn out to hear them read. As conditions in Ireland became increasingly bad in the early 1800's, thousands of Irishmen and their families decided to make the long, wretchedly uncomfortable trip to what they called "the Land of the Young," where a chance to work and get one's belly filled were promised.

The migrants' experience was filled with misfortunes. They were fleeced by their own countrymen at ports of departure like Londonderry, Belfast and Cork while they waited for a ship. Landing at Boston or New York or Philadelphia, they were fleeced once more, this time by countrymen pretending to be helpful to greenhorns. The immigrants would be conducted to nearby boardinghouses by runners, some wearing jaunty green hats. The rents, they would later discover, were piratical, forcing some heads of households to become indentured to landlords in America, just as they had been in the old country. If they escaped boardinghouse bondage, they lived in great, crowded groups in cellars, attics, warehouses and ancient houses which inevitably became disease-ridden ghettos.

The potato blight of 1846 and 1847 forced a million and a half more Irishmen to emigrate, the greatest portion of them coming to America. And America, in particular the coastal cities, was not at all kind to its visitors. Without education or white-collar skills, the Irishmen were channeled into primitive manual

work. "No Irish Need Apply" was a sign they were often confronted with. So some found work as laborers or factory sweepers or in stables. Wages were excessively low. Some of the enterprising ones used what capital they had to establish grocery stores specializing in foods regarded as staples by the Irish. Because some of the store owners manufactured raw whiskey, some of these stores metamorphosed into saloons.

Away from the coastal cities the Irish found their presence more welcome and the work better paid. In a time of violent American expansion west and south, canals were being dug, macadamized roads were being laid, railroads were being built. The Irish, sturdy and desperate, a generation or less away from starvation, furnished the unskilled labor that most native sons disdained. The Irish constructed the National Road from Cumberland, Maryland, to Vandalia, Illinois, and dug DeWitt Clinton's Erie Canal—and found themselves yet again cheated. They were forced to pay piratical prices to company stores for tobacco, clothing, shoes and comestibles. When the labor supply began to exceed the demand, they were paid off in whiskey. And when there were more laborers available than could be used, Irishmen from one county would battle with Irishmen from another in an effort to keep or acquire the backbreaking jobs. One fight for work—on the Chesapeake and Ohio Canal—grew so bitter that President Jackson was forced to summon Federal troops to stop it.

Despite their mental and spiritual stagnation as they were viciously exploited in the promised land, the Irish found a way to survive. That was by obtaining the vote and by voting in great blocs.

Before 1822 in New York State a male citizen could not vote unless he owned property, which automatically eliminated almost all the Irish population. But in that year an amendment to the state constitution waived the property requirement. Tammany Hall, the state's as well as New York City's most powerful political club, shortly discovered the value of the monolithic Irish vote and wooed the Irish, who soon became the will behind Tammany's voice in politics. Other well-oiled political machines —in Boston, Chicago, Philadelphia, San Francisco and Detroit—followed New York's lead.

Boxers—proud to be of service to whoever offered them money—were found to be useful in the helter-skelter, poorly supervised arena of politics, particularly Irish politics. On election day, boxers helped stuff ballot boxes; and they stole those not stuffed enough. Drunks were wheeled in to vote. Voters known to vote the wrong way were chased away from the polling places. Peace was kept at political meetings by boxers, and hecklers were bodily expelled. Political arrangements were made and alliances formed at saloons where boxers hung out. John Morrissey, Yankee Sullivan, Lew Baker and James Turner—all splendid boxers—worked actively for Tammany Hall. Tom Hyer and Bill "the Butcher" Poole broke with Tammany because of its domination by "foreigners." (When Poole was murdered in a saloon by Tammany fighter Lew Baker as a result of a political-*cum*-grudge argument in 1855, five thousand admirers of the Butcher marched down Broadway from Bleecker Street to the Battery in Manhattan as several brass bands propelled his soul to heaven.) John Carmel Heenan, one of the greatest of American boxers, was assigned the task of busting open the head of anyone who heckled an orator at Tammany political shindigs.

Raging feuds marked the personal relationships of the early American champions and their challengers. Tom Hyer, the former butcher boy who beat Country McClusky at Caldwell's Landing on the Hudson in 1841 and is accounted the first "official" American champion, despised Yankee Sullivan; Morrissey loathed Heenan; and Joe Coburn was not too crazy about any of them.

Yankee Sullivan was as willing to fight out of the ring as in it. In a New York saloon he overheard someone remark that he was afraid of Tom Hyer. Afroth, he promptly set out to locate and destroy his rival and found him in a saloon at Park Place and Broadway. It was a mistake. Hyer, presumably more sober than Sullivan, knocked him out in three minutes. When he could talk again, Sullivan challenged Hyer to a formal fight for the American championship. While Hyer was the larger man— four inches taller and thirty pounds heavier than Sullivan and with a much greater reach—the latter had by far the more experience, having never been beaten in bouts in Ireland, England and Australia.

The rivals planned to meet at Pool's Island, on the Maryland border, on February 6, 1849. However, a boatload of police from Baltimore landed there in time to threaten them with arrest and prevent the fight. Both men escaped by posing as their own seconds and boarded steamboats loaded with spectators. After a nautical chase, the constables' boat foundered providentially on some rocks, and the spectators' boats anchored off a deserted stretch of Maryland beach. There a ring was set up, and as snow swirled down, Hyer proceeded to demonstrate that the saloon fight had been no fluke. He stunned his opponent with blows that Sullivan was unable to block, and after sixteen rounds Sullivan's second, Country McClusky, seized his man to save him from further punishment. Hyer was declared the winner, and Sullivan went to the hospital.

The most colorful, enterprising and ambitious of American champions in the middle of the nineteenth century was John Morrissey. Born in Templemore, Tipperary, in 1831, he came to America at the age of three. The family settled in Troy, New York, where the elder Morrissey worked as a day laborer. John, the only son among eight children, sought employment early. At twelve he labored in a wallpaper factory for $1.25 a week, then in a rolling mill. (John C. Heenan, a local tough, worked with him.) In 1846 he worked in the molding room of a converted stove foundry, helping make bombshells for the Mexican War. Strong and thick-skinned, John became the most prominent "rounder" in the city, taking eager part in gang fights. These were mainly between the Up Town roughs and the Down Town rowdies. Morrissey was the leader—"chief devil" —of the Down Town group. John

O'Rourke, a well-known fighter, was leader of the Up Towners. Inevitably the two battled it out in a saloon. O'Rourke tripped Morrissey and laid him flat on coals spilled from an overturned stove. Between getting burned on his back and being strangled from in front, Morrissey was hard put to weather the match. But, kicking and clawing, he squirmed out from under and proceeded to give O'Rourke a thorough lacing. During the following months he beat up the rest of O'Rourke's gang, one by one. From the stove incident he acquired the nickname "Old Smoke."

He then became in turn a bartender, a runner for a boardinghouse in New York and a deckhand on a Hudson River steamboat. Meanwhile he taught himself to read and write. Hearing about the gold being dug up in California, he stowed away on a ship headed there. But he was discovered, and rather than being returned to New York in a brig, he sneaked off at Panama. There, unable to raise fare by gambling, he stowed away on another ship and was again apprehended. Morrissey was threatened with being put off at inhospitable Acapulco, but he helped quell a mutiny by the passengers over the poor food aboard, and the grateful captain delivered him to San Francisco. In that picaresque city he opened a gambling house, which was only moderately successful because Morrissey valued his popularity over riches. Then he heard about a gold strike on Queen Charlotte's Islands, lying to the north off British Columbia. With friends, Morrissey bought a schooner and weapons, including a cannon, and sailed away on what amounted to a piratical venture. Embarking without papers, Morrissey and his crew of gamblers, miners and thugs located the islands, which they found inhabited by an artistic tribe of Indians, the Haida, but barren of gold. Returning disconsolately to San Francisco, he sold the schooner and returned the band's investment.

He was in the mood, as it happened, to take up the offer of one William Thompson, who had enjoyed some success in the California ring, to fight anyone in California for a two-thousand-dollar side bet. Though he was not in

Yankee Sullivan

shape for a formal fight in the ring against a professional, Morrissey was convinced by admirers that he could handle Thompson, and he consented to the meeting. The two men fought on Mare's Island on August 31, 1852. Thompson, more experienced and a cleverer boxer, plastered Morrissey much as he pleased for the first eleven rounds, though Morrissey stubbornly pursued him, not much bothered by the beating. His followers were bothered, however, and the gang of toughs, miners, gamblers and saloon fighters made such threatening noises that Thompson became terrified and deliberately fouled Morrissey. The latter's backers collected their bets and hailed Morrissey as the coming champion. Flushed with victory and imbued with confidence, Morrissey returned to New York to challenge Tom Hyer for the championship of the United States. Hyer declined, but Hyer's archenemy,

Yankee Sullivan, who was seeking the title, agreed to fight.

Sullivan was not a true Yankee, nor was his name Sullivan. It was James Ambrose. Born of Irish parents in London's East End, he had scores of fights as a youth but then fell afoul of the law and was transported to Botany Bay in Australia as a felon. Finding manual labor arduous, Sullivan escaped, made his way to San Francisco and eked out a living with his fists. Then he returned to London, where he won a fight but fled back to America when he learned that the police were hot on his trail. Back in America, he boldly claimed the American championship, Hyer having retired.

For all his evil ways, Sullivan had both courage and a sense of humor, as he showed in a fight with Vincent Hammond, a boxer of no great merit. Hammond managed to surprise Sullivan in the first round by whipping out a straight right that smashed Sullivan's lower lip against his teeth, severely lacerating the inside of his mouth. Since there was a tradition at the time of betting on "first blood," Sullivan, to save his friends' wagers, swallowed the bubbly fluid—like Eurydemus centuries before—so that no red would appear on his face. Then, attacking fiercely, he managed to cut open Hammond's cheek. "Sullivan draws first blood!" sang out the referee, the arbiter in these matters, and Sullivan's supporters whooped and cheered. A moment later Sullivan spat out a mouthful himself and cried through swollen lips, "And there goes second!" Hammond was soundly drubbed after that and at the end of eight rounds was unable to come to scratch. It was a glorious night indeed for Yankee Sullivan.

The battle between Sullivan and Morrissey, held at Boston Four Corners in New York on October 12, 1853, was a strange one. Morrissey was younger, taller and heavier; Sullivan, who wore an American flag around his waist to show his patriotism, was the more crafty. Sullivan hit Morrissey as he pleased in the early rounds, cutting Old Smoke's face up and belaboring him in the body, but no punch was hard enough to keep Morrissey from return-

ing to scratch after the respite. In the thirty-eighth round, Morrissey, still strong, seized his lithe opponent around the waist and throat and held him against the ropes. Half supported by the ropes, his back bent nearly in two, Sullivan was growing black in the face when his seconds entered the ring and tried to force Morrissey to release him. Morrissey's handlers then leapt in and started to fight with Sullivan's. One of the latter was getting pummeled by a Morrissey second named Awful Gardner, so Sullivan, by now freed, started to help him. Meanwhile Morrissey had repaired to his corner, ignoring the other fight in the ring. The referee called "Time!" and Morrissey strode to scratch. Sullivan, however, was too busy scrapping with Awful to keep the engagement. The referee thereupon awarded the fight to Morrissey. Dismayed, Sullivan leapt out of the ring and Morrissey was acknowledged the champion of America.

Sullivan shook the dust of the East from his heels and voyaged west to San Francisco, where he soon became involved with gamblers who took gold miners' money. He had the bad luck to appear at a time when vigilance committees were in the process of restraining criminals, jailing some and publicly hanging others. Sullivan was arrested

John Morrissey

32

and thrust into jail to await trial. There he was found hanged one morning, presumably the victim of vigilante impatience.

Morrissey's fortunes continued to prosper. The recognized titleholder, he opened a profitable public house in New York, where no gambling was allowed. He married the daughter of the steamboat captain for whom he had worked as a deckhand, and he kept a hand in politics, in particular opposing Bill Poole and his Native American Party. He and the Butcher decided to have it out one night on the dock at the foot of Amos Street. Poole arrived with his gang; Morrissey showed up alone. Morrissey more than held his own, but whenever he went down, some of Poole's cronies kicked him. Still Morrissey got up, poked a few strange noses and returned to his battering of Poole. He won the fracas, and Poole swore he would never fight him again.

Meanwhile John Carmel Heenan had, like his townsman, traveled a long way from Troy. A tall, strong, handsome man who could have been successful in a dozen fields, Heenan was taught mechanics by his immigrant father but was lured by the prospect of finding gold in California. He journeyed there but, being of practical bent, decided to go to work instead. He was hired as a mechanic in a workshop of the Pacific Mail Steamship Company, in Benicia, across the bay from San Francisco. He engaged in fights in his spare time, having learned his apprenticeship in Troy, and became popular as "the Benicia Boy." His western reputation established, he returned to New York panting for a fight with Morrissey. The champion was willing to fight his rival, and the meeting was arranged: five thousand dollars a side, for the American title, to take place on October 20, 1858. The fight was to be held, for purposes of avoiding jail, on Long Point Island, an island in Lake Erie belonging to Canada.

Fight fans, thugs, pickpockets, gamblers and supporters of both parties debarked in steamboats from Buffalo the night before, and the ships weighed anchor far offshore. The spectators rowed to the strand, and the ring was pitched near the island lighthouse.

Neither fighter had a great deal of trust in his opponent, so by mutual agreement fifty guards stood by to see that foul play was minimized, and a second ring, twenty feet beyond the first, was set up to keep spectators from mixing it with the pugilists.

Heenan, the heavier by twenty pounds, forced the fighting, his fists carrying the explosive force of a wrecker's ball. But Morrissey weathered the blows, concentrating his attack on Heenan's body. He knew that the Benicia Boy was not in the best of condition because of a recently healed leg ulcer. Heenan smashed Morrissey to the sand in the fifth round, but Morrissey, heartened by the urgings of his constituents, returned to scratch and kept pounding Heenan's stomach. In the ninth round Heenan threw a desperate straight right which Morrissey ducked. Heenan's fist shot into a ring post, and he broke his hand. Unable to use his right hand thereafter, his attack faltered as Morrissey kept hammering home blows. In the eleventh Heenan collapsed and, despite the ministrations of his seconds, was unable to face the champion for the twelfth. Morrissey had retained his title.

It was his last fight in the ring. He then became friends with John Hunter and William K. Travers and opened a racetrack at Saratoga. The following year he helped found a jockey club. In 1861 he began dabbling in Wall Street stocks. Meanwhile he had become a serious political candidate, discovering that his popularity as a prizefighter, a sporting-house owner and a racetrack founder were useful assets in obtaining the loyalty of the electorate. He was elected twice to Congress and twice to the New York State legislature, where he was a staunch opponent of Boss Tweed and was noted for his compassion for the taxpayer.

Heenan, for his part, accepted the American crown that Morrissey had decided to forswear, and then sought the world title. For a while he traveled around the country giving boxing exhibitions. Then in 1859 he began negotiations for his fight in 1860 with Tom Sayers, the English champion, for the world's championship.

John C. Heenan

In this endeavor, Heenan was encouraged by Adah Isaacs Menken, whom he had married a short time before. Actress, authoress, poetess and lecturer, the Menken, as she was called, was one of the most accomplished women of her time. She had even boxed with Heenan to see what that experience was like. She was not unaware of the publicity that would accrue to her if her husband should become champion of the world. Later she would achieve international fame by playing the daring role of Mazeppa in the historical drama of that name, based on a poem by Lord Byron. The story concerns a Tartar prince, Mazeppa, who loves the daughter of a Polish nobleman. The nobleman strenuously disapproves of the romance. Mazeppa is taken captive and, as punishment for his audacity, is lashed to a fiery steed which runs off to the hills. Playing the male role onstage, the soft-eyed Menken was actually lashed to the steed, face upward. The animal then noisily galloped off, to the screams and applause of packed houses. Witty and intelligent as well as strikingly pretty, the Menken would also become the good friend of Algernon Swinburne, Charles Dickens, Walt Whitman and Dumas *père*.

As the monumental fight approached, since Heenan carried on his shoulders all the prestige and honor of young America, that topic took precedence in Eastern papers over the wise saws of Abraham Lincoln, who was about to be nominated as the Republican Presidential candidate. When the news arrived by steamship that the fight had ended in a riotous draw, however, the publicity that the Menken had thought would prove useful was not worth much. Heenan, moreover, deserted his wife and ran off to Chicago with a young lady. After that he went back to England, where he became a bookmaker.

A section on one phase of American boxing in this era—from 1850 to about 1880—might be called Farces, Nonfights and Intimidations, for that is indeed what many contests were. The list of these bouts, many of them for championships, is impressive. Among the highlights:

On May 15, 1863, Joe Coburn fought a riverman from Cincinnati named Mike McCoole, known as "the deckhand champion of America," for the American championship. The fight took place near Cumberland, Maryland. Coburn was the better boxer, McCoole the more powerful hitter and able to withstand more punishment. However, during the sixty-seven rounds of fighting, McCoole was continually harried by Coburn's enthusiastic friends at ringside. They not only hurled gross insults at the riverman but added to his distraction by hitting him from time to time. Somewhat confused, McCoole took a number of punches from Coburn that he might otherwise have avoided, and little by little Coburn wore him down. At last Coburn knocked him to the turf with such finality that one of McCoole's seconds threw in the sponge.

McCoole nonetheless claimed the championship, and in 1868 he and Coburn decided to have it out. The fight was scheduled to be held in Cold Spring, Indiana. Despite a drizzle, about five thousand respectable citizens were present for the epic affair. A good portion of pickpockets attended as well. Before the fight started, the pickpockets, who had been very busy, expressed their pride in their calling by sending a shower of wallets and billfolds like flying bats in the general direction of the ring. When this ceremony was over, McCoole climbed through the ropes and went to his corner. Coburn was heading toward the ring when he was arrested by an agent from the Treasury Department. It developed later that Coburn did not feel well, was sure he would be beaten and arranged for the "arrest" to avoid facing McCoole. McCoole thereupon informed the crowd that he was, by default, the heavyweight champion. The crowd, fleeced, wet, cold and disgusted, did not much care.

Tom Allen, an English invader, was several times made aware of the whimsical activities of his opponents' backers. In 1869, in a fight with McCoole held near St. Louis, he showed a degree of prescience by declaring to the spectators before the bout that he intended to become an American citizen and hoped to receive fair play. Then he proceeded to plunge his fists into the sluggish McCoole, cutting him up thoroughly. Before he could extinguish the riverman's light entirely, however, McCoole's gang broke through the ropes, flourishing guns, and demanded that the referee give their man the decision. The referee fled and announced the verdict several hours later, from St. Louis. After rumination, he awarded the decision to McCoole on a foul.

Allen, who became champion of America, was twice more involved in bouts where violence erupted at critical points. In 1873 he fought Ben Hogan, a German soldier of fortune (originally named Hagen) who had spied for both sides in the Civil War. The fight took place in Pacific City, Iowa, and Hogan came equipped with a party of toughs who announced that their man had better win. Allen knocked him down for eight successive rounds, but in the ninth the ropes parted and the referee was informed by Hogan's supporters that he ought to give Hogan the decision. The referee refused to do so, however, and left without awarding the decision to anybody. That night, from a safe vantage point, he gave the decision to Allen, who thus retained his title.

Some of Allen's enemies in St. Louis, where he kept a saloon, decided in 1876 to rid him of some of his alleged conceit by having him licked in the ring. Old Joe Goss, another invader, was selected as Allen's opponent, and the fight was scheduled to be held near a railroad track (for ready escape from the blue-nosed authorities) about fifteen miles from Cincinnati. The militia arrived before the battle got under way, so spectators and principals traveled fifteen more miles down the track and detrained. The ring was pitched near the rails. Allen, now an American citizen, bashed Goss from stake to stake, closing an eye and breaking his nose, despite threatening howls from Goss's supporters in the crowd. The howls got increasingly loud as the twenty-first round ended. It did not seem as though Goss, who had been slammed to his knees, would toe the mark for the twenty-second. The threatening sounds increased, and metal glinted ominously in the audience. Then Allen, to the surprise of all, deliberately struck Goss twice in the forehead as Goss knelt in the middle of the ring. The referee awarded the fight and "the championship of America" to Goss, while Allen retained his life. He considered it a fair trade.

In 1864 Joe Coburn went to England for the express purpose of fighting Jem Mace, then the British champion. But when Mace refused to let a good friend of Coburn's act as referee, as Coburn insisted, the fight was called off and Coburn returned to America. Seven years later Coburn emerged from retirement to have another go at Mace, who was now preaching the gospel of British boxing in America. The bout, held at Long Point, was one of the most nonsensical on record. Coburn, a clever boxer, had been informed that Mace's great skill lay in his ability to counter after his opponent jabbed or made any kind of lead. Coburn reasoned that if he refused to lead, no matter what opening was offered, Mace would be stymied. As indeed he was. Coburn did not throw a single punch, and the two jigged around the ring, making head feints, shoulder feints and eye feints as though intent on doing furious damage. Mace was just as stubborn as Coburn. The crowd became restless, and after an hour and seventeen minutes of the harmless war dance, the weary referee finally capitulated and called the bout a draw.

In 1879, with the sport relatively stagnant and the championship apparently going begging, two relative unknowns fought for it. One was Johnny Dwyer, brother of the political boss of Brooklyn, who had sparred creditably with Coburn and Allen. The other was "Grayback" Jimmy Elliott, who had nearly killed a man during a robbery and had just been pardoned from a Philadelphia prison. The two met at Long Point, with five hundred spectators on hand.

Dwyer had things his own way for nine rounds, easily avoiding Elliott's wild swings, and at one point hit his opponent so hard a blow to the temple that the crowd thought Elliott's skull had cracked. In desperate straits, Elliott in the next round maneuvered Dwyer close to the ropes and tried to gouge his eyes out. Dwyer screamed so loud that the referee was constrained to separate the two, whereupon Dwyer's seconds pointed out that Elliott's fingers were adrip with turpentine. Time was called while Dwyer's eyes were rinsed with water. When he could see somewhat, the two resumed the battle. In the twelfth, the desperate Elliott tried to take a chunk out of Dwyer's kidney with his teeth. As he made his lunge, Dwyer caught him under the chin with a right uppercut. Elliott staggered back and Dwyer seized him around the waist, hoisted him up and flung him to the ground, landing on Elliott's chest with both knees. Elliott was no good after that, and Dwyer won the thousand-dollar side bet and the championship. He fought no more, so it is difficult to assess his worth as an American champion.

The dearth of good American heavyweights and the casualness with which the title was bandied about is illustrated by the somewhat phenomenal career of Paddy Ryan. Born in the town of Thurles in Tipperary, Ryan came to America with his family when young and grew up in that Bristol of America, Troy, New York. In his teens his strength and cleverness at wrestling earned him, in local circles, the title of "the Trojan Giant." Some of his strength was developed by sculling.

At six feet one-half-inch tall and weighing, in his prime, 210 pounds, he later became so successful at grappling and in informal saloon fights that he issued a bold challenge to Americans everywhere that he would fight any man for a thousand dollars a side, the winner to be proclaimed the national champion.

Ryan's backers wanted him to fight Johnny Dwyer of Brooklyn, who had had such a troublesome time with turpentine in his bout with Jim Elliott, but Dwyer had retired. Despite the fact that he had fought but one professional fight (and had lost it), Ryan was confident that his wrestling ability and saloon-fight knowledge were enough to see him through the toughest bare-knuckle bout.

Joe Goss, the ex-champion of England and, by default, the recognized American champion, agreed to lay his title on the line. He and Ryan met on May 30, 1880, at Collier Station, a small town on the West Virginia–Pennsylvania border. Youth, strength, and gameness, along with a height and reach advantage, made up Ryan's arsenal against Goss's vast experience.

The forty-two-year-old Briton had things his own way for the first sixty rounds, pummeling Ryan at will, but he managed to exhaust himself in the process. Ryan had the better of it when he could get close enough to Goss to squeeze him or trip him. Goss, ringwise enough to fall down when grazed by one of Ryan's awkward swings, was nonetheless in trouble when the rounds reached the eighties. In the eighty-sixth a roundhouse swing by Ryan caught Goss on the chin. As he staggered backward, Ryan seized him around the waist, lifted him and threw him to the turf, landing on the champion's ribs with all his weight. Breathless, dazed and full of aches in his chest, Goss could not toe the mark despite the valiant work of his cornermen, and Paddy Ryan was declared the winner and American champion—the only man in history to have won a heavyweight prizefight title in his second fight. In his third he had the bad luck to come up against John L. Sullivan. ■

THE BATTLE *between CRIB and MOLINEAUX, fought at Thistleton Gap in the County of Rutland Sept. 28th 1811 for 600 Guineas a side 11 rounds, fought in 19 minutes, in which Crib was Victorious, he Moor was carried off senseless with a broken Jaw. Crib was but little the worse*

THE CLOSE OF THE BATTLE or the CHAMPION TRIUMPHANT.

Tom Molyneaux, born a slave in South Carolina, won his freedom by boxing. Above, in an engraving by George Cruikshank, he loses his second match with Tom Cribb at Thistleton, England, in 1811. Molyneaux died in Britain at the age of thirty-four.

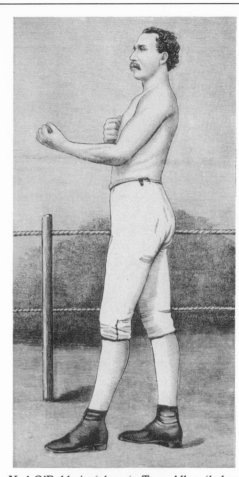

Tom Sayers (above); Johnny Dwyer (below).

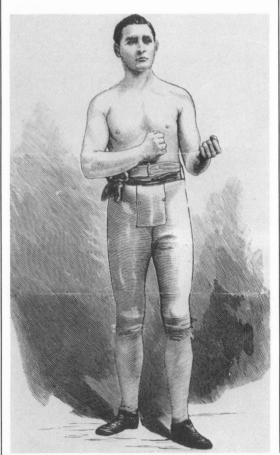

Ned O'Baldwin (above); Tom Allen (below).

After the Prince of Wales became King George IV in 1820, British boxing began *to fall into a decline. But across the ocean a young America welcomed immigrants*

Tom Hyer (above); Charles Gallagher (below).

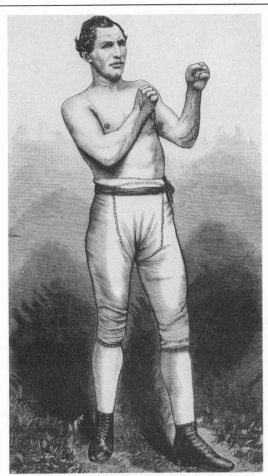

Joe Coburn (above); Jem Mace (below).

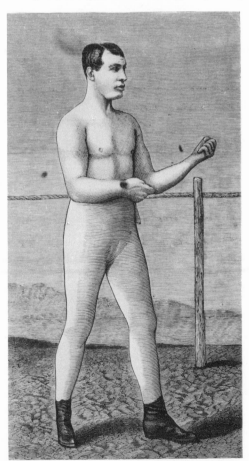

and provided the perfect setting for contests in which a man could prove his worth with his fists. Some of the great boxers of this period are shown above.

THE GREAT FIGHT,
between TOM HYER & YANKEE SULLIVAN, for $ 10.000.

On February 7, 1849, Tom Hyer knocked out Yankee Sullivan in sixteen rounds at Rock Point, Maryland. The winner got $10,000. Doubtless this set the standard for later purses that stirred the imagination of American fans.

John C. Heenan and Tom Sayers at Farnborough, England, April 17, 1860. Lithograph by Currier and Ives. Courtesy of the New York Public Library.

The first International Championship Bout was held April 17, 1860, at Farnborough, England. American Champion John Heenan fought British Champion Tom Sayers. After forty-two rounds the contest was declared a draw.

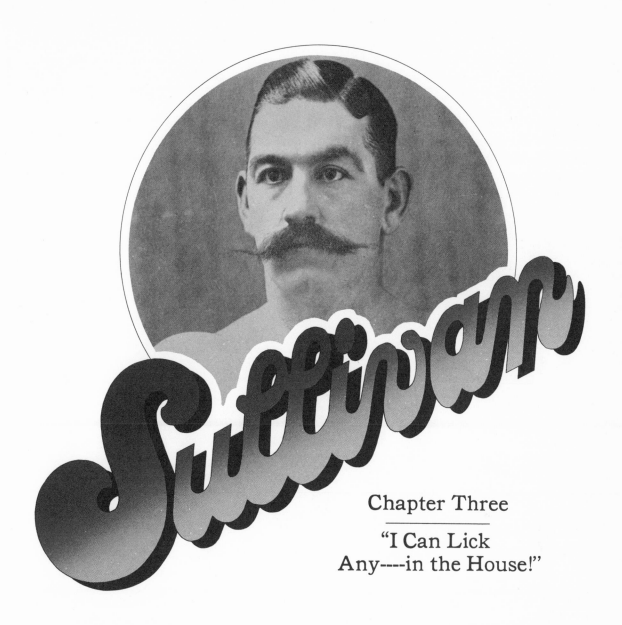

Chapter Three

"I Can Lick
Any----in the House!"

John Lawrence Sullivan was a boozer and a bully and a braggart and as such was loved by every red-blooded American. That is, with a few dramatic exceptions. Two enemies were the governor of Mississippi and the editor of the extremely powerful and wildly imaginative *Police Gazette*. Then there were a few bluenoses, some clergymen and some do-gooders who disliked him as the dominant representative of a sport they abhorred.

He wrote his signature in the air after making a pronouncement: Yours truly, John L. Sullivan.

When he visited England in 1887 (he came away richer by ten thousand dollars for exhibiting his "sparring" to doting Englishmen), they would say to one another, "Shake the hand that shook the hand of John L. Sullivan." He was such a good saloon fighter that Teddy Roosevelt, then the New York Police Commissioner, often asked Diamond Jim Brady, whom Sullivan admired, to wheedle him out before he wrecked the place. Some time later Roosevelt carried Sullivan's gold-mounted rabbit's foot—a gift—to Africa for luck.

Sullivan was noted for his sense of humor. It was his practice, when moving from saloon to saloon in a city, to walk up behind a patron preoccupied with his thoughts or deep in conversation and throw a roundhouse blow at his derby hat, sending it sailing along the bar. One night young Lionel Barrymore, after performing in *The Brixton Burglary*, was relaxing at the bar of Jack's, a New York restaurant frequented by actors, when Sullivan came in and impishly tried to knock his hat off. But Barrymore saw the blow coming and moved, getting his face in the way of the swing. He was knocked out for an hour, and a newspaper headline the next day read: NOTED ACTOR KNOCKED OUT BY SULLIVAN. Sullivan, remorseful after the KO, kept buying drinks for everybody. Barrymore took up boxing and wrestling in a gym to keep in shape lest a similar incident recur.

Brawling, rowdy, robust America—with its Manifest Destiny, free enterprise and good fellowship enhanced by bad whiskey; Conestogas fording rivers and hurtling down hills; vast waterways being dug to link lakes and rivers; rails being laid down by coolies moving east and by Irish immigrants moving west—seemed to be epitomized by the personality, in the ring and out, of the swaggering, supremely confident, never-take-a-back-step Boston Strong Boy.

He liked the ladies, and they flocked to him at the hotels he stayed at: "If she's a looker, send 'er up." He looked the part of a conqueror—a florid-faced, black-browed, black-haired, mustachioed man with an aggressive fighter's jaw.

He was immortalized in poetry. Listen:

Just fancy what mingled emotions
Would fill the puritan heart
To learn what renown was won for
     his town
By means of the manly art!
Imagine a Winthrop or Adams
In front of a bulletin board,
Each flinging his hat at the
     statement that
The first blood was by Sullivan
     scored.
Thy bards, henceforth, O Boston!
Of his triumph of triumphs will sing!
For a muscular stroke has added a
     spoke
To the Hub, which will strengthen
     the ring!
Now Lowell will speak of the "ruby"
And Aldrich of "closing a match,"
And Longfellow rhyme of "coming
     to time"
Of "bunches of fives" and "the
     scratch."

(The "ruby" is what is today called the "claret," slang for blood. "Closing a match" is pursuing one's opponent in the final struggle. "Coming to time" is emerging from one's corner at the referee's beckoning. "Bunches of fives" are fingers. "The scratch" is the mark the fighter must reach at the referee's call of "Time!" to start each round.)

He never failed to draw enthusiastic crowds. He dared anyone to last four rounds with him. Was a broken jaw worth a thousand dollars? Only one man picked up the prize, an Englishman named Tug Wilson. Wilson did it by crouching and "crawling" (vernacular for going down without being hit).

Sullivan was a master of gasconade. In a saloon, when the amber liquid rendered him expansive, he would proclaim, "I can lick any son-of-a-bitch in the house." His companions would roister and laugh and shout and drink Gaelic toasts to the boast, the bill being defrayed by Sullivan.

He tried his hand at acting as well as fighting. Although his most dramatic stint onstage was shaping horseshoes while playing a blacksmith, he had enough faith in himself to say, "I don't want to sound egotistical, but I hope someday to be as great an actor as [Edwin] Booth. . . . I've just begun this business now and of course I'm not up on all points. But they'll come along, all right. . . . None of the great actors had to study much."

He shook hands with the Prince of Wales—the future Edward VII—and by doing so elevated the sport of prizefighting. John L. had it in him to say, "Well, Prince, next to your champion, Jem Smith, whom I'm anxious to whip, you're the fellow I most wanted to meet while in England."

In America, everything he did—getting arrested for fighting in the ring and out of it, issuing challenges, refusing challenges and defending himself to his critics—was reported widely in the press. Boston saloons featured a spring-operated John L. Sullivan Athletic Punching Machine—"How Hard Can You Hit the Great John L.?" Posters of him looking fierce in a boxing pose covered unsightly spots on the saloon walls. After James J. Corbett dethroned Sullivan, in many saloons a hand kinescope was available to show jumpy pictures of the fight to disbelievers. And so great was the impact of John L.'s career and personality and the extent of his popularity, that there remained quite a few.

———————

The first great American boxing idol was born in Roxbury, Massachusetts, a suburb of Boston, on October 15, 1858.

He was as Irish by heritage as you can get, his father hailing from Tralee in County Kerry and his mother from Athlone in County Roscommon. He was never allowed to forget that his paternal grandfather had been a famous Celtic wrestler and handy at swinging a shillelagh in less formal encounters. His mother was a giant of a woman, nearly as big as her son became in his early fighting years. His father, Michael, though small, was a fiery, pugnacious man who built his muscles by working as a hod carrier and was a champion fighter among his colleagues.

In high school John was no student, but he was strongest of all and especially skilled at baseball, boxing and wrestling. Because his mother wished him to become a priest, John dutifully attended Boston College for a time. But he found the theological concepts too complex for his taste and left after sixteen months.

Through his father's influence he became a hod carrier. He found two recreations a welcome relaxation from that somewhat dull and monotonous labor: friendly wrestling matches, and amateur "sparring exhibitions" in Boston theatres. The latter were allowed by the local constabulary because they were fought for only three or four rounds under Queensberry rules, which were becoming popular in the East. The wearing of gloves—called "pillows" by the cynical—made a difference to the city fathers. Also, the term "sparring" has a noncommercial, friendly tone. But the blows struck were extremely violent.

Forsaking the hod, John became successively an assistant plumber and a tinsmith. He adopted the latter trade after being fired by his plumber boss. The pair had an altercation, and the head plumber, who had thought he could teach the young man a fistic lesson, discovered when he came to that his jaw was broken in several places.

When away from the tinsmith shop, Sullivan began thinking about a career in baseball. He showed so much ability on local semipro teams that there was talk of his being signed with the Cincinnati Reds, the first of the truly impressive barnstorming professional ball clubs (fifty-six wins and one tie in 1878). But Sullivan never found out how he would have fared as a batter in the somewhat disorganized, somewhat suspect ball games of the time, for he was propelled willy-nilly into prizefighting.

One night he attended a sparring exhibition at the Dudley Street Opera House in Boston. A fairly experienced boxer, Tom Scannel, challenged anyone in the theatre to stay three rounds with him. Scannel was looking, or possibly leering, at Sullivan while making his speech. Sullivan being the local hero, cries of "Go get him, lad!" and "Murther him, Johnny!" came from all parts of the audience. The young man grinned self-consciously, took off his jacket and tie, rolled up his sleeves Kerry-style and sprang up onto the stage.

After the light gloves were donned, he moved over to meet the relaxed-looking Scannel and learned his first lesson in serious prizefighting: never take anything for granted. He assumed Scannel would shake hands before the battle started, or at least touch gloves. But Scannel started a swing before Sullivan could think of protecting himself and landed a left hook high on Sullivan's cheek, staggering him. As future boxers were to learn, Sullivan was a man of extremely explosive temper when stung with a blow or fouled. He roared toward the snickering Scannel with the charge that was later to be his most characteristic fighting tactic and flung a right fist at Scannel's jaw. It propelled Scannel off his feet and sent him soaring into the orchestra pit. The audience could not have been more pleased.

At the age of twenty, Sullivan was broad of chest, stout of arm and strong of wind. He was five feet ten-and-a-half inches tall and weighed a sturdy 190 pounds. An early notable victory that showed his ferocious punching power was over Johnny "Cocky" Woods, a fighter who at one time had been matched with the great John Heenan. Undaunted by Cocky's reputation, Sullivan sprang at him, accepted a straight left without blinking and slammed his right at Cocky's jaw. Cocky crumpled and failed to rise. Other victories followed in quick succession, including those over Tom Dwyer, the

Massachusetts champion, and an experienced heavyweight named Tom Chandler. What the public was learning was that Sullivan loved a scrap, and that if he managed to land his right where he aimed, the bout was over.

Early in Sullivan's career, "Professor" Mike Donovan, middleweight champion of the world, visited Boston and looked around for an opponent to spar with. (The academic title was an honorary one, in recognition of Donovan's scientific use of his fists and his footwork. Donovan later became boxing instructor at the New York Athletic Club. Like many boxers of the era, he was familiar with the interiors of jails as a result of engaging in his unlawful profession.)

Sullivan anxiously applied for the job. At first Donovan, who had thrashed many heavyweights, was unwilling to take on the broth of a boy, lest the bout prove too one-sided. But William Muldoon, the wrestling champion who was to figure so large in Sullivan's fortunes, convinced the professor that the young man was sturdy enough to accept whatever Donovan might throw at him and in addition had a pretty fair wallop himself when it landed.

When the bout got under way, to Donovan's consternation Sullivan rushed straight across the stage at him without the least sign of deference and started flailing away so enthusiastically that Donovan could not use his vaunted footwork or land blows of his own. He was pursued, cornered and belted unmercifully. If he had not been such a successful boxer *without* depending on footwork, he would have been knocked out. Later he was to say of Sullivan's hitting power, "It was like being kicked in the head by a runaway horse!"

Then came an exhibition with Joe Goss, the Englishman whom Paddy Ryan had beaten for the American heavyweight title the year before. Despite Goss's cleverness, Sullivan smashed him in the mouth so hard in the second round that Goss sat down bedazed. He would refuse to continue the exhibition, he murmured through swollen lips, unless Sullivan pulled his punches. This was as hard for the Bostonian to do as it was to be later for Jack Dempsey, but Sullivan agreed, and the fight went to its prescribed three rounds. Goss's analogy regarding the Sullivan punch was, "It was like the kick of a mule."

Now the Strong Boy's fame reached far-off Cincinnati, where the sports-minded editor of the *Enquirer,* Macon McCormick, decided that Sullivan must be witnessed by the local fans. His opponent would be another "Professor"—John Donaldson, considered the best heavyweight in Ohio. Nothing loath, Sullivan undertook the trip, admired the city's slaughterhouses and river traffic and stepped into the ring with Donaldson. His attack was so savage and his punches so shattering that Donaldson wanted to leave after three rounds. But he became frightened at the crowd's noisy protest—violence was promised if the bout did not continue—and he faced Sullivan again. After a few more blows he decided to risk the crowd's violence, and he quit. The spectators were pacified by his promise that he would get into better shape and fight Sullivan again in the near future.

As good as his word, the professor reappeared and became the first fighter to adopt the tactics that frustrated Sullivan and later served a number of the Strong Boy's opponents so well: He ran, clinched, sidestepped, crouched, fell before being hit and sprinted backwards. Panting, Sullivan finally caught him in the tenth round and knocked him out.

Arrested for breaking the state law, Sullivan confronted a local judge who, like so many practitioners of the law, was all in favor of watching a good scrap. The judge seemed to have been in attendance and had cheered the knockout. He acquitted Sullivan on the grounds that it had not been a prizefight at all; it had been a footrace. To the applause of the gallery Sullivan marched out of the courtroom. Those spectators who had been rounded up by the police were likewise acquitted.

Billy Madden, a Boston boxing manager, was shrewd enough to see a great future for Sullivan. There was a possibility that if Sullivan could catch up with the elusive Paddy Ryan he could become the American champion. Ryan had been ducking Sullivan until—in

the classic ploy—the challenger could "get a reputation."

To this end, in 1881 Madden took the twenty-three-year-old Sullivan on tour, publicized his ferocity in the ring and offered fifty dollars to anyone who could last four rounds with his man. Those who tried became Sullivan's supporters for life after the first few blows. "It was like being hit in the face with the bottom of a telephone pole," one shattered victim commented. Some, after receiving the first punch and fearful of what damage might be further inflicted, scampered offstage, to the raucous delight of the audience and over Sullivan's shrug and moue of dismay.

During the tour there occurred one of the most earth-shattering nonconfrontations in the history of sport. Sullivan, with justification, had a high opinion of himself. His self-esteem was matched by that of Richard Kyle Fox, a grandee of the sensational-magazine field, who was riding high on the astonishing success of his *Police Gazette.* Covering sports, theatre and vivid crime, the magazine was visible in barbershops, firehalls, police stations, saloons—everywhere he-men gathered—and it was a huge seller when hawked on the streets by urchins.

Fox was twenty-nine when he arrived in this country from Dublin, impoverished but aburst with ideas. He worked for a New York newspaper, saved his money, borrowed more and bought the *Gazette,* the oldest weekly in the country. To boost its ailing circulation he started a sports section devoted mainly to prizefighting—a sport that appealed to many males because of its illegality. Fox gave full coverage, including lavish artwork, to the Goss–Ryan fight of 1880. Sales zoomed. A special edition covering only the fight in all its ramifications completely sold out. Thereafter, in the field of publishing at least, Fox was not to be headed.

The dapper Fox, perhaps the most influential sports figure in the country, was a backer of Paddy Ryan and a compulsive presenter of championship belts. Nor did the awarding of them go unnoticed by the *Gazette.* To the end of making himself famous as a sportsman, Fox gave away more than a quarter of a million dollars in cash prizes, medals, belts and trophies to various "champions" of one sort or another. Often, out of wily caprice, Fox picked a new face to challenge an established champion. Those who thus won awards included George A. Sampson, who, to outshine Florenz Ziegfeld's strong man Sandow, supported a *Police Gazette* ferris wheel on his chest; and Lawrence M. Donovan, who jumped off the Brooklyn Bridge to make bridge-jumping fans forget Steve Brodie. Fox's own portrait adorned the championship belt he awarded to Billy Wells, champion of allowing his head to be pounded through an iron block by means of a sledge hammer.

The confrontation between Sullivan and Fox took place at Harry Hill's Dance Hall and Boxing Emporium, a cluster of two-story buildings at the corner of Houston and Crosby streets, near New York's Bowery. It was a favorite watering place for stage and sporting people, politicians, and gang leaders and their doxies. Among its regular clientele were such notables as P. T. Barnum (actually its landlord), Oscar Wilde, James Gordon Bennett, Lillian Russell, Thomas A. Edison, Diamond Jim and, of course, Richard K. Fox. William Muldoon wrestled all comers on its stage. But its major attraction was boxing, officiated usually by Hill himself. Sullivan made his New York boxing debut there.

Shortly after having saved fifty dollars by knocking out a good bareknuckler, Steve Taylor, in the second round, Sullivan was basking moistly in his success at a table at Hill's filled with admirers and hangers-on. Fox was seated a few tables away. Expansively, he asked a waiter to trot over and ask the young fighter to come to Fox's table. "Mr. Fox would like a word with him."

The summons fell hard on Sullivan's ears. "You go tell Fox," he roared, "that if he's got anything to say to me he can come over to my table and say it!"

Fox bristled at the ultimatum. The gall of the pug! The snub so rankled that Fox attacked Sullivan in his magazine for years. He also searched constantly for a fighter who could demolish Sullivan. As it turned out, from a fight

fan's viewpoint the feud was one of the most salutary things that ever happened to the boxing game.

———————

The Strong Boy cut a wide swath over the country and more bodies fell: John Flood, "the Bull's Head Terror," who fought Sullivan on a barge near Yonkers in the Hudson; James Dalton, tugboat captain and waterfront bruiser; Jack Burns, "the Michigan Giant," a clever three-hundred-pounder; another three-hundred-pounder, lumberjack Fred Crossley. The impressive series of victories and Madden's ballyhoo put the fighter's name on the lips of sportsmen everywhere. Finally Ryan, feeling the pressure of public discontent over his refusal to meet Sullivan, signed articles for a championship contest with him. The fight, to a finish, was to be held on February 6, 1882, under London Prize Ring rules—no gloves to be worn, of course—for twenty-five hundred dollars a side. The site chosen was New Orleans.

Excitement filled the land. Every saloon, every hangout for followers of the Fancy, every bailiwick where red-blooded men gathered, resounded with strong opinions as to the respective merits of the two fighters. Many times the bout was fought vicariously as the tempers of the arguers got the better of them. Thousands of fans began to drift south at the end of January, certain they were going to see one of the epic clashes of the century. American newspapers for the first time in history hired famous writers, dramatists and even clergymen to cover the fight. The list included Henry Ward Beecher, T. DeWitt Talmadge and Nat Goodwin.

The excitement increased as the gladiators arrived in New Orleans to complete their training, and local papers fanned the fires of speculation. Speculation was so blazing, in fact, that it was deemed wiser not to hold the bout in New Orleans at all but at some secret spot nearby. With prizefighting illegal in Louisiana, city fathers fretted about the unwelcome publicity the city might receive if the fight came off.

So early on the morning of February 7, a train chugged into the New Orleans depot. It was slyly packed with sporting men, some even clambering atop roofs. Each fighter was accorded a special car, in which he could shadow box or meditate, as he chose, during the trip.

The mysterious journey ended in Mississippi City, Mississippi, just beyond the Louisiana border. The fans piled out or jumped down or staggered off with nothing but pleasant memories of the train ride. A ring was quickly pitched in a small valley overlooked by a resort hotel. Some spectators hung from trees. A still-picture camera was positioned in a high booth, looking down on the ring. Attention was paid to a proclamation by the governor of Mississippi that was nailed to a tree. It warned that the fight was illegal and that good citizens were constrained to prevent it from taking place. The laughter, as they say, was general.

When the fighters ducked through the ropes it was clear that Ryan was larger than Sullivan, but Sullivan appeared to be in the fitter condition. Under London rules wrestling was legal — a factor Ryan counted on — so perhaps sheer bulk would be of importance.

Spectator Fox was one of those most chagrined when Sullivan sprang from his corner like a hungry tiger and landed a right flush on Ryan's jaw, sending him to the turf and ending the first round. In the second, Ryan carefully avoided Sullivan's swings, moved in close and flung the challenger heavily to the ground with a hip lock. The third round ended with Sullivan flinging Ryan earthward with a similar hold. But in the following rounds there was little wrestling. Ryan, at the mercy of Sullivan's fists, was harried and sent staggering from post to post as the crowd cheered and Fox seethed, screaming at the champion to inflict some damage on the publisher's mortal enemy.

Bloody, his breath coming in gasps, Ryan rallied somewhat in the eighth. However, under the wilting sun, he fell behind in the exchanges with the heavier-hitting, battle-hardened challenger. A right to the side of the jaw sent Ryan toppling over, and he lay inert till his handlers sprang forth to drag him to his corner. Courageously he staggered forth to the mark at the call of "Time!" Sullivan, seizing his chance and fired with new zeal, threw a left to Ryan's temple, moved in and followed with a right that crashed behind Ryan's ear. Ryan hit the turf with a thud, and the crowd sent up its victory roar. In the center of the ring a weary Sullivan exulted, as well he might. It had been a long, difficult road, but now he was

At New Orleans on February 6, 1882, John L. Sullivan fought Paddy Ryan.

the champion of America.

Completely different from Ryan in temperament, Sullivan reveled in public combat and the adulation and riches it brought. Two months after winning the title he was charging across the ring again. He knocked out John McDermott in three rounds; three months later, the Jimmy Elliott of turpentine fame was also knocked out in three rounds.

Then, in a sense, Sullivan got his comeuppance, and through the hands of none other than Richard K. Fox. The playboy-sportsman imported "Tug" Wilson from England to fight Sullivan in one of the latter's stay-with-me-four-rounds dares. Only now the reward was a thousand dollars. (After he won the title, Sullivan's price, perforce, had to go up.)

The bout was held at the Old Madison Square Garden, at Twenty-Sixth Street and Madison Avenue, on July 17, 1882. At Wilson's insistence, London Prize Ring rules were to prevail—rules that he was a genius at using to his advantage. The biggest crowd ever to see an American fight—ten thousand spectators—was wedged into the Garden, while another ten thousand loudly clamored at the gates outside. Among the thick layers of smoke that beclouded the arena, silver-headed canes, opera hats and stiff white shirtfronts were prominent, for New York swells were out in force, partly as a tribute to Fox. But Sullivan also had his supporters, who resented Wilson's statement for the papers, "The purpose of my visit is to thrash that insolent puppy, Sullivan."

Wilson, three inches shorter and thirty pounds lighter than Sullivan, for the most part slithered around the ring in a deep crouch to keep his head safe from the champion's blows. He also hugged, sidled off and ran backwards. If he was slightly jarred by a punch, down he went for a half-minute's respite. He lasted the four rounds, and though he did not add much to the majesty of the British lion, he collected his thousand dollars. He journeyed back to England with his ill-gotten spoils and opened up a popular pub, where he regaled his customers with his account of the fight. It was probably not an entirely accurate one.

Chortling over Sullivan's discomfiture, Fox then imported another Englishman, Charlie Mitchell, to destroy the champion. The fight, held under Queensberry rules this time, again took place in the Garden. To everyone's surprise, especially Sullivan's, the lighter Mitchell knocked the champion down in the first round with a short right to the face. Then Sullivan battered the Englishman about the ring for the next two rounds, knocking him through the ropes in the second and onto the boards in the third. Mitchell was saved from a knockout only by the fortuitous appearance of a Metropolitan police captain.

Fox then placed his faith in the far-off Antipodes, importing a New Zealander, Herbert Slade, called "the Maori." Again the battleground was the Garden. Though Slade towered over Sullivan and outweighed him, the champion disposed of him in three rounds, doubling him over with body blows and taking him out with a right to the back of the neck—a reincarnation of the deadly "chopper."

At this point in his career Sullivan, never a teetotaler, began to drink more than he could accommodate, and he paid less and less attention to training or the control of his ballooning weight. He set a record one evening by finishing off six quarts of whiskey in five hours. He was able to continue his heavy drinking during a new nationwide tour of exhibitions and serious bouts because his opposition was too poor to force him to train. It consisted largely of bandy-legged unknowns in widely scattered cities over most of the country—Butte, El Paso, San Francisco, Memphis and Boston among them. During this tour he helped popularize the use of gloves for prizefighting and emphasized the soundness of the Queensberry rules. But what he did mainly was impress the mythos of John L. Sullivan's invincibility on the minds of the American public.

There were two ominous portents, however, in 1884. Again challenged by Mitchell, Sullivan agreed to a Garden fight on June 30. At the appointed time, however, Sullivan had failed to arrive. Mitchell was sitting in his corner fretting over Sullivan's nonappearance when, in a scene that would live in New York memory, Sullivan entered the ring not in knee breeches but in a tuxedo and obviously in no state to walk, let alone engage in a prizefight. He explained rather slurringly to the audience that he felt "shick" and would have to postpone the bout. He was soundly booed as he staggered back up the aisle.

Five months later he met John Laflin in the Garden. Having neglected to train and vastly overweight, Sullivan was at Laflin's mercy for two rounds and absorbed the type of cuffing he usually dished out. But in the third round, rage compensated for his lack of condition and he counterattacked, driving Laflin to the ropes with a barrage from both sides. With Laflin erect but helpless, the dependable police hopped inside the ropes to halt the fight.

Sullivan gave old and somewhat plumpish Paddy Ryan a return go in 1885 and was pummeling him soundly when the New York police once more made their appearance. This time they got inside the ring in fifty seconds.

In the fall of 1885, he met Dominick McCaffrey for "six rounds or to a finish" in Cincinnati. In a rather confusing affair, the two fought evenly for six rounds and through a postprandial seventh. When the bell for the eighth rang, Sullivan refused to continue. "I've had enough for today," he growled to the referee. That unfortunate gentleman was beseiged by McCaffrey's handlers, whose claims were countered by some of Sullivan's noisier backers. In the general melee the referee slipped through the pack and sped back to his home in Toledo without venturing to render a decision. Two days later, via the press, he awarded the fight to Sullivan.

The following year the champion knocked out his old rival, Paddy Ryan, in three rounds in San Francisco. The two gladiators, both somewhat gone to fat, were watched with interest by a good-looking young bank clerk, James J. Corbett, who was beginning to make a local name for himself as a ring scientist.

But if he was not in the best of shape, Sullivan still maintained his courage, as shown in a Minneapolis bout with Patsy Cardiff, "the Peoria Giant." Sullivan broke his right arm by hitting Patsy's tough head, and the limb was useless to him for most of the bout. He kept jabbing out with his left while hardly able to defend himself from Patsy's left-hand blows. However, he managed to attain a six-round draw.

By now another challenger, Jake Kilrain, had appeared on the scene. With Fox to urge him on, Kilrain was noisily challenging Sullivan for a title fight, especially through the medium of the *Gazette*. Kilrain, who had developed his muscles through sculling as well as boxing and wrestling, was a reasonably good boxer and hard hitter. The same age as Sullivan, he felt he had an edge because he did not train as hard in saloons. He had fought a four-round draw with Mitchell in Boston in 1884, and he had engaged in a gruelling 106-round draw with Jem Smith, the English champion, in des Souverains, France. (The contest had been called because of darkness.) Many fans, their opinions shaped by the vindictive policy of the *Gazette,* were sure that the bloated Sullivan would be slaughtered if he ventured into the ring with Kilrain.

With Sullivan continuing to ignore the challenge, Fox took it upon himself to pronounce Kilrain the American champion by default and award him an expensive championship belt. But Boston fans, outraged at this, chipped in and presented Sullivan with an even fancier one. So rewarded, Sullivan expressed contempt for Kilrain's belt. "I wouldn't put it around the neck of a Gah-damn dog," he announced.

In 1887 the champion decided to visit England, ostensibly to fight Mitchell for revenge, but actually to meet Jem Smith, the English champion, so Sullivan could justify his claim to the world title—which some people (notably in the British Isles) did not think he deserved. When a reporter asked him why he was going, Sullivan grew livid above his celluloid collar and declaimed: "I've been abused in the papers, I've been lied about and condemned by men who, for commercial reasons, wanted to see some true American, a son of the Stars and Stripes, whipped by a foreigner. [Obviously a knock at Fox.] So now I'm intending to get even by unfurling Uncle Sam's victorious flag in the land from which my enemies brought men they hoped would conquer me. If there are any fighters abroad who think they can whip me, I guess I'll give them a chance. That goes especially for Charlie Mitchell and Jem Smith!"

On arriving at Liverpool with a new manager, Harry S. Philips, and Jack Ashton, his trainer and sparring partner, Sullivan was accorded a tremendous welcome; and the cheers rang out equally loud as his train chugged from town to town on the way to London. At the London station, the crush of eager Englishmen swarming aboard his cab to shake the mighty Sullivan hand was so great that the floor broke through. Struggling up from the bottom of the pile, the champion bellowed with good-natured laughter at his predicament, and the cheer was deafening.

A few evenings later, at a banquet, Sullivan publicly challenged Smith and Mitchell. Smith would have none of him. Mitchell, however, agreed to do battle. Before Sullivan started off on an exhibition tour of England and Scotland, he and Mitchell signed articles for a fight. It was to be under London Prize Ring rules, five thousand pounds a side, and the winner would be proclaimed world champion. (Jem Smith did not like this one bit.) On his return to London Sullivan met the Prince of Wales and sparred for him and members of the nobility at the Pelican Club. He was graciously presented with a gold watch by His Highness, who was not much of a boxing fan.

For the fight with Mitchell, as with so many others, a secret site had to be found. Arrangements were made to hold it on the estate of Baron Rothschild at Chantilly, twenty-five miles north of Paris. To keep the principals from being apprehended by gendarmes, the precise location was kept secret to all but a few. The result was that only about forty spectators were present to witness the "world championship" bout. Most of them were Britishers who had bet on Mitchell. But one spectator was Billy Porter, the noted American bank robber, who carried a pistol in each overcoat pocket. He informed Mitchell's

backers that he was there to see his compatriot get a fair shake. Another member of the select audience was Sullivan's actress girl friend, Ann Livingston. To avoid trouble, or possibly panic, she came dressed as a boy.

Both boxers had spent days soaking their hands in walnut juice to toughen them, and both wore spiked shoes. Unfortunately for both gladiators and spectators, heavy rains had made the area selected—a patch of ground behind the Baron's racing stables—a quagmire. From the start of the bout, the feet of the fighters kept sinking deep into the mud, and footing was precarious. Sullivan managed to knock Mitchell down several times in the early milling, but he could not get sufficient leverage to put him down permanently. And Mitchell, as was his fashion, often fell to the turf after being hit by a glancing blow, thus avoiding a second one and gaining his respite. At one point Mitchell spiked Sullivan on the foot, putting the champion into an extra black rage. According to the American columnist Arthur Brisbane, who was present, Sullivan snarled, "Be a gentleman, you-- --- --, if you can!" Rain descended from time to time, and Sullivan often shivered from the cold. Both fighters were forced occasionally to disengage and rest, holding onto the ropes.

The miserable conditions as well as Mitchell's stratagem were not conducive to a worthwhile contest, and at the end of thirty-nine rounds, with both fighters threatening to die of exhaustion and pneumonia, the handlers got together with the referee and the bout was declared a draw. Thereafter both Mitchell's and Sullivan's backers claimed that their man had won. It was Heenan–Sayers all over again. Brisbane, however, said Sullivan won handily. Sullivan, already disgusted with Mitchell's tactics and the decision, underwent the further ignominy of being carted off to a Gallic jail. Mitchell went, too. However, both were shortly released.

Despite the decision, great acclaim was showered on the American when he returned home. But with the necessity for strict training being over, he sought solace and companionship from the bottle in increasing doses. The result was that in August, 1888, he suffered a physical collapse, afflicted with a combination of typhoid fever, liver trouble and a mysterious itch. He was ill until November, and fans speculated worriedly whether he would survive, and if so, whether he would ever fight again. Sullivan surprised them on both counts.

━━━━━━━━━━

The battle against Jake Kilrain was doubtless John L.'s noblest hour in the ring (three hours, actually). Sullivan had been accosted, while downing a stein of bourbon in a Boston saloon, by William Muldoon, that looming presence. Muldoon informed him, with menace in his voice, that articles were about to be signed for him to fight Jake Kilrain in July, six months away. Sullivan, now weighing 240 pounds and desperately out of shape, protested mildly, but few people said "No" to Muldoon.

Undertaking the most tortuous training of his career at Muldoon's health farm in upper New York State, Sullivan dried out, worked out and dieted down to a reasonable 207, very little of it fat. His eyes became clear, his punch began to carry its old authority and his wind was good.

Once again New Orleans was the jumping-off place for the heavyweight championship. At dawn on July 8, 1889, a secret train pulled into the depot. The fans, loudly shushing themselves, piled in and atop, the fighters stole into their special cars and eventually the train reached the chosen site. This time it was Richburg, Mississippi, on the estate of Charles W. Rich, a wealthy lumberman. For the convenience of spectators, he had set up a wooden arena. Twenty Mississippi Rangers, Winchesters at the ready, stood around the ring. When Sullivan demanded to know why, he was informed that they were necessary "to keep the peace." The referee was John Fitzpatrick, later to become mayor of New Orleans. In Kilrain's corner were Charlie Mitchell and Mike Donovan. Sullivan's cornermen were Mike Muldoon and Mike Cleary. His bottleholder, whose chief function was to keep anyone from slipping poison into the liquid,

was "Handsome Dan" Murphy. His timekeeper was Tom Costello.

Kilrain's timekeeper deserves some attention. He was William Barclay "Bat" Masterson, the generally calm, moustached Western sheriff, marshal, peace officer, buffalo hunter, Army scout, hired gun, boxing referee and promoter, newspaperman and theatrical impresario—one of the most versatile Americans who ever lived. He got his nickname from hitting recreants over the head with his cane. While his connection with boxing was far from casual, he was a poor judge of talent: He wagered heavily on Kilrain over Sullivan, Mitchell over Corbett, Corbett over Fitzsimmons and Willard over Dempsey. Far from a large man, he seemed to think that usually size—when the smaller man was unarmed with a cane—was one of the most important factors in the ring.

Along with Wyatt Earp, Masterson is reputed to have tamed Dodge City, Kansas, "the wickedest little town in America," but his major incursions into prizefighting took place in Denver. Denver was probably even wickeder than Dodge.

Denver in the late nineteenth century was chockablock with saloons, bordellos, snuggeries where the sweetish smell of opium was wafted about and drugstores where morphine and other narcotic drugs were sold over the counter. Tourists were the special prey of bunco artists, steerers, shills, cappers, bartenders (through knockout drops), pickpockets, drunk-rollers and corpse-rollers, numbers-game salesmen and drunken cowhands who "hurrahed" the town (shot it up) as a means of celebrating payday. The one honest gambling house in the city was duplicated exactly inside and out by enterprising gamblers to deceive the unknowing tourist.

As a boxing promoter, Masterson had a rival in Soapy Smith, a black-bearded villain who, before coming to Denver, had run the town of Creede, Colorado, which might have been even wickeder than Denver. Soapy's first offering to the Denver public was unique: a bout between two contestants wearing sabots. "Boxers will Battle in Wooden Shoes," ran the promotional material with which

Denver was plastered. The fighters were the Oklahoma Sausage and the Platteville Terror. Knowing that the Terror was a native of France and had worn sabots during his youth, Soapy and his colleagues bet heavily on him. To insure there would be no foul play in the ring on the part of the Sausage, Soapy appointed himself the referee.

Unfortunately, the Frenchman's deft footwork was not speedy enough to keep him away from the Sausage's blows for ten rounds, and the latter won the fight handily on points—or should have. Seeing something that the audience did not, Soapy awarded the fight to the Terror on a foul. The fans rioted, nearly tearing to pieces the Central Theatre.

Appalled by the travesty, Masterson helped organize the Colorado Athletic Association. One of the backers of the firm was tricky "Kid" McCoy, who was to become world welterweight and middleweight champion from 1896 to 1898. McCoy was famous for his corkscrew punch, a strange fight with Corbett, his marriages (nine) and a charge of murder, which he beat.

When Masterson was frozen out of the organization a month later, mainly by its vice president, Otto Floto, he formed the Olympic Athletic Club, with himself as president and chief promoter. In this capacity it was one of his functions to obtain injunctions to prevent fights from being stopped by Denver's notably corrupt Fire and Police Commission. There was also the problem of halting riots started by customers who resented the way a decision went. They were apt to tear up seats and hurl heavy objects at the ring and its environs.

To stop the flow of illegal money into the Fire and Police Commission's coffers, the state legislature legalized boxing, but the fixes and double X's and the lack of true talent caused apathy on the part of fans. Both Masterson and Floto were losing money as promoters. One of Bat's last acts before leaving Denver was to cane Floto, who, not having a cane himself, fled down the street so fast that Bat could not catch him.

Masterson then came to New York, where his admirer, President Roosevelt, appointed him deputy U.S. Marshal for the southern district of the state. After that he became a columnist and boxing authority for the New York *Morning Telegraph,* and a bon vivant on the Great White Way.

⸻

Under a blazing Mississippi sun the starting gong clanged at high noon. Sullivan, in green knee-breeches, long stockings and fighting boots, launched himself at Kilrain. He threw a long left which Kilrain blocked. The challenger sent Sullivan's head back with a left of his own and then, seizing him by the shoulders, tripped him. Sullivan fell heavily to the turf. The first round had taken five seconds.

An enraged Sullivan went after Kilrain in the second. In a struggle to apply wrestling holds which had both warriors puffing and perspiring in the nearly airless pocket of the arena, Sullivan tripped Kilrain. In the next round, to cheers, Kilrain drew first blood, a roundhouse right that nearly tore Sullivan's ear off. Wisely, Kilrain dropped to the ground lest Sullivan reply with a roundhouse of his own. After that, respectful of Sullivan's wrestling and boxing prowess, Kilrain fought a Mitchell-type battle—he moved away, threatened a punch and changed his mind, flitted about and made Sullivan do all the pursuing. One spectator described Kilrain's tactics as like those of a "man entering a saloon, seeing somebody he owes money to, and beating a hasty exit." Sometimes the challenger would not throw a punch for minutes at a time; one dull round lasted fifteen minutes. His plan seemed to be to outfoot Sullivan until the latter dropped dead of exhaustion. But Sullivan, perhaps in a show of bravado, refused to sit down between rounds. "What's the use?" he snarled at his handlers. "I've only got to get up again."

By the twelfth round it was evident that Kilrain was the one feeling the violent heat, and more and more of Sullivan's blows pounded at his body. It was reported by one spectator that when one of these blows landed, the impact could be heard for seventy-five yards. In one round Kilrain spiked Sullivan, which put the champion into such a fury that

John L. Sullivan and Jake Kilrain fought an epic seventy-five-round bout lasting two hours and fifteen minutes. That fight signaled the end of the bareknuckle era.

he almost lost the fight; he pursued Kilrain so enthusiastically that he started to gasp from the effort, and it looked as though he might fall down from lack of breath.

There followed some immensely dull rounds. In the twenty-seventh Sullivan connected with a roundhouse right that sent his opponent backwards and earthwards. After that, action again turned slow, and the spectators, quite warm themselves, started to boo and hoot. When the forty-third round ended, one of Sullivan's cornermen, feeling his hero needed nourishment, fed him some tea that was laced with whiskey. Sullivan came out with a charge but a few moments later became violently sick in the ring. "You want to quit?" demanded Kilrain, noting Sullivan's plight. "No!" bellowed Sullivan, and he threw a straight right at Kilrain's mouth, flipping him onto his back.

In the forty-fifth round Sullivan not only knocked Kilrain down but stomped on him—a breach of the rules that the referee overlooked. Perhaps he was feeling some of the effects of the heat himself.

In the sixty-eighth, Sullivan, somehow rejuvenated, feinted with his right, and Kilrain, as was his wont, recoiled from it. But Sullivan shrewdly stepped

in and caught him under the jaw with a right uppercut that lifted the challenger off his feet and sent him sailing backwards. Dazed, Kilrain lasted only seven more rounds. During the rest at the end of the seventy-fifth, a doctor at ringside remarked to Kilrain's seconds, "If you keep sending that man of yours out there, he will surely drop dead of exhaustion." Regretfully, Donovan tossed in the sponge, and Sullivan retained his title.

Both fighters were in bad shape from the sun as well as from general fatigue and their wounds. Kilrain's back was covered with lobster-red blisters, while Sullivan's back was more of a beet red. Nor did the fighters' miseries end with physical discomfort. On his triumphant way back to New York by train, Sullivan was suddenly yanked out of his berth to face eight Tennessee policemen, guns drawn. Sleepy and suffering from a hangover, he was told that Governor Lowry of Mississippi had ordered his arrest for breaking the antiprize-fight statute of that state. Too bewildered to take on his captors, Sullivan allowed himself to be handcuffed and trundled off to a Nashville jail. He was released the following day, however, and permitted to return to New York. There he was hailed as a worthy cham-

54

pion, but his glory was short-lived. He was appalled to learn that at the request of Governor Lowry, New York's governor was allowing Sullivan's extradition to Mississippi, where he would be tried in court. "My God," Sullivan growled. "Haven't I been voting right all these years?"

Sullivan was convicted despite the influence of friends and sentenced to a year in prison. He appealed, however, and got off with a thousand-dollar fine. Kilrain, too, was tried in Mississippi on a charge of assault and battery. He was sentenced to two months in jail. But since Mississippi allowed citizens of the state to hire convicts as laborers, Kilrain was "sold" to Charles Rich and spent his time at Rich's home as his pampered guest.

Years later an admiring Vachel Lindsay, the "vagabond poet" who strolled vast distances trading rhymes for food, gave Sullivan's feat Homeric treatment. The poem was called "John L. Sullivan, the Strong Boy of Boston."

When I was nine years old, in 1889,
. . . .
I heard a battle trumpet sound.
Nigh on New Orleans
Upon an emerald plain
John L. Sullivan
The strong boy
Of Boston
Fought seventy-five rounds with
    Jake Kilrain.
. . . .
In mystic, ancient 1889,
Wilson with pure learning was
    allied.
Roosevelt gave forth a chirping
    sound.
Stanley found old Emin and his
    train.
Stout explorers sought the pole in
    vain.
To dream of flying proved a man
    insane.
. . . .
Johnstown was flooded, and the
    whole world cried.
We heard not of Louvain nor of
    Lorraine,
Or of a million heroes for their
    freedom slain.
Of Armageddon and the world's

birth-pain —
The League of Nations, and the
    world's one posy.
We *thought* the world would loaf
    and sprawl and mosey.
The gods of Yap and Swat were
    sweetly dozy.
We thought the far-off gods of Chow
    had died.
The mocking bird was singing in
    the lane . . .
Yet . . .
"East side, west side, all around the
    town
The tots sang: 'Ring a rosie'
'LONDON BRIDGE IS FALLING
    DOWN.'"
And . . .
John L. Sullivan knocked out Jake
    Kilrain.*

On his second triumphal return to New York, the champion, to his delight, was deluged with theatrical offers. He graciously consented to appear in a melodrama written especially for him, *Honest Hearts and Willing Hands*. While Sullivan was several light-years away from being an accomplished actor, he bellowed his lines with such vigor and struck horseshoes with such bravado that theatregoers flocked to see him. Actor, hell! He was John L. Sullivan, champion of America, the world and the universe, and it would be fascinating even to see him slip on a sleeve garter.

Under the aegis of the young theatrical impresario William A. Brady, the play went on a nationwide tour which culminated, rather fatefully, in San Francisco. (After that engagement, the troupe was to sail to Australia.)

In that cosmopolitan city Sullivan was invited to box a four-round exhibition with a local fighter, one James J. Corbett. Corbett, Sullivan knew, was one of those upstarts making noises about a title challenge. Rather sourly, he consented to the exhibition — but since the fight was going to take place in the ornate Grand Opera House, he insisted that the principals be

---

*Reprinted with permission of The Macmillan Company from *Collected Poems* by Vachel Lindsay. Copyright 1920 by The Macmillan Company, renewed 1948 by Elizabeth C. Lindsay.

dressed properly in formal evening clothes, and that heavy gloves be worn. The psychological purpose was to show the world in what little regard he held the San Franciscan as a challenger for his crown. Corbett had no choice but to acquiesce, but one can imagine what was being said in the Corbett household as his excited parents and brothers and sisters watched him struggle into his white tie.

Both fighters removed their jackets while onstage, but the sparring was immensely dull. Sullivan, the international figure and show-business personality, did not wish to exert himself against the stripling. As for Corbett, he had something else on his mind besides looking good for his friends in a sparring match. He merely feinted and sidestepped and measured the timing of Sullivan's punches and determined what preparations Sullivan made before launching them. Hardly a blow was struck in the four rounds, and when Sullivan offered his jaw to be hit, Corbett waggishly offered his own. The spectators showed their displeasure at the lack of action with catcalls and boos. But as Corbett emerged from the theatre, he was humming a lively jig.

Sullivan almost immediately thereafter boarded the *Maripose* with his troupe for the Australian tour. Just before it sailed, a package was delivered to him. Opening it, he saw it was a box of expensive Havana cigars. He sniffed one appreciatively, then glanced at the card of the sender. It read, "Bon voyage! James J. Corbett." "That California dude!" Sullivan exploded. He opened the porthole and flung the box out into the bay.

To his chagrin, when he arrived in Australia he found that dwellers in that outspoken land did not like *Honest Hearts,* did not appreciate him in it and especially did not relish his claim that he was heavyweight champion of the world. Had he beaten Charlie Mitchell? No; a draw was the best he could get. Had he beaten Jem Smith? Never got into the ring with him. And what about the Australian coves? Wasn't Australia part of the world? What about Frank Slavin? And the impressive black who came from Jamaica, Peter Jackson? No, there was very little awe expressed for Sullivan in Australia.

Sullivan was never noted for a prejudice against blacks, but in the fashion of many white fighters of his day and for years thereafter, he drew the color line when it suited his convenience. Peter Jackson desperately wanted to fight him, but Sullivan would not hear of it. "I will not fight a Negro," he declared. "I never have and I never will. Yours truly. . . ." And that was that as far as Jackson's immediate heavyweight title hopes were concerned.

On his return to Boston, Sullivan, piqued by the darts cast at him by Lilliputians, wrote an open letter that appeared in many newspapers in America and was picked up by some papers in other countries. It went, in part:

I hereby challenge any and all bluffers to fight me for a purse of $25,000 and a bet of $10,000. The winner of the fight to take the entire purse. I am ready to put up the $10,000 now. First come, first served. I give preference in this challenge to Frank P. Slavin of Australia, as he and his backers have done the greatest amount of blowing. My second preference is that bombastic sprinter, Charles Mitchell of England, whom I would rather whip than any man in the world. My third preference is James J. Corbett, who has uttered his share of bombast. But in this challenge I include all fighters.

The Marquis of Queensberry must govern this contest, as I want fighting, not footracing, and I intend to keep the championship of the world.

John L. Sullivan, CHAMPION OF THE WORLD.

Peter Jackson was of course not mentioned, but one reader was delighted to see his own name listed. And what delighted him even more was the phrase, "First come, first served." As sure that he could beat Sullivan as Sullivan was that he could squash him like a bug was: The dude from California. ∎

In the 1880's John L. Sullivan left an indelible imprint on America. "The Boston Strong Boy" epitomized a nation beginning to feel its muscle as a world power. Sullivan became a hero to millions who saw in him their condition as the sons of immigrants battling for a place in the New World.

John L. Sullivan

John L. Sullivan was born in 1858 in Roxbury, a suburb of Boston. A boozer and a bully and a braggart, his temperament ideally suited late-nineteenth-century America. This was a society that set its own standards and created its own styles. Great champions gain notoriety through conflict, and Sullivan was no exception. The owner of the Police Gazette developed an early hatred for Sullivan, and the magazine's constant search for Sullivan's conqueror kept John L. in the public mind. In Mississippi a hostile governor saw to it that a Sullivan match carried the threat of police action. "I can lick any man in the house," Sullivan's famous brag when he honored a saloon with his vast presence, became his trademark and was echoed clear across the land. He was seldom challenged.

Above, Sullivan beats "Professor" John Donaldson in 1880. For John L. it was a further step on the road to fame.

THE SULLIVAN-RYAN PRIZE FIGHT.

WHICH TOOK PLACE AT

BARNES' HOTEL, MISSISSIPPI CITY, MISS.

FEBRUARY 7TH, 1882.

From an instantaneous photograph taken on the spot by Messrs. Moses and Scnby, Photographers, Canal street, New Orleans, La.

On February 7, 1882, Sullivan fought Paddy Ryan for the title. Originally set for New Orleans, their match had to be moved secretly across the border into Mississippi. In wilting heat, Sullivan outwrestled and outpunched Ryan and scored a knockout in nine rounds on the lawn of the Barnes Hotel in Mississippi City to become the champion.

Above, Sullivan launches a blow against British Champion Charles Mitchell on March 10, *1888. The bout was held privately on Baron Rothschild's estate in Chantilly, France.*

Nine days before his epic contest with Jake Kilrain, Sullivan is seen at camp in upstate *New York. Seated are trainers Mike Cleary (left) and Dan Daly (right).*

On July 8, 1889, Sullivan fought Jake Kilrain in Richburg, Mississippi. It was undoubtedly Sullivan's finest hour. Following a physical collapse from chronic drinking, Sullivan went into rigorous training and shed thirty-three pounds. The upper photo shows Sullivan landing a pulverizing blow. In the lower photo, Kilrain hits the dirt.

The Sullivan–Kilrain contest was a fitting climax to an era that was passing. In an age when brute strength and endurance were the tests of excellence, these two men fought under a torrid sun for seventy-five rounds. After more than two hours of debili-

tating combat, Kilrain's corner threw in the sponge. Sullivan became the undisputed bare-knuckle king. John L. left his mark on other victims (see overleaf), who included water-front brawlers as well as men who themselves were formidable fighters.

John Flood

Herbert A. Slade, the Maori

Dominick McCaffrey

Paddy Ryan

Jake Kilrain

"Professor" Mike Donovan

Charlie Mitchell

"Professor" John Donaldson

The shock of James J. Corbett's victory over Sullivan at the Olympic Club in New Orleans on September 7, 1892, cannot be overestimated. Corbett was a new kind of hero. Above, Corbett, an unemotional executioner, beats the weary Boston Strong Boy by a knockout in Round 21 of the first title match to use Marquis of Queensberry rules. Prizefighting was now to enjoy the reign· of its most scientific student.

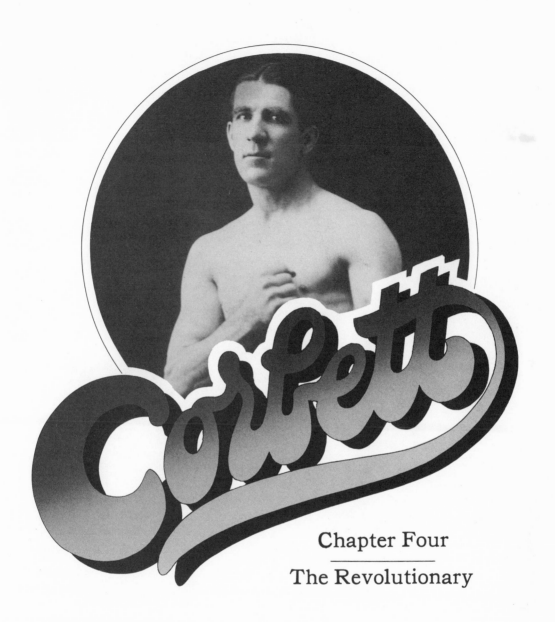

Chapter Four

The Revolutionary

If John L. Sullivan had known the manner of man who was stalking him, stubbornly dedicated to removing the crown he wore, either he would have undertaken the most strenuous training of his career; or he would never have insisted on a winner-take-all stipulation in the fight's articles of agreement; or he would have chucked everything and devoted his life to acting. James J. Corbett was the greatest boxer of all time among the heavyweights and one of the greatest ring generals of any weight. No heavyweight ever approached him in the ability to ride with a punch (and so remove part of its sting); slip a punch; make his opponent lead before he was ready and then counter with a series of pistonlike left jabs; feint an opponent into committing a defensive maneuver and then attack the newly vulnerable area; or drift just out of reach of a punch a split second before it reached its intended target. No other heavyweight—and few fighters in the lighter weights—ever approached his clever, gliding, instinctive footwork.

Corbett had other useful attributes. A genius at improvising in the ring, he could discourage an opponent from making use of a dangerous weapon (as he did with Peter Jackson); force his opponent to move in the direction he wished (as with Joe Choynski); make him charge like a wild bull (as with John L. Sullivan).

He was a master of practical psychology, and the methods he used were varied and ingenious. Any fool in trunks can make his opponent wait fretting in the ring or call him and his kin nasty names, but Corbett was infinitely more subtle. Adopting Clausewitz's maxim that the winning general is the one who can impose his will on his enemy, Corbett plotted and schemed before fights to chip away at his opponent's confidence, throw him off balance, enrage him, destroy his concentration. He could be intensely stubborn about getting his way just before a fight. In attacking his opponent's nerves in these ways, Corbett made use of his talents as an actor and his own particular temperament. It has been said that lack of confidence in himself was not a Corbett fault.

And finally, no boxer was ever more dedicated to perfecting his craftsmanship than Corbett. As a result of his constant study and spectacular success, he completely revolutionized the science of prizefighting.

Corbett was born in one of the less pretentious sections of San Francisco—"south of the slot (Market Street)"—on September 1, 1866. His parents, in the great tradition, were Irish. His father, Patrick, came from the town of Tuam in Galway County, and his mother, Kate, came from Dublin. Patrick, who never walked away from a fight but desperately wanted his sons to become gentlemen in the new country, had sailed for New Orleans in 1854. Finding nothing to his liking there, he moved west and settled in San Francisco. After a few business enterprises failed, he took the family and the family cow (led sobbingly by embarrassed young Jim) to the other side of the slot and settled in Hays Valley. There he set up a livery stable and, as an adjunct, an undertaking parlor.

San Francisco at this time was cosmopolitan but far from sophisticated. Violence was an accepted fact of life, and street fights and lot fights among youngsters were a frequent form of daytime relaxation. Many fine fighters came from there, including Jimmy Britt, who gave Battling Nelson some tough battles; Jimmy's brother Willus, once the national amateur lightweight champion and later manager of Stanley Ketchel, the great middleweight; and Willie Ritchie, at one time the professional lightweight champion. From the nearby suburb of Benicia, where almost every saloon boasted its shrine to John C. Heenan, the Benicia Boy, two members of the baronial Mizner family had flings at the game. Addison Mizner, later noted principally for his architectural work in Florida, fought in Australia under the name of Whirlwind Watson. And Wilson Mizner—con man, faro dealer, miner, playwright, saloon singer, hotel owner and so on—fought in the ring, managed Stanley Ketchel at one time and also managed Jack Kearns, who in turn was to manage Jack Dempsey to a world championship. Wilson Mizner, a veteran of many bar fights, always tried to avoid using his fists lest he lose his skill at dealing cards. He recommended in such situations hitting an opponent on the head with a ketchup bottle. The sight of the flowing ketchup, resembling one's own blood, was guaranteed to knock the aggressiveness out of anyone.

The fourth of ten children, Corbett fought in streets, lots and school yards and eagerly watched his older brothers and their friends spar in his father's livery stable. Even then—a sort of Wolfgang Mozart of pugilism—he was picking up moves, tricks and shifts that would prove valuable to him later. His parents wanted him to become a priest, but his interests ran more to track, gymnastics and baseball.

His ability to absorb boxing knowledge became evident when he was twelve. While attending St. Ignatius College, he offended the school bully, Fatty Carney, a boy much larger and older than he. The "I'll-get-you-after-school!" threat was made, and Corbett, though scared, forced himself not only to show up but to act tough. Even at that age he realized it was better to seem aburst with confidence in a situation involving violence. Followed by half the school, the two sauntered to a lot next to the U.S. Mint. Nervous but cool, Corbett staved off Fatty's rushes with jabs and sidestepped deftly to keep from being bowled over. He had picked up from his older brother Frank the trick of looking at his opponent's stomach and hitting him in the face, which baffled Fatty. Corbett won the fight, but both he and Fatty were expelled from school. His father, though he deplored fighting in the street, was not displeased that Jim had beaten up "that big Carney boy."

The next year Jim attended Sacred Heart College, where he acted peaceably enough but accepted slights from no one. However, when a Brother gave him a sharp crack on the hand with a stout pole for talking in class and then threatened to give him another, Corbett, who felt an athlete's concern about his hands, ran out of the school, outracing pursuit. He never returned. Through his father's influence he got a job as messenger for a bank. Sharp at figures and polite, he worked his way up to assistant cashier.

During this time he continued to spar in the livery stable and with his bank colleagues during lunch breaks. He also played considerable baseball. One day, after several hours of work on account books, he noticed that his left hand ached. It struck him that, like most right-handers, he was neglecting the development of his left hand. To remedy this, at home he began to smack his fist into a pillow, striving for accuracy in his punching. At lunchtime, in friendly bouts with fellow employees, he practiced shooting left jabs at various face and body targets.

At this point in Corbett's career, a friend of his named Lew Harding, who fancied himself something of an impresario, began to take Corbett to various blacksmith shops and fire-engine houses, where some of the toughest citizens of San Francisco were wont to hang out. He would introduce Corbett, who was wearing natty clothes and a white collar, as a pretty fair fighter. And would anyone care to mix it with him? There were always plenty of applicants, and Corbett, while he was often hard-pressed, managed to handle them all. Then, running out of opponents for his charge, Harding boldly took Corbett, still dressed like a dude, to the dives and dens of the notorious Barbary Coast, where the challenge was repeated.

The boundaries of the Barbary Coast —from 1850 to 1870 the most villainous piece of real estate in the world—have changed with the years, but at that time it was bordered roughly on the east by the waterfront and East (now Embarcadero) Street; on the south by Clay and Commercial streets; on the west by Grant Avenue and mysterious Chinatown; and on the north by Grant Street. It was still throbbing with corruption and violent criminality when Corbett made his fistic incursions. In earlier years, outraged vigilance committees would from time to time rampage and hang people, frightening the smaller-time crooks out of town; and at times depressions and earthquakes would reduce the amount of loot to be squeezed out of the unwary. But swindling, arson, mugging, robbery, shanghaiing, drunk-rolling and crooked gambling were trades too profitable to lie dormant for long. Criminals of all types and all nations congregated there after the Gold Rush because of the ease with which miners were separated from the dust in their kicks, and the peculiar vulnerability of sailors who came into port.

When ships began to arrive in great numbers in the 1850's, carrying immigrants and prospectors from the East, business (in particular gambling) boomed. The streets and alleys became littered with bagnios, dives, wine dens, deadfalls, fandango parlors, concert saloons, dance halls and groggeries. In Corbett's time these places of entertainment and pleasure included the Billy Goat, run by Pigeon-toed Sal; the Opera Comique, run by Jack Harrington, the Beau Brummel of the Coast, who wore a plug hat, a frock coat and tight purple pants and flaunted a mustache so long he could tie the ends of it beneath his chin; the Cobweb Palace, run by a man who loved spiders and let them spin their webs whithersoever they wished; the Morgue, a headquarters for hoppies (drug addicts); Denny O'Brien's, which featured bouts between terriers and devil-may-care rats gathered from the waterfront; and the Every Man Welcome, the Dew Drop Inn, the Bull Run and the Bella Union.

Many saloons specialized in shanghaiing sailors, or landlubbers who were about to embrace a new profession. One saloon, run by a Miss Piggott, had a trapdoor adjoining the bar. If a customer walked in and stood over this subtle engine, he was sold a drink laced with opium. After he had downed it, Miss Piggott would slug him from the front with a club and a confederate would slug him from the rear. The trap was released, and the customer plummeted onto a mattress and was then borne to the hold of a ship. Awakening, he would find himself a deckhand. Miss Piggott's regulars avoided this section of the saloon, so there was always space at the bar for strangers. Shanghai Kelley's saloon on Pacific Street had *three* trapdoors. He not only sold his clients drink (beer seasoned with laudanum) but gave them a cigar doped with opium,

referred to by the knowledgable as "the Shanghai Smoke."

For entertainment in many of these establishments there were singers, pianists, actors, acrobats, guitarists in the fandango parlors, dancing in the dance halls and conversations with the versatile ladies employed there. There were also odd characters to wonder at—like the man who would eat anything at all for a small fee, and Oofty Goofty. Oofty Goofty, who had acting ambitions but settled for less, would go from saloon to saloon and let anyone who wished hit him, for a small token, with a baseball bat. He carried the bat around with him.

Crime in the streets was carried out openly, and policemen, who seldom dared to travel alone, always carried an arsenal of weapons, including long, sharp knives. Young hoodlums cut off and collected the queues of Chinese and set fire to their laundries. If an alleged criminal was apprehended, he or his friends generally had enough political influence to get him off. In the bay, it was the practice of some professional boatmen, hired to transport a passenger from ship to shore, to row out to a deserted stretch of water and threaten to throw him overboard if he did not part with a sizable sum of money. Some bodies that washed ashore were thought to have belonged to unwilling victims of this ploy.

Several famous heavyweight prizefighters had adventures there of varying degrees of seriousness. Yankee Sullivan, mentioned earlier, was found hanged in a San Francisco jail; John Morrissey, while heavyweight champion of America, was chased out of a poolroom and down the stairs by a zealous 120-pound political worker armed only with a billiard stick; and Oofty Goofty, importuning John L. Sullivan to hit him, was cracked so hard over the back with a billiard stick that he was never the same thereafter. He became a fervid Corbett rooter.

Somehow Corbett, for all his dudish appearance and foppish manner, never suffered an accident in one of these places, and he outboxed their best men. One presumes that learning he could confront, size up and handle the toughest of the saloons' representatives did not lower his self-confidence any.

Inevitably he got his comeuppances. A good ballplayer, he had been asked by San Francisco's Olympic Club to play on its team, but a line drive injured the fingers of his left hand, and he realized his baseball career was over. (His younger brother Joe later pitched for the Baltimore Orioles.) So he decided to specialize in boxing. Accompanied by his impresario friend, he accosted the club's boxing instructor (always known as the Professor) and asked him to box, to see if he knew his business.

"Have you had any experience?" asked the Professor.

"Plenty!" answered Corbett, blacksmith-shop and saloon triumphs fresh in his mind and impatient to put on the gloves.

Once the two started to box it became apparent to Corbett that outmaneuvering the wild swingers of the Coast was far different from outfoxing an extremely adept specialist. Time after time his head was sent rocking back with straight lefts. "He hit me so often," Corbett wrote in his autobiography, "that I thought there was a shower of boxing gloves like big hailstones coming through the air." Some friends of the Professor's who were watching buckled over with laughter every time he landed a stiff jolt, which seemed to inspire him to greater efforts. Finally Corbett, usually cool, lost his temper and started to scuffle. The Professor indicated the match was over and warned Corbett that if he did not behave he would get thrown out of the club. Corbett controlled himself.

Undaunted, the next day he returned to the gym and noticed a large man with an impressive black beard sparring with an opponent. It looked like easy pickings for Corbett, so he asked Harding to set up a sparring match for him. With a bland expression, the Professor gave his permission. Once the gloves were donned, Corbett did some fancy footwork and launched a blow directly at the whiskers. The next thing he knew he was sitting in a chair with water being splashed on his face, his legs being rubbed and smelling salts being jammed at his nose. He had been knocked out for

Jim Corbett—young and determined

the first time in his life. Not quite accepting it, he stood up and indicated he was ready for another go. The bearded man, who turned out to be the club heavyweight champion, said no, the brash young man had had enough. To prove he hadn't, Corbett started to jog around the track bordering the gym and promptly smashed into parallel bars, side horses and gymnasts on the flying rings, causing great consternation among the exercisers. As Harding took him home, Corbett realized he had a great deal to learn about boxing.

Fortunately, the club shortly engaged a professor more compatible with Corbett's temperament, Englishman Walter Watson, and Corbett began taking lessons twice a week. He practiced what he learned in front of a mirror at home (to the amusement of his older brothers) and when not taking a lesson watched other pupils taking theirs. He also attended every professional fight held in San Francisco, most of them being presented at the rival California Athletic Club. He had the knack of adopting what was useful to him and weeding out what was inefficient or outdated, and he assembled an impressive repertoire of punches, feints, shifts and clinching tricks—a quality of selection extremely few boxers have.

After a few lessons Corbett demonstrated his newfound knowledge by tendering a friendly beating to his two older brothers in the livery stable, and a little later he knocked out the middleweight champion of the Olympic Club, much to the delight of Watson. Corbett later won the heavyweight championship, though at six feet one inch, he weighed only about 160 pounds. He became so proficient that none of the members would fight him in tournaments. To make up for this lack, Corbett stationed himself over the Golden Gate like a Colossus of Rhodes, managing to fight, either privately or in a public exhibition, every good heavyweight and middleweight who came to San Francisco. He built up an impressive record for an amateur, beating Buffalo Costello of Australia in three rounds and Big Mike Brennan, "the Porta Costa Giant," in eight. He fought a draw with Jack Burke, the Irish lad, in eight. The reputations of these fighters were formidable, and Corbett was the underdog in every fight. Costello, a superb middleweight, had twice held Frank Slavin, the number two Australian heavyweight, to draws—but Corbett showed himself to be faster than Costello. Burke had fought a draw with Jack Dempsey, "the Nonpareil," and three draws with Charlie Mitchell, the noisy Englishman. Brennan had fought forty rounds with Joe McAuliffe, "the Mission Boy," considered to be one of the outstanding heavyweights on the West Coast.

At the club one afternoon Corbett was pressed into service as a sparring partner for the visiting Nonpareil, considered one of the greatest middleweights who ever lived; and he held his own for a half hour of steady boxing, until the Nonpareil gave him a bloody nose by means of a professional trick—hitting with his wrist while coming out of a clinch. While staunching the flow of blood, the Nonpareil said, "If I were as big as you, I'd be heavyweight champion of the world."

All these battles were good preparation for Corbett's bout on a barge with Joe Choynski—probably the most gruelling ever fought by either contestant in their entire careers. What started as a kind of teen-age feud—the two toughest kids in town, living within blocks of each other, inconclusively scrapping in lots—had developed into an intense and publicly acknowledged rivalry. Choynski had joined the California Athletic Club and had turned professional, knocking over Pacific Coast opponents with impressive regularity. Corbett was still juggling figures at the bank but was working hard to improve his boxing skills. Whenever one of Choynski's supporters claimed that Joe was the best fighter in town, a Corbett supporter would counter with, "Yeah, but he never licked Jim Corbett." Because of the many factions involved—club rivalry, economic rivalry (Choynski was a candy puller in a candy factory), neighborhood rivalry and amateur versus professional rivalry—interest in a formal fight between the two was intense. The newspapers fanned the flames by having Choynski call Corbett yellow and Corbett assert Choynski was much overrated as a pugilist. Corbett finally got his father's permission to engage in a fight, and arrangements were made in a newspaper office. It was to be to a finish for two thousand dollars a side, under Queensberry rules, the contestants to wear two-ounce gloves.

Joe Choynski was a Pole of Jewish faith, a stocky young man who weighed about 165 pounds. He was nowhere near the boxer Corbett was, but he was a shrewd ring general and a tremendous natural puncher. If he had fought in a different era from this—which has been called the golden age of heavyweights—or if he had been luckier, he might have been heavyweight champion of the world. He was later to knock out George Godfrey, who was called "the American colored champion," in fifteen rounds, and a none-too-experienced Jack Johnson in three. Johnson called Choynski's punch to his temple the hardest punch he received in his ring career. In a tough twenty-round draw with Jeffries before Jeffries became champion, Choynski hit the Boilermaker the hardest punch Jeffries had ever received and convinced him to change from his standup style to "the Jeffries crouch." Choynski also fought Joe Walcott, Kid McCoy and Bob Fitzsimmons. He is credited with a loss against Tom Sharkey in 1896, but the rules of the fight were rather strange. It was agreed—since Sharkey, though much heavier, did not have Choynski's experience—that if the Sailor lasted through eight rounds he would be awarded the decision. Choynski belted Sharkey all around the ring for two and a half rounds and probably would have scored a knockout had not Sharkey, probably inadvertantly, fouled him. Choynski's seconds screamed "Foul!" and, the referee consenting, Choynski was allowed a rest period to recover from the effects of the low blow—in defiance of all tradition. When the fight was resumed, he began battering Sharkey again, even knocking him out of the ring, with Sharkey landing on his head. However, the Sailor crawled back in and weathered successive rounds. Since he was still erect at the end of the fight he was termed the victor. But few victors were ever so damaged in comparison with the loser.

Since the Corbett—Choynski battle was to be to a finish, it could not legally be held in a California sports club, and a secret site had to be found. Finally an old barn near Fairfax, in Marin County across the bay, was selected, and privileged parties were told of the location. Word leaked out, however, and on the day of the fight a great many more people than had been counted on pulled up in carriages and on horseback. A large number of people were already installed in the barn, awaiting action, and these had to be shooed out to make room for those who had paid admission. Because of the high feelings aroused by the fight, guns were removed from the spectators before they were allowed to enter the barn. Corbett was a little annoyed to find that the Nonpareil had consented to become one of Choynski's seconds. Dempsey explained that he had no hard feelings against Corbett—it was merely

a job he was being paid a thousand dollars for. The ring was pitched in the barn loft, and about a hundred spectators were crowded around it, from gamblers and pickpockets to factory workers and wealthy businessmen. Just before the principals met in the center of the ring for instructions, a friend of Corbett's pressed five hundred dollars into his hand, saying, "Bet Choynski this that you'll beat him. If you win, keep it." Corbett, aware of the psychology involved, jauntily made the offer and was pleased to see that Choynski refused. So did the Nonpareil.

The bout started, each contestant feeling the other out, and finally they clinched. "Jim, let's break nice and easy," Choynski said. Corbett suddenly remembered something Choynski had told him a while back, when the two were engaged in a friendly conversation —how Choynski would throw his opponent off guard by getting him to break clean a few times and then, as a surprise, would shoot over his right quickly on the break. The moment Choynski finished talking, Corbett brought his own right over, hitting Choynski on the chin and knocking him down for a count of five. This surprised many of Choynski's backers, who had thought of Corbett merely as a clever boxer.

The rounds continued at a faster pace, with neither man showing much advantage. The most notable occurrence was Corbett's injuring his right thumb in the fourth against the top of Choynski's head. At the end of the fifth the local sheriff made his entrance, apologized and said he had to stop the fight. A fan himself, he suggested that the bout be continued in the next county. Fighters and spectators, disappointed but resigned to this sort of persecution, made for the railroad station to take the train to nearby San Rafael, but a huge crowd was at the station, suspecting such a move. Where great crowds assembled on fight day, sheriffs were sure to appear, so it was decided to postpone the fight until another secret site could be found.

After nursing his extremely sore thumb for a week, Corbett was finally told that the new site would be the deck of a huge wheat barge anchored off

Benicia in Carquinez Strait, an arm of San Francisco Bay. The position of the barge—near the boundaries of Solano and Contra Costa counties—was supposed to sow confusion in the minds of the respective sheriffs. The day before the bout, Corbett entrained for Benicia and spent the night in the country home of the Mizners.

Choynski was aboard the barge by the time Corbett was rowed out the next morning. A ring had been pitched on the wooden deck, and the barge was acrawl with spectators. Excitement was such that skiffs, rafts, sailboats and steam launches surrounded the barge like Barbary pirates. Several notables, in trying to get aboard, had fallen into the water. Strangers who tried to assault the barge were repelled with boathooks.

A serious hitch developed after the principals had dressed and were standing in the ring. It seemed that Choynski's gloves had disappeared (actually, they had been thrown overboard). "I lost them," Choynski said sheepishly. The Nonpareil suggested the fight be conducted with bare knuckles. Corbett saw through the trick and said that Choynski could fight that way if he wanted to but that he, Corbett, was going to wear gloves. Finally a bystander chucked a pair of driving gloves to Choynski. Corbett agreed to Choynski's wearing these (much to his regret later), and at noon, with a cheery sun beaming down and reflecting off the placid waters of the strait, the fight got started.

Knowing that Corbett's right thumb bothered him, Choynski started with a rush and tried to belabor Corbett's head with a flurry of punches. Corbett kept him off with straight lefts to the face, but as a result of Joe's persistence, after two rounds Corbett's face was raw and bloody. In the third round a disaster befell Corbett. In jabbing for Choynski's face as Joe ducked, he hit him a smashing blow on the forehead. Corbett felt a sudden sharp pain in his left hand and knew he had broken at least one finger. The hand got sorer and sorer as the fight progressed, but he had no choice but to use it.

Because of Corbett's lack of offense, Choynski was beginning to land more and more. The driving gloves he was wearing had three seams across the back, and every time he landed a blow on Corbett's body he left three parallel ridges. In about the tenth round Corbett discovered he was wearing the wrong kind of footwear for a fight on the torrid deck of a barge. The heat penetrated the rubber soles of his shoes, causing the bottoms of his feet to become a great mass of blisters which broke, healed and rebroke as the fight continued.

Choynski was coming at him so strongly that Corbett decided he must devise a new tactic. He told his trainer, Billy Delaney, to holler, "Jim! It's time to use the right now!" in order to fool his opponent. Delaney did as he was ordered, and Corbett cocked the right as though he were going to throw it. Choynski moved away from the wild swing—to Corbett's left—enabling Corbett to use effectively a punch he had just invented, out of necessity. This was the left hook. Since it pained him considerably to hit with the third and little fingers, he found he could save them if he bent his arm and swung from the side, hitting with the first knuckle and the side of the hand. When Choynski moved that way the blow hit him with double force.

However, Choynski pressed on despite profuse bleeding, and whenever Corbett was forced to use a straight left he nearly fainted from the pain. In the fourteenth Choynski landed a terrific left squarely on Corbett's right eye, nearly closing it and causing the cheekbone to swell alarmingly. Nearly out on his feet, Corbett merely stood in place, arms dangling. Suspecting a trick, Choynski paused, but then he was all over Corbett, raining blows on him. Corbett could do nothing but instinctively dart his head from side to side to reduce the effectiveness of the punches. Finally the round ended and his seconds led him, completely groggy, back to his corner.

During this round Frank Corbett, anxiously looking for his brother Harry to discuss the progress of the fight, found him at the stern of the barge, crying. "I can't stand to see Jim licked," he said. "That's a hell of an attitude when Jim needs you!" Frank said, and smacked him in the nose. The two started to scuffle but soon realized, from the roar that went up, that they were missing a better fight on another part of the deck.

Corbett now made an important geographical discovery: The barge's lookout house formed a small pool of shadow into which the broiling rays of the sun did not pour down so sharply. Corbett backed into it and did most of his fighting from that vantage point. When the seventeenth round started he was annoyed to see Choynski rush toward the spot and station himself there, waiting for Corbett to come to him. The battle became one as much for holding a choice piece of territory as for victory in the field. Round piled on round, with the blood on the deck making the footing precarious. Corbett gradually forged ahead, even though his broken hands, his blistered feet and the cuts on his body and face, attacked by the sun, caused him almost unbearable agony.

A policy Corbett always followed, when he thought his opponent was beginning to tire, was to watch him as he returned to his corner. At the end of the twenty-seventh round he noticed that the spring had gone completely out of Choynski's legs. He determined that if he could land a good solid left hook, he might end the fight. Delaney kept hollering for him to use the right, and Choynski moved away from it. Timing the move precisely, Corbett put everything he had into the punch—not caring if he broke every finger in his hand at this point—and it landed on the side of Choynski's jaw. Down he fell. Corbett stood dazed and blinking while the referee counted out his opponent. When Delaney, to the cheers of fans, sprang into the ring and hugged Corbett, Corbett asked him what had happened. "You knocked him out!" Delaney screamed above the uproar.

The two boxers were taken aboard a tugboat, where, when he had his strength back, Corbett congratulated Choynski on the fight he had put up. After the tugboat docked, Corbett was whisked off to a Turkish bath, where he could mull over his injuries. He had no feeling in either hand, his right cheek was puffed out to twice its normal size,

he could hardly see through either eye and he had welts and painful cuts all over his body. He learned later that Choynski was in equally bad shape. For seven hours Corbett sat in a steamer chair, his feet soaking in two pails of hot water, his hands in two more, his face and body covered with hot towels. "Joe Jabbed to Death," proclaimed the San Francisco *Examiner*.

The Choynski fight, painful as it was, led indirectly to Corbett's fight with Jake Kilrain. Corbett did not fight for a year but worked in the auditor's office at City Hall, meanwhile engaging in mild exercise at the Olympic Club. During this period a new weekly paper called *The California Illustrated World* appeared. The first issue featured a cover picture of Corbett, labeled "The Coming Champion of the World." A copy of the issue found its way shortly afterward to New Orleans, a stopping-off place for William Muldoon's boxing and wrestling troupe. Kilrain, a year and a half after losing to Sullivan, was the star of the troupe and was casting about for someone to box with during Mardi Gras week. Someone in the group discussing the problem, which included the New Orleans gambler Bud Renaud, suggested Dominick McCaffrey, but Kilrain wanted an easier opponent. Another member noticed the paper with Corbett's picture, and after the group had recovered from laughing at the article, Corbett was hit on as a likely possibility. A telegram was dispatched to him in care of the paper's editor. If he would come to New Orleans and fight six rounds with Kilrain, Muldoon would pay his train fare coming and going; the winner of the bout would get two thousand dollars, the loser five hundred. Corbett, despite the misgivings of his friends, accepted with alacrity. The Nonpareil, however, was confident. "Kilrain will never lay a glove on you," he predicted.

Two weeks before the fight, Corbett set out on the four-day journey, sprinting alongside the tracks whenever the train stopped. Bud Renaud met him at the depot and assumed a look of intense dismay when he saw what the telegram had wrought. Corbett weighed about 165 pounds and had a long thin neck at the time; Kilrain, on the other hand, was a stocky 215. The Renauds, thinking Corbett was going to be killed in the ring, treated him very hospitably.

On the night of the fight, Corbett was putting on his shoes in his dressing room at the Southern Athletic Club when Muldoon burst in and told him to hurry; the referee and Kilrain were waiting for him. It suddenly struck Corbett that he had had no say in the selection of the referee, and now he demanded to look him over. A worried delegation of club officers and Renaud came in. They feared Corbett had turned yellow and was backing out. Corbett told them not to worry but that he was not satisfied with the referee. Since it seemed as if he would sit in the dressing room all night if he were not allowed to have his way, he was permitted to pick somebody himself. Selecting blindly from the group, Corbett happened to choose an amateur champion of the club who was also a respected cotton broker.

As the fight started and a confident Kilrain marched toward him, Corbett feinted twice and then poked Kilrain six times in the nose before Kilrain could raise his hands to protect himself. Corbett kept hitting his opponent wherever and whenever he pleased, confusing him with the speed of his attacks and cutting his face up. Corbett won an easy decision, and after the bout he was carried off in triumph to the Pickwick Club and toasted in champagne. The victory gave him a good deal of publicity in the East, where it counted, and it was thought by some that if Sullivan were to retire and Corbett were to put on about forty pounds, he might make a worthwhile successor to the champion.

Now the idol of San Francisco, Corbett was appointed professor of boxing at the Olympic Club and spent most of his time working out and trying to put poundage on. When Peter Jackson, the great Australian heavyweight, was brought to San Francisco by the California Athletic Club, the two were introduced, but they did not get along at all well, though Jackson was an extremely polite, modest personage. Jackson was so annoyed with Corbett, in fact, that he challenged Jim to meet him in the ring. Corbett demurred, say-

ing he wasn't heavy enough yet. It was a sound decision.

A word about Jackson. He is considered by many experts to have been the greatest heavyweight who ever lived. Writing years later in a national magazine, Corbett ranked him with Jeffries as one of the two greatest heavyweights of all time. The fighters in Australia, America and England who ventured into the ring with him when he was in his prime—1883–92—would hardly argue the point. Jeffries later used the memory of a punch Jackson had thrown at him as a basis for comparison with all the other single devastating punches he had received.

Born in the West Indies in 1861, Jackson came to Sydney, Australia, at an early age. As a teen-ager he became a merchant seaman, learning to fight

Peter Jackson

on the waterfront and aboard ship. He first came into public notice when Australian papers ran an account of how he quelled a mutiny with a single blow of his right fist. Then an event occurred which virtually forced him to take up another profession. Displeased about something Jackson had done, a ship's officer slapped him in the face and called him a dirty nigger. Jackson, even then a courtly, considerate man, did not retaliate but obtained permission from the captain to engage in a shipboard bout with the officer.

At the call of "Time!" Jackson moved out carefully, threw punches with a kind of pumalike grace, stalked his man around the ring, avoided blows with consummate ease and then hit his opponent so hard a blow on the chin that a quart of whiskey had to be poured down the officer's throat before he revived.

Jackson was an extremely well-built athlete, six feet one inch tall, and at his most successful weighing about 210 pounds. Ashore, he was taken in hand by the foresighted Larry Foley, who ran Sydney's most popular sporting saloon. Foley, who had attended the Sydney boxing school set up by the great Jem Mace, taught Jackson the refinements of boxing and launched him on a fistic career. The black man tore through the ranks of Australian heavyweights like a hurricane, knocking out everyone he faced, and then turned to exhibitions. These were with "right hand barred"; that is, Jackson was forbidden to throw a punch with his right hand. This gave considerable assurance to his opponent, partly because they could be attacked from only one wing, but mainly because the rule eliminated Jackson's best attacking weapon, one that no fighter had been able to stop: the one-two.

Probably the most effective weapon in any fighter's arsenal, if he can develop it, the one-two consists of a left jab, generally thrown high to obstruct the opponent's vision, followed instantly by a straight right to the opponent's chin. Its effectiveness depends partly on the marksmanship of the right but mainly on the speed with which it is thrown. Jackson's two blows (like Car-

pentier's in a different era) landed almost simultaneously. The jab tilts the opponent's head back at a vulnerable angle, putting extra pressure on the neck while causing the chin to rise. If the right lands at the proper instant—before the head can be lowered to protect the jaw—a knockout or knockdown often results. Jackson often varied the combination by shooting a right to the body as his opponent's guard went up to protect his face from the left.

Frank "Paddy" Slavin, considered to be Australia's top fighter, continually found excuses not to meet Jackson (though they met later in England), as did other prominent Australian heavyweights. Finally Jackson cornered the titleholder, Tom Leeds, beat him soundly and became champion of Australia. He came to America in 1888, desirous of conquering enough Americans to warrant the acceptance of his challenge by the great John L. American fighters, knowing his reputation, were not eager to meet him, but Joe McAuliffe finally acquiesced. Unable to cope with Jackson's specialty, he absorbed a severe beating in California.

Later, in Sullivan's Boston, Jackson found a second opponent, George Godfrey. In the Godfrey fight, Jackson's first appearance in the sophisticated East, he entered the ring wearing a tattered bathrobe and a nervous expression, aware that critical eyes would be resting on him. Once in the ring, however, he was all business. He stunned the crowd with his lightning-like straight rights and lefts, his economy of movement in delivering or avoiding a blow and his deadly accurate one-two. Godfrey had never faced an opponent so lithe and purposeful or one who hit with such jolting force. He stood up under the punishment for nineteen rounds. Then Jackson, eager to end Godfrey's suffering, snapped a right to Godfrey's heart, feinted with his left and crossed with his right, smashing Godfrey on the side of the head. Godfrey reeled toward the ropes, Jackson pursuing him. But Godfrey held up his hand in signal of defeat. He refused to go down, but he knew that continuing would be fruitless.

When word was taken to Sullivan

by Arthur Chambers, perhaps the foremost boxing authority in the country, that Jackson was a remarkable fighter, Sullivan merely grunted. "What's that to me?" he asked. "He's colored, isn't he?"

Once Corbett had put on ten solid pounds, however, he was eager to fight Jackson, for several reasons: as a test of his own ability; to see if he could learn something new about the art he had dedicated himself to mastering; to enhance his reputation on a national scale; and to show John L. Sullivan that he, Corbett, was willing to fight a man whom he, John L. Sullivan, seemed to be afraid of. A match between the two was arranged for May 21, 1891.

A few months previously Corbett had had an epic meeting with Sullivan. He had gone to New Orleans to see Fitzsimmons fight his friend the Nonpareil for the middleweight championship and then had stopped off in Chicago, where Sullivan was playing in *Honest Hearts.*

Knowing that Corbett was in the audience, Sullivan graciously asked him backstage. In his dressing room he tried to break Corbett's hand with a handshake—a kind of hobby with Sullivan—and offered him a drink. Corbett refused but Sullivan kept attacking the bottle, finally feeling so expansive that after the curtain was rung down he insisted on taking Corbett on a tour of Chicago saloons. After introducing Corbett as "the fellow who's going to fight that nigger, Jackson," he would have a few drinks and then utter the defi he was so famous for. After a few bibulous stops, Corbett got tired of hearing it. In Mat Hogan's, a favorite hangout for politicians, sportsmen and other notables like Bill Pinkerton, the detective, Corbett virtually told Sullivan to shut up, although he was tactful about it. Sullivan looked shocked, and Hogan's clientele held their collective breath, not knowing but what they were about to see the American championship settled then and there. But Sullivan's temper reached a plateau and finally dissipated. He suddenly became more respectful toward Corbett and ceased making his boast in Corbett's presence. It was Corbett's round.

Corbett's match with Jackson was to be held at the California Athletic Club. The articles called for a fight to the finish, for a $10,000 purse—$8,500 to the winner and $1,500 to the loser. Queensberry rules would be followed.

Before the match, Jackson had the bad luck to sprain an ankle, which cost him about a week of training. His manager, the shrewd Charles E. "Parson" Davies, suggested that he postpone the fight, but Jackson, perhaps a little overconfident, felt he could beat Corbett "standing on one leg." The betting was 5 to 1 on Jackson; Corbett's supporters bet merely on how many rounds he would last. Corbett, knowing he was the underdog, the lighter man and the less experienced man, trained hard and long for the bout. On the psychological side, he made disparaging remarks about Jackson's ability whenever he was interviewed, to arouse the black man's ire. In the locker room just before the fight, he made it a point to show Jackson that he was not at all in awe of him. When the question of hitting in the clinches came up, there was an exchange of snapped phrases like "Any way *you* want it!" Corbett could see that Jackson was wondering why Corbett was so cocky. The question of corners came up. Corbett said Jackson could have any corner he wished. This settled, Jackson then politely requested that he be allowed to enter the ring last—it was a superstition he had. Eyebrows raised, Corbett refused point-blank. Forty-five minutes passed while the two argued or sat in brooding silence. Finally the directors of the club came in and pleaded with the fighters to enter the ring. A compromise was reached: they would go through the ropes together. When they got to the ring apron, Corbett gave a nod and put his head under as if to enter. Jackson climbed through, but Corbett slyly slipped back; Jackson's irritation, when he saw Corbett grinning at him, was plain to see.

When time was called, Jackson swarmed all over Corbett, trying to knock him out as quickly as possible—partly out of pique and partly to win bets for those who had felt Corbett would not last ten rounds. Jackson chased him all around the ring, shooting his one-two. No one had ever made Corbett move so fast to escape punishment. He ducked, sidestepped, clinched, tried to keep Jackson off with jabs; but these methods were only partly effective. Finally Corbett found a solution. When Jackson rushed, Corbett would thrust his left shoulder into Jackson's chest. It did not bother the black man for a few rounds, but finally he complained to the referee. "If you don't like it," snarled Corbett, "keep out of the way!" Since Jackson was himself providing the momentum that propelled him into the shoulder, Corbett's maneuver was a legal one.

In the sixteenth round Jackson's left snaked toward Corbett's face and was immediately followed by a terrific jolting right to the body. It was the hardest punch Corbett had ever received up to that time; he felt chills running up and down his back. Somewhat desperately after that Corbett cast about for a way to stop Jackson from landing his devastating right to the body after his left

lead. Again he arrived at a solution. Instead of trying to block the left, Corbett merely turned his head away, and before Jackson could bring home the right, Corbett shot his own left to Jackson's stomach, causing Jackson's right to be deflected by Corbett's arm. Except for a few instances the maneuver effectively stopped this particular combination of Jackson's.

But Jackson was a thinking fighter, too. Once when Corbett shot his left to the body, Jackson unleashed a terrific right uppercut that came within an ace of taking Corbett's head off. To discourage Jackson from using the uppercut—which he recognized as a most formidable weapon—Corbett continued to throw his left to Jackson's body and, anticipating the uppercut, moved his head a little farther to the right each time, so that Jackson kept missing by wider and wider margins. One time, instead of shooting the straight left, Corbett hooked with that hand to the side of Jackson's jaw, staggering the black man, and that was the last he saw

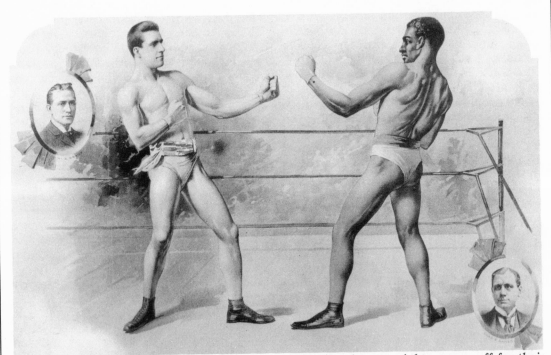

James J. Corbett and Peter Jackson, the great Australian heavyweight, square off for their battle in 1891. In the upper left insert is William Brady, who as Corbett's manager guided the Barbary Coast fighter through his fantastic career. Charles "Parson" Davies, Jackson's mentor, appears in the lower right insert. Listed as a "fight to the finish," the bout was declared "no contest" after sixty-one rounds.

of the uppercut.

In the twenty-eighth round Jackson hit Corbett a hard shot to the side of the head, and the latter, partly stunned, realized he would either have to attack furiously or be knocked out. Drawing on his last reserves, he unleashed punches from every angle and drove Jackson across the ring. The onslaught left Jackson nearly helpless, but Corbett was in too much of a hurry to punch with the accuracy demanded. The bell saved Jackson, and Corbett cursed the impetuosity that had cost him a knockout.

The rounds passed and the fighting slowed down except for occasional spurts of activity, with one and then the other fighter holding the advantage. Corbett's arms were getting heavy, and he could not tell, so numb were his hands, whether his fists were clenched or not when he launched a blow. Jackson was equally weary, as he revealed by dropping his hands to his sides every now and then to rest his arms. Those who had bet that Corbett would not last ten rounds were now betting that he would not last twenty—then thirty and forty. At times there was almost as much activity in the audience and at the betting booths as in the ring.

In the sixty-first round the referee, to the surprise of nearly everyone, stopped the fight and called out, "No contest! All bets off!" Jackson's seconds immediately started pulling off his gloves. Corbett protested mildly about the bout's having been stopped, but he was too weary to kick up much fuss. Later he contended that the fight had been stopped to save the wagers of those doubters who had bet he would not last ten, twenty, thirty or forty rounds. Because of the referee's no-contest decision, the club, indulging in a singular feat of rationalization, paid only twenty-five hundred dollars to Corbett and the same to Jackson, instead of splitting ten thousand dollars down the middle—for four hours of the finest fighting ever seen in America. The action so displeased many of the members that they resigned. Newspapers all over the state denounced the club's officers for their cheapness, and the internal squabble that resulted caused the or-ganization to break up entirely.

Corbett later apologized to Jackson for his newspaper statements and his conduct in the locker room, saying it was only part of his plan to equalize the odds. Jackson, ever the fine gentleman, readily accepted the apology. Each fighter later admitted to newspapermen that his opponent was the hardest man he had ever faced.

Because Corbett's many friends and supporters in California felt he had gotten jobbed in this matter, they arranged for a testimonial benefit for him at the Grand Opera House. It was here that Sullivan consented to spar with Corbett, provided both contestants wore dress clothes. And it was here Corbett learned that if he ever got into the ring with Sullivan, he would have no trouble beating him.

After the Corbett fight, Jackson crossed the continent again and sailed to England. There he knocked out Jem Smith in two rounds at London's Pelican Club, and Frank Slavin at the National Sporting Club. Slavin lasted for ten rounds, and the fight was pronounced by some veteran spectators the best ever held at the National; by others the best they had ever seen anywhere. Jackson then journeyed to Dublin, where he sparred for three rounds with Peter Maher, the Irish champion. Although he was able to hit Maher at will, Jackson was so impressed by the Irishman's right-hand power and aggressiveness that he urged him to come to the United States—which Maher did, playing no small part in American boxing history.

Unfortunately, Jackson contracted consumption while abroad. Discouraged by unaccustomed physical weakness and the failure of his crusade to gain him either glory or affluence, he began drinking more than he should. Returning to America, he was not fit enough to stand up to the buffets of the plodding Jim Jeffries of 1893. Though Jackson showed flashes of his former speed and punching power, he was knocked out by the Boilermaker in three rounds. Now, in the classic tradition, Jackson began to forsake training and lose to second-raters. Frank Slavin generously paid his fare back to Australia, where there was hope that the sun might effect a cure for his consumption. But it did not. Jackson, who might have been world champion under different circumstances or in a different era, died a pauper in Queensland in 1901.

===

The travesty of the sparring match with Sullivan and the difficult bout with the great Jackson brought Corbett unexpected rewards. He was asked to go on the road with a minstrel company and spar between the acts, which he was delighted to do. Then a childhood friend of his, bustling William A. Brady, who was basically a theatrical impresario, asked him to do a fight scene in the British melodrama *After Dark*. Noting Corbett's stage presence and poise, Brady decided to transform him into a box-office star in the theatre— but of course it would be better if Corbett were the heavyweight champion. So Brady set about helping Corbett achieve this ambition.

The partnership between the ambitious Corbett and Brady—billiards hustler, candy butcher, actor in saloon theatres of the Far West, manager of Yousouf, "the Terrible Turk," improviser, expert at con, mighty discoverer of stage talent—was as successful as that between Kearns and Dempsey and Descamps and Carpentier. Following his stage stint, Corbett, under Brady's canny aegis, fought short bouts in some of the country's major cities, getting his name known and acquiring a steady income. He finished the tour in Madison Square Garden, where he took on three opponents the same night. He knocked out one, outpointed another and fought a no-decision bout with the third.

Corbett was back in San Francisco when Sullivan's bombastic advertisement appeared in the newspapers. He entrained for New York a week later, pondering and puzzling how he could raise ten thousand dollars. It turned out to be quite easy. Corbett simply went to Koster and Bial's Music Hall, on Twenty-Third Street near Sixth Avenue, a theatre that was patronized by sporting people and men-about-town, and asked. Some of the regular patrons there were young Jacob Ruppert; Al

Smith, the gambler; "Honest John" Kelly (to figure later in Corbett's stars); Richard Canfield, the gambler; Frank and Phil Dwyer, the racehorse owners; Stanford White, the architect and courter of Lillie Langtry; and Diamond Jim Brady. All were free spenders. Corbett received the promise of five thousand dollars from Colonel Frederic McElwee, manager of Louis Ehret's racing stables, and the rest of the money came in as readily.

The details of the match were settled in the office of the New York *World*. Acting for Sullivan, Jimmy Wakeley insisted that the entire twenty-five-thousand-dollar purse should go to the winner. To his surprise, Brady, acting for Corbett, readily acquiesced. (It was not entirely bravado; Brady had immense faith in Corbett.) Other terms were agreed on: The fight was to be held at the Olympic Club in New Orleans on September 7, 1892. It would be fought under Queensberry rules, with the gloves "the smallest the club will allow." Thus the historic match—the first heavyweight championship to be held under Queensberry rules—was made. It was also the first championship fight to be held under the protection of the police, made legal because gloves were to be worn by the contestants.

For a few weeks, while Sullivan was playing to packed houses in *Honest Hearts*, Corbett went on tour with Brady, offering two hundred dollars to anyone who could stay with him four rounds. An indication of Brady's confidence in Corbett as a fighter—and of his (Brady's) true interests—was the fact that while Corbett was training for Sullivan he was also in rehearsal for a play called *Gentleman Jack*, written at the behest of Brady by a hack playwright he knew. Brady figured that Corbett, as the star, would draw full houses in theatres all over the country once he was champion. That the play was reasonably palatable and that Corbett was a convincing actor were all lagniappes. After the tour, Corbett plunged into serious training (and rehearsing) at Brady's home near Asbury Park, New Jersey. Sullivan finished his dramatic stint, went on a week-long spree in New York and then settled down to the unpleasant task of rounding into shape at Canoe Place Inn, in Bay Head, Long Island. By playing handball with the international champion, Phil Casey, he took off nine pounds, getting down to 218 ten days before the fight.

To celebrate Mardi Gras week properly, the Olympic Club had arranged for three championship bouts to follow one another on successive nights. The first was between George Dixon and Frank Skelly for the featherweight title. The second was between Billy Myer and Jack McAuliffe for the lightweight championship. And the climactic one, which had the entire country agog, was the fight for the heavyweight championship.

Sullivan took up quarters at the Young Men's Club of New Orleans, while Corbett stayed at the Southern Club, the site of his victory over Kilrain. Trainloads of sportsmen, gamblers, business tycoons, gunmen, show people, financiers and con men poured into the city days before the fight. Wagering was heavy, with the odds wavering between 4 to 1 and 5 to 1 on Sullivan. On the night of the fight, the Olympic Club was packed to overflowing, with thousands clamoring for admittance outside. All roads leading to it were jammed with vehicles of every sort, and the streets of the city were black with people. The name "Sullivan" was on everyone's lips. Corbett came to the club dressed every inch the gentleman—light summer suit, straw boater and a little bamboo cane. If he had been spotted by a bookmaker, the odds might have shot up to 8 to 1.

In the locker room some decisions had to be made—one quite unusual. Sullivan wanted to wear a heavy bandage around his stomach, but Corbett demurred, saying that after a few rounds it would harden, giving Sullivan extra protection. He won his point. Sullivan demanded the lucky corner, the one in which the winners of the two previous nights—McAuliffe and Dixon—had sat. Corbett demurred. A coin was tossed and Sullivan lost. Sullivan demanded to enter the ring last. Corbett refused. (He did not want to be around when the huge Sullivan ovation volcanoed up;

but it was also a useful tactic to further enrage his opponent.) Stubbornly waiting, Corbett was told that a coin had been tossed, that Sullivan had lost and that Sullivan would enter the ring first. Corbett, all unsuspecting, left the locker room and walked down the aisle. He noticed suddenly that Sullivan was *not* in the ring. He waited patiently in the aisle until Sullivan appeared and told him calmly that he (Corbett) was not going in the ring first if they had to stand there all night. This did not sit well with Sullivan's notorious disposition, but, emitting a menacing growl, he marched down to the ring and climbed in. He got a tremendous ovation. Corbett's was quite mild. The crowd was pleased that he had shown up at all.

Sullivan, wearing green tights and high shoes, scowled at Corbett as Referee John Duffy explained the rules. Corbett, wearing drab-colored trunks held up by a red, white and blue belt, smiled and waved cheerily at total strangers to show Sullivan how unimpressed he was at the champion's façade of ferocity. When the "hitting in the clinches" subject was brought up by the referee, Corbett made some direct queries of Duffy without deigning to look at Sullivan, referring to him with a sneer as "this fellow." After his questions had been answered to his satisfaction, he looked Sullivan very aggressively in the eye and was pleased to see that Sullivan was disturbed by the lack of reaction his scowl was getting.

When the fight started, it was Corbett's plan to let himself be worked into a corner. He wanted to find out, while still fresh, what Sullivan's tactics would be in that situation. A few minutes after the first round started, he learned what to expect when cornered and how to anticipate Sullivan's right-hand punch and just how far to move his head to avoid it. Corbett did not strike a blow, however, and when the second took on the same flavor—Sullivan lumbering after what looked like an abject coward —the fans started hooting at him. So, like a confident matador, he turned his back on his opponent, waved to the audience and shouted, "Just wait a minute! You'll see a fight!" Sullivan's face grew black with rage at this presumptuousness and he charged Corbett again, only to find the challenger tantalizingly out of reach. Corbett was filled with confidence as he returned to his corner, but his second, Billy Delaney, warned him not to be careless. "Remember, this guy can take you out with one punch," he said. "My God, Jim!" Brady implored, "Remember *Gentlemen Jack!*"

Now Corbett promised himself, for the sake of his self-respect, that he was going to land at least one good shot before the next round was over. Again he allowed himself to be worked into a corner and glanced around as though looking for an escape route. Sullivan, intent on seeing that he did not get away, was not ready for the straight left Corbett launched at his face with all his power. As Sullivan recoiled in consternation, Corbett followed up with a fast series of punches, driving him across the ring. By the time he had finished the flurry, Sullivan's nose was broken.

In the ensuing rounds Corbett continued his tactic of making Sullivan pursue him and miss. The champion's swings became wilder and wilder. Sometimes there was so much force behind them as they tore up the air that he almost fell down. At one point, exasperated, he stopped in the center of the ring and called, "Come on and fight!" Looking like Puck, Corbett refused to attack, and the crowd booed. Sullivan once more advanced.

Then Corbett, when he saw Sullivan puffing and noticed how his swings had slowed down, became bolder. He moved close to Sullivan and feinted. Sullivan overreacted to the feint (a characteristic Corbett had noticed in the testimonial-dinner match). Bang, bang, bang, bang—four rapid jabs to the champion's swollen nose. A few rounds later Corbett felt it was time to stand close and damage Sullivan with some hooks and straight rights; he felt confident that Sullivan could not reach him with a hard punch. But in the seventeenth Sullivan did land his only good blow of the bout, a hard right that bowled Corbett over. The crowd stood up with a roar. This was the Sullivan they had waited to see! But the bell ended the round, and Corbett made his way back to his corner without any difficulty.

When the twenty-first round came up, Corbett—amazed at Sullivan's endurance—was not sure how much longer the fight would last. In an attempt to end it, he moved toward the champion, feinted with his left, brought it back and hooked it alongside Sullivan's jaw. Sullivan's eyes glazed. Unwilling to let him escape, Corbett went after him, pummeling with both hands. Since Sullivan was not covering himself effectively, Corbett set himself and put everything he had into a right that hit Sullivan on the side of the jaw. Sullivan toppled to the turf, where he lay motionless, and was counted out. As Corbett, the referee and Sullivan's seconds deposited Sullivan in his corner, a thunderous, astonished roar went up from the crowd, and a maelstrom of hats, coats, canes and belts swirled into the ring, a kind of spontaneous homage to the new champion.

Unmarked, unruffled, magnanimous in victory, Corbett stood in the center of the ring and acknowledged the cheers. Then he went to Sullivan's corner to shake hands. Sullivan, close to exhaustion, his face battered, his body a mass of bruises and welts, rose to his feet, raised his arms for silence, and as the crowd hushed, announced hoarsely, "Gentlemen! It's the old story. I fought once too often. But I'm glad it was an American who beat me and that the championship stays in this country!" A cheer went up for Sullivan's gallantry, his supporters forgetting their monetary losses in this electric moment. Later, in his dressing room, Sullivan had a change of mood. He kept shaking his head, wondering aloud how he ever could have lost to that kid Corbett.

As for the new champion, suddenly plunged into glory and affluence, he declined to go out on the town with the ecstatic Brady and company, winners of thousands of dollars in bets. Instead, he went to the Southern Athletic Club (as he had said he would after the fight). There he was offered champagne but drank milk—a footnote to the battle that the newspapers did not miss. A new era in prizefighting had begun. ∎

When James J. Corbett became champion in 1892, boxing acquired a new image. Previously fighters had been known for brute strength and crude behavior, but "Gentleman Jim" provided a different profile. His dress, manner, and style were reminders of early British champions who gained the adoration of royalty.

In 1891 Corbett fought the great Australian Peter Jackson. After sixty-one grueling rounds the referee stopped the fight.

In 1898, the year after he lost his title, Corbett fought Tom Sharkey. Sharkey, right, won as the result of a foul.

This sketch of Corbett's first title defense against Charlie Mitchell, in 1894, is a case of artistic license. They wore gloves.

While on tour in a play called The Naval Cadet, *Corbett married a lovely lady named Vera Stanhope. So began a tradition that champions should win the favor and hand in marriage of ranking beauties.*

Jim Corbett, born in 1866 in San Francisco, had early set his sights on succeeding John L. Sullivan. His was a carefully planned campaign based on study and discipline. Sullivan, who had become slow and ponderous, had never faced a man like Corbett. In Sullivan's mind fighting was a manly art depending on the relentless imposition of force, whereas footwork and defensive skill were the essence of Corbett's talent.

On January 25, 1894, Corbett defended his title against Charlie Mitchell at the Duval Athletic Club in Jacksonville, Florida. Cor- bett had been touring for a year in a play called Gentleman Jack, while challenges came from all sides. Corbett consented to

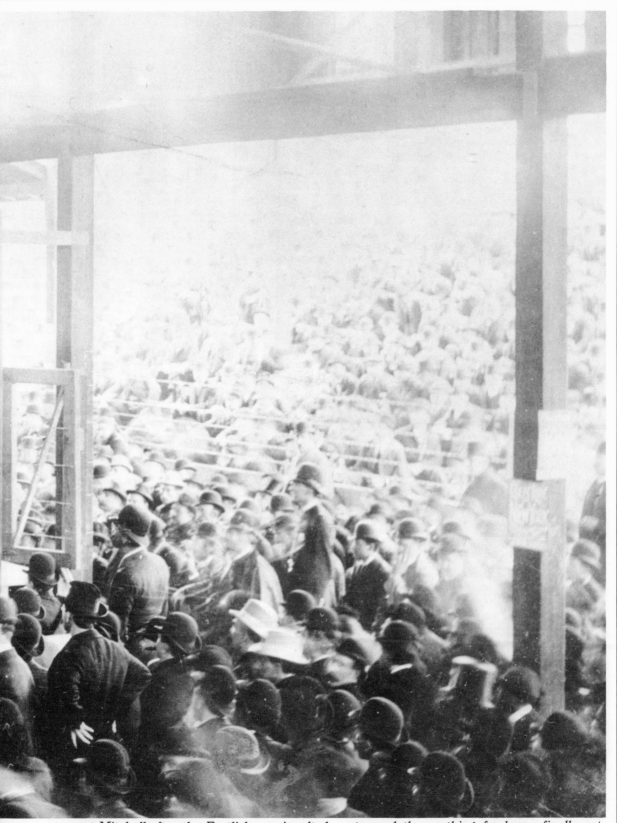

meet Mitchell after the Englishman insulted him. Mitchell's press campaign demanding a showdown helped inflame Corbett's wounded ego, and the seething feud was finally settled in the ring. The Englishman, a vastly inferior performer, got his comeuppance.

Gentleman Jim, in the bikini-like trunks, is seen above with Peter Courtney in Orange, New Jersey. The extraordinary thing is not that Corbett is fighting the New Jersey champion but that they are performing before a motion-picture camera. The year was 1894, and Thomas Alva Edison had just perfected the remarkable Kinetoscope.

The odd structure at left, known as the Black Maria, housed the Kinetoscope and the mobile padded stage, fifteen feet wide and six feet high, on which Corbett and Courtney fought. The building was mounted on a pivot and could be swung around slowly to follow the changing position of the sun, since the film was shot by natural light. For barely working up a sweat Corbett received $5,000. There were six rounds of one and a half minutes each, matching the duration of the film that the camera held. When film ran out, time was called and Edison took off two minutes to reload his camera. Corbett won by a "knockout" in six rounds. The inventor and the invention that was to change the habits of an entire civilization are shown at left (center).

Three gentlemen stroll the boardwalk in Atlantic City in the summer of 1914. The man on the left is Jackie Wilson. In the center, as always, is Gentleman Jim Corbett, still dapper at forty-eight. And on the right is Joe Choynski. Corbett and Choynski fought four times—their bouts were lessons that ultimately led Corbett to the crown.

At the turn of the century the link between boxing and drinking establishments was firmly founded. The man who was champion attracted the public. Above, Jim Corbett's place in New York, which later became the site of Saks Fifth Avenue.

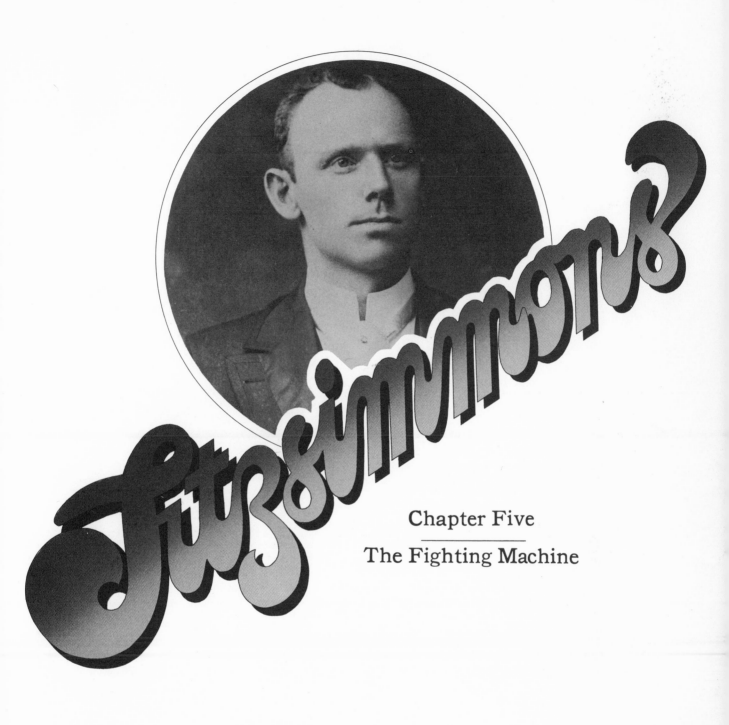

Chapter Five

The Fighting Machine

After winning the championship, Corbett reveled in it in a quiet way, resented by some for dethroning America's hero, and not too eager, in the fashion of boxing champions, to risk losing his title. The plotting done so carefully by Brady bore rich fruit: Sullivan's conqueror starred in *Gentleman Jack* in cities all over the country, and the money rolled in. He was a poised actor, tall and dark, with Gaelic good looks and a sonorous voice. These qualities, combined with the aura that surrounded him as the most destructive man with his fists in America, made many a lady theatregoer's heart flutter. He was the prototypical matinee idol, with a few pluses added. He paid for his glory from time to time. One theatre fan, enraged at finding Corbett's picture on his beloved's dressing table, took a shot at him with a revolver but missed. In another city Corbett was sued for alienation of affection but won the case with ease.

His picture appeared on cards put out by cigarette companies. He was one of the earliest endorsers of manufacturers' products. A plaster case was made of his right hand and used as a model for a metal replica, which was sold as a paperweight. Corbett realized a thousand dollars on the deal. He bought some real estate in the Bronx and made a huge amount of money from it years later. His praises were sung in vaudeville turns:

> You may talk about your champions
> in the good old days of yore,
> The heroes of the prize ring in
> savage mills galore,
> The gallant gladiators, who battled
> doggedly
> As brave as jungle lions, and game
> right to the core;
> But for splendid speed and science,
> none of them could compare
> With him who holds the title now,
> a true American,
> Jim Corbett of the Irish breed, the
> wizard boxing lad
> Who took the fighting crown away
> from John L. Sullivan!

Where Sullivan's style had been to throw silver on the bar and order drinks for everyone in the house, Corbett's largesse was of a more sophisticated nature. He would enter a posh, crystal-lit restaurant in a high-class hotel and order wine for the patrons; it was part of his plan to elevate the image of boxing. His father's advice to "always act the gentleman" was diligently adhered to. Delmonico's, New York's ritziest restaurant, was frequented by Corbett's friends in the theatrical, legal, business and financial professions and by handsome society folk, and it was Corbett's favorite place to dine. Soon after he sat down, his table would be aswarm with celebrities.

Nor did he forget the plight of the ex-champion. Sullivan had realized nothing from the fight and had lost his shirt betting on himself. Corbett consented to spar with him at a Sullivan testimonial at Madison Square Garden — a magnanimous gesture that put twenty thousand dollars in Sullivan's pocket, including a thousand dollars Corbett laid out himself for a box so that his eminent friends would have a good view.

There was no end to Brady's enterprise. When the Chicago World's Fair opened in 1893, the showman had Corbett engage in sparring exhibitions with Jim Daly, and then, as a change of pace, matched Daly with a kangaroo. (How the Greek gods of irony must have laughed!) Before an astonished audience, Daly feinted the kangaroo with a left, then hit it with a right alongside the head. The kangaroo promptly reared back on its muscular tail and kicked Daly with a hind leg, nearly eviscerating him and propelling him across the ring. The audience began rooting for the kangaroo, but Daly sailed into it with both hands and knocked it out.

Meanwhile, hungry hounds were constantly yapping at the heels of Sullivan's thespian conqueror. Those making the most to-do in the press and wherever their sporting friends gathered were Frank "Paddy" Slavin, Peter Maher, the Irish champion, Bob Fitzsimmons and Charlie Mitchell. Peter Jackson had thrown down a gauntlet, but since he was spending more time in cafés and saloons than in training, his challenge was not taken too seriously.

Fitzsimmons had been the most direct. After the Sullivan benefit, he dropped into Corbett's dressing room unannounced. "Corbett, I can lick you" he asserted, "and you've got to give me the first chance!" Corbett shouted at the Cornishman to get out. He did not like Fitzsimmons, perhaps because the Cornishman had beaten (nearly to a pulp) Corbett's good friend Jack Dempsey for the middleweight championship. None of the challengers, oddly enough, was an American. Conceivably Corbett felt that by not fighting any of them he was making sure (as a true patriot) that the title stayed in America.

But after a year of preoccupation with other pursuits, Corbett finally consented to fight Mitchell—possibly because he wanted to kill the Englishman. Mitchell had first aroused Corbett's ire before the Sullivan fight in New Orleans. Because of his eminence in America at the time, Corbett had been accorded a sparring spot at Miner's Bowery Theatre in New York, pre-empting a scheduled exhibition between Mitchell and Slavin. Brooding over their joint grievance at the celebrated Hoffman House bar opposite Madison Square, they decided to pester Corbett. The pair accosted him in the lobby of the theatre, where Mitchell, noted for his waspish tongue and command of Billingsgate, insulted Corbett and his relatives until the latter's face grew mottled with rage. As his peroration, Mitchell challenged Corbett to fight him then and there, but the prudent Corbett refused. Mitchell advanced toward him, and Corbett might have had to throw out his left to defend himself had not Mr. Miner himself intervened. The newspapers dutifully reported that Mitchell had given Corbett a dressing down and had challenged him on the spot, but that Corbett had "turned yellow."

Returning to England, where he was recognized as the top heavyweight even though Jem Smith held the title, Mitchell pressed his challenge through the newspapers. His manager, Squire Abingdon Baird—a wealthy theatrical entrepreneur most of whose productions seemed to star Lillie Langtry, the devastatingly beautiful actress from the Isle of Jersey—dispatched a formal challenge to Corbett. The side bet was to be ten thousand dollars, and the winner could claim whatever purse was forthcoming. The squire inferred that regarding wagers, the entire wealth of the British Empire stood back of his man. Corbett accepted, and the squire, Mitchell and their retinue sailed for America.

In the office of the New York *World* on Park Row, gambler Al Smith (by way of gambler Richard Canfield) laid down fifty thousand dollars in thousand-dollar bills in support of Corbett. The squire seemed to have only ten thousand dollars, however, to place on Mitchell. To cover his manager's discomfiture, Mitchell unleashed his tongue and soon worked Corbett into a froth of rage. The two fighters were held apart by cooler heads, but Brady was so enraged by the Englishman's manners that he wagered two thousand dollars to one thousand dollars that Mitchell would not show up for the fight. By the time the imbroglio ended, the side bet, to Brady's mystification, had been whittled down to five thousand dollars.

The Duval Athletic Club in Jacksonville, Florida, made the best offer for the bout—a purse of twenty thousand dollars—which was duly accepted. While an arena was being constructed in the city, Mitchell pitched camp at St. Augustine and Corbett at Mayport. Corbett trained hard for the fight and relaxed by playing croquet with Jack Dempsey, who was still a little woozy from his fight with Fitzsimmons. The hiring of Dempsey as a companion and sparring partner seemed like an act of charity on Corbett's part, but it was Dempsey who would save his title for him.

Because the governor of Florida disapproved of the bout, the city of Jacksonville took the case to court. Thereupon the governor called out the state militia and deployed his troops around the newly built arena. When Brady considered holding the fight in Georgia, the governor of that state arrayed his troops on the Georgia-Florida border. The night before the bout, the Supreme Court of Florida declared that the governor had no legal right to stop it. But the legal squabbling and the martial moves had discouraged fans from the North from making what might be a fruitless trip. Attendance was relatively sparse, and many seats were occupied by Florida militiamen who sat with their guns on their laps. They did not buy tickets. Bat Masterson and a gunfighter named Converse sat in Mitchell's corner to make sure that the Englishman was not given a raw deal. The referee was a former baseball umpire named "Honest John" Kelly, who brought a fresh mind to refereeing—a lucky thing, as it turned out, for the champion.

While in training, Corbett had received a jolt from his brother Harry, whom he had backed in a saloon-*cum*-betting parlor for sporting types in San Francisco, Corbett's Café. Jim was confident he could beat Mitchell, who was only five feet nine inches tall and weighed 160 pounds, and he so advised his brother. Harry sent back word that he had put every nickel he owned on Jim, plus a substantial sum he had borrowed. The fact that Harry might lose everything he owned preyed on Corbett's mind as—leaving the psychologizing to Mitchell—he entered the ring first. He was given plenty of time to worry.

Mitchell did not appear for an hour as Corbett, wearing a light robe, alternately stewed and shivered in the chill wind. When Mitchell appeared, Corbett was in far from his best humor. Wearing a clown hat and totally unconcerned, Mitchell (richer by two thousand dollars) smiled and winked at him, then laughed and whistled and waved at the crowd. When Honest John summoned them for their instructions, Mitchell took the opportunity to invoke his choicest pejoratives in a loud voice, and Corbett grew so angry that he saw Mitchell through a red haze. The instructions finally given, Corbett snarled to the referee, "No shaking hands!" Dancing in his corner, he shouted at the time-keeper, the well-known jockey "Snapper" Garrison, to get on with banging the gong. As the gong sounded, Corbett —in complete accord with Mitchell's plans—tore across the ring and swung with both hands as Mitchell backed away and carefully covered up. Then, spotting an opening, the Englishman let fly a hard left hand that homed in on Corbett's lip—first blood, with all that entailed, for Mitchell. The fact that he had been lured into playing the other man's game, the dull pain in the lower part of his face and the fact that he was continually being insulted as the Englishman milled on the retreat enraged Corbett still further. The first round was Mitchell's.

Corbett did not decrease his pace in the second, and his greater size and ability to place his punches began to tell. He landed a right to the body, the effect of which all Mitchell's ring generalship could not hide. It hurt. The Englishman began backing away, still hurling vituperation, and went down for the count near the end of the round. While on his knees, waiting for "Nine," Mitchell kept the flow of invective coming. "Count faster!" Corbett shouted at Honest John. The insults got to be too much for the champion, and, shoving the referee aside, he smacked Mitchell in the head while the challenger was on his knees. Immediately the gunmen in Mitchell's corner sprang to the ring apron, flourishing their weapons, and the crowd stood on their seats and howled in confusion. The Nonpareil and Brady leapt into the ring. Dempsey got between Mitchell and Corbett, slapped the champion in the face to restore him to a semblance of sanity and pushed him toward his corner. Kelly was so confused he did not think to award Mitchell the fight on a foul. He chased Brady and the Nonpareil out of the ring and beckoned the fighters to continue where they had left off. The round ended a moment later, and Corbett walked to his corner. But Mitchell pursued him and struck Corbett a savage blow behind the ear. Corbett fought back, and the two brawled for a few seconds before their handlers pulled them apart.

In the third round Corbett continued his assault and, caring not a jot for the damage to his hands, launched a hard right at the point of Mitchell's jaw— probably the hardest he ever threw. Mitchell grew stiff, then toppled forward on his face. Without waiting for the count to finish, Corbett strolled to his corner and had his handlers unlace his gloves, confident that Mitchell would be a long time coming around.

In his dressing room after the fight, Mitchell talked to Bat Masterson about the battle. "You sure got him mad, Charlie," Bat said by way of comfort.

"I got him mad, all right," Mitchell said ruefully, with a shake of his aching head. "But I didn't care to get the bloke *that* bloody mad." Whereupon Mitchell turned all gracious for the press and called Corbett "the greatest fighter who ever stood in a ring." "I don't care who goes against him," he asserted. "If he keeps his health he will never be beaten." The *Police Gazette* proclaimed Corbett the greatest modern fighter, and the press in foreign lands accepted him as the first heavyweight champion of the world.

Following the fight, the principals were arrested and arraigned before a Florida magistrate for their sins. The trial took place three months later. The state district attorney acted as prosecutor, and Corbett was given the unusual privilege of selecting the jury. He picked the right panel, and after ten minutes of deliberation the members found Corbett, Mitchell and all concerned not guilty. What took them so long? "We just wanted to make it seem like we were thinking it over," a juror confided to Corbett a little bit later.

Brady then escorted Corbett, Daly and *Gentleman Jack* to Europe, Corbett taking the opportunity to allow his parents to visit their home island and greet old friends. The play had a successful run at Drury Lane in London but fared poorly in other cities, including Dublin, Glasgow and prizefight-conscious Birmingham. The British apparently were not ready to accept Corbett's dual role of actor-fighter. He had better luck with his boxing. After sparring in London with Jem Mace, British heavyweight champion of a bygone era, Mace told him, "Young man, you are the most scientific boxer I have ever seen." In France, Corbett and Daly put on boxing exhibitions at the Folies Bergère, delighting the French, to whom the sport was a great novelty. Brady made arrangements for Corbett to fight the French *la savate* king, Charlemont, but

the Frenchman backed out at the last minute. Arrangements were made for Corbett to spar with Leopold II, King of the Belgians, a fine amateur boxer, but Corbett was in a hurry to return to America, so the bout was canceled.

Back in America, Corbett starred in a new play, *The Naval Cadet,* married a pretty blonde lady named Vera Stanhope, whom he had met while on tour in Kansas City, Missouri, and on September 7, 1894, fought the second most historic bout of his entire career. It was against Peter Courtney of Trenton, the champion of New Jersey, and it took place inside a mutuscope—the world's first motion-picture studio. The bout was fought at the behest of Thomas A. Edison's Kineograph Company, which was pioneering in the production of films for the kinetoscope, a peephole machine in which the viewer, after inserting a coin, could see what amounted to a silent motion picture. Edison did not invent the motion picture, but he coordinated the ideas of other inventors—such as Auguste Lumière of France and Dr. Coleman Sellers of Philadelphia—and developed, in his busy laboratories, a motion-picture camera (the kinetograph) and the kinetoscope.

Edison's mutuscope, or "kinetoscopic theatre" (nicknamed the Black Maria), built at the plant near Llewellyn Park, New Jersey, was a structure that looked something like a huge German tank of World War I. It was covered with tar paper on the outside and painted black on the inside to bring the actors (or athletes) into sharp relief. A large section of roof could be opened up to let the sunshine in, and the studio swung on a graphite center, the ends being held up by iron rods extending from a center post. This allowed the structure to be moved to follow the path of the sun as it swept across the sky, creating maximum natural illumination. The first movie Edison shot inside the Black Maria was "Fred Ott's Sneeze." Ott, an Edison lab assistant, was noted for his uncontrollable sneezing, and Edison felt he would make a lively subject for the revolutionary entertainment form.

John L. Sullivan was the first eminent fighter to whom Edison offered the boxing job, but he turned it down because he did not think the fee was sufficient. Corbett, believing it would be useful to see himself in action (the same lure that cajoles stage actors to Hollywood), readily accepted.

With Edison directing in the best style of David Wark Griffith—"Keep your face to the camera, Jim! Hold up that right-hand punch till you get him in the middle of the ring!"—and John P. Eckhardt refereeing, the two battlers fought for six rounds. Rounds were limited to two minutes each, because that was when the film ran out. Rest periods were two minutes long, because it took that length of time to reload the camera. The extra respite was welcome, because the heat inside the primitive studio was stifling. A single one-ton camera was used.

Corbett began with a rush, jabbing the overawed Courtney at will and darting about at four times Courtney's rate of speed. When the New Jersey champion seemed to be in dire straits, Corbett restrained himself so that the fight would last as long as had been planned. In the sixth round, to furnish a proper climax, Corbett cornered Courtney at the ropes, measured him with a left and flung a straight right to the jaw. Courtney had the distinction of being the first man tolled out before the motion-picture camera. Corbett received $4,700 as winner and Courtney $250 as loser.

After polishing off Courtney, Corbett repaired to a nearby railroad depot to catch the train back to New York. There he was accosted by a local sheriff, who had been tipped off that an illegal prizefight had taken place that he had somehow missed. He wanted to arrest somebody involved, so he asked Corbett who he might be. Corbett affected theatrical disdain at the sheriff's ignorance. "Don't you recognize me?" he intoned. "I'm Maurice Barrymore." The sheriff stared in puzzlement. "Maurice Barrymore, the actor." The sheriff turned on his heel and left, hunting for easier prey. Barrymore, who once acted in San Francisco in *Camille* with a callow Corbett, would have been proud of his protégé.

Boxing thereafter became closely tied in with the infant film industry. Motion pictures of prizefights were a staple of kinetoscopes of the late 1890's and early 1900's, before the advent of projection screens and "the story picture" (such as *The Great Train Robbery*). They were ideal from the standpoint of the kinetograph operator and director; action was confined to a small space, there was plenty of motivated movement to help the viewer ignore the "flicker" between individual frames and only a small cast was required. Additionally, there has always been a psychological link between violence and the movies; kinetoscopic films like Edison's "The Execution of Mary, Queen of Scots" was a tremendous hit in the 1890's.

In 1895 came the development of the film projector ("vitascope") by Thomas Armat of Washington, D.C. These machines, manufactured by Edison, showed Edison's kinetoscopic films to large audiences and were instrumental in changing movies from a novelty toy into a gigantic industry. The first commercial picture ever shown on the screen was a bout between Young Griffo, the imcomparable Australian featherweight and lightweight who fought some of his best fights when inebriated, and Battling Barnett, in May, 1895. Later, motion-picture films of championship bouts found a public feverish with anticipation to see its heroes in action and brought tens of thousands of dollars to the principals, their managers and the film producers. The Corbett-Courtney bout was exhibited in kinetoscope parlors and after vaudeville acts, and it attracted customers to traveling carnivals and amusement parks. Corbett—photogenic and poetry in motion when he boxed in the ring—signed the world's first "exclusive star" contract with Edison's Kinetoscopic Exhibition Company. In March, 1897, Enoch Rector exposed eleven thousand feet of film in recording the Corbett-Fitzsimmons fight, the first championship fight ever filmed and the longest film made up to that time of a single event.

═══════════

If Corbett abominated Mitchell, he detested (for reasons he could not quite explain) Fitzsimmons. Yet pressures grew stronger on him week by week to accept the Cornishman's persistent challenges. Newspapers demanded that Fitz be given a title shot. Whenever Fitz could assemble a group of sportsmen around him, he asserted that Corbett was afraid to fight him. When Corbett performed in *The Naval Cadet,* members of the audience were apt to heckle him with, "Why don't you fight Fitzsimmons?" Sullivan's admirers—who remained legion even with the passage of time—wanted to see Corbett get his block knocked off. There has always been something distasteful to the fight fan about the champion who continually avoids his most eligible challenger, and sportswriters are always willing to take up the cudgel for that challenger.

Sensitive to the signs of the fans' dissatisfaction and seeing box-office receipts falling off, Brady, in the great tradition, told Fitzsimmons to get a reputation. The procedure was to be this: Fitzsimmons was to fight an Australian named Steve O'Donnell, in whom Brady had a financial interest. If he beat O'Donnell, he would fight Corbett. To build up O'Donnell, Brady arranged a match for him with Jake Kilrain. Unfortunately for Brady, Kilrain, though old and shaky, beat the tar out of O'Donnell. In this he was helped spiritually by John L. Sullivan. Screaming insults and threats at O'Donnell from Kilrain's corner, the ex-champion so upset the Australian's concentration that he became an easy mark for some of Kilrain's elephantine swings.

Resigning themselves to the caprices of whatever muses run prizefighting, Corbett and Brady finally accepted Fitzsimmons's challenge. Articles were signed on October 11, 1894, at the New York *Herald* Building for a side bet of ten thousand dollars and the largest purse that any club might offer, the winner to get it all. Fitzsimmons and his manager, Martin Julian, were present, as was Brady. But Corbett refused to come. At the meeting, Fitzsimmons began to rail at the absent Corbett. Brady threatened, quite daringly, to throw him out the window if he didn't shut up. Brady reported the incident to Corbett, and Corbett fumed. There was no dissimulation in the notices given to the public that this was a grudge fight. Curiously enough, it was nearly two and a half years before the two fighters were to meet inside the ring.

Few prizefighters have been so jeered at as Bob Fitzsimmons. His appearance was the chief cause for merriment. He was gangly, knock-kneed and walked with a shambling gait. He was freckle-faced, bald except for a fringe of pale reddish hair that circled his small head like a tonsure and had whitish skin that looked as though it had been decorated by a pointillist. After being in the sun his skin became one huge freckle. His spindly legs thrust him to a height of six feet; with his barrel of a chest he looked top-heavy in the ring. His weight was a problem; he was fighting professional heavyweights when he weighed as little as 150 pounds. He was known by a dozen nicknames, few of them flattering. One was "Ruby Robert," because of the general impression of reddish ocher that his hair, brows and freckles gave. "Lanky, freckled freak" and "knock-kneed crane" were epithets accorded him in the newspapers; "a fighting machine on stilts" was John L. Sullivan's thoughtful description of him; "bald-headed kangaroo" was the way a few rival fighters referred to him. When he stepped into the ring, some fans seeing him for the first time laughed; others started worrying about the wagers they had risked on him.

Fitz had several attributes working for him, however. While nowhere near the boxer Corbett was, nor close to Jack Johnson as a defensive fighter, and while sometimes given to wild, ineffective swings, he was rugged, determined and, above all, crafty in the ring. He had enormous shoulder, back and arm development. And he could hit. How he could hit! He could punch effectively with either hand from long range or short and while off balance. Jack Johnson, who defeated Fitz in their only bout (when Fitz was forty-five years old), rated the Cornishman over Jeffries and Sam Langford as a puncher. He recalled one left-hand blow—which he narrowly got out of the way of—that "hummed past like a swarm of bees." For his weight Fitz was probably the hardest puncher who ever lived.

Guarding his chin with his raised left shoulder, he was willing to accept punishment patiently for rounds on end if eventually he could find an opening for one of his paralyzing blows. When the climax of a bout came, with both fighters tired and hurt, he found in himself a drive to hit harder and last longer than his opponent. Like the great Tom Cribb, he was gifted with tremendous powers of recuperation; after absorbing a thorough battering, he would return to battle refreshed from his single minute's respite. Sometimes he would lure a foe into becoming careless by pretending to be hurt and then lash out with a stiff right or left which would change the course of the fight.

Gene Tunney tells the story of an unusual training technique that Fitzsimmons made use of. He would go off alone somewhere and, concentrating his utmost, would close his eyes and imagine himself to be drowning in the ocean. At the moment when in his mind's eye he was about to perish, he would quickly thrust out an arm and pretend he was being saved by seizing a plank on the surface. Desperation gave his thrust great power, and he attributed his ability to punch hard, from every position, to his constantly practicing his escape from death.

Fitzsimmons was basically a good-natured, nonviolent, home-loving, animal-fancying individual. A man of enormous appetite when he was knocking over heavyweights, he ate well even while in strict training for a fight. Often supper would be half a chicken, some toast, a cup of coffee and a bowl of stewed fruit. His favorite food was calf's-foot jelly, which was prepared for him by his wife, Rose—a training-camp habitué—and which he devoured by the pound.

One time at his house in Bath Beach, near the Brooklyn Bridge, his kindness towards members of the animal kingdom got him into trouble. The story is related by Robert H. Davis, the author of *Ruby Robert* and a newspaperman who covered the Corbett fight for the Hearst press. Davis, a good friend of the Fitzsimmonses, was rousted out of his bed one night by a mysterious phone call. It seemed that Fitz, either drunk or crazy, was claiming to be training a macaw to talk. After the caller hung up, Davis sped over to Fitz's house. The report was true all right, but Fitz was more obsessed than drunk or crazy. The bird had gorgeous plumage, red eyes, a sharp beak and ferocious claws. Fitz showed Davis how friendly it was, then fed the macaw bananas and plums. A storm broke outside, which upset the bird, who gave all his food back. Seeing that the bird was ill, Fitz gave up and went to bed. Davis slept on the couch.

When Fitz was deeply asleep, the bird, perhaps upset by being kept up so late, or by the thunder and lightning outside, or by too much mental pressure, attacked the champion. It sank its claws in his thigh and began pecking away at his kidney. Fitz woke up and, unable to dislodge the bird, ran outside and fell face down in the mud. Davis, awakened by his cries, yanked the bird off and chucked it into a closet. In the bathroom, Fitz examined his wounds. He had deep cuts all over his thighs and punctures over his kidney. Davis bandaged him up, and the two went to bed.

A few hours later Davis went to the closet and found the bird exhausted and dispirited. He picked it up and flung it out of the window. The bird wobbled off, never to be seen again.

Fitz was dismayed that the bird had acted the way it did, after the prizefighter had tried to teach him to talk.

"What did you want him to talk about?" Davis asked.

Aching and bloody, Fitz did not think the issue was one to be discussed. "Oh, 'ell," he replied. "Let's go back to bed."

Ruby Robert was born on June 4, 1864, in Elston, a town in Cornwall in southwest England. When he was nine his family migrated to Lyttleton, on the east coast of New Zealand's South Island. At the local school Fitz showed himself to be a star sprinter and soccer player. Occasionally poked fun at because of his frail appearance, he had informal sparring matches with his schoolmates and began to feel that his vocation, when he grew up, might lie in this direction. At an early age he was apprenticed to a blacksmith and earned his muscles by pounding a sledge on an anvil to shape sizzling sections of iron.

When Fitz was eighteen, Jem Mace visited New Zealand to supervise an amateur boxing tournament. In a bout a short while before, Fitz, weighing 140 pounds, had shocked his neighbors by knocking out Tom Baines, a blacksmith known as "the Timaru Terror." Now he informed Mace that he wanted to enter the tournament as a heavyweight. Mace told him he should enter as a lightweight, but young Fitzsimmons stubbornly refused. Mace let him have his way, certain that he would suffer at the hands of the first brawny competitor he met. But Fitz knocked out four large opponents with ease and became amateur heavyweight champion of New Zealand. The next year Mace brought Herbert A. Slade, "the Maori," to Fitz's island and made the mistake of letting him enter the ring with the local hero. Fitz attacked him so viciously that in the second round Mace scrambled through the ropes to stop the fight before his man lost his memory.

Turning professional, Fitz beat three local fighters and then looked about for greener pastures. Having no money for frivolities, he stowed away on a two-masted schooner and landed in Sydney. There he got a job as a blacksmith and spent his spare time trying to locate opponents. He found two, beating one and losing to the other in a four-round knockout. (The latter was Jem Hall. Fitz later claimed—such is the pride of champion boxers—that he had thrown the fight at the request of gamblers.) He had enough money now to book passage for San Francisco and even greener pastures—specifically, the California Athletic Club. There his request to officials to be given a fight met with nothing but polite chuckles. Insistent, he was matched in an informal bout with a hard-hitting middleweight named Frank Allen, highly respected in the locality.

Fitzsimmons, eager to please, stepped onto the gym floor and jabbed Allen into a state of confusion for a few moments, then threw a short right that sent him rolling across the gym floor. Not only was Allen knocked out, but his wrist was broken when he landed, and the blow had shattered to bits a dental bridge he wore. Allen was an early attester to the power of Fitz's punch. An official fight was promptly arranged for Fitz at the C.A.C.

His first formal victim in America was an Australian named Billy McCarthy, considered the second-best middleweight in America (after Dempsey). McCarthy made the mistake of poking fun at Fitz and found himself reeling around the ring under a fusillade of short, savage punches. Repeatedly knocked down, he lasted nine rounds before being counted out. Fitz's five-round demolition of Arthur Upham at the Audubon Club in New Orleans on June 28, 1890, so impressed the sports of Louisiana that he was matched with the Nonpareil at the same club for the middleweight championship. The purse was twelve thousand dollars, the highest ever offered for a fight up to that time—and very tempting to Dempsey. Fitzsimmons would have fought for nothing.

Jack Dempsey was one of the greatest middleweights of all time. Conqueror of many much heavier battlers, he had held the championship for seven years. During the course of a career filled with triumphs, he had taken part in one of the strangest bouts on record, and he was once beaten in the most bizarre way conceivable.

On a wintry day in 1887, Dempsey fought challenger Johnny Reagan of New York. The secret site was a small piece of land extending into Huntington Bay on the north shore of Long Island. Spectators (to the number of about twenty-five), principals and their entourages arrived by tugboat. There was a tide factor that looked ominous— a small portion of the ring was beginning to be covered with water—but the fight went on anyway. Dempsey mauled Reagan thoroughly for several rounds but then found his shin cut deeply by a blow from one of Reagan's boxing shoes, which had thoughtfully been outfitted with track spikes by his seconds. Showing immense restraint, Dempsey's handlers insisted that the spikes be made duller, and while the Nonpareil was being patched up this was taken care of. The fight resumed, but by this time the surf was beginning to roll, and half the ring was covered by water from the sound. The contestants whaled away at each other until the water was nearly to their knees. Then the referee halted the bout. After a conference, everyone boarded the tug and sailed to another spot, the trip taking about an hour. Between the chill and the lack of activity, however, Dempsey's leg had stiffened to the point where he had to be carried from the boat to the new location, atop a knoll some distance away from the beach. The Reagan faction was pleased. But once he got to moving about in the ring, Dempsey found his circulation and mobility restored and proceeded to give Reagan a thorough drubbing.

Two years later, at the California Athletic Club, Dempsey had the misfortune to be on the receiving end of the deadly "pivot punch." His opponent was George La Blanche, a Canadian known as "the Marine." Outweighed by thirty pounds, Dempsey jabbed and cut the slow La Blanche to ribbons for thirty-one rounds. It seemed that the Canadian would never stagger through the thirty-second. Dempsey stalked him carefully, measuring him for the knockout blow, when La Blanche—remembering an unorthodox move he had been taught by his trainer, the English lightweight Jimmy Carroll—launched the pivot punch. He missed purposely with his left and used the momentum of the swing to pivot on his heel all the way around to his right, thrusting his right arm straight out as he whirled. As he completed the circle, his extended right elbow hit Dempsey on the chin. Tremendous power is imparted to this punch, partly because of the distance it travels and partly because of centrifugal force, so that it would not have mattered whether La Blanche hit Dempsey with his fist, wrist, forearm or elbow. Dempsey dropped flat on his face, breaking his nose on the ring floor. Every person in the audience was stunned at the sight of the fighter who a moment before had been seeking an inevitable knockout, now flattened by a punch that had traveled about eighteen feet. The referee looked from Dempsey to La Blanche and back again. La Blanche stood paralyzed, his right arm held straight out. It was a long time before Dempsey could be revived, and La Blanche was declared the winner. So much fuss was raised in the papers about the blow, however, that Dempsey's crown was restored to him and the punch was declared illegal. (The fact that La Blanche was over the somewhat loosely defined middleweight limit gave Dempsey supporters further grounds for denying him the title.)

The Nonpareil was a useful man to have in one's corner, as Corbett well knew from his barge fight with Choynski. He was chief second for Jack McAuliffe when the American lightweight champion fought Jem Carney, the British champion, for the world title before an unruly crowd of twenty-eight in a Revere, Massachusetts, stable. The year was 1887. As the fight progressed, Dempsey kept insisting to the referee that Carney was fouling McAuliffe, but the referee ignored him. Finally, in desperation—since Carney was piling up a lead on points—Dempsey bit McAuliffe on the shoulder, leaving teeth marks. When the thirteenth round began, McAuliffe managed to pull Carney's head down to his shoulder, yelped and shouted to the referee, "Look! He's biting me!" The referee stared at the teeth marks and then at Carney, who, by grinning, revealed that he had no teeth to bite with. Sighing, the referee bade the boxers to continue. The fight continued for seventy-four rounds, until finally the spectators, all wildly partisan, broke into the ring. The fight was declared a draw.

When McAuliffe later fought Jimmy Carroll, the Englishman who had taught La Blanche the pivot punch, out of friendship for the Nonpareil he cut and sliced his opponent to ribbons before mercifully knocking him out in the forty-seventh round.

Courageous, popular, tricky, Dempsey was somewhat overconfident for the Fitzsimmons bout and did not train as hard as he usually did. He wished he had when he saw what faced him at the weighing-in—a perfectly conditioned fighter, wasp-waisted and all sinew, with the legs of a welterweight and the upper body of a heavyweight. Fitz was three pounds heavier than Dempsey, at 150½, and a few inches taller. More of a boxer than a slugger at the time, when the bout began Fitz toyed with Dempsey, skillful as the Nonpareil was, for twelve rounds. Dempsey was badly cut and nearly out on his feet. Had Fitz wanted to end the bout earlier, he could have. When he was informed by his handlers that Dempsey's men were about to throw in the sponge, he saved them the trouble by dashing out for the thirteenth, driving the Nonpareil into a corner and slamming a right to the chin that knocked him out.

As middleweight champion Fitzsimmons found pickings so slim and purses so small that he cast a longing eye on the heavyweight title, though he knew the road would be rocky and full of detours. In this ambition he was greatly encouraged by his manager, Martin Julian, and Julian's sister Rose, whom Fitz had married. Rose and Frank had done an acrobatic vaudeville turn in San Francisco—the muscular Rose was the understander in the act—before Rose married Fitz. The trio became very devoted to one another.

The Cornishman's first impressive heavyweight victory was over the Irishman Peter Maher, on March 2, 1892, at the Olympic Club in New Orleans. Maher had been born in Galway in 1869, won the Irish heavyweight title in 1889 and came to America in 1891. In knocking out some of this country's second-raters, Maher, who was six feet tall and weighed 190 pounds, showed a splendid right-hand punch and a fair ability to box. His trouble was that he was inconsistent as a fighter, sometimes a whirlwind and sometimes a placid striking bag.

Fitzsimmons, though outweighed by thirty pounds, chose to slug with Maher—a tactic which the Irishman at first welcomed, since he did not wish to chase Fitzsimmons around the ring. But it soon became apparent to the crowd and to Maher that Fitzsimmons was landing the heavier blows and with finer marksmanship. In the twelfth he cornered Maher and knocked him out with a left hook to the jaw and a straight right to the body.

Fitz's ability to flatten a man quickly was demonstrated in his bout with George Godfrey, whom he put away in one round. (Not discouraged by his loss to Fitzsimmons, Maher did the same thing a short while later.)

The Cornishman next took on hard-hitting Joe Choynski in Boston on June 17, 1894, the same year that squat, muscular Tom Sharkey, discharged from the Navy, began his cumbrous fighting in San Francisco. According to the best sources, Fitz and Choynski had made an agreement beforehand to box six fast rounds but not to do significant damage to one another—a discreet move, since both had reputations for punching power. The match was friendly until the third round, when Choynski espied an opening and uncorked a terrific right to the point of Fitz's chin. Fitzsimmons fell down in a heap, a look of surprise on his face, and barely got up before being counted out. His powers of recuperation and ability to clinch were all that allowed him to finish the round. In the fourth he charged at Choynski, forgetting the agreement, and launched a barrage of blows that soon had the Californian reeling. Fitz was getting set for the knockout in the fifth when the police leapt into the ring. The fight was declared a draw.

The site chosen for the long-awaited Corbett-Fitzsimmons battle was Dallas. The promoter was Dan Stuart, a gambler and business associate of Diamond Jim Brady's. He exuded confidence and seemed to have plenty of money. He had obtained Governor Culberson's permission to build an arena and stage the fight, offering a purse of forty thousand dollars, plus five thousand dollars extra for each camp for training expenses. Corbett blithely started training in San Antonio and Fitzsimmons in Corpus Christi. Interest in the fight was growing daily. Then bad news came. The governor reversed his position and declared the fight could not be held in Texas. Stuart, Brady and the newspapers all argued that Texas did not have an antiboxing law, therefore the

Five-cent song sheets celebrated the combatants in the Fitzsimmons–Corbett fight.

fight could not be stopped. The governor obliged by calling a special session of the legislature and jamming through a bill that prohibited boxing.

Stuart forsook his half-built arena in Texas and persuaded the citizenry of Hot Springs, Arkansas, that it would be profitable to hold the fight at that popular resort. He got Hot Springs' permission. Corbett and his entourage moved to Arkansas, but Fitzsimmons stayed in Texas. Brady felt that Fitz was dilly-dallying because he wanted a share of the film rights—the original agreement had awarded all revenues from the fight film to Brady and Corbett. (Brady also suspected that Stuart was interested in the film rights.)

From Little Rock, the capital, came the pronouncement from Governor Clark that there would be no fight in Arkansas. The sheriff of Hot Springs, favoring the fight, assured Corbett he would assemble vigilantes to keep the state militia out of the city if the governor attacked. Corbett started to build an arena just outside Hot Springs, using his own funds. Then the sheriff got a dressing down from the governor and decided not to promulgate a civil war. Fitzsim-

mons at this point journeyed to Texarkana, gave himself up to the law and was transported to Little Rock. The governor held a meeting with the principals and their managers to clear the air, telling them that they would be shipped out of the state in pine boxes if Corbett and Fitzsimmons attempted to engage in a prizefight while on Arkansas soil. Noting the casualness with which revolvers were displayed, the fighters and their retinues left the capital as quickly as possible and relaxed only after they had crossed the state line.

The fight was put off for eight months—for all the principals knew, forever. During this time Corbett, rather disenchanted with the boxing game, acted in his play and fought an out-of-shape four-round brawl with Tom Sharkey, which was declared a draw. Fitzsimmons was more active. He had a rematch with Maher—the preparations for which resembled those for the siege of Sevastopol—and an extremely strange fight with Sharkey.

Corbett showed his distaste for Fitzsimmons in a peculiar way. On November 11, 1895, Maher fought Steve O'Donnell, who was highly regarded by the champion and often used by him as a sparring partner. After Maher, enjoying one of his very good days, hammered O'Donnell into unconsciousness in one round, Corbett leapt into the ring and publicly announced his retirement— no doubt influenced by the fiascos in Texas and Arkansas. Since that left a kind of vacuum in heavyweight ranks, he declared that he was awarding the title to Peter Maher. The proffering of titles is something a champion has no right to do, but some of them make the gesture.

Fitzsimmons thereupon challenged Maher, and canny Dan Stuart, recovered from his legal wounds, signed the two to fight "in or near" El Paso, Texas. Governor Culberson averred that he would not permit the fight, but Stuart paid no heed. Fitzsimmons trained in Ciudad Juárez, just across the border from El Paso, and Maher trained at Las Cruces in New Mexico. There was immense activity, not all of it military, on the American side of the border. The shrewd Stuart became very interested in films and arranged, after some experiments, to have motion pictures of the fight taken. Gambling establishments and saloons proliferated as visitors from far-off places arrived in droves. The attorney general of Texas moved in with a dozen stalwart Rangers. The governor of New Mexico arrayed troops at the Texas–New Mexico border to prevent the fight from taking place in New Mexico. Bat Masterson, a loyal friend of Stuart's, swept into El Paso with his personal army, a small one, all of whom were bound by oath to aid Stuart in whatever enterprise he engaged. Stuart kept selling tickets for the fight in his office in El Paso. Scheduled for February 15, the fight was postponed to the twenty-first because Maher developed an eye infection from alkali dust. But on what planet would it be held?

Then, on February 20, the resourceful promoter posted a notice outside his office announcing that anyone who wanted to see Maher versus Fitzsimmons was to report that night either at his office or at the railroad depot. The destination was a secret; the entire package was twelve dollars. Hundreds boarded the train Stuart had chartered, including Rangers and Masterson's army. During the all-night trip, the passengers amused themselves by drinking, speculating on the outcome of the fight and playing cards and shooting dice. The next day the train arrived at Langtry, Texas, 350 miles to the southeast of El Paso and close to the Mexican border. The town, dusty and without vegetation except for sagebrush and tumbleweed, normally had a population of one hundred. It was named after Lillie Langtry, the actress whose taste in fashion half the social world slavishly imitated. She had smitten Judge Roy Bean, "the Law West of the Pecos," as he liked to be known, who held court in his saloon. (The saloon was called "The Jersey Lily" in Mrs. Langtry's honor.) Judge Bean, who had never met Mrs. Langtry, tacked up every picture he could find of her in his saloon and collected articles about her exploits, which he pasted in a huge scrapbook. He trimmed his beard so that he would look more like the Prince of Wales, a member of Lillie's regiment of notable friends and party companions, and he carried on a brief correspondence with her. Lillie was quite honored when she learned that the judge had changed the town's name from Vinegaroon to Langtry. (She finally visited the town two years after the judge died and was presented with a pistol he had used to keep order while holding court in the back of the saloon.)

Stuart ordered the passengers to detrain, and then he and Judge Bean had a talk with the U.S. marshals and other officials who had been instructed to keep the peace and prevent the fight. Bean convinced them that the passengers were merely "tourists" and should be allowed to cross the Rio Grande. Finally the officials acceded, and Stuart led the tourists across a pontoon bridge into Mexico. The Rangers had no jurisdiction on Mexican soil, and the Mexican federales were too far away to make their presence felt. The ring was pitched on a flat area between two hills, with the spectators scrambling up the slopes to find the best view. The kinetoscopic cameraman set up his machine and signaled he was ready.

A short time before, Fitzsimmons, noting the cinematographic preparations, had asked Stuart if he could have a share of the film rights. "No," Stuart told him. Fitzsimmons accepted the reply in silence, but presumably he decided there was going to be damn little film for anyone to enjoy the rights to.

Referee George Siler tossed two pairs of five-ounce gloves to the contestants, gave them their instructions and the fight started. Fitzsimmons, his eyes ominously narrowed, moved to the center of the ring and accepted a right thrown by the Irishman. Clinching, he took another right, and Siler warned Maher about hitting in the clinches. On the break, Fitz snaked out a left that jarred Maher and followed it with a right and left to the body. Maher struck back with his right and once more they clinched. Fitz broke and backed off. Advancing, Maher swung a long left at Fitzsimmons's head. Fitz moved out of the way, pawed with his left and slammed a right to Maher's jaw. Maher toppled over onto his back, and Siler counted him out. The round had lasted a minute and a half. The kinetograph operator shrugged and started to disassemble his camera.

Elated at the quick result, Fitz's manager, Julian, stepped into the ring and pompously announced that Fitzsimmons, as the new champion of the world, was ready to defend his title against any and all challengers. The oration was interrupted by the frantic announcement that the bridge over the Rio Grande was being swept away by the torrential current. The crowd rushed down the slopes and to the riverbank and safely scrambled back across to Langtry and the judge's saloon.

Fitzsimmons was realistic about the status of his world title, however. He realized that he was champion only of Peter Maher, and that to gain glory, the money coming to him and personal satisfaction he must get Corbett into the ring. An incident that occurred in Philadelphia sharpened his resolve.

Shortly after the Maher bout, Corbett happened to be staying at the Green Hotel in Philadelphia with his brother Joe when Joe pointed out Fitzsimmons talking to the room clerk at the desk.

Corbett, putting on his boldest front for reasons of psychology, strode over to Fitz, slapped him on the back and said in a scathing way, "Here, you! You can't register just by making your mark." As Fitzsimmons looked up, startled, Corbett turned to Joe. "Joe," he ordered, "you take the pen and write Mr. Fitzsimmons's name for him. He doesn't know how to."

Fitzsimmons grew extremely upset at this, but whatever he might have replied was cut short by Corbett's next speech. In *Roar of the Crowd,* Corbett relates that he cannot recall his exact words, but they were something like this: "When you come down here, under the circumstances, you show you're inviting trouble. There's been a lot of talk in the paper about punching faces and pulling noses and all that; and it's time someone had his nose pulled at least." And so saying, Corbett reached over, seized Fitzsimmons's nose between two fingers and gave it a monstrous tweak. A riot followed, with Corbett's friends holding him back and Joe wrestling with Fitz to keep him from attacking his brother. Fitz broke away and, darting into the dining room, hurled a caster full of bottled condiments at Joe. Joe ducked and it splattered against the wall. The manager then appeared and quieted everybody down. Fitzsimmons did not stay at the Green Hotel.

Fitzsimmons's fight with Tom Sharkey on December 2, 1896, in San Francisco, as they say in the lexicon, smelled. Before the battle Frank Julian claimed loudly that he had heard on reputable authority that the outcome had already been arranged by local gamblers: Sharkey was to win, however possible. It was significant that members of the press were not seated at ringside but farther back. Wyatt Earp, the hero of Dodge City and a man who stood for no nonsense, was the referee.

Fitz easily outboxed the clumsy ex-sailor for several rounds, though he could not knock him out. In the eighth round he drove home a powerful body punch that sent Sharkey to the floor. Sharkey writhed and Earp promptly disqualified Fitzsimmons, asserting that the blow had been low. Fitzsimmons went for Earp, who wisely drew a revolver, and that was the end of protesting from Fitzsimmons's side. All witnesses not involved in the fix maintained the blow was not a foul, and evidence supports the contention that Earp had been bribed to end the fight in this manner if Sharkey found himself in trouble. It was a blot on Fitzsimmons's escutcheon but a worse one on Sharkey's.

———

The Corbett-Fitzsimmons bout has been called the battle of the century, and in many respects it was. It was characterized by many firsts. No fight in history had the advance publicity of this one, nor was coverage of any previous fight so massive. Both Corbett and Fitz were hired—by the New York *World* and the Hearst papers, respectively—to write their own daily reports of training procedures, stratagems and so on. (Presumably, like later athletes so engaged, they had help.) George Siler, the referee, doubled as chief correspondent for the Chicago *Tribune*. It was the first fight of which motion

pictures were taken for showing by projectors on screens. It marked the first time a woman (Rose Fitzsimmons) shouted advice to a principal from that principal's corner. It was the first time an outdoor arena was completely erected especially for a prizefight.

This time the site chosen by promoter Dan Stuart was Carson City, Nevada (named after the famous Kit), overlooked by the majestic, snow-capped Sierras. The purse was fifteen thousand dollars, winner take all, and the side bet was twenty-five hundred dollars. Constantly reassuring the fighters' managers that the bout would take place (Governor Sadler proved to be extremely cooperative), Stuart constructed the arena in the middle of a racetrack about a third of a mile from the city.

Inevitably the excitement attracted hoboes, grifters, loafers and small-time con men, most of whom were rounded up and jailed as a favor to the respectable fight fans who flocked into town. No restraint was put on opportunities to gamble or carouse in other ways, however. Special trains from the country's major cities began arriving a week

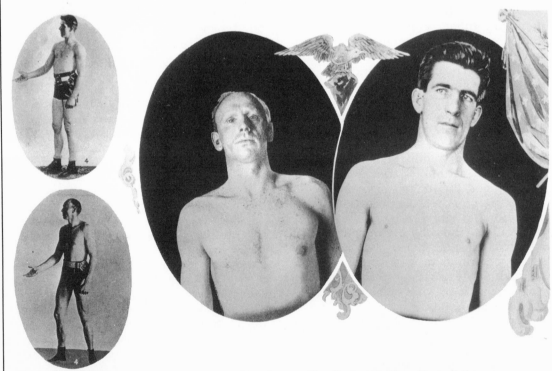

"Ruby Robert" Fitzsimmons (left) and Gentleman Jim Corbett before their fight

before the fight. Newspapers dispatched their top correspondents. Former Senator John J. Ingalls of Kansas was hired by the Hearst press to report on the fight from an intellectual standpoint. Fitzsimmons's supporters included copper and tin miners, late of Cornwall, who bet their combined resources on their countryman. The best odds they could get were 4 to 5, with Fitzsimmons the slight underdog. But he had started at 6 to 10.

It is possible that rumors of friction in the Corbett camp were a factor in the dropping of the odds. There was a feud going between Charlie White, a trainer whom Brady had brought to camp with him, and Billy Delaney, Corbett's regular trainer. White had trained Fitz in two of his fights, and Brady thought his knowledge of Fitz's style and temperament might be useful. Corbett wasted a good deal of energy trying to appease both men. There was also a feud between Corbett's regular dog, a mongrel, and a fine collie Jim's brother Frank had sent him to keep him company while training.

Some amusement was furnished by one of Corbett's sparring partners. This was a large, clownish fellow, a bumpkin hailing originally from Ohio, named Jim Jeffries. Just approaching twenty-three, Jeffries had a good left hand and was a willing punching bag for Corbett, but he did not know the first thing about boxing. He had been recommended by De Witt Van Court, boxing instructor at the Los Angeles A.C., as a good man for Corbett to practice "roughing it" with. Jeffries impressed Corbett with his doggedness in running long distances (he was at least the equal of the dedicated champion) and his ability to take punches without a whimper. Corbett spent part of his time trying to teach the awkward fellow some of the fundamentals of his chosen sport.

About a week before the fight Corbett went for a stroll with Brady and Delaney to have a look at the arena, a huge structure built to hold twenty-five thousand people. Delaney spotted a cloud of dust, which it turned out was being raised by Fitzsimmons and his retinue, who were jogging toward the Corbett party. Fitz's great dane, Yarum, accompanied them. When Fitz reached Corbett, he clapped him on the shoulder, smiled and offered to shake hands. Ever the tactician before a battle, Corbett growled, "I'll shake hands when I meet you in the ring." Fitz looked nonplussed. Corbett added, indicating the dog, "You'd better bring along that fellow, too. You'll need him!" Fitz quietly turned on his heel and walked away. When his party had jogged off, Corbett told his friends with some satisfaction that he was sure that Fitzsimmons, thus intimidated, did not think he could win the championship. It is conceivable, however, that there is such a thing as a psychological backfire.

On fight day, March 17, 1897, Bat Masterson and his deputies, who had been engaged by Stuart, relieved spectators of their guns and other weapons in orderly fashion, giving out receipts. Regarding corners, Corbett had his usual luck. Delaney won the toss, which meant that Fitzsimmons would be boxing while facing the sun until he could maneuver his way out of it. John L. Sullivan and Governor Sadler were introduced from the ring to large ovations. Through his manager, Billy Madden, Tom Sharkey issued a challenge to the winner. Fitzsimmons, wearing a Japanese bathrobe, chewed gum to calm his nerves. Corbett, wearing a gray robe, showed the poise of a champion by calmly waving to his friends and family members at ringside. His father and brothers Harry, Joe and Frank were on hand to lend their vocal support. The weights were announced as 183 pounds for Corbett and 167 for Fitz. After the fighters received instructions from Siler in the center of the ring, Corbett extended his hand. Fitzsimmons, remembering past slights, ignored it.

At the bell, both fighters moved forward cautiously, Corbett aware that he was pitted against a crafty foe who was never more dangerous than when hurt, and Fitzsimmons knowing that he was fighting the most scientific boxer in the history of the sport. Corbett shot out a light left jab, then transformed another jab into his favorite left hook, which Fitzsimmons took in the stomach. Corbett drifted backwards to avoid Fitz's counter. Corbett kept jabbing at

Fitz's face, keeping him off-balance and maneuvering easily out of the way when Fitz sought to retaliate. At long range, Corbett was clearly Fitz's master. The Cornishman's face began to grow red from cuts, and his swings became wilder as Corbett jabbed, hooked, neatly avoided punches by slight movements of his head and shoulders or quickly stepped backward out of reach.

The pattern continued for five rounds, with Fitz accepting the punishment in a kind of stolid, flat-footed way. Corbett seemed to sense the precise moment when Fitz was about to launch one of his blows. Committed, Fitz would throw it, but Corbett, wraithlike, would be just out of reach. In the sixth round, Corbett saw an inviting opening and slammed a hard left hook at Fitzsimmons's chin and knocked him down. Bleeding from the nose and mouth, dazed and nearing exhaustion, Fitzsimmons clutched Corbett's legs with his arms for support. Corbett tore himself away and Siler began the count. Rose Fitzsimmons, a rather Brunhildean figure, leaned over the ropes and loudly pleaded for her husband to get up. "You're counting too slow!" Corbett said angrily to Siler. (Both Corbett and Brady later claimed that Fitz had been down at least thirteen seconds before he got up.) At Siler's toll of nine, Fitzsimmons struggled to his feet and went into a peculiar defensive stance, wrapping his arms around his head. Corbett tried to finish him before the bell but could not land the vital blow. The odds, as Fitz sat panting and in a semi-stupor in his corner, rose to 10 to 4 on Corbett.

Recuperation in a hurry was the Cornishman's stock-in-trade, however, and he came out nearly whole as the seventh round started. He aimed a series of right-hand swings at Corbett's head. They missed, but they were not expected to land; it was part of Fitz's stratagem. Corbett, becoming weary himself, began to raise his guard to block these blows. It was then that Fitz hurled his potent left into the pit of Corbett's stomach. Hurt, losing some control over his reflexes, Corbett tried to disguise the effects of the punch by some rapid footwork and jabs, but the knowledgeable members of the audience were aware of the damage inflicted. In his front-row seat, Brady borrowed a bottle of whiskey from a patron and attacked it in frantic gulps, but the alcohol did not elevate his spirits any.

In the following rounds the change in Corbett was apparent. He was moving more slowly and with less éclat, even though he had transformed Fitzsimmons's face into a scarlet mask and was keeping Fitz from getting close with his precise hitting. Fitz continued to swing for Corbett's head, stoical about the blows he took and the blood he shed. Then, in the fourteenth round, with Corbett's guard once more raised to ward off a high blow, Fitz landed a left hook with immense force behind it to Corbett's stomach. This was the famous "solar plexus punch." Corbett collapsed to the ring floor, conscious but unable to control his lower limbs. This is Corbett's description of the punch:

"All at once [in the fourteenth] he began to swing so hard that when he missed he spun around as though on a pivot. Several times he did this and I jumped so far out of his way that I couldn't reach him when he came back to his original position.

"At last I figured on staying in line the next time he turned that trick and decided, instead of jumping back, just to pull my head a bit back. Then when he pivoted around I'd have my right ready and shoot over the blow that would end it all. It was a grand idea and on it the championship was to depend.

"To tempt him into the trick I thrust out my head, and he started his old vicious right, but as I had planned, just at the beginning of the swing I pulled my head back sufficiently to be out of reach.

"As one does when getting off to a wrong start, he pulled his punch and started for my head. Again I jerked my head aside, and this time, seeing he was going to miss once more, again he pulled his punch. Now a man with the natural fighting instinct that Fitzsimmons possessed will never let any arm be idle, so as my head flew back and he checked his right, he let his idle left try something, just started it haphazard and landed on the pit of the stomach. Quicker than all this takes to tell, I sank to my knees."

Corbett heard Siler count up to eight, growing frantic over his inability to rise from the floor. He groped for the middle rope to try to haul himself to his feet, missed it and fell on his face. Again he reached for the rope—but too late. "Ten!" cried Siler, signaling the knockout as the gong repeatedly clanged the message. Fitzsimmons's backers tossed their hats in the air and yelped and pounded one another's backs in exultation. The Cornish miners were happiest of all, save for Rose Fitzsimmons and Martin Julian, and Fitz himself. Corbett struggled to his feet, wild with rage. He rushed over to Fitzsimmons, who was surrounded by his handlers and friends, and would have continued the battle had he not been restrained. Corbett shouted wrathfully over the tumult, "That was a lucky punch! You'll have to fight me again!"

"I'll never fight you again," Fitzsimmons said.

"You'll have to fight me," Corbett shouted. "Or I'll lick you every time I meet you on the street!"

"If you ever hit me again," Fitzsimmons said, "I'll shoot you!"

In the locker room, Fitz told Governor Sadler, "He outboxed me completely those first seven rounds. His speed was incredible. I never believed any man could hit me as often as Corbett did." In his locker room, Corbett (like Sullivan before him) could not understand how he had lost. "It was a lucky punch," he kept telling himself, his voice somewhat choked. Mourning bitterly over his defeat, Corbett left for his hotel before the governor could visit him. But the two met later. "It was a fluke punch that beat me," Corbett told the governor. "I know I can beat him if I can just get him in the ring with me again." The governor promised that as long as he was in office, Nevada would welcome a return bout between the two.

A San Francisco physician named John W. Gardner was the man who described the debilitating blow as a solar plexus punch—one that struck the large network of nerves behind the stomach that controlled all the abdominal viscera and affected muscular movement and breathing. Newspaper writers seized on the scientific term and gave the blow a mystic quality. But many experts believe there was nothing new about it; Jack Broughton had found the spot in 1730, calling a punch to that area "the projectile," and it was known to other British bareknucklers as "the mark."

When Brady returned to New York he was aghast to learn that Stuart had managed to get complete control of the movies of the bout. He had incorporated the project without Brady's knowledge, assuming the office of president of the company. Nor would he discuss the matter with Brady. The enraged showman engaged a lawyer and forced Stuart, finally, to allot him and Corbett one quarter of the profits made by the film. The motion picture, clearly showing the esoteric punch as well as Corbett's boxing magic, took in three quarters of a million dollars—the first movie to realize a gross of that size. (It opened at the Academy of Music in New York, an important social and sporting event.) But, as Brady complained, by the time Stuart, as company president, got through juggling the books, his and Corbett's shares were pitifully small.

Now began Brady's attempts to lure Fitzsimmons back in the ring. But Corbett was more interested in a high-class saloon he owned on Broadway, near Thirty-fourth Street, than in what seemed like an aimless pursuit. Brady did not think the business was Corbett's métier (he was right) and the two gradually drifted apart, Brady becoming completely involved in theatrical ventures. Fitzsimmons was no more eager than he should be to defend his title. With his wife he starred in a play especially written for him, *The Honest Blacksmith,* which featured his skill at the anvil. Sometimes he took extra time while onstage to construct horseshoes for his friends in the audience.

Meanwhile Jim Jeffries, on the West Coast, was mulling over what he had learned as Corbett's sparring partner in Carson City, earning his nickname of "the Grizzly Bear of Ringdom" and wondering wistfully if he would ever learn enough to become a contender for the title. ∎

Born in Cornwall, England, in 1862, Bob Fitzsimmons moved with his family to New Zealand when he was nine. As a youth he was an apprentice blacksmith, and it was then that he developed powerful arms and shoulders that later made their mark in the ring.

Never a true heavyweight—in his prime he weighed 165—from the waist down Fitzsimmons was built like a spindly lightweight. John L. Sullivan, whose opinion counted, cast a pall on Fitz's credentials. Sullivan called him "a fighting machine on stilts."

When Bob Fitzsimmons came upon the scene, his diametrical opposite, Gentleman Jim Corbett, set the standard by which other boxers were judged. Corbett was a man of style and grace and savoir faire. Fitzsimmons was known as Ruby Robert because of his freckled countenance, which became a brilliant crimson when it was subjected to the stress of combat. Fitzsimmons was a thoroughly unlikely successor to the glamorous Gentleman Jim and was given small chance against him.

Courage, willingness to take punishment, and remarkable recuperative powers were the components of Fitzsimmons's talent.

Fighting Gus Ruhlin in 1900 at Coney Island, Ruby Robert demonstrates his power in the sixth-round knockout above.

In 1909, ten years after he lost the heavyweight crown, Fitzsimmons fought Bill Lang in Sydney, Australia. Long past his prime, the former champion was knocked out in the twelfth round.

In February, 1896, Fitzsimmons met Peter Maher in Mexico. Originally scheduled for Langtry, Texas, the bout was held across the border by order of the Texas governor. With Bat Masterson commanding a small army of deputies, fans were taken to a secret destination in Mexico where the fight was held. Fitzsimmons, who earlier had beaten Maher in New Orleans, this time won by a knockout in the opening round.

Bob Fitzsimmons, the man jogging in the lead, prepares for his historic meeting with James J. Corbett in 1897. On this country road outside Carson City, Nevada, a few days before the fight, the challenger met the champion and offered to shake hands. "I'll

shake hands when I meet you in the ring," Corbett replied, certain that he had gained a distinct psychological advantage. This pre-fight encounter only served to heighten the drama of a match that had gained more publicity than any in previous boxing history.

On March 17, 1897, Corbett and Fitzsimmons come out for Round 1 in Carson City. The fight, which was more than two years in preparation, was billed as "The Battle of the Century." Despite accounts to the contrary, this photo unmistakably reveals that few fans

traveled to the foothills of the Sierras — probably because after so many postponements fans were doubtful that the bout would be held at all. This was the first title match to be recorded on film; with Corbett as star, the success of the production was largely assured.

The motion picture of Corbett and Fitz, which earned $750,000, was the first movie ever to realize that kind of return. In the extremely rare frames above, the pictorial quality is sufficient to give a vivid idea of the fight. In the early rounds the advantage was all Corbett's. His deft footwork and swift jabs made it seem only a matter of time before he would dispose of Ruby Robert. Bottom frame, a confident Corbett returns to his corner at the end of Round 13, planning to knock Fitzsimmons out in the fourteenth.

Round 14 begins uneventfully as the two fighters dance before the camera. Then Fitzsimmons moves in with a pistonlike left to

Corbett's body. With delayed reaction because he wants to continue the fight, Corbett sinks to the canvas in stunned disbelief.

Clutching his side and having lost control of his limbs, Corbett vainly tries to rise as Referee Siler continues to count.

Fitzsimmons's paralyzing blow, which ended the reign of Corbett, became known as the solar-plexus punch.

Bob Fitzsimmons, once reviled for lack of style and stature, poses as a country squire. Once again those qualities that can best be described as intangibles—character, determination, and will—produced a champion who was truly legendary.

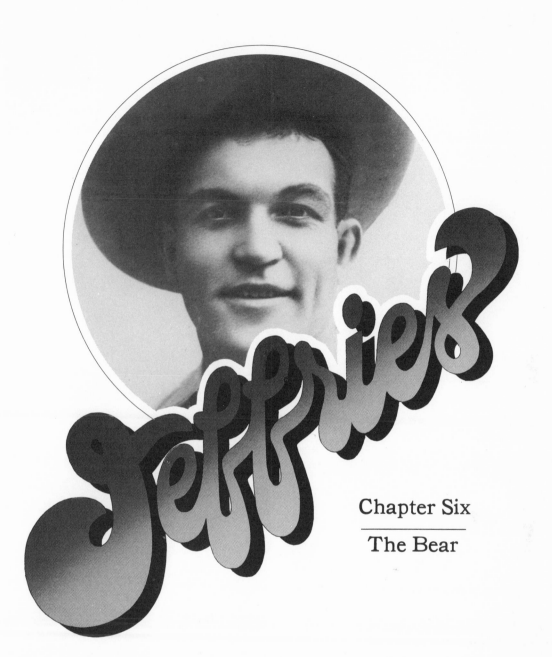

Jeffries

Chapter Six

The Bear

There is no question that if it had not been for the manipulations of William A. Brady, the Machiavellian showman who once handled Corbett, Fitzsimmons never would have risked his title against Jeffries.

Getting Fitzsimmons into the ring after he defeated Corbett took immense conniving and not a little luck. He had been seeking the title so long that he was in no hurry to take a chance on relinquishing it. The press hooted at him for refusing to defend his title for more than two years, putting boxing in the doldrums and forcing sportswriters to report on such activities as bicycle racing, sculling and professional baseball, which was in its embryo state. None of these was as exciting or as emotion-arousing as boxing from the standpoint of anticipation, analysis and hindsight.

Corbett was making the noisiest challenges, but Fitzsimmons had said after their fight that he would never fight the gentleman again, and he was a man of his word. As for Brady, for a time he was more interested in the theatre than in prizefighting. He produced a thriller called *Way Down East,* a terrifyingly bad melodrama which, after being rewritten by the famous play doctor, John R. Grimer, became a valuable piece of stage property for twenty-one years. A violent mechanical snowstorm which awed audiences and battered the heroine from flat to flat helped sell tickets. (D. W. Griffith would pay $175,000 for the film rights and make a memorable tearjerker out of it, starring Lillian Gish.)

Just before the Spanish-American War, however, the theatre business fell into a slump, and Brady, ever sensitive to the public's pulse, considered going back into the fight game. The country's martial mood seemed to demand violent activity in the ring. Brady looked, as usual, for a future champion—anything else was a waste of time. Periodically he would wander to the Broadway Athletic Club and the Lenox Athletic Club or travel to Maspeth, L. I., where another boxing club was located. On these visits he reveled in the billowing smoke, the knowledgeable fight talk, the thwup of leather on flesh as a hard blow landed, the thud of the heavy bag being punished and the pervasive tattoo of the light bag being toyed with by specialists; the rope-skipping, the shadowboxing, the greetings of old friends and presentations by enthusiastic managers of their latest tigers. Brady compared the last with his fond memories of Corbett, the ballet master, and rejected them out of hand. For months the visits were merely a pleasant journey back into time.

When it reached his ears that Jeffries, the Western sequoia who had beaten, among others, Tom Sharkey, Joe Goddard and Peter Jackson, was going to appear in an exhibition at the Lenox Athletic Club, Brady made it a point to purchase a ringside seat. He remembered Jeffries chiefly as the bumpkin who had come to Corbett's Carson City camp to rub down Corbett's legs and accept his punches. In his favor was the young man's demonstrated ability to take a walloping without falling; and he was as much a fetishist about training as Corbett had been. But he was clumsy and ponderously slow in the ring, for all his running speed outside it. The question was, would his ability to punch compensate for his obvious weaknesses? The wheels inside the shrewd showman's head began to revolve slowly.

To impress the cynical sportsmen of the East, Billy Delaney, Corbett's former trainer who was now Jeffries' manager-trainer, had arranged for him to fight two men the same night—Steve O'Donnell of Australia, a former pupil of Peter Jackson's, and Bob Armstrong, a large Negro with a fair record. Unfortunately, Jeffries was overzealous in his efforts to knock out the wily Armstrong. He flailed wildly at him, and though he won the decision, he broke his thumb and injured his knuckles on Armstrong's head and was unable to face O'Donnell. The sad fact was announced from the ring. After Jeffries was hustled up the aisle under an umbrella of hoots and boos for his cowardice, Brady pushed his way to Jeffries' dressing room and was allowed to enter. The bandages were off Jeffries' hands. There was no doubt of the injury; his left hand was blotched with purple and swollen to the size of a melon. Brady had never seen anyone so depressed. "What do you intend to do now?" he asked the dejected warrior.

"I'm going back to California," Jeffries growled. He was angry about the boos he had gotten and the cries of "Fake!" and "Clumsy bum!" He would be even angrier when he saw the scoffing appraisals of his talents in the New York press: Never had a more inept heavyweight trod on Manhattan soil; never had there been a less auspicious debut. "The hell with New York!" Jeffries snapped at Brady. Disgruntled, he swept back to his favorite state and resumed his favorite recreations—hunting and fishing in the wilderness, out of sight and hearing of sycophants, hypercritical newspapermen, obtuse fans and wily promoters and managers.

Despite the fiasco, Brady was impressed by Jeffries' huge size, his ability to absorb punishment, his endurance and ability to throw a punch—even if he seldom met his target. He had immense destructive potential, if his skills could be channeled in the proper direction. That his New York appearance was so ignominious was grist for the Brady mill; it gave him a lever to convince Fitzsimmons to step in the ring with the bumpkin.

First Brady arranged for the use of the Coney Island Athletic Club outdoor arena, which would hold about twelve thousand customers. Then he wooed a number of politicians, including Tammany Hall's Big Tim Sullivan, in order to obtain a license to promote a fight. Then he wired Jeffries, who was stalking grizzlies in the California mountains, to hold himself in readiness for a championship match. The stipulation was that he would allow Brady to manage him for two years. Jeffries wired back acceptance of the terms.

Now came the difficult part. Brady spent weeks trying to convince Fitzsimmons and Julian that everyone would profit from a fight between the champion and Jeffries. Jeffries and Brady would enjoy a payday; Fitzsimmons could answer his newspaper critics, have an excuse for avoiding Corbett and gain some glory in the East. Since it would be New York's first heavyweight championship fight, the gate promised to be large and Fitz would earn some easy money. Brady used a fifth column to good effect—he had friends of his who knew Fitzsimmons din it into the champion's ears that Jeffries was ungainly, an ineffective hitter and a likely punching bag. Fitzsimmons finally acquiesced—for 65 per cent of the fighters' share of the purse—and the fight was scheduled for June 9, 1899.

Brady immediately began to exploit Jeffries' status as a challenger. He sent him on an exhibition tour with Jack McCormick and Jeffries' brother Jack as sparring partners. The tour helped get Jeffries in fighting trim and made money for both the Boilermaker and the impresario. Weary of travel, Jeffries then repaired to Elmhurst, New Jersey, for serious training. The camp was grim, according to Jeffries' wishes, with no time for horseplay. His regimen was strict. He rose at six, worked with pulley weights for ten minutes, ran wind sprints for twenty minutes, then had breakfast (basically a lamb chop and two soft-boiled eggs; no coffee, tea, milk or water). He rested till nine, ran fourteen miles, got a rubdown and rested till noon. At two thirty he rose, played a few games of handball, skipped rope and punched the heavy bag for twenty minutes. Immediately afterwards he got into the ring with members of his sparring stable, who had orders to slug as hard as they could. Jeffries himself held back his punches, not out of compassion but to keep from damaging a useful training aid. He boxed as many as sixteen three-minute rounds, then skipped rope, threw the medicine ball and finished with a high-speed shadowboxing session—all under the eagle eye of Delaney, the nonpareil of trainers. Following that, a rubdown, a shower and supper: steak or lamb chops, spinach or asparagus and no liquids. After supper, a long walk to unwind, a slowly imbibed glass of water and, at nine o'clock, bed. Jeffries felt that by cutting down on liquids he would improve his speed in the ring.

He considered himself lucky to have as a sparring partner and sometime trainer Tommy Ryan, the English welterweight whom he considered the world's greatest ring general and a better boxer than Corbett. With Ryan, he developed the defensive crouch that became his trademark. Jeffries realized, after a bout with Choynski which nearly resulted in his jaw becoming unhinged, that his defense needed improving. In the crouch, he bent over from the waist and shuffled forward, his left arm extended like the trunk of a cautious elephant. His face was protected by his right forearm, and his torso, being horizontal, was difficult to hit unless his opponent moved in close—where, of course, he came within range of the peaceful-looking trunk that could deliver such deadly blows. Ryan's strategy was for Jeffries, with his cast-iron jaw and tough hide, to absorb all the punishment his opponent could dole out. Then, when the latter was arm-weary, his knuckles smarting and his enthusiasm at a low ebb, Jeffries would counterattack. Jeffries developed a left hook and a straight left which he could deliver from that seemingly awkward position and which wreaked devastation from only inches away—possibly the most effective body punch developed by any fighter in history.

To prevent facial cuts from Fitz's slashing blows, Jeffries devised another ritual. Twice a day he rubbed his face and neck with beef brine and borax. He would massage the ingredients into his skin after his workout and let the sun dry them, after which he would wash the brine off with salt water and borax. It left his skin soft but extremely tough, with something of the texture of tanned leather.

By this regimen he worked himself into the best condition of his life. Old John L., stopping by with a covey of newspapermen, shouted, after seeing Jeffries spar with Ryan, "Here's the next champion! I never saw anyone move so fast!" Jeffries was careful not to show it, but beneath his mask he glowed.

Before the fight, Jeffries did something which earned him a great deal of criticism: He arranged for a friend to bet five thousand dollars for him on Fitzsimmons. Jeffries answered the shocked people who confronted him with this irregularity that if he lost, the money he won on Fitz would repay him some-

what for the time and effort he had put into training for the bout; if he won, the opportunities coming his way would be such that the five thousand dollars would never be missed. He also contended that it was fairly common practice. But if it was, it was not widely known or countenanced.

The most encouraging thing of all, as the Jeffries camp saw it, was that Jeffries' hands were in fine shape. As a result of successful experimenting with light bandages rather than the heavy tape he had been wearing under his gloves, Jeffries found that his hands stood up well under the punishment they received from the heavy bag and an occasional blow to the head of his sparring partners.

Brady, having ensnared the champion, overseen his man into awesome condition and supreme confidence and otherwise prepared for a grand entertainment, on fight night proceeded to instill a few doubts in the mind of Fitzsimmons. The champion had never seen Jeffries fight and was unaware how massive he was. Scene One was laid in the corridor between the contestants' locker rooms. Brady summoned Julian and launched into a wild diatribe about the clinching rules. Julian was mystified by all the fuss, but Fitz came charging out of his quarters, suspicious that something might be put over on him. Brady affably led him into Jeffries' locker room, where Scene Two was to take place. Jeffries lay virtually naked on the rubbing table, a muscular giant with arms like oak trees, a body rippling with sinew, a forest of hair on his chest, and legs like the pillars of the Temple of Zeus. Donning some pajamas Brady tossed him, Jeff listened to the discussion and on Brady's cue moved toward the champion. He seized Fitzsimmons around the back of the neck with one hand and around the waist with the other, paused, and then threw him against the wall. "That's what Mr. Brady was talking about, I think," he murmured with the deference due a champion. Fitzsimmons and Julian left in silent bewilderment. Aware that Fitz had been shaken by viewing the monstrous proportions of the man he was to meet, Brady allowed himself a smile.

Jeffries yawned and relaxed on the rubbing table.

The gate was seventy thousand dollars; it would have been more had not the threatening weather discouraged some fans from attending. Despite Jeffries' weight advantage of thirty-eight pounds, a height advantage of two inches and a youth advantage of thirteen years, the odds were 10 to 6 on the champion. Brady, flushed with the anticipation of victory, did a good turn for Jesse Lewisohn, the stock speculator, who was a good friend of both Diamond Jim and Lillian Russell.

"Do you think Jeff has a chance?" Lewisohn asked from his seat as Brady marched down the aisle ahead of the Jeffries entourage. Brady, who knew Lewisohn had bet heavily on Fitz, confided, "Jeff will murder him." Lewisohn arose and promptly hedged his bet with a twenty-thousand-dollar wager on Jeffries.

Fitzsimmons received a huge ovation as he entered the ring in light trunks supported patriotically by a belt of American flags. A large floral horseshoe stood in his corner, his friends' way of wishing him luck. Jeffries, his corner unadorned, received the polite hand accorded to a well-built animal who courageously enters the slaughterhouse.

George Siler, one of the most famous and certainly one of the gutsiest referees of all time, was the third man in the ring. In a day when some referees at the end of a bout were wont to flee the ring in the face of a hostile crowd and render their decisions a day later and a hundred miles away, he refused to be intimidated. In 1891 he refereed a fight outside Chicago between two heavyweights of no great stature, Pat Killen and Bob Ferguson. The assigned referee had not appeared and Siler, a spectator, was pressed into service. Each fighter was represented by a heavy-betting mob.

In the second round Ferguson was in dire straits from Killen's blows. Someone in the crowd shouted "Time!" in an effort to end the round. Siler, realizing the cry had come from a Ferguson supporter, ordered the fighters to continue. Hating to lose momentum, Killen charged at Ferguson and threw a hard right to his ribs. The bell rang—a signal for the spectators to erupt into activity. Ferguson's camp hollered "Foul!" and Killen's people called Ferguson's supporters dirty welshing liars and worse. Chairs were swung and heads were smashed. Fortunately, revolvers were used only as blackjacks. Ferguson's chief second rushed at Siler and said he was going to kill him. Siler was cool about it, awaiting death in a neutral corner of the ring.

The free-for-all among the fans continued as the bell rang for the third round. Siler managed to clear the ring of partisans and ordered the fighters to fight. As he moved around the ring to watch the pair, whenever he came within range a Ferguson supporter jabbed him lightly in the back with a long knife. "If Ferguson loses," the fan muttered, "you'll get this in your belly."

Killen knocked out his opponent in the sixth, giving Siler no choice but to declare him the winner. Though threatened with death by Ferguson's rooters, Siler, with great equanimity, strode straight at them and through them, pretending not to hear their threats. He headed for the depot. A few shots were fired at him, but Siler did not look back or increase his pace. He got on the train and calmly rode back to Chicago.

====================

The Fitzsimmons–Jeffries fight was a shocker for the knowledgeable Eastern fight fans who attended. They had never seen a crouch like Jeffries', nor a fighter who could absorb such severe, well-aimed punches nor hit so effectively from minimal distances. Fitzsimmons moved out at the bell, hands held high in an orthodox stance. Approaching him was a stooped-over creature, seemingly passive in nature but muscular beyond belief. Fitz feinted, then threw a hook which the creature ducked. He moved forward to clinch, and Fitzsimmons felt again the immense strength of his opponent. After the break, Jeffries swung his ponderous left at Fitz's stomach, but Fitz moved away from it. Fitz launched a quick one-two—left to the stomach, right to the head. Jeffries accepted the blows without blinking. A moment before the round ended he flung forth a remark-

128

ably quick straight left, smashing Fitz-simmons in the mouth. A few members of the audience wondered about hedging their bets.

Given frantic advice by Julian, Fitz rushed toward Jeffries at the bell, feinting and swinging his deadly hooks. But Jeffries withstood the assault; the blows either bounced off the shell that was his body or slid off the top of his head. Overextending himself in his eagerness to penetrate the challenger's defense, Fitz left himself open for a straight left to the chin. It traveled only about six inches, but it was powerful enough to lift Fitz in the air before he toppled to the floor. Fitz was up without a count and flailing away with both hands as the bell rang. During the minute's respite Fitz's supporters took comfort in the fact that their man had the greatest recuperative powers of any fighter in the world and that he was most dangerous when conditions looked blackest.

Fully recovered, Fitz sprang toward Jeffries to open the third round, hooking with his left. But the occasional blows in the face he received snapped his head back and slowed down his assault. At the end of the round, Fitz espied his opening and instinctively shot a hard right hook that smashed against Jeffries' neck. Jeffries could feel his neck swell. Fitzsimmons showed his surprise when Jeffries not only refused to fall but countered with a straight left to the heart.

The pattern continued, with Jeffries seeking to make Fitzsimmons lead and then driving home quick counters. Fitz was landing more punches, but Jeffries seemed to be doing the greater damage. In the sixth round, Jeffries, weary from crouching, stood up, a more open target for Fitz's blows. Fitz feinted, hooked, moved away, jabbed and hooked. Thinking he had found an opening, he flung a hard right at Jeffries' chin. But before it landed, Jeffries smashed a right at Fitzsimmons's heart. The blow echoed through the amphitheatre, and Fitzsimmons visibly shuddered. Some of the fight went out of him. In the same round, Jeffries weathered, without being affected, the same solar plexus blow that had destroyed Corbett.

Curiously, it was a blow that Fitzsimmons delivered rather than one he received that marked the beginning of the end for the champion. In the eighth round, when Jeffries moved his chin for an instant from behind his shoulder, Fitzsimmons landed his best punch of the fight, a vicious left hook that struck Jeffries square on the jaw, immediately raising a large lump. When he saw that this blow—the one he had been waiting to land for eight rounds—had not knocked Jeffries down or even made him react, Fitzsimmons lost enthusiasm for the contest.

In the tenth Jeffries pounded the champion without provoking much retaliation. But he was cautious, for he knew, and his handlers repeatedly warned him, that Fitz was most dangerous when hurt. Near the end of the round Jeffries caught Fitz under the chin with a left uppercut. Fitz swayed, hands at his sides, and fell to the floor. He was up at seven, and Jeffries smashed him in the face with his ponderous left. This time Fitz was down for nine. He staggered toward his corner when the round ended, and his handlers worked furiously to restore his strength.

He was not yet through. In the eleventh he used everything in his repertory of maneuvers and blows to find a vulnerable spot in Jeffries' armor. But Jeffries was less cautious now. The champion's punches had lost much of their force. Jeffries shifted his attack from Fitzsimmons's body to his head. He moved forward inside a Fitzsimmons hook and landed a straight left to the champion's chin. Fitz's hands dropped. If he was feigning, it was a magnificent performance. Jeff threw a left hook that nearly took Fitzsimmons's head off. Still advancing, he followed with a right uppercut that caught the champion on the point of the chin. Fitzsimmons's eyes grew glazed and he fell to the floor. Nervous, elated, supremely confident, Jeffries waited for him to push himself to his feet. The crowd, sensing history was being made, was on its feet and then on the chairs in a frenzy of excitement, roaring its approval as Fitz was counted out by the tolling arm of Siler. Jeffries' arm was raised in triumph. America had a new hero.

Brady was not one to let grass grow under his feet or even allow a lawn to be seeded. To capitalize on his investment, he already had had lithographs printed up advertising Jeffries as the new heavyweight champion and had made arrangements for an extended boxing-*cum*-theatrical tour. Jeffries won the title on Friday, was allowed to rest and wind up his affairs on Saturday and on Sunday was again Brady's man. The tour was most strenuous for Jeffries, and not many men could have survived his schedule. He would box an exhibition and umpire a baseball game in one city in the morning, travel to another in the afternoon to box and umpire and travel to a third for a boxing exhibition, after which he would play the lead in a melodrama, generally *The Man from the West*.

After a few months, having exhausted the American public with Jeffries' thespian ability, Brady piled the weary champion and his entourage onto a ship and journeyed to England. There he and Jeffries dolled up in evening clothes with bosomed shirts that looked like spinnakers, high silk hats and shoes that pinched. Thus adorned, they confronted English society. Jeffries met the Prince of Wales (the sportsman who had acted so jolly with John L. years before), Lord Beresford and a number of other peers of the realm, most of whom he got along with swimmingly. A commoner gave him trouble, however.

At a banquet given in Jeffries' honor, who should show up in the middle of Jim's gracious thank-you speech but Charlie Mitchell with his gang of toughs. Embarrassing Jeffries' English hosts and such American notables as cartoonist Homer Davenport and actor Nat Goodwin (a good friend of Diamond Jim's and Buffalo Bill's), Mitchell railed at Jeffries for being a bloody cheese champion and if he would just get his bleedin' carcass into the ring with old Charlie, we would see who was really heavyweight champion of the world. Luckily for Mitchell, who was by that time a middleweight grown to fat, Jeffries paid no serious attention to the challenge, then or ever. Mitchell's father-in-law, the English sportsman Pony Moore, rose after Mitchell had stormed out and remarked, "I hope the fight never comes off, because I don't want to see my daughter a widow." The laughter was general. If Jeffries was annoyed at Mitchell he showed it only in the English ring, quickly knocking out a half-dozen of Britain's best and bravest and awing followers of the Fancy.

The troupe then went to Paris, where Jeffries fought a Frenchman who was said to be champion of that country. He wanted to kick as well as box (*la savate*), and Jeffries told him to go ahead. The Frenchman, kept off-balance with jabs to the nose, hooks to the body and light raps to the chin, never got a kick away. When he began to stagger around the ring, Jeffries refrained from finishing him off—he just pushed him through the ropes. He had been told it would be indiscreet of a visitor to knock out such an eminent athlete.

Next came a tour of Scotland, then Ireland. At the railroad station at Dundalk on the west coast of Ireland, Jeffries was told a man wanted to see him. It turned out he was "little Jimmy Sharkey," a short but very broad man who was the father of the Fighting Sailor, Tom Sharkey.

"Are you going to give me boy Tom a go at the title now?" the elder Sharkey asked as the pair shook hands.

"You bet I will," said Jeffries heartily. "He's a strong, rough fighter and I expect a great battle out of him."

"Well, not wishing you any ill luck at all, Mr. Jeffries, but I hope the lad beats the bejazus out of you."

And back in America, Tom Sharkey nearly did.

Jim Jeffries was Tom Sharkey's greatest admirer. Jeffries had won a decision over the short, immensely broad ex-sailor in twenty rounds in Mechanics Pavilion in San Francisco on May 6, 1898, the day after the War Department received Admiral Dewey's telegram that he controlled Manila Bay. The bout was more like a waterfront brawl than a boxing match, characterized by the rough, often foul tactics Sharkey specialized in; but Jeffries could be equally rough if he had to. The two stood toe to toe for a good part of the first nine rounds, Sharkey trying to drive Jeffries back with hooks and Jeffries refusing to give ground. Neither fighter paid much attention to defense. The two were so occupied in trading blows in the tenth round that neither noticed a section of seats in the balcony dangerously swaying and finally collapsing with a splintering crash. Hundreds of spectators were hurled to the floor amid much screaming and groaning and cries of alarm from the persons below they happened to land on. Panic was somehow averted—perhaps because of the entertainment being furnished in the ring—and the fight continued. Jeffries won simply by outlasting the Sailor. Sharkey was bitterly disappointed, feeling Jeffries had taken as much punishment as he had, but he got some satisfaction out of Jeff's promise that the Boilermaker would give him the first shot at the title if he should win it.

In his autobiography, written with Hugh Fullerton, Jeffries twice puts Tom Sharkey's name in capitals in listing and appraising the major heavyweights of his time; Corbett, Choynski, Fitzsimmons and Jack Johnson have to be content with lower case. He called his second fight with Sharkey the hardest he ever fought. More than that, it was "the greatest combat ever waged in a ring between two human beings." Apart from calling Sharkey the roughest, gamest and most willing fighter in the world, he considered him the greatest audience pleaser of all until Jack Dempsey came along. (Tom pleased the audience in one of his fights with Corbett by picking up both Corbett and the referee, dumping them on the floor and falling on top of them.)

The ex-sailor earned his chance at the title mainly because of his strange defeat of Corbett the year before. In a bout at the Lenox Club on November 22, 1898, Corbett, somewhat out of condition, was manhandled unmercifully by Sharkey, who countered Corbett's greater boxing skill by wrestling him all about the ring. Corbett's protests were ignored by the referee. Yet despite being hurled to the floor several times, Corbett cut Sharkey up considerably, and the decision could have gone either way—except that one of Corbett's handlers excitedly jumped in the ring during a late round and Corbett was disqualified. Sharkey had also knocked out Gus Ruhlin, "the Akron Giant," with one punch and flattened the clever Kid McCoy in ten.

At the time of his second fight with Sharkey, Jeffries was not in the best of condition. He had been keeping late hours as an actor and had been wined and dined in Europe. In addition, to help him train for the brawl he expected, he had hired a clownish wrestler, Ernest Rober, as a sparring partner. One afternoon Rober playfully hurled a medicine ball at Jeffries as the champion was clambering upstairs. To protect himself Jeff flung up his left arm, and the ball struck it. Jeffries had a high threshold of pain, but his arm hurt him considerably. Rober rushed to him, noting Jeffries' grimaces and the rapidly swelling elbow area. He seized the arm and tried unsuccessfully to twist the joint back into place. In the training room, hot and cold compresses failed to ease the champion's anguish. He suffered for two days, then went to a specialist in New York City, who told him he had a dislocated elbow and would not be able to fight for six months. Jeffries insisted on fighting. Ryan was against it, but Brady and Delaney were for it. "You can beat the bum with one hand," Delaney assured him. Jeffries knew better. It was hard enough to keep Sharkey from swarming all over him with *two* arms; with one it might be impossible.

The fight was held at the Coney Island Athletic Club on November 3, 1899, for a twenty-five-thousand-dollar purse put up by the club. As Jeffries and his small army strode down the aisle toward the ring amid cheers and friendly greetings, Jeff wished he had taken Ryan's advice and ducked out. The promoters, who had not told anyone they would be taking motion pictures of the fight—the first ever shot at night—had installed huge lights directly over the ring. From any portion of it, Jeffries could reach up and touch them with his glove. The heat was intense; it reminded Jeffries of the searing blast from the furnace of a locomotive when the fire door is opened. Perspiration immediately began flowing off him in rivulets, and he felt as though he were inside a brightly lit baker's kiln. At times it seemed his hair was on fire. Somehow Sharkey's manager had learned of the motion-picture lights and, to Jeffries' dismay, had placed two large electric fans behind the challenger's corner.

Since no one relished the heat, referee George Siler quickly gave his instructions, the fighters returned to their corners and the bell rang. Sharkey, a much improved fighter since their last set-to, sprang forth with the determination of a famished tiger and started to slug. There was an exchange of hooks and straight rights, with Jeffries unable to fend off the attack because of his nearly useless left arm. He gave ground before the challenger's ferocity and pawed weakly at him with his left to set him up for a straight right. The crowd was wild with anticipation as they saw Sharkey bull Jeffries from ringpost to ringpost. When the debilitating round was over, Jeffries, sweating profusely in his corner, envied Sharkey his electric fans.

Sharkey rushed again at the bell. After a flurried exchange, Jeffries spotted an opening. Seeking to end the fight quickly, he smashed his left upward from his crouched position. It crashed against Sharkey's chin, and the Sailor virtually did a back somersault and lay on his back. He was up at nine, however, and covered up as Jeffries, his left arm a cauldron of pain, sought to land the finishing blow. The champion knew that from that moment on he would have to depend solely on his right. Sharkey weathered the round.

Aware that this might be his last chance to win the championship, Sharkey kept pressing forward in succeeding rounds, accepting punishment as he tried to find an opening for a knockout punch. Round after round Sharkey wobbled back to his corner, but he always returned for the next one refreshed. He sought to land his favorite punch, a left hook to the head, but Jeffries beat him time after time with a right to the body. In the tenth Jeffries opened up a cut over Sharkey's left eye. From the eleventh through the sixteenth rounds, exchanges were less frequent and less vicious as weariness slowed down both boxers. Then in the seventeenth, as Sharkey renewed the attack, Jeffries stepped back. Sharkey

was lured forward and Jeffries threw all the muscle he possessed into a roundhouse right that smashed into Sharkey's body. Jeffries heard something crack and, from the grunt emanating from the Sailor, knew that he had broken several of his opponent's ribs. The damage inflicted forced Sharkey to carry his left low to protect his damaged side, which allowed Jeffries to aim for his jaw. Sharkey buried this vulnerable piece of anatomy behind his hunched left shoulder, however, and Jeffries' blows landed on the Sailor's temple or left ear. Blood began to flow freely from the lacerated eye and rapidly swelling ear, and soon both fighters were covered with it. Hardly able to see, bleeding profusely, his ribs hurting painfully, Sharkey renewed the attack. On one occasion, in his eagerness to come to close quarters, he smashed Jeffries' forehead with his own. On two other occasions he butted Jeffries in the nose and knocked out one of his front teeth. Siler, too, was occasionally suffering damage from Sharkey's wild blows.

In the twenty-third round of the blood-spattered melee, Sharkey caught Jeffries' glove under his right arm. Jeffries, in jerking his hand away to prevent further injury to his aching left arm, had the glove yanked off. Seeing this, Siler waved Sharkey back and tried to replace the glove. Sharkey was not to be dissuaded from his mission. He moved quickly around the referee and took a swing at Jeffries' head. Jeffries ducked and instinctively jerked his left hand free of Siler and struck at Sharkey's face with his bare fist as hard as he could. The pain was excruciating, and Jeffries almost lost consciousness. Siler finally got the glove on again. Soaked with sweat and covered with Sharkey's blood, it seemed to weigh half a ton.

Sensing he would lose the decision if the fight went the limit, Sharkey strove mightily for a knockout in the twenty-fourth. But Jeffries summoned strength from some unknown source and managed to beat Sharkey to the punch, taking the sting from his blows or making him miss. The last round was a repetition of the twenty-fourth—both fighters nearing complete exhaustion from the penetrating heat and the punishment absorbed, yet both trying to score knockouts, Sharkey because it was his only means of winning, Jeffries out of a champion's pride. At the final bell the two were toe to toe in the center of the ring, battering each other about the face and body. Siler pulled them apart and raised Jeffries' hand in token of victory. Sharkey stood by, disgruntled, bloody, aching in every joint, each breath causing him anguish. He was taken to a hospital, and Jeffries, his face cut, his mouth and nose swollen, was ordered by a detective not to leave the city until the Sailor was out of danger.

The heat had been torturous not only for the gladiators (Jeffries lost twenty pounds) but for the spectators as well. Reporters at ringside nearly passed out. Back as far as the tenth row sweltering fans removed hats, coats, collars and even their shirts. During the twentieth round a spectator in the twelfth row wondered aloud how the fighters could stand it. Then he fainted. Within a week after the fight the hair of both fighters began to fall out because of the torrid blast of the lamps. It was a memorable evening.

———————————

Compared to adventures he had in the wilderness, the forests and the mountains and to his near-brushes with death and serious injury, what Jeffries endured in the ring must have seemed relatively mild to him. No prizefighter of any era loved to hunt, fish, trail game or walk along mountain paths as much as he, especially in the company of outdoorsmen like himself. He reveled in the wonders of nature and saw his victories and the crown he wore in comfortable perspective. Nor was any prizefighter so impatient with the sycophants, hangers-on and fair-weather friends that comprise one of the burdens a champion must carry.

An excellent shot with rifle, shotgun and revolver, Jeffries hunted bear, deer, mountain lions, catamounts, boars and mountain goats. He ventured into the Colorado rapids in a canoe, was chased by a fiery, maddened horse, nearly drowned in a whirlpool and was nearly killed in a fight with a badger.

The horse incident occurred when he was in his teens. He was visiting the ranch of a friend of his father's in the Tehachapi Mountains of California. An ancient horse owned by the rancher was selected to be killed and used as a lure to trap a bear, that animal relishing horsemeat above all else. The rancher did not want to shoot it, so young Jeffries volunteered. He led the horse down the mountain to an oak tree in whose branches platforms had been constructed for night shooting. He lifted his rifle, aimed between the horse's eyes and fired. The horse fell, and Jeffries started back up the trail. After a few minutes he heard a strange, terrifying noise behind him. It was the horse charging his way, eyes wild with vengeance, blood streaming down its nose. The young hunter took one glance and then sprinted for a quarter of a mile—in the belief that it was the horse's ghost that was chasing him. The horse was slowly gaining. Just when Jim could feel its breath on his neck, he came to an opening at the side of the trail, leapt aside and, as the horse steamed past, shot it in the back of the ear, killing it instantly. His first shot, Jim realized, had glanced off the horse's skull, merely stunning it. It was the worst fright he ever had in his life. He had nightmares about the event for a while, and though he became a good rider, he never really felt comfortable with horses afterwards.

The bout with the badger took place when Jeffries was older. As he and a group of friends were returning from a hunting trip in the hills north of Los Angeles, shooting rabbits from the car in the moonlight, Jeffries spotted a pair of eyes gleaming in the dark. He had the driver stop, seized a shotgun and approached the creature. It was a badger. The animal darted from the bush it was hiding behind and started scurrying across the field. Jeffries pursued it and when it turned back, fired both barrels at the animal. The badger rolled over into a kind of ball and lay still. Jeffries gave it a kick to see if it was dead. It was not. It charged at him like Sharkey had at Coney Island. Jeffries hit it with the stock of the shotgun but it kept boring in, eager to sink its teeth in Jeffries' throat or claw his thighs. He dodged and kept swatting it with the shotgun as his friends in the car roared with laughter at his predicament. Jeffries began to get winded from his exertions but managed to knock the badger out with the barrel of the shotgun before it could claw him. He waited for a minute, then picked up the animal by a hind leg and carried it to the car. "Sharkey gets the decision!" one of his friends shouted, breaking everybody up. He dropped the badger to the ground and once more it came to life, baring its teeth and seeking to close. Jeffries pounded at its head with the shotgun barrel—by now remarkably bent—and once more it went down. Taking no chances, Jeffries clubbed it several more times, then chucked it in the back seat to raucous congratulations from his friends. Before the car could start, the badger came to life in the back seat, and the hunter sitting there yowled in terror. Jeffries seized it by a hind leg and hurled it from the car. A friend shot it with his revolver. After a moment the badger got up and, realizing it had had enough, darted off toward the brush. Jeffries got out of the car, chased it and shot it with a rifle. This time the animal did not get up. One of the hunters took it home and had it mounted. He named it Tom.

Jeffries was born on a farm near Carroll, Ohio, in the hilly southern part of the state, on April 15, 1875. His mother, Rebecca, a strong-willed, capable woman, was Pennsylvania Dutch. His father, Alexis C. Jeffries, who was both Dutch and Scottish, was principally a farmer, but he was also something of a traveling preacher and a student of the world's religions. They were stern, righteous parents, but Jim and his four brothers and three sisters were immensely fond of them. Farming being uncertain in that part of Ohio, when Jim was seven the family moved to a ranch near Los Angeles. Another reason for the move was that young Tom Jeffries was crippled from curvature of the spine, and his parents thought the milder climate of southern California might benefit him.

Jim grew up solid and strong, and in the few fights he had, he always found himself pitted against older boys. He did not lose these fights, however, being as stubborn as he was powerful. He was not a poor student, but he despised his teacher, the feeling being mutual. One day at recess he was playing second base while the teacher pitched. Jeffries happened to be looking toward the outfield, and the teacher whacked him in the head with the ball. "Anytime a player isn't watching the game," the teacher intoned, "hit him with the ball. It will teach him a lesson." Three weeks later, while Jim was pitching, the teacher, who was playing third base, was talking to the base runner. Jeffries fired the ball at the back of the teacher's head, flattening him. As the latter approached Jim, fists clenched, Jeffries remarked, "You told us to hit anybody with the ball who wasn't paying attention to the game."

The feud got warmer, with the teacher humiliating Jim in class whenever he could. One afternoon, when Jim slipped a note to a girl in class, the teacher slapped the desk with his ruler and demanded to see it. After the girl refused, the teacher approached her and started smacking her on the knuckles with his ruler. Jeffries sprang up, smashed his slate over the teacher's head, jerked him across the room, wrestled him to the floor and started pummeling him. His brothers finally pulled him off. It was Jeffries' last day of elementary school. His father investigated the affair, decided Jim was in the right and set him to work around the ranch, an arrangement satisfactory to Jim. He studied by himself, then attended Los Angeles Business College for a year, his ambition at the time being to learn mine engineering.

At fifteen, a young man of enormous energy and uncertain ambition, he left home and got a job in the Timecula Tin Mines in Timecula, California. Most of the miners were Cornishmen who, in their leisure time, were intensely devoted to sports. Jim soon established himself as the best wrestler and the fastest runner (he ran barefooted) and occasionally won sums of money for those miners who backed him in contests. The mine did not produce enough tin for a profit, unfortunately, and the owners closed it down. Jeffries, despite his youth, thereupon got a job as a helper in the boiler works of the Santa

Fe Railroad in San Bernardino. When he was asked if he wanted to shovel coal on a locomotive, he leapt at the chance, feeling it was a first step toward becoming a locomotive engineer. For three months he was in a sooty paradise, marveling at the power of the engine. Then one day, as the train was speeding down a mountain, a horse wandered onto the tracks. The horse was not thrust aside by the cowcatcher but got somehow wedged between the front of the engine and a culvert. The engine started to buckle and the engineer cried, "Jump!" Jeffries jumped from the cab, and the engineer landed on top of him. Both watched the engine and fifteen cars topple over into a ditch beside the tracks.

The accident cured Jeffries of further railroading ambitions. He got a job as a boilermaker in a steel plant, then took another as a meat-packer at the Southern California Packing Company in Los Angeles. At the latter he worked up to twenty-four hours a day, going swimming or boxing in a gym in his free time instead of wasting time on sleep. The boxing was done in a small gym called the East Side Athletic Club, and Jeffries' reputation grew locally, though he never hit any opponent as hard as he felt he could. One of his admirers asked him if he would fight a professional Negro boxer named Hank Griffin, and, all unwitting, the nineteen-year-old Jeffries cheerfully accepted.

The fight took place at the Manitou Club in Los Angeles, Queensberry rules, to a finish. The winner was to get 75 per cent of the fighters' purse and the loser 25 per cent. The arrangements were all pleasantly baffling to Jeffries, who had never considered becoming a professional.

As his buddies cheered him on, Jeffries was made to look ridiculous by Griffin, a wily, experienced professional. Nervous, bewildered by Griffin's speed of hand and foot, Jeffries was hit repeatedly in the face and body without being able to counter with a blow of his own. For the first few rounds he stumbled about the ring like a blind man, entirely at the black man's mercy. There was this to be said for Jeffries: Like Corbett, he had the faculty of watching

the match objectively and learning as he boxed. Except that where Corbett was interested in subtleties, Jeffries, far from a natural boxer, picked up the rawest fundamentals. But, given Jeffries' extraordinary physical skills, fundamentals were enough.

After absorbing Griffin's blows for ten rounds, Jeffries realized that Griffin could not really hurt him; nature had furnished him with nearly impenetrable armor. He bided his time, waiting to land one solid punch. In the fourteenth, Griffin moved in quickly to throw a fast left and right. The right never landed. Jeffries, solidly based, ripped home a straight left to the mouth. As Griffin recoiled from the force of the blow, Jeffries advanced a step and hit him with a right to the jaw that knocked him out. His cohorts pounded one another on the back and set about collecting their odds-on bets.

At breakfast the following morning in the Jeffries household his mother read about the fight in the paper, frowned in disapproval and sternly told him not to fight again professionally until he was twenty-one—an injunction Jeffries faithfully obeyed despite the fact that he was being offered many fights by promoters. His brothers were delighted at his interest in professional fighting, the national hero then being James J. Corbett; his sisters were aghast, prizefighting being held in some circles as one step below bank-robbing.

He continued working as a boilermaker and packager and boxed at the Los Angeles Athletic Club, where the coach, De Witt Van Cort, foresaw great possibilities in him, so long as he did not overmatch himself while learning his trade. At twenty-one Jeff was a superb athlete. He was six feet two inches tall, weighed 220 pounds, and could run a hundred yards in a little over ten seconds, high jump five feet ten inches, outwrestle the roughest wrestlers in Los Angeles and outlift the most dedicated weight lifters. He reveled in hard physical work and welcomed challenges to his strength. For the next few years he would undoubtedly be the strongest man to enter the ring.

His term of desuetude ended, Jeffries,

sponsored by Van Cort, defeated Dan Long. Then he was sent by Van Cort to Corbett's training camp to act as a general helper and sometime sparring partner. Bill Delaney accepted him gladly; at the least he could serve as a human punching bag while Corbett made ready for Fitzsimmons. The sophisticated Corbett regarded him as a bumpkin and, according to Jeffries' account, one time used him cruelly. Generally when the two sparred, Corbett would pull his punches, and sometimes he would not punch at all but look for practice in escaping from the tight corners that Fitzsimmons might place him in. But one morning Jeffries was instructed by a Corbett assistant, Charlie White, to lead with a right-hand blow to Corbett's body. Jeffries protested, knowing this broke a basic boxing maxim. "It'll be all right," White assured him. "Fitzsimmons does it."

Shrugging, Jeffries agreed to act as ordered. He was no Fitzsimmons, however, and just as he started the punch, Corbett smashed him in the mouth with his own right with all the force he could put behind it. Jeffries' head rocked back and he was shaken to his heels. Enraged, he sprang forward, drove Corbett into a corner and began to pump home punches as fast and hard as he could. Corbett fell into a tight clinch, but Jeffries broke loose and flung Corbett against the wall of the gym. Delaney repeatedly hollered, "Time!" and tried to hold Jeffries back. Finally Jeffries cooled off and, mouth aching, strode to the dressing room.

Later Corbett asked Jeffries if he had hurt him.

Jim Jeffries, seated second from right, is shown in training for his battle royal with Jack Johnson. So intense were the passions of white America that an entire nation begged Jeffries to leave his farm and "wipe that golden smile off Johnson's face!" Jeffries responded, but less for racial reasons than for the tinkle of gold. Retired five years, the fabled "Boilermaker" had ballooned to 320 pounds.

"All you did was bust up my mouth," Jeffries said sourly. Putting on his coat, he added, "If that's as hard as you can hit, you're going to have a lot of trouble with Fitzsimmons."

Corbett's had not been a happy training camp, and Jeffries' prediction was correct. He saw the fight from atop the stands at Carson City (not wishing to be part of the coterie in Corbett's corner) and noted that Corbett was missing blows he should have landed. He remarked early in the fight, despite Corbett's lead in rounds, that Fitz would knock the champion out. Which, of course, he did.

Though so low in the pecking order at Corbett's camp that he did not even get to meet Bill Brady, Jeffries found a friend and admirer in Bill Delaney. On his return to Los Angeles, Delaney got him fights with T. van Buskirk, whom he knocked out in two rounds, and with Slaughterhouse Henry Baker of Chicago, who got his nickname from his habit of felling steers with a blow of his fist. Baker hit Jeffries with his famous punch and acted shocked when Jeffries refused to topple over. In the ninth round Jeffries caught up with him and fired a short left hook. Baker flew backwards, turned as he fell and wound up lying over the middle rope. Jeffries pulled him back into the ring, where he was counted out.

Moving up in class, Jeffries then fought Gus Ruhlin, a leading contender among the heavyweights. In this bout Jeffries learned another lesson. Despite the fact that he knocked Ruhlin down several times, he began to feel more tired than his experienced opponent, and his punches were losing some of their force. At the gong at the end of the twelfth, Jeffries dropped his hands and turned toward his corner—to be greeted with a terrible surprise. Ruhlin had moved up behind him and swung a well-aimed roundhouse-right haymaker that struck Jeffries on the right ear. For a second Jeffries thought the building had fallen on him. Delaney, consternated, kept hollering "Foul!" at the paralyzed referee, but Jeffries convinced him the damage was negligible —though his ear kept ringing for hours afterwards—and set out, his energy renewed, to demolish Ruhlin. He pursued him for the next eight rounds and succeeded in knocking him down. Ruhlin always got up, however, and fought defensively for the rest of the fight. It was declared a draw.

Moving up still another step, Jeffries then fought the great Joe Choynski. The San Franciscan made him look like an awkward amateur and delivered severe punishment for nine rounds. In the tenth he gave Jeffries the opportunity to learn still another lesson. Affecting timidity, he was running away from Jeffries, his back to him, as Jeffries pursued closely. Then Choynski ran straight into the ropes and ricocheted backward. As he was propelled toward Jeffries he quickly pivoted and hit Jeffries with a right to the mouth that broke his nose and wedged his lower lip between his teeth. Jeffries stopped dead in his tracks, thinking his neck had been stretched a full foot—but he did not go down. In the closing rounds Jeffries kept trying to corner the tiring veteran. Though he floored him three times, Choynski always got up. Referee Graney called the bout a draw, a decision Jeffries was happy to get.

In quick succession he was matched with Joe Goddard, the black "Barrier Champion" from Australia; Peter Jackson, for the boxing lesson he might learn; Peter Everett, a villainous-looking opponent; and, as topping for the cake, the Sailor, Tom Sharkey, considered the second-best fighter in the world.

Jeffries kept knocking down Goddard with punches to the body and won a decision in four rounds. Jackson was far past his prime and had lost his great speed and hand quickness, and Jeffries solemnly put him away in three rounds. (It was while training for the Jackson bout that Jeffries met Tommy Ryan, who had come to San Francisco to fight George "Young Corbett" Green.) The Everett bout was a comical one, with "Mexican Pete" sprinting around the ring as Jeffries pursued him. Jeffries knocked him down one time with a right to the spine; he finished him in the third round by cornering him and hitting him on the jaw with his left as Everett tried to slip past him to more open pastures. Then there was the successful roughhouse with Sharkey, and Delaney felt his man was ready to invade New York.

————————————

There was little rest for Jeffries while he was under Brady's aegis. After the second Sharkey fight he signed articles to meet Corbett at the Seaside Athletic Club at Coney Island on May 11, 1900, and was promptly put on tour around the country, starring in a terrible vehicle called *Eighty Minutes in New York*. While visiting West Baden, Indiana, to soak in the baths, he was signed by Brady to take on Jack Finnegan in Detroit. Annoyed because of a dispute about the gloves he was supposed to wear, Jeffries flattened Finnegan with two punches.

At this point in his career the psychology that besets most champions affected Jeffries. He began to feel that his efforts to reach the top should be rewarded, and he regarded training as unnecessary drudgery. He drank too much champagne, stayed up too late and when he went into training for the Corbett bout, his camp at Elmhurst, New Jersey, was more casual than it should have been and was peopled by pranksters. Jeffries had been told that Corbett was working like a demon to put himself in shape for the fight—constantly sparring with Gus Ruhlin—but he paid little heed.

One of the characters in Jeffries' camp was Ed Dunkhorst, "the Human Freight Car." Dunkhorst was himself in training to fight Fitzsimmons. When he came to the camp he weighed 260 pounds and with assiduous effort he pushed his weight up to 287. His usual dessert after a workout was a gallon of ice cream. Jeffries' cook, as a joke, loaded Dunkhorst's plate with the richest foods he could find. But Dunkhorst got so tired of the jokes played on him—including being hit in the nose with a croquet mallet wielded by Tommy Ryan—that he demanded to box Jeffries, to teach him a lesson.

"This is what Fitzsimmons is going to do to you," said Jeffries affably as they touched gloves. He feinted twice to bewilder Dunkhorst, then hit him a left to the stomach and a left to the chin. Dunkhorst landed in a sitting position in a far corner of the ring, got up and left. Ryan scolded Jeff for hitting Dunkhorst so hard; he might have hurt his hand. When Dunkhorst fought Fitzsimmons, the aging Cornishman knocked him out precisely in the manner Jeff had predicted.

A week later, on the day of his fight with Corbett, Jeff was immersed in a sea of his own troubles. He knew he was in for a frustrating afternoon. Although the odds were 3 to 1 in his favor and it was even money that he would score a knockout in ten rounds, Jeff finally was worried about his physical condition. Besides that, he was still somewhat in awe of Corbett, in the sense that his mentor had been at one time his foremost idol. The day was hot and muggy, with a scent of rain in the air. Jeffries wondered if his vitality would be sapped.

When the two met in the center of the ring to be given instructions by Charlie White, Jeffries recollected for a moment the trick that had been played on him at the Corbett camp and resolved to gain a measure of revenge. When he saw the magnificent shape Corbett had gotten himself into—much better than he had been in for the Fitzsimmons fight—he wondered if he could get Corbett to stand still long enough to enable him to land a couple of punches.

A roar of encouragement went up for Jeffries as he moved swiftly toward Corbett. Corbett jabbed, sidestepped, slipped punches, broke clinches and fled—all part of his plan to wear Jeffries down so that he could be attacked with impunity in the final rounds. When Jeffries did land a punch it was while Corbett was in flight, and its force was minimized. Corbett's footwork and his judgment of distance were never better. He splashed jabs into Jeffries' face like a trip-hammer, throwing the champion off-balance and making him look awkward and ineffectual. The jabs did no marked damage, but were a source of immense annoyance, like a swarm of gnats that cannot be swatted. Sometimes Corbett would land six fast blows and be out of reach before Jeffries could make ready to retaliate.

At the end of the sixth, a disgusted,

discouraged Jeffries told his friends at ringside, "You better hedge your bets. I can't catch him inside of ten rounds." At the end of the tenth, with Corbett not only having survived but shown himself clearly the champion's master, the crowd rose and gave him a standing ovation.

Jeffries now began to stalk Corbett rather than waste his strength in wild rushes, ever on the lookout for the opening he required for his power-laden left. The fight's pace slowed; fewer blows were struck. Then a welcome cooling wind came up, and the pound of thunder could be heard far off in the west.

In the eighteenth Corbett became more aggressive, repeatedly moving in toward Jeffries and landing fast combinations, despite warnings from his corner: "Not yet!" "Wait!" "Be careful, Jim!" The margin between the two seemed to be growing. In the twentieth Corbett saw a need for caution; Jeffries missed his chin by the merest fraction of an inch with a blow that would have sent him through the ropes. Corbett's supporters gasped, then cheered his skill in avoiding the blow.

Outside, the storm broke, thunder roared and in a moment water started pouring in the entrances to the arena and running down the aisles. Jeffries found the cool air refreshing, and he gulped it gratefully. Corbett, knowing he had won every round so far, planned to move in with everything he had in the twenty-fourth and twenty-fifth, whether he broke his hands or not. He would make sure of the decision and give the crowd an exhibition of the science of boxing. Brady was gnawing his nails, and Delaney was frantically ordering Jeffries to corner Corbett and get home a solid punch.

Corbett came out fast and aggressively for the twenty-third, feinting, sidestepping, throwing a series of jabs. Delaney and Brady were frantically shouting, "You've got to knock him out, Jim!" Jeffries concentrated on his target, oblivious to other sounds and sights. Corbett smugly danced forward to fling a jab in Jeffries' face. To add force to the blow he had drawn back his left shoulder a little. It was the opportunity Jef-

fries had been waiting for. He struck without thinking—a straight left to the jaw, followed instantly by a left hook to the jaw. Corbett saw the first punch coming and tried to pull back, but too late. When his head came forward he caught the full impact of Jeffries' hook. He went down as though shot, and the referee began his count. When it reached seven, against all rules one of Corbett's seconds threw a bucket of water in his face and started to climb into the ring. Jeffries, not wanting to win on a disqualification, ran toward the second and began kicking him. The storm raged outside in counterpoint to the wild excitement of the crowd over the change in the fight's fortunes. Many were unbelieving, so swift had been the blows, and it was only after Corbett had been helped to his corner and revived that they could credit their senses. The champion had retained his title. When Jeffries' hand was raised, Brady for once was silent.

After his astonishing victory over the world's greatest boxer, Jeffries took a well-earned rest. He visited his family at the ranch near Los Angeles, looked up old friends and then, on a tip from a mining engineer, decided to go hunting in Mexico, near the lower Colorado River. He was warned repeatedly about cutthroat American bandits and hostile Indians, but he did not think they could be much worse than the villains he encountered in the fight business, and he went anyway. The peerless outdoorsman got along fine with the bandits and with the Indians, shot boars and snakes, clubbed ducks and dynamited fish, the last to make sure the Indians he was staying with had an ample food supply. They regarded this huge, barefooted man as some kind of god. Jeffries pronounced the two months he spent in the delta and the surrounding forests the finest time he ever had in his life. When he returned to civilization he could not get his shoes on.

The ubiquitous Brady then harnessed him to appear in *The Man from the West* and committed him to three fast fights, against Hank Griffin, Joe Kennedy and Gus Ruhlin. This time a more experienced Jeffries pounded Ruhlin to the floor in five rounds. Then it was

Fitzsimmons again.

Fitzsimmons had been bombarding Jeffries with challenges in the newspapers, and the champion, grateful for the chance Fitzsimmons had earlier accorded him, agreed to a bout on July 25, 1902, in San Francisco. The fight was to be twenty rounds. It was held in the Mission District, under a huge circus tent packed with seats. When Jeffries entered the ring he was so upset by the flimsy qualities of the ring floor, which shook and shivered every time he took a step on it, that he railed at Delaney and kicked into the aisle a bouquet of flowers from one of his admirers.

As has been noted, fighters used many tricks to advance themselves and to take advantage of opponents in the early and middle 1800's. This was no less true in the early 1900's—except that technology lent assistance. A fighter's hands were generally bandaged in the locker room without the supervision of the opponent's manager or trainer, although the gloves were generally put on in the ring in the presence of the referee. As a result of this tradition, or oversight, some enterprising trainers, with the blessing of the fighter's manager, placed plaster of Paris, gum arabic or "tea lead" (lead foil wrapped around packages of tea) beneath their man's hand tape. When water was poured down the fighter's wrist, the plaster of Paris or gum arabic quickly hardened, making the fist heavier, giving it more leverage and making its impact harder. Lead foil rendered some blows nearly lethal. When Jack "Doc" Kearns, later to become Jack Dempsey's manager, was a lightweight, his manager once wrapped his hands in lead foil before putting on the gloves for a fight. Kearns had a good first round, mystifying his foe with the power of his punches. But his arms got so weary in succeeding rounds that he could not raise his hands for defense and took a fearful shellacking. It convinced Kearns he should become a manager.

To add to his chances of regaining the crown, Fitzsimmons allowed plaster of Paris to be placed under his bandages before his second fight with Jeffries. The shrewd Delaney, visiting Fitz's locker room before the fight, saw the foul deed and rushed back to Jeffries to inform him. Jeffries shrugged. "The hell with it," he growled. "I'm bigger and tougher than he is and if he wants to use plaster of Paris, let him. I'll flatten him anyway."

As a result of his magnanimity toward Fitzsimmons, Jeffries took the worst cutting-up of his career. Fitz, following a plan to slice Jeffries to pieces rather than attempting to batter him into insensibility, was content to rake the champion's face and head with his lethal gloves. As the rounds progressed, Jeffries felt his face sting and knew he was bleeding from a dozen lacerations. In the seventh Fitz landed a hard right on Jeffries' left eye, laying the flesh open and allowing the blood to pour out. Today the bout would have been summarily stopped; then it merely delighted the Fitzsimmons faction.

In the eighth a desperate Jeffries, frightened at his blood loss and unable to see out of his left eye, sprang from his stool and drove Fitz into a corner. He feinted with his left and, as Fitz started to block it with his right, quickly changed direction and landed the solidest blow of the fight, a crunching left to the liver. Fitz slowly sank to the canvas, clutching his body, his face ashen, his mouth agape. Gasping for breath, he could not struggle to his feet before the count of ten.

It took a little over a month for Jeffries to recover from the deluge of cuts on his scalp, face and body. So good-natured was he that he not only forgave Fitzsimmons for the trickery but suggested they go on an exhibition tour together. He found Fitz a great source of fun and a fine companion as they took on all comers, offering fifty dollars to anyone who could stay four rounds with either. The tour ended when Fitzsimmons received a telegram saying his wife, Rose, was ill with pneumonia in Philadelphia. She died a few days after his arrival, and all the remaining bookings were canceled. Before Jeffries left for his home in California, Fitzsimmons told him that he would like to help train him for Jeffries' upcoming fight with Corbett. Fitz had never forgotten Corbett's slight in Carson City.

Jeffries' second fight with Corbett

was to be held at the Yosemite Club in San Francisco on August 14, 1903, and the crowd was expected to be enormous, since the bout was between the two most famous men in California. Delaney, Corbett's former trainer, was still with Jeffries, spilling Corbett's secrets as best he could. And then a kind of "equalizer" developed. This was the defection to Corbett's Alameda camp of Tommy Ryan. Always volatile, Ryan had gotten into an argument with Jeffries over a small matter and had left in pique. Corbett, who realized he was getting older with each passing moment, welcomed Ryan, as much for his boxing skill as for any secrets he might impart. Corbett had noticed that when he sparred he was not as quick to move out of the way of blows as he had been. His wife suggested his eyes might be going bad on him. "You squint when you read the paper," she told him. Corbett mulled it over.

Ryan's appearance infused new life into the camp. He informed Corbett he would work for nothing if he could be in the challenger's corner during the fight —such was his antipathy toward Jeffries. Since Ryan had worked with Jeffries on the crouch, Corbett paid close attention when Ryan devised a way to attack it. And together they devised a way to block the deadly effective left hook that Jeffries delivered from this position. Ryan advised Corbett to place his right hand by his side in such a way that, when Jeffries swung, Corbett would turn to his left and catch the blow with his hand. Although Corbett had heretofore relied solely on his own knowledge, intuition and experience to devise defensive maneuvers, he felt Ryan's tactic was sound. He practiced the movement, with Ryan imitating Jeffries, until he felt he had it perfected.

As Jeffries and Corbett were given instructions by referee Eddie Graney in the center of the ring under the huge canvas top, Corbett felt he was too calm and envied Jeffries his keyed-up nervousness. Jeffries ignored Corbett's handshake and was too wrought up to speak when Corbett wished him luck. Fitzsimmons, Delaney and Tom Sharkey were in Jeffries' corner; Ryan, Yank and Tom Kenny were in Corbett's. Cor-

bett at 180 pounds weighed 48 pounds less than Jeffries. He was ten years the Boilermaker's senior.

In much better condition than in their first fight, Jeffries tore forth at the bell, launching his attack. Corbett, to save his legs, did less dancing than in previous fights, being content to slip punches, take them on his arms, roll with them or duck. He jabbed repeatedly to keep Jeffries off-balance. Jeffries, prancing about like an overbred racehorse, apparently eager to show the fans that he was Corbett's equal as a boxer, changed style in the middle of the round and got much the worse of the flurry of exchanges.

In the second round, as Jeffries advanced, Corbett figured that while he was still fresh, he would try Ryan's defense for the hook. He saw Jeffries set himself, and as though it were moving in slow motion, Corbett watched the punch coming. He twisted to his left and dropped his right hand to smother the blow. But he did not have his hand in the right place, nor did he move away with the celerity required. The punch ripped into his side—harder than Peter Jackson's best—and Corbett dropped to the floor. It felt as though every rib on his right side had been broken. Corbett realized he could not get up before the count of ten, but friendship is a powerful drug. The timekeeper was an old friend of his, and so was Eddie Graney. Corbett caught his eye, the glance meaning, "I won't be able to get up unless you count very slowly." Graney obliged by giving Corbett one of the slowest counts on record as Jeffries fumed, hitting his gloves together. Corbett rose shakily at "Nine" and Jeffries rushed at him. Corbett managed to duck a blow and fall into a clinch until the round ended.

He was obviously through. In his corner, as his worried handlers sponged him off and fanned him, Corbett cursed himself for following Ryan's advice instead of relying on the instincts that had served him so well in a score of previous bouts. However, there was nothing for it but to step forth again and brace himself for the pounding he knew he was going to take. When he rose at the gong, he found he could not stand erect because of the pain in his ribs, so he adopted a kind of crouch to protect his injured side. In addition, he found the muscles in his neck were sore and stiff from his fall to the floor, and he could not move his head to avoid punches in his customary way. He could not rely on footwork or use his right hand as a weapon because of his broken ribs. As a consequence of these handicaps, he had to bore in rather than dance away, and he accepted a great number of hard blows. His defense became verbal. He laughed at Jeffries and told him he was a poor fighter; he taunted him, saying he could not possibly score a knockout. Jeffries tried. He knocked Corbett down five times in the next few rounds, but Corbett always gamely rose to sally forth again.

In the seventh a strange thing occurred. Instead of bounding across the ring to press the attack, Jeffries walked midway and stared at Corbett. To the challenger, this indicated that Jeffries must be weary himself and wanted to conserve his strength. Calling on his last reserves, heedless of his aches, Corbett launched a desperate counterattack, throwing his hardest punches at Jeffries. Surprised, Jeffries retreated as he accepted the blows. The crowd, sensing a dramatic turn of fortune, rose to its feet, stood on its seats and let out a concerted roar. It would have been the most popular victory in the history of San Francisco had Corbett won. What the fans did not perceive—as Jeffries did—was that Corbett's punches had no sting to them, and they had no effect on the champion. As the round ended, Corbett received the greatest ovation of his career.

Ryan was ecstatic as he placed the water bottle in Corbett's mouth. "You've got him licked, Jim! You've got him licked!" he cried. Spitting out, Corbett knew better. And he suspected Jeffries knew it. The tide changed again in the eighth and ninth, Jeffries pursuing and hitting, Corbett weathering the blows as best he could, bone weary and suffering intense pain in his right side. In the tenth Jeffries feinted with a right and, as Corbett reacted, launched his terrible left hook. Corbett managed to get his ribs out of the way but took the force of the blow in his unprotected stomach. He doubled up with a groan and sank to the floor. Up at nine, he was felled by another left to the stomach and a right to the jaw. When Graney tolled off "Seven," Ryan threw in the sponge in acknowledgment of defeat. For all he knew, Corbett might have been killed by the next bombardment. It was Corbett's last fight. He became a vaudeville performer, a lecturer and an advocate of physical fitness. Later, along with John L. Sullivan, he would be in Jeffries' corner in Jeffries' most important fight.

Somewhat to Jeffries' dismay, by 1904 and 1905 a legend of invincibility had risen around him like mist on a moor, and he simply ran out of opponents. His only fight in 1904 was a two-round knockout of Jack Monroe, a Canadian who had no business in the ring (though he later became a war hero with the Princess Pat Regiment, killing the Boche with a lumberjack's ax, his favorite weapon).

At this time nearly every state had a ban on boxing, California and Nevada being the notable exceptions. But though Jeffries and Delaney scoured those states for opponents, as well as South Africa, Australia and England, no worthy competitor could be located. Delaney made a sweeping challenge: Jeffries would fight Sharkey, Corbett and Fitzsimmons on successive nights, and the first one to beat him could have the crown. They all had fought a brace of fights with Jeffries, however, which seemed to be enough to last a lifetime, and the defi went unheeded.

Jeffries devoted himself to the theatre once again, playing the title role in *Davy Crockett*. The drama was enlivened by the presence of wolves, bloodhounds and deer onstage. The finale was a clinch between Jeffries and his eighty-five pound leading lady; the sight sometimes caused laughter to break out through the tears of the audience as the curtain fell.

The play tour over and no reasonably competent challenger having turned up, there was nothing for Jeffries to do but retire as the undefeated heavyweight champion. He made the announcement to the press and returned to his ranch in Burbank to farm and raise cattle and, in his spare time, to hunt and fish.

The moment his retirement was made known, a scramble began to seize the abandoned crown. The two most promising contenders of a quite mediocre crop were Marvin Hart of Louisville and Jack Root, who had emigrated to the United States from Austria and lived in Chicago. Root, a smart, fast fighter but no heavyweight, had beaten Kid McCoy (Norman Selby) in ten rounds to become the world's first light-heavyweight champion (the division was instituted in America in 1903). Hart had beaten Tommy Ryan as a middleweight and had won a twenty-round decision over a gangly Negro named Jack Johnson—though the referee had not put himself out to give Johnson the best of it.

Hart and Root were matched for the mythical crown, the bout taking place in Reno on July 3, 1905. Lou Houseman, a writer for the Chicago *Inter-Ocean,* was also Root's manager and a good friend of Jeffries. He prevailed on the Boilermaker not only to referee the fight but to name the winner the new heavyweight champion. Unfortunately for Houseman, Hart won by a knockout after twelve lackadaisical rounds, thereby gleaning whatever glory there was to be had from this exploit.

Hart, as champion, had two fights. The first was with Pat Callaghan, whom he knocked out in two rounds; the second was in Los Angeles against Noah Brusso, better known as Tommy Burns, who won an easy decision in twenty rounds. Burns was a fighting champion, but there was one man he would not fight: Jack "Li'l Arthur" Johnson, the golden-toothed black man. When Johnson finally caught up with Burns and defeated him, thereby becoming champion, the world shook on its axis. Many thought that Jeffries was the man to repair it.

Jeffries' pleasant idyll on his ranch began to be interrupted at the end of 1908. He was urged, for anthropological, psychological, patriotic and possibly genetic reasons, to shuck off retirement and remove this mote from the public eye. Jeffries seemed at the time the most formidable of the White Hopes, that army of Caucasians recruited by the dozens all over the world in an attempt to find a contender who could dethrone the black man. Badgered by friends, by newspapermen in their columns and by imploring letter writers, Jeffries mulled the situation over on the porch of his ranch. He was not sure he could get in shape for the contest. In his five years out of the ring he had ballooned up to 320 pounds. Training for the fight would be an ordeal. He did not especially need the money, though he sensed the gate would be enormous.

In common with many Americans of the time, Jeffries did not have a high opinion of Negroes, for the most part an impoverished, suppressed, poorly educated minority. Caucasians expected to see them cuddle their caps in their hands whenever the two races met. Jeffries had fought blacks before—Griffin, Goddard and Jackson. But Griffin had been his first opponent, and Goddard and Jackson were *Australians.* The novelist and correspondent Jack London made a plea in the New York *Herald:* "[Jeffries] must now emerge from his alfalfa farm and remove the golden smile from Jack Johnson's face." The great old-timers of the ring—Sullivan, Corbett, Choynski—backed London up. Johnson's flamboyant life style disturbed the majority of white Americans.

Beyond his willingness to accede to the appeals of his admirers, Jeffries had another reason for returning to the ring. Word was continually reaching him that the black man was noising it about that if he ever got the chance he could whip Jim Jeffries, because he already had beaten his brother Jack. The fight had taken place in Oakland, Jack Jeffries lasting only five rounds. "I already got Jim's number," Johnson was reputed to chortle when in the company of sporting men.

Jeffries did not have a high regard for the new champion's ability. Marvin Hart had beaten him. Joe Choynski had flattened him, although because the bout had been interrupted by Texas Rangers, it had been declared a draw. The champion's other victories Jeffries dismissed —they had been against smaller men, inexperienced men, overconfident men. Thinking it over, Jeffries guessed he hated Jack Johnson more than any man alive. Yes, he would fight him. ■

James J. Jeffries, once Corbett's sparring partner, began to have designs on the heavyweight crown. Born in Ohio in 1875, Jeffries made an early reputation based on strength and a capacity for absorbing punishment. Following the Corbett–Fitzsimmons bout, Jeffries set out to learn his craft. For Jeffries, it was lucky that Fitzsimmons didn't enjoy the acclaim once showered on Gentleman Jim. It was equally fortunate for Jeffries that Fitzsimmons vowed never again to step into the ring with Corbett.

Luring Fitzsimmons into the ring was the chief concern of William A. Brady, the sly theatrical impresario who had managed Corbett to success in the ring and on the stage and took over as manager of Jeffries at a time when Jeffries was fed up with prize-fighting. Pressured to defend his title, Fitzsimmons chose Jeffries as his opponent because Brady had painted an image of the contender as being ponderously slow and easy to hit. He neglected to reveal several of Jeffries's redeeming qualities.

Jeffries's camp at Allenhurst, New Jersey, two days before the Fitzsimmons fight. Left to right are brother Jack Jeffries, Tommy Ryan, Bill Delaney (seated), Jeffries, and Jim Daly.

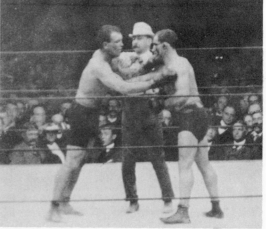

For two years Fitzsimmons had chosen to tour the country and make horseshoes on the stage in a melodrama especially written for him rather than risk his title. In selecting Jeffries over Corbett, Kid McCoy, and Tom Sharkey, Fitzsimmons paid little attention to the fact that the Boilermaker was thirteen years his junior and nearly forty pounds heavier. The match was to be held at Coney Island, New York, on June 9, 1899. Top, Jeffries and Fitzsimmons solemnly pose for the camera after signing. Above, challenger and champion shake hands.

Jeffries, on the left, is seen fighting Tom Sharkey. Jeffries won both fights against the opponent he most admired.

On August 14, 1903, Jeffries fought Corbett a second time in San Francisco, and for the second time Jeffries was the winner by a knockout. Though he was long past his prime, Corbett's fame lingered; thus grew the myth of Jeffries's invincibility.

The mettle of Joe Choynski, that persistent goad of great heavyweights, was shown in San Francisco in 1897 when he battled Jeffries to a twenty-round draw, hitting him, the Boilermaker recalled, the hardest blow he ever received in his career in the ring.

For drama and intensity of feeling, no contest ever reached the fever pitch that followed
Jeffries's return from retirement in his quest
to dethrone Jack Johnson. And few fighters
were surrounded by so many advisers who
felt it was Jeffries's sacred mission to win

back the crown. At Jeffries's training camp, above, are some of the interested parties. Foreground, left to right: Dick Adams, Promoter Tex Rickard talking to Jeff's business partner Sam Berger, and Clarence Berry conferring with Jeffries.

Jeffries, in training for Jack Johnson, is seen with Jim Corbett, above, right. Corbett was Jeffries's principal adviser.

In the sequence above, taken from film, Jim Corbett spars playfully with John L. Sullivan at Jeffries's camp in Reno, Nevada. Right (middle), Jeffries chats on the porch. Right, Jeffries as a hunter.

Jim Jeffries, in the center, is seen doing road work in preparation for his bout with Jack Johnson. For a man who had been out of action five years, and who had gained one hundred pounds, getting into fighting trim was a monumental effort.

At Reno, Nevada, Jeffries is seen with John L. Sullivan and Jim Corbett in what proved to be the reconciliation of a seventeen-year feud between Sullivan and Corbett. John L., the bulky man with a mustache, was hired as a correspondent by The New York Times.

Jeffries's training regime for the 1910 fight with Jack Johnson was perhaps the most avidly followed in the history of boxing, with correspondents daily sending lengthy dis-patches to their papers and Reno overflowing with fans. Above and on the following pages, the Boilermaker goes through his chores on the day before the fight in front

of a thousand of the faithful who have paid to watch. Jeffries skipped rope and punched the bag, and as a fitting and exciting climax, he sparred with Joe Choynski. Not only had Choynski held Jeffries to a twenty-round draw, but in 1901 Choynski had knocked out Jack Johnson in three swift rounds.

910-RENO

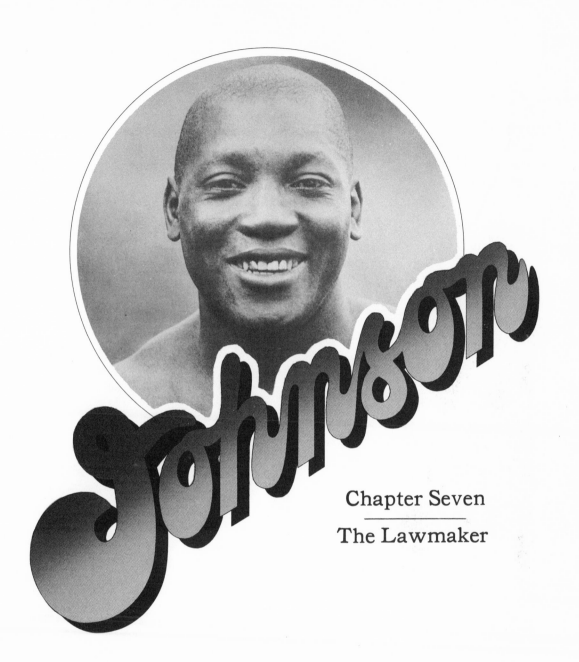

Chapter Seven
—————
The Lawmaker

Jack Johnson, the first Negro to win the world heavyweight boxing title, was the central figure in the most dramatic event in sports history, the event that caused more national repercussions than any other. Without consciously trying to, and without being quite aware of what he was doing, he struck a slashing blow for the prestige of his race, investing his brothers with a sense of pride and identity, a *machismo,* that they did not dare to hold until he captured the championship from a white man—and retained it against an "invincible" white ex-champion! He is adjudged by many to have been the greatest heavyweight ever to have donned gloves. Few men in any field, of any color, were so arrogant as he. Few got so much pleasure out of publicly flouting law and custom as he. Few seemed to be as harried by the law and legal minions as he. He claimed to be persecuted, and he was. But circumstances were ideal for persecution. It was partly the era in which he lived, partly his own impulsive, perverse behavior and partly the nature of the beast he made it his business to gain mastery over.

But he had his good times, too. He reveled in adulation and received his share of that. He liked to flaunt his riches, and he made and spent huge amounts of money. He bought his mother a house in Chicago. He beat the four fighters he most violently hated (three white, one black) in his fifteen-year career as a prizefighter. Despite all the disasters that engulfed him, like the hurricane-brought floods that blasted his native island, Johnson was immensely amused by his life on this planet. What an effect he had, what a glorious splash he made!

John Arthur Johnson was born on March 31, 1878, in Galveston, a bustling port on the north end of Galveston Island, twenty-four miles off Texas in the Gulf of Mexico—an island so attacked by the sun throughout most of the year that it was sometimes called Devil's Island. Johnson was the son of a school janitor and part-time preacher who had fought on Lee's side during the War Between the States and, while helping to check Sherman's march, had contracted rheumatism. Jack, as a consequence, had to don a dirty apron and assist his father in sweeping out the school buildings. His schoolmates, on their way to go swimming to escape the murderous heat, would stop by to jeer at him at his work. Tall, gangly, fearful, he was regularly beaten up by bullies, though his older sister defended him when she could, always urging him to strike back at his tormentor. It was not only bullies he feared. After a losing bout, his mother—a small, compact woman called Tiny—would give him a hiding with a two-by-four when he came home bloody and disheveled. His was not a joyous childhood.

Still, the future seemed reasonably bright for a fairly intelligent Galveston Negro who did not mind manual labor. The port was the second largest in the United States, with ships from South America and the West Indies daily unloading their cargoes. Some days Jack would skip school, with its ignominy and torment, and wander down to the wharf to watch hulking stevedores at work. There were also cotton warehouses, lumber mills, cottonseed refineries, jute mills, breweries, oil wells and chemical plants, all simmering in the sun.

When Jack was twelve he decided he had had enough of Galveston. With two dollars in his pocket, he climbed out of his bedroom window, slid down a drainpipe and made off in the night. He rode the rattlers, evaded the long steel rods used by railroad guards to poke at nonpaying passengers and begged for food at back doors on his long journey north. He held a series of odd jobs, the best of which was working as a trainer in the racing stable of a wealthy Bostonian. Then, cold and homesick after an absence of five years, he decided to return to Galveston and was willing to accept a beating to earn the money for the trip. Two black boxers, Joe Walcott and Scaldy Bill Quinn, were about to perform in Woburn, north of Boston, and Jack offered himself up as a sparring partner. First he applied to Quinn, who summarily chased him out of his camp, and then to Walcott, who took him on. Walcott, "the Barbados Demon," who was to become the world's welterweight champion in 1901 (and beat quite a few heavyweights before reaching that pinnacle), was a short, thick-necked, strong-chested man with a formidable reach and a tremendous punch. Like Johnson, he had run away from home at an early age and had taken to boxing as his best way to earn a living, fighting for purses that at times were as little as $2.50. Walcott took a liking to Johnson, although this did not prevent him from handing the thin lad a walloping in their sparring sessions. The punishment meted out by Walcott, however, was a minor annoyance compared to riding the rods and racing on top of freight cars to avoid the cruel bludgeons of railroad guards. In the meantime Johnson was absorbing a great deal of fighting knowledge, particularly learning how to defend himself. Walcott admired Johnson's ability to take a punch, predicted great things for him and arranged to have him in his corner for the Quinn fight.

Walcott had no trouble in lambasting Quinn around the ring, but Johnson's advice—because he hated Quinn after his rejection—was for the Demon to keep pressing. "The fight's goin' about even," he said, sponging off Walcott. "You better make sure and keep hittin' this baby." Which Walcott did, finally metamorphosing Quinn into a bloody hulk that dropped unconscious to the floor in the seventeenth round.

A few days later Johnson bade farewell to the Walcotts and, money jingling in his pockets, shipped on a boat to Galveston, where he got bawled out by his mother for running away from home. However, he had gotten bigger and healthier looking, he had money to buy food for the family and he had brought back with him the biggest bass viol Tiny had ever seen—so he was shortly forgiven. One of the jobs he found after his return was mixing paint in a nearby paint shop, where he found an employee his own age who liked to box. Daily sessions when the foreman was out of sight helped further develop Johnson's defensive skills, which were quite unique. He fought in a stand-up style, careful never to be caught off-balance, and he invented a way to stop a punch that no

one had ever thought of: A split second after an opponent's blow was launched, Jack snapped a sharp counter to the biceps of the extended arm. The jolt stopped the fist in midair, and it was not only painful but it sapped some of the strength from the arm that received it. After several knocks in the same place, the opponent did not want to, nor could he, throw as many punches or throw them as hard. The blow has been likened to a pitcher firing a ball into the precise center of a catcher's mitt.

Johnson got his chance to test his ability in a classic way. A circus played Galveston that featured a man named Bob Tomlinson, who offered five dollars to anyone who could stay with him for four rounds. After seeing some aspirants go to their doom, Johnson accepted the challenge. He managed to withstand Tomlinson's assault for three rounds by blocking blows and by clinching in the polished Joe Walcott manner. In the last round he counterattacked so viciously that Tomlinson's manager had to ring the bell ahead of time to save his tiger from a knockout. With part of his winnings Jack treated the Johnson family to a dinner of fried chicken, chitterlings and yams.

To supplement his paint-shop income, Johnson began to take part in Battle Royals—wild brawls with five or six Negroes in the ring, staged for the entertainment of Texans at stag affairs. Every contestant struck out in all directions; the one who remained on his feet after the rest were out cold was declared the winner and collected five dollars. Losers received nothing for their wounds. Jack's trick was to find a brother slightly off-balance and clobber him on the side of the head. When the others wisely ganged up on Johnson, he jeered at them, broke their concentration, took their best shots while keeping the ropes to his back and managed to knock them all out anyway.

By this time he had developed an effective, snakelike left that he could redirect in midair if his opponent tried to move out of the way or pick the punch off, and he fashioned the greatest right uppercut in prizefight history. He would lean forward, weight on his toes, left ready to parry any blow aimed at his face, and launch the blow in a nearly vertical direction with all the power of his massive shoulder, back and thigh muscles behind it. In more formal fights he fought a draw with Jim McCormick, called "the Galveston Giant" (an apposition that Jack was later to usurp), and won a ten-round decision over the veteran Sid Smith.

The black man was getting too good for local talent, promoters figured, so in 1901 they imported a fighter of some skill and experience to see if he could give Johnson a proper tussle. This was Joe Choynski, the West Coast champion. It seemed like a splendid opportunity for Johnson. If he could whip Choynski he would be on his way to fistic notoriety and might make a respectable amount of money in the ring, something no black heavyweight had ever done. And of all sports popular at the time, boxing was the only one in which blacks were permitted to compete against white men.

Johnson shortly learned he had set his sights too high. His vaunted defense was no protection against the veteran's pumping arms and iron fists, and in the third round the dark-haired San Franciscan struck him a left-hand blow on the temple—a sensitive point in any man—that knocked Johnson flat and left his head ringing. Choynski stood over him, ready to pounce the moment Johnson arose—but suddenly five Texas Rangers leapt into the ring, brandished revolvers and covered the fighters and the referee. They announced that the governor of Texas had ordered the principals arrested. Reinforcements sprang in, followed by the local sheriff. Johnson and Choynski surrendered and, engulfed by cheers and catcalls, were trundled off to the Galveston jail.

Johnson always had the happy faculty of making the best of adversity. Imprisonment did not upset him. He received three squares a day and found good company in Joe, who gave him boxing lessons during the exercise period in the prison yard. When reporters asked Choynski about Johnson's ability, they were informed that he might someday become champion—always assuming, of course, that he could lure the white titleholder into the ring.

On his release, Johnson headed for Chicago, at that time the city furnishing the most action for the heavyweights. Local talent included Jack Root, Peter Maher, Billy Stiff, Frank Childs, Marvin Hart, Tom Sharkey and Packy MacFarland. Johnson immediately got a job as Root's sparring partner but was discharged for being too clever with his fists. Fights were hard for him to get—he was black and he was dangerous in the ring—and he froze and starved on windblown streets of Chicago in the terrible winter of 1902. Frank Childs, a compassionate black man and fellow boxer, rescued Jack from dying a pauper's death in a Chicago gutter, but after Jack had warmed himself by Childs's stove and eaten a few meals, Frank abruptly threw him out to make room for a relative from Memphis. Once again the wind blasted through him as he shivered his way along the streets of the city. Then to his immense joy he found a nickel in his tattered pants. He burst into a saloon, slapped the nickel on the bar, sipped a beer and helped himself to all that the price of a beer entitled him to: pickles, cheese, sausage and pumpernickel. He feasted for nearly an hour, and a new man strode out to face the benumbing Chicago night.

But Johnson had had enough of Chicago and decided to move west. California might not provide him with a livelihood from fighting, but at least it would be warm. Jack arrived there after long, bone-shaking rides curled up under freight cars, outwitting railway guards and risking his life by dropping in on hobo jungles for a plate of Mulligan stew. Then fate threw Frank Childs into his lap. The two men fought a twenty-rounder in Los Angeles that was largely ignored by fans and the press. Childs would remember it, however. All the resentment Jack harbored for being thrown out of Childs's apartment into the wintry night gave his fury wings, and he cut Childs to pieces, meanwhile scoffing at his former benefactor's inability to find his target or avoid Johnson's bombardment. Making sure that Childs stayed erect until the punishment had been completely administered, Johnson jabbed with his left, moved forward, lowered his right arm and brought it up in his devastating uppercut. Childs went down and out and did not recuperate from his beating for weeks.

Johnson then served his apprenticeship by toppling over the massive Negro boxer known as Klondike (because he was not fazed by cold weather); knocking out Jack Jeffries, brother of the champion, with considerable relish; fighting two draws with the rugged veteran Hank Griffin; and earning a decision over the speedy George Gardner.

The last victory gleaned Johnson something of a reputation. Born in Ireland, Gardner had defeated stocky Frank Craig in England. (Craig had earlier beaten clever Kid McCoy.) In the United States, Gardner defeated Joe Walcott and Jack Root. He then claimed the world's light-heavyweight title, although the title meant little to Americans at that time—they identified with middleweights and heavyweights. Gardner had to make a payday, and so he consented to give Johnson a bout. The grinning Negro whose delight was in whipping Caucasian fighters did not train seriously for the fight, even though he was aware that a victory over Gardner would be a long step toward the title he really coveted. Nine days before the fight, Jack contracted an agonizing stomach ailment and could not hold down any food but biscuits and milk. In pain and weak from his diet, Jack fought a defensive battle for the first seven rounds, catching punches and slipping punches and accepting Gardner's rapierlike jabs in the face when his speed of hand played him false. As the rounds wore on Jack's confidence in his ability to endure increased, however, and he began driving home blows of his own. Gardner was the fastest boxer he had faced, but he was not a heavy man or a heavy hitter; one of Johnson's hooks or right crosses was equal to a dozen of Gardner's. In the twelfth round he struck the Irishman over the heart with a straight right that stopped him in his tracks and nearly toppled him over. The champion weathered subsequent attacks by retreating and covering his face with his hands and his body with his elbows as

Johnson stalked him. He finished the fight standing up, but there was no question about the decision. Johnson could lay claim to the world's light-heavyweight championship.

With his spirits at their zenith, Johnson pursued his quest. He beat two black fighters, Denver Ed Martin and the crafty Sam McVey. Then he traveled to Boston to whip a pair of whites, Sandy Ferguson and Joe Butler. He lost to Joe Jeannette, a polished black fighter, on a foul. The money rolled in and rolled out just as fast. Johnson was indulgent toward himself after so many years of harrowing privation, and he spent what he made on clothes, on champagne suppers for his swarm of girl friends, on presents for his favorites among the hangers-on that cluster around every winning prizefighter, on golden teeth of which he was inordinately proud. The latter, a unique trademark, lent elegance to the taunts that poured from his mouth when he was handily beating an opponent.

Like Peter Jackson before him, he traveled the country seeking a fight with the white champion—in this case, Jeffries. It was never forthcoming. The bout would not draw, he was told. Jeffries would demolish him in two rounds, he was assured. Holders of the most coveted title in sport simply did not risk their crowns against black men. That was tradition, but Johnson kept knocking at the sacred gates. He suffered a setback in 1904 when he lost to the relatively unknown Marvin Hart in San Francisco. At the age of twenty-six, Johnson was six feet one inch and weighed 210 pounds. He was at the height of his physical powers. It is unlikely that Hart would ever have consented to the bout if he had not known something.

Starting cautiously, as was his habit, Johnson let his opponent lead and countered with his biceps blow or moved away, peppering his opponent's nose with fast jabs. He quickly saw he had little to fear from Hart, and beginning in the sixth round he started to pummel him all over the ring. By the fifteenth round, moving at full speed, Johnson had cut Hart to ribbons—the Kentuckian's eyes were nearly swollen shut, his body was blotched with red and the area around his mouth and nose was puffed and bloody. Hart did not go down, however. Johnson stared at the referee, wondering why he did not stop the slaughter, for Hart could hardly defend himself. Then Hart suddenly recuperated. He began to attack Johnson in the body and did not pause until the twenty rounds of the fight were over. Johnson kept backing away or tried to clinch to avoid punishment, and the last rounds went to Hart. In spite of this Johnson was relatively unmarked, while Hart had suffered grisly wounds. There was no question but that Johnson should have gotten the decision, but the referee, Alex Greggains, awarded it to what was left of Hart. When Johnson complained, he was told that the referee thought he had loafed in the early rounds. There was no appeal, and the crowd was largely satisfied with the verdict. Johnson added this grievance to the many others he nurtured. Then Hart beat Root for the title that Jeffries had chosen to abandon, and Johnson grew even more bitter.

Hart was not the champion very long.

———————————

Tommy Burns, born Noah Brusso of French-Canadian stock in Hanover, Ontario, Canada, was a much better fighter than he has been given credit for. He was a short, extremely compact man with a reach that belied his height. Facially he resembled Napoleon Bonaparte, and his hair lay in triangular fashion over his forehead to add to the impression. The shortest of Queensberry heavyweight champions, Burns was five feet seven inches, and his best fighting weight was 175 pounds. He turned to boxing after acquiring a reputation in lacrosse and hockey. He soon showed himself to be quick on his feet, a wise ring general who was able to throw a powerful punch with either hand. Typical of determined men his size thrust up against taller, heavier opponents, he learned to absorb punishment stoically, accepting cuts and bruises in the hope that he could maneuver within range for close infighting, of which he was a master. His tongue was as vitriolic as Charlie Mitchell's.

He began professional fighting in 1900 as a lightweight, put away almost all opposition and in 1905, while in California, decided to pursue the largest prey, which was where the biggest money was. Hart, flushed from his victory over Root, knocked out a monster from Butte, Montana, named Pat Callaghan and figured he was ready for a second title defense. Of course he was not considering fighting any gentleman of color, such as Johnson, Sam Langford, Joe Jeannette or Sam McVey. Promoter Tom McCarey, after seeing Burns knock out Dave Barry in San Francisco, urged Burns to take on Hart for the championship. Aware of the disparity in their sizes and not yet confident of his ability to maul large opponents, Burns was hesitant until McCarey offered him fifteen thousand dollars—more money than Burns knew existed—for his appearance. Burns grabbed it.

On February 23, 1906, the two met in a sluggish match, with Jim Jeffries, grown somewhat fat, refereeing. Burns, pacing himself and holding back his most formidable punches, was content to outbox Hart so convincingly that Jeffries had no choice but to award him the title. Hart thereupon joined the Louisville police force. Johnson seethed.

Now began the great chase. As Burns worked to establish his right to the crown after so easily winning it, Johnson clamored for a chance to get in the same ring with him. He taunted Burns and insulted him. He gave notice to the world that Burns was afraid of him. Unheeding, Burns knocked out Bill Squires of Australia in a round, flattened Fireman Jim Flynn in fifteen and Joe Grim, "the India Rubber Baby," in three. He fought a draw with Philadelphia Jack O'Brien and then, in a second meeting, torpedoed O'Brien's claim to the championship belt by defeating him handily in twenty rounds. Burns then rid himself of Johnson's pestering by sailing to England, where he engaged Gunner Moir, the champion of that country. After seeing Moir box in an exhibition at the National Sporting Club in London, Burns rushed out to find a bookmaker and bet a fast two hundred pounds on himself. He toyed with the Gunner for nine rounds to give the swells in attendance a treat, and then put him away in the tenth. On St. Patrick's Day in Dublin, in 1908, he set a record of sorts by knocking out the Irish champion, Jem Roche, in eighty-eight seconds. In Paris he stopped a South African heavyweight, Jewey Smith, in five rounds and Bill Squires in eight. Johnson by this time had pursued Burns to England; so Australia suddenly seemed attractive, and Burns promptly placed half the world between himself and the black contender.

In Australia Burns put himself in the hands of Hugh D. "Huge Deal" McIntosh, a remarkable entrepreneur interested in promoting boxing in the Antipodes. McIntosh had been a bicycle racer, a boxer, a newspaper owner, a member of Parliament and a theatrical producer. An example of his enterprise was his buying up all the American and Australian flags in Australia before the arrival of a U.S. goodwill fleet during Christmas week of 1908. Store owners and citizens had to buy them from him at fairly steep prices if they wished to show their own goodwill. Guided by McIntosh, Burns beat his old friend Squires and Bill Lang, the Australian champion. Then came McIntosh's coup.

Knowing that the American fleet was about to arrive and aware that American sailors would be ravenous for an action-packed spectator sport in which an American was involved, McIntosh sounded out Burns on fighting Johnson. Australian papers were enthusiastic for the bout, and the public clamored to see someone who might put up a battle against the cocky little titleholder. Burns accepted—if McIntosh would pay him thirty-five thousand dollars. McIntosh said he would, though it was a preposterous sum to pay a fighter at the time. Then he cabled Johnson, who had just knocked out Ben Taylor in Plymouth in eight rounds. McIntosh offered Johnson five thousand dollars and expenses. Johnson accepted. He would have paid to be allowed in the ring.

The fight was to be held in a bowl-like stadium, built by McIntosh, on Rushcutter's Bay, outside of Sydney, on December 26, 1908. This was Boxing Day by British and Commonwealth custom, so named because it was the traditional time for householders to give Christmas boxes to tradesmen, servants and minor officials.

Johnson's gold teeth shone in happy expectation when he strode down the gangplank. He happily wagered on horse and dog races and went into casual training. Then for some reason—possibly he began to doubt his ability, under white man's rules, to take the crown—he turned morose and surly. First Johnson was afraid he would not be paid his share of the purse. McIntosh soothed him. The next thing that troubled him was the choice of referee. Many names were suggested, none satisfactory to Johnson; finally he chose McIntosh himself, who obtained Burns's approval. The promoter worried, then made a thorough study of Marquis of Queensberry rules. And Johnson stewed in his training camp because he had failed to receive a share of the film rights—another example of the white man's duplicity.

Burns was the favorite at odds of 7 to 4, and in the world's most intense betting community, eastern Australia, little Johnson money showed. Burns was amazingly confident. The police would of course stop the fight if one of the fighters had to be saved from a terrible beating; in such a case how then should the decision go? "If the fight is stopped, no matter when," the champion announced, "let the referee pick the winner. I don't want a no-contest decision." Hearing this, Johnson wondered what sort of decision the referee, who happened to manage the champion, would render. There were many imponderables to ruminate over as he tried to relax in the days and nights before the fight.

Every male in Sydney with the price of a ticket showed up for the fight, along with sundowners and diggers from the billabongs and outback. Twenty thousand fans crowded into the stadium, including Jack London, battler for the common man and a worrier over what would happen if a black man took the title. At least forty thousand more milled and pushed and traded opinions in the streets outside. In the ring, Johnson smiled at Burns. It was not an ominous smile, but Johnson's thoughts were unfriendly. The man had led him on a very long chase. In keeping with his reputation as a mouth-fighter, Burns had insisted to the press and his cronies that Johnson was yellow, had impugned his parentage and had thought up a number of racial slurs.

At one in the afternoon, the sun beamed down as the pair nodded to the referee's instructions, retired to their corners and awaited the gong. The gong exploded, and the world stood on its toes. Curtain finally up. Johnson sprang across the ring, measured his man with a few extended jabs, clinched to determine Burns's strength, feinted with a long left, then brought up his right under Burns's chin. Burns flew up in the air and toppled with his back to the floor. His head hit with a popping sound that could be heard all over the arena. The crowd, stunned, rose with a roar. Burns was implored to get up by men who were risking seven pounds to win four; shaking his head, at the count of eight he did.

Burns's only tactic, because of Johnson's size and reach, was to move in close to the black man and pump home blows to his body. But Johnson, who relished any aggressive move on the part of an opponent, met his charge, fended him off with jabs, feinted with the left hook again and smashed a right against the Canadian's jaw. Burns recoiled as though his head had been partly severed, then retaliated with a hard body blow of his own that Johnson accepted with a smile. Now he began to taunt Burns. "Poor little Tommy," he said, his voice carrying beyond the ringside seats. "Who told you you were a fighter?" Burns advanced again, his lips moving in an insult, to be met by a series of hammerlike blows on his face and numbing ones on his arms. At the bell, Burns wandered to his corner, rolling his head to place his cerebrum where it belonged. Johnson pranced back to his own corner.

As the second round began, Johnson stood in mid-ring and beckoned Burns to come within range. He talked a little. When Burns accepted the invitation he was struck with a quick left-right in Peter Jackson style that sent him to his knees. He was up in an instant, mouth-

ing persiflage of his own. In a clinch Burns shouted in Johnson's ear, "Come on and fight, nigger!" But it was Burns who was doing the holding. Johnson threw him off and Burns skipped about in unaccustomed defensive postures. "Let's fight, you yellow gray man!" Johnson riposted. "You been runnin' away from me long enough. Now I caught you. Show me if you got any guts." Burns was too weary to react to Johnson's taunts, and the round ended quietly.

The third round saw a different Burns—chin ensconced behind his left shoulder, crouching so low that his only vulnerable spot was the top of his Napoleonic head. But suddenly he raised up and startled Johnson with a sharp right to the chin. The 7-to-4 men inhaled deep breaths, and their hopes in the champion rekindled.

Johnson's imaginative vocabulary took over in the fourth, a counterpoint to the damage he was inflicting. Burns's left eye began to swell, and blood dripped from his mouth. When the two clinched, Johnson left no doubt as to who was the stronger man, flinging Burns from him the way a man in temper flings away an importuning beggar.

In the fifth, Burns, miraculously rejuvenated, flew at Johnson and slammed a series of pistonlike blows at Johnson's body. Johnson did not react as expected. He poked fun at Burns's lunges, holding him off with his left and hurling imprecations as he practiced feints with his right.

Johnson was all business in the sixth, as though he had to put his personal stamp of utter superiority on the white upstart who claimed the world's heavyweight championship. He rocked Burns's head back with the long snakelike left—the "sneaky" punch that landed before it was seen and that carried so much power. He aimed the next punch for Burns's swollen eye, redirected it toward the body. It sank in, making Burns wince, and then Johnson followed with a straight right to Burns's mouth. Dramatically vocal, Johnson stood in the middle of the ring, challenging anybody, challenging he knew not who, and urged the damaged champion to come toward him. Burns cautiously advanced.

Splat! The right-hand punch that sent Burns rocking and reeling against the ropes in the fourteenth was no ordinary blow. It carried all the savagery and venom that had been stored up in Johnson for years, not only against Burns for leading him on the long chase, insulting him for his color and calling him coward, but against all white men. It was for the years of humiliation he had suffered because of his pigment, the years of subjugation his race had had to put up with: Moving off the sidewalk when a white man strolled by. Tipping the cap to show deference. Segregated schools, stores, railway depots, restaurants. The memory of the command, "Shuck down!" The stigma of being thought untouchable. The danger of being lynched. The scarcity of decent jobs and the limited chances for advancement. Some white men spat when they said the word "Nigra." Well, the Nigra had spat back. It was a punch that shook the world.

Police swarmed into the ring to save Burns from total destruction. Yet Burns, as they held him back, still screamed vilifications through torn lips and swore he could go on fighting. No one can deny his courage. The weight of the world had lain on his shoulders, and he felt a responsibility (as Jeffries, goaded on by world opinion, would later). Johnson was awarded the decision.

Burns was never much of a fighter after that. He blew his thirty thousand dollar purse at the Sydney racetracks and later turned preacher, one of his sermons being on his experience with Johnson. "Race prejudice was on my mind," he would declare. "The idea of a black man challenging me was beyond enduring. Hatred made me tense. It wasn't Jack Johnson who beat Tommy Burns but Tommy Burns who beat himself."

Now began a pair of parades on collision course. One was led by Johnson, who strutted about, grinning at the world and its rules for black men, his gold-headed cane flourished like that of a French monarch, his flashy clothes adrip with gems and jewels, with his entourage of frail, pale, blonde white ladies (forget the reputation of most of them), his stable of fast cars (at a time when most whites could not afford even one car), his successful stage appearances.

The other parade was that of the White Hopes, eager for a chance to "whack the nigger" and make a fortune for so doing. They were advertised for in the papers and dredged from every coal mine, farm, ranch, city slum, locomotive cab, carnival, hobo jungle and blacksmith shop in the land. Burns searched for some. Walter "Good Time Charlie" Freedman scoured China. The best of them were Luther McCarty, Arthur Pelkey, Gunboat Smith (so called because of the astonishing size of his feet), Tom Cowler, Frank Moran (who had a terrific punch he called "Mary Ann"), Philadelphia Jack O'Brien, Al Kaufman, Carl Morris, Boer Rodel, Tom Kennedy, Billy Wells, Fred Fulton and Al Palzer. Some of the White Hopes more or less eliminated themselves, knocking out one another. Black Hopes like Sam Langford and Joe Jeannette discouraged some. Pelkey killed possibly the best of them when he hit McCarty with a left to the head while McCarty was looking the other way. Suffering from an earlier injury, McCarty died from a brain hemorrhage. Pelkey was no good afterwards, either. Johnson eliminated some of them himself—Victor McLaglen (later to star in *The Informer*), O'Brien and Kaufman—all the while training on booze and in general living high.

One man nearly got him. He was, curiously enough, not a heavyweight but a middleweight, Stanley Ketchel, "the Michigan Assassin," probably the greatest fighter, pound for pound, who ever lived. Born Stanislaus Kiecal of Polish parentage in Grand Rapids, Michigan, Ketchel ran away from the farm chores he hated and hoboed his way west, learning his trade as he went and enjoying it. He was a devastating hitter with both hands, and the majority of his fights, whether in the ring or a saloon, usually ended in fast knockouts; he had not the patience of Johnson nor the temperament of the gentle giant we will meet later. He won the middleweight title by beating Billy Papke, "the Illinois Thunderbolt," in 1908, then lost it to Papke in a strange way. With

Jim Jeffries refereeing, Papke forgot to shake hands at the bell and got in a first shot to Ketchel's throat before Ketchel thought of defending himself. It won the fight for the Thunderbolt then and there, since Ketchel was hardly able to suck in oxygen and for a while thereafter was an easy target for the Papke's ramming blows. He went down four times in the first round; in succeeding rounds his nose was smashed and his eyes were cut. He endured, however, unable to see and groggy from blows to the head, until the twelfth, when Jeffries mercifully stopped the fight. The beating he took would have meant the end of the career of anyone else, but the Assassin came back for a return bout ten weeks later. Springing from his corner at the bell he gave Papke a beating that virtually retired him from the ring.

The Johnson-Ketchel fight, held in Colma, California, on October 16, 1909, was supposed to make money for everybody. With motion pictures on nearly everyone's mind, it seemed logical and fair that the current heavyweight champion and the great middleweight should make a film. A commercial film not being very profitable if it lasts only a few minutes, the principals arranged among themselves that the bout should last at least a half hour. The heavyweight would knock Ketchel out at the end of that time, and profits would roll in for years to come.

The fight began with Johnson blithely countering the Michigander's charges. The pair pirouetted around like a ballet act; there was much movement, little damage. Then in the twelfth Stanley saw a way to earn permanent fame. He forgot about the cameras, forgot about the agreement and shot across the ring at Johnson, swinging the overhand right that had pulverized so many opponents. Hit in the jaw, Johnson went back and sat down abruptly, as anyone would when taken by such surprise. A less tough man would have found his chin broken and might have disappeared from the scene. But Johnson arose almost immediately, a black god of vengeance, and lent support to the apothegm that a good big man can always beat a good little man. He rushed

across the ring and smashed Ketchel in the face with a straight right. It was so hard a blow that four of the Assassin's teeth were sheared off, and Ketchel was out for the night. There is a canard that the four teeth were stuck to Johnson's glove when he withdrew it. The fact is, though, that Johnson was not only a fine defensive fighter; when he wanted to hit, he could *hit*. The double-X did not increase his affection for the white man. Ketchel met a strange end. A ladies' man, he was shot dead by a jealous farmhand, Walter A. Dipley, the following year.

Curiously enough, at this time the three best fighters in the world, after Johnson, were black men. They were Joe Jeannette, Sam McVey and Sam Langford. Most white fighters drew the color line against them; hence they constantly fought one another. If by some chance they were allowed in a ring with a white man, it seemed politic for them either to lose or at least not to tear their opponent to ribbons. Because most white men refused to fight him, Jeannette exiled himself to Paris. Frenchmen were becoming avid fans of the sport and gladly paid to see two skillful black men fight. In one encounter in Paris a record was made by Jeannette and McVey: There were thirty-eight knockdowns in the fight, Jeannette hitting the floor twenty-seven times and McVey eleven. Jeannette won the fight.

The best of the three nonchampions was Sam Langford, who some say was better than Johnson. But boxing is a funny business, a showman's business, and it did not seem profitable to Johnson, at the height of his earning powers, to grant a title bout to Langford. Langford, born in Weymouth, Nova Scotia, on March 24, 1886, was a short, squat, gnomelike man with an incredibly long reach and incredible strength. Never attending school a day in his life, he ran away from home at the age of ten and worked in a logging camp, in a brickyard and as a porter in a Boston cafe. After he beat up someone called "the Champion of Cambridge Street," he took up fighting as an amateur. This provided him with some sort of income, since the watches he won could be sold back to the donor.

Langford's natural style and ferocity in the ring found an admirer in Joe Woodman, who ran a gym in Boston, and so he was granted a series of bouts with whites and blacks. His zeal was his downfall. He beat up everyone in sight and caused white opponents to hide. In his boxing career of twenty-one years he wandered around the civilized world fighting anyone who would get into the ring with him, and he beat nearly all. As a lightweight he beat the great Joe Gans (later the world lightweight champion) and George "Elbows" McFadden, who would hit you with his elbow if he missed with his glove. Weighing only 160 pounds when he fought heavyweights, Langford beat O'Brien, George Godfrey, Fireman Jim Flynn, Gunboat Smith, "the Hussar," and Tiger Smith. Like many another person, one supposes, he happened to be born at the wrong time. In a later era he might well have been the world's heavyweight champion.

Not long after their first and only fight, which Johnson won by outpointing Langford in twenty rounds, the two happened to meet in a South Philadelphia saloon. Langford threw down the gauntlet to the new champion. "Jack," stated the Tar Baby, "you either give me a match or I'm goin' to take my coat off and beat the stuffin' out of you in front of all your buddies here. And they can tell everybody how I did it." Lighting up the room with a banjo smile, Johnson replied, "Sam, of course I'll give you a fight. I'm expectin' a call from San Francisco about a fight there. But if you'll wait five minutes we'll sit down and talk over arrangements about a fight between you and me. Don't worry— you'll get your shot at the title." Johnson left. Langford waited the requested five minutes, then ten, then twenty, then thirty. It struck him finally that Johnson would not come back at all. Langford felt like a jilted bride. One could say that Johnson was afraid of Langford; or perhaps he was too shrewd a businessman to fight him. Certainly he had everything to lose and nothing to gain in such a bout. Living was too easy— he was making $2,500 a week for his theatrical performances—and the pres-

tige he carried as champion was gaining him many new friends.

Langford, always broke, always begging for fights, kept plugging away at his trade and was good enough, when well past his prime in 1923, to beat Andrea Balsa and so become the heavyweight champion of both Mexico and Spain.

Finally the Caucasians did find a White Hope, invincible Jim Jeffries, who finally acceded to the blandishments of the press and his friends and particularly to the plea of Jack London: "You've got to come back, Jeff!"

The man who brought off the encounter was George L. "Tex" Rickard. Tex, later to become the world's greatest fight promoter, had a checkered career. He was born and raised in Clay County, Missouri, on January 2, 1871. The family's farm was next to that of Mrs. Zerelda James, the mother of Frank and Jesse. George's sleep as a youngster was sometimes disturbed by the horses and gunshots of posses galumphing by, and he saw men lynched and murdered by the dozen. Human life did not mean a great deal. As a result of his early conditioning, George dabbled in many fields (including running a cattle ranch in Brazil), but he was primarily a gambler and chance-taker, one of the greatest the world has ever seen. He was a prodigy trail cowboy at the age of eleven, and he stayed a prodigy throughout his life. At twenty-one he was a town marshal. He trekked to the Yukon Valley before the Klondike Gold Rush of 1904, prospected, made a fortune and lost it. It seemed more sensible to him thereafter to cater to the miners' yen for excitement than to compete with them in their panning, and so he opened The Northern in Nome, reputed to be the only honest gambling saloon in Alaska. Rickard acquired, in any case, an invaluable reputation for honesty, though he was not above pulling sly tricks when necessity demanded.

His first boxing promotion involved Joe Gans and Battling Nelson. This was in 1906 and came about by accident. He had dropped down to Goldfield, Nevada, which was running out of gold.

Business was slow.

"Why don't we put on a fight," one of the saloonists asked, "and bring in some customers?"

Rickard mulled it over and went into action. He had foresight, patience and nerve. He wired the lightweight champion, Joe Gans, who was black, and the Nordic challenger, Battling Nelson, that he would proffer thirty thousand dollars to the principals if they would fight in Goldfield. The distribution of the pie was to be settled by the fighters or their managers. Rickard had going for him, in the classic time of the big con, the mark and the hustler, an immense respect for his word. If Rickard said a deal was set, it was set. Showman to the core, Rickard backed up his offer with a display of thirty thousand dollars in gold pieces in the windows of gambling houses—a different house each day. Unbelievers gaped. Business in Goldfield boomed. Receipts for the fight—seventy-eight thousand dollars—

were the highest ever totaled for a fight between lightweights.

The fight was a bloody one. Gans, weakened by having to make weight, managed to punch Nelson around the ring for thirty rounds. Then the hard-headed Nelson's strategy asserted itself. The Durable Dane endured the beating and came back strong in the thirtieth round. He smashed the black man from ringpost to ringpost, but Gans, even though defenseless, did not go down. The pattern continued: Nelson trying to floor his opponent, the black man stubbornly managing to stay upright. Then Gans, summoning mysterious reserves, began to belabor Nelson again. In the forty-first round Nelson became desperate. The fight was not proceeding according to plan. Gans was snapping jabs in his face, and Nelson's best blows had no effect. In the forty-second round Nelson clinched and smashed blows at Gans's groin. He was warned by referee George Siler. As the warning

Jack Johnson and Jim Jeffries sign for their historic struggle on July 4, 1910. Jeffries is on the far right. Standing behind the black champion is "Tex" Rickard, whose flair and gambler's instinct saw this contest as the way to make a million dollars.

179

was being given, Nelson shot a hard right below the belt. Gans fell in great pain. Siler pushed Nelson to his corner and, returning to the fallen champion, raised his arm. Gans was winner on a foul.

The fight showed Rickard two things: There was a large amount of money to be made in promoting fights, and a heavyweight white-black fight promised a drama that no other could match. The casting was easy. There was the black heavyweight champion, threatening the white race with his airs and his flouting of his coloredness; and there was the former white champion, who had tossed away his title like Prinny scattering largess to the crowds cluttering Bow Street, and who was thought to be the most invincible fighter who had ever lived. The match seemed as natural as that between Desdemona and Othello. Rickard was not the only promoter who saw the possibilities; he had powerful rivals who gaped at the potential profits in it. But he was the man who arranged it. How? By the simple device of backing up his talents as a salesman with something tangible. Anybody can *talk* money; Rickard produced it.

Rickard's great talent, actually, was being able to borrow money without furnishing collateral. He found a backer in Thomas F. Cole, a Minnesota mining millionaire with whom he had done business. Then, pockets loaded with thousand-dollar bills, he entrained for Pittsburgh, where Johnson was doing his theatrical bit—talking about the Burns fight and about outrunning a kangaroo, skipping rope, shadowboxing and playing the bass viol. A high spender, Johnson was broke. "This is the situation, Mr. Tex," he said. "No matter what the papers say about the big money for the fight, nothin' is set for damn all. What would be useful to me, Mr. Tex, is about twenty-five hundred. To settle up some bills and things." Without a blink, Rickard rolled out two thousand-dollar bills and one five hundred, and the wide-eyed Johnson accepted them. No signature, no handshake, no obligation was demanded; but Rickard the psychologist had Johnson in his pocket.

He knew, from Johnson's estimate,

that the bidding price of the fight would be one hundred thousand dollars. A meeting was held at the Meyer Hotel in Hoboken to determine who would promote "the battle of the century"— though it was kind of early in the century to make that assertion. (The meeting was held in Hoboken because the law in New York contended that not only was boxing illegal but that *talk* about promoting a fight was illegal.) Robert F. Murphy, the amiable Broadwayite, acted as sachem. On hand were Fat Jack Gleason; Eddie Graney, built like a balloon; Uncle Tom McCarey of Los Angeles; Phil King, representing "Huge Deal" McIntosh of Sydney; Li'l Arthur, teeth agleam; moustached George Little, Johnson's manager; Sam Berger, the lightweight fighter and clever businessman who represented Jeffries; the press and sportsmen, and slim Tex Rickard, the hard-eyed gambler from the Klondike and points west. Jeffries himself wasn't there.

There was a lot of envelope talk as the bids, all of them huge, were made. Graney, a referee with ambitions, offered the fighters 80 per cent of the gate receipts as against a $70,000 guarantee, plus all film rights. Gleason offered a choice of $125,000 with no film rights, or $75,000, plus two-thirds of the film rights. McIntosh offered $55,000 for the fight if it was staged in America—but $100,000, plus a fourth of the film rights, if it was held in Australia. McCarey's offer was: "On behalf of the Pacific Club of Los Angeles. I offer the entire gate receipts and fifty per cent of the movie rights, or a guaranteed purse of $100,000 with fifty percent of the movie rights." It all seemed very tempting to Little and Berger. How could Tex top these bids?

He handed Murphy an envelope, saying, "Be careful with this one, Murphy. It's got some real money in it." Murphy ripped it open and spilled out the contents: A certified check for five thousand dollars, and fifteen thousand-dollar bills. Johnson's eyes bugged. Seeing the reaction, the other promoters knew they were in trouble. When Rickard's message was read, they knew they were licked. The message was: "We offer the fighters the price guarantee of $101,000 with 66⅔ per cent of the movie rights. The bout will be staged on July 4 in California, Nevada or Utah. In addition to the $20,000 contained in the envelope, $20,000 will be deposited sixty days before the fight and an additional $50,000 forty-eight hours before the encounter." Johnson nodded, and the following day the transaction was finalized. Rickard would be the promotor.

Then Tex made the biggest error of his career. He let Jack Gleason talk him into putting the fight on in San Francisco. The governor of California, the Honorable James J. Gillett, promised that the fight would take place there, no matter how much smoke the reformers made. The law stated that "only sparring exhibitions" were allowed, but everybody knew this was no sparring match. The rumors began to spread. The most pervasive and disturbing was that the match was fixed. Johnson would lie down for the white man and pick up a boodle.

Then the reformers' voices were heard. Governor Gillett was besieged, assaulted, engulfed, annoyed by letters, phone calls and telegrams. White against black in the ring was unnatural —especially *this* black; white women would not be safe in their beds, and so on. Gillett, with his eyes on more fascinating political spoils, threw the fight out of California. Rickard stewed and threatened to sue but realized he was overmatched. The governor turned righteous suddenly and expounded for the press: "If Tex Rickard is looking for a fight with me he will get a bigger one than advertised for the Fourth of July. We've had enough of prizefights and prizefight promoters. They've been breaking the law long enough and we'll have no more of it. When the fighters lick the state of California they can go ahead and lick each other, but not before."

Now there had to be a change of venue. The money accompanying ticket orders, which had been coming in from all over the world, had to be returned. Rickard's half-built thirty-thousand-dollar arena on an empty lot on the corner of Market and Sixth streets had to be abandoned. The governor's decision was an expensive one for the

promoter.

And the two principals, what of them? Neither was doing much training as rumors of a fix spread throughout the city. Jeffries was grumpy in his camp at Rowardenna, high in the mountains, trying to get into shape by letting his sparring partners hit him rather than by throwing punches himself. Sometimes he would just wander off to fish. Johnson's was a good-natured camp with plenty of clowning and singing. Johnson himself played the bass viol at the choral sessions. It seemed to the press that he was irresponsible. But he was just magnificently confident.

Governor Denver S. Dickerson of Nevada promised Rickard that the fight could be held in that state without any fuss, and three desert towns—Ely, Goldfield and Reno—pleaded for it. Tex chose Reno because of its spider web of railroad junctions. "There'll Be a Hot Time in the Old Town Tonight!" blared through trumpets and tubas when Tex arrived, and the air rang with hearty greetings from his friends of gold-mining days. A twenty-thousand-seat stadium was miraculously built for him in two weeks. But again pressure was applied by reformers for the governor to stop the fight. For his part, Dickerson did not want his state to bear the stigma of a major fixed fight. Somewhat worried, the governor approached Tex and asked if the fight was on the level. Tex assured him it was. "Then that's good enough for me," said Dickerson, and he refused to come to heel for the reformers.

Reno was a gaudy circus in that summer of 1910. Everyone who was anyone showed up: Cincinnati Slim, the sterling bank robber; Won Let, the number-one executioner of the Hip Sing Tong, who had already tucked away thirty Chinamen in hatchet wars; Jack London and Watertank Willie; Indians, miners, ladies there for divorces, cowboys, Mexicans, swells, gamblers, pickpockets, the great and the near-great. Four private railway cars were hired by Payne Whitney to transport Wall Street moguls there.

The city was a hustlers' and a thieves' paradise. Gutters were filled with cheap watches filched by the pickpockets in attendance, who did not think them worth fencing. The best way to carry money, if you wanted to keep it, was to stuff it under porous plaster around the chest. The crowd was a Jeffries crowd, raucous, boisterous, filled with zeal. The bands were applauded when they played "All Coons Look Alike to Me." Bookies shouted their odds, with few Johnson takers—though Pullman porters on the trains that staggered into the city to unload their jovial passengers made quite a cleaning. The cry, "Jeff, it's up to you!" was heard all over the city. And crowds! The biggest little city in the world was inundated by fight fans. They slept in hotel lobbies, in the halls, in the bathrooms. They lined up patiently for hours outside restaurants waiting for the simplest fare. They dropped off to sleep in the bars, at the gambling tables, in the bagnios. And they discussed the fight. How could Jeffries lose? True, he had burgeoned up to three hundred pounds; but he had taken seventy pounds off by attending the Carlsbad Spa in Bohemia, where he had met Edward VII, who had predicted that he would have no trouble with the black fellow. And he had in his corner an amazing array of helpers. They included Jim Corbett, the chief of staff; Farmer Burns, the wrestler; Joe Choynski, who was acting as one of Jeff's sparring partners, and Bob Armstrong, the Negro who had been indirectly responsible for Jeff's getting the title in the first place and who, during the fight, was to act as a kind of punkah wallah to keep the sun from attacking Jeff's head.

Tex had invited all the great fighters to come to the event gratis, and they swarmed into town by the carload. Most of them were not pleased with Jeffries' training methods. Ketchel was escorted out of the ex-champion's camp by Farmer Burns for criticizing them. John L. Sullivan, writing for *The New York Times,* said the fight looked like a frame-up and as a result nearly got into a battle with his old friend Corbett.

Jack Johnson loved to perform. Even while in training for Jeffries, a bout threatened by racial violence, Johnson was always ready with a quick smile.

(Corbett's ghost-writer sent out daily lies about Jeff's fine condition but put all the money he had on Johnson.) Langford was there, pestering Johnson for a fight, but that was the only gravel in Johnson's craw. Jack was getting into fine shape, impressing Dickerson and other notables with his speedy hands and footwork. Yet most fans still picked Jeffries out of sentiment. Even Rex Beach, the outdoors author, wrote that he could not imagine a man as well-built and strong as Jeffries falling down defeated.

On July 4, 1910, a blazingly hot day, Johnson looked radiant as he entered the ring, brushing off the insults and jeers of the fans like a man good-naturedly shooing gnats. Jeffries by contrast looked drawn and haggard when he marched down the aisle, and he was glum as the pair stood in the center of the ring listening to the straw-hatted Rickard's instructions. (Rickard had been chosen as referee by the two fighters and his own financial backers.)

To the dismay and shock of most of the crowd, which had bet heavily on Jeffries, the Boilermaker was helpless against the black man. He simply could not find his target. Sometimes fighting erect and sometimes in his crouch, always looking clumsy as he moved forward, he had his blows slipped or blocked and then received terrific counters in return. As the fight wore on, he took a terrific beating around the face, and he became more sluggish-looking as the fight progressed. Corbett was screaming insults at Johnson to distract him, but the black man had the leisure time to smile and deliver repartee of his own. "How do you like this jab, Mr. Jim?" he would call, pecking at the Boilermaker's nose. He kept taunting Jeffries, too. When the latter tried to clinch, Jack would say, "Now stop lovin' me like that, Mr. Jeff," and either wrestle him around the ring or smash his face with three or four quick jabs. Once he leaned over the ropes and remarked to Sullivan, "Captain John, I thought this fellow could *hit!*" Jeffries fans got their only satisfaction in the eleventh when, face puffed and bleeding, the Boilermaker made a desperate rush and landed a left and right to Johnson's body.

A yell of anticipation arose, but the punches did not bother Jack, and the crowd realized it could only wait for the idol to fall.

The end came in the fifteenth. After a clinch, Jack flashed out a one-two that struck Jeffries on the chin and made him stagger back. In an instant Johnson was on him—lefts and rights pumped to body and head that had Jeff reeling. Another quick series sent him down. The audience stood up and roared its apprehension. Jeff was lying between the top and middle ropes, partly hanging over the ring apron. Looking dazed, he got up on one knee as Rickard counted. He was up and as quickly down again as Johnson pounced like a tiger. "Stop it! Stop it!" cried the audience to Rickard. "Don't let him be knocked out!" They also shouted imprecations at Jeffries' opponent. Jeff staggered about the ring, assaulted by additional short, chopping blows. Again he was sent sprawling between the ropes. At the count of seven, one of his seconds illegally placed a foot inside the ring. Rickard saw it and raised Johnson's arm in triumph. It was clear, though, that Jeffries could not have gotten up till long after the ten-count. The black man had proved himself better than the white man's best.

The victory gave black persons' spirits a lift and unleashed the smoldering resentment they had held for decades against their overseers. Riots broke out like measles all over the land, almost the moment after Rickard raised Johnson's hand in victory. *"Après moi le déluge,"* the king of promoters might have ruefully said. After viewing the national carnage, Rickard swore he would never promote a fight between a white man and a Negro again—and he never did.

In Keystone, West Virginia, Negroes exultantly took possession of the town. In Pueblo, New Mexico, every policeman in town was rousted out to restrain the rioting at the Bessemer Steel Works. Macon, Georgia, Negroes were so boisterous in celebrating Johnson's victory that the constabulary deputized loyal whites to tone down the disturbances. In Mounds, Illinois, Negroes with illegally obtained firearms shot up the town to express their joy. In Wilmington, Delaware, a passive white man was attacked by a gang of Negroes and sliced with a razor.

The blacks did not have everything their own way. "Let's lynch the first nigger we meet!" cried a tough outside a saloon at Eighth Avenue near 135th Street in New York City. A crowd of militant and slightly soused Caucasians loudly supported the suggestion. They seized a Negro who was passing by in his auto and severely beat him up before he was rescued by the police. The Pearl Button Gang of 99th Street and Columbus Avenue smashed in the heads of Negroes who lived in nearby tenements. Two Negroes in Charleston, Missouri, charged with the murder of a white man, were forcibly released from jail and summarily lynched by a white mob. There was talk of burning the Negro section of Charleston, but cooler heads prevailed.

Because of the deaths and injuries, Congress thereupon passed what might be called the Johnson Law. Fearful that films of the fight would again stir up trouble, legislation was hastily passed prohibiting interstate passage of fight films. Johnson figured the ban cost him about $500,000.

Still, it was a good payday for both men. Johnson received 60 per cent of the purse ($60,600); plus a bonus of $10,000 for lending his signature to the contract; plus $50,000 for his share (one-third) of the movie rights. Jeffries received 40 per cent of the purse ($40,400); plus a bonus of $10,000; plus $50,000 for his share (one-third) of the movie rights. The reason that Johnson's share of the motion-picture fee was smaller than Jeffries was that, when the dickering was being done with the producer's agent, Jack was involved in a high-stakes dice game. He was too involved in making his point to ask what Jeffries' share was. Altogether, Jeffries realized a total of $192,066 for the fight— far and away more than he had ever earned previously. Later he would say the beating he took was not worth it.

Pockets jingling, Johnson continued his flamboyant ways out of the ring and his insolently efficient ways in it. He wore a blue beret and smoked cigars in a long holder. He established the Café de Champion in Chicago and catered to customers of all persuasions, drawing no color line. He sipped vintage wine through a straw. He bought more cars and drove faster. He bought a sizable home for his mother in Chicago. He clowned through a fight with Jack O'Brien because he knew no decision would be given, and he half-derided the fans for attending. In 1911 and 1912 he tested the patience of the white man; part of the test in 1911 was his marrying the first of his three white wives, Etta Duryea, in Pittsburgh.

The year 1913 was a good one for Krupp and other munitions makers, but a bad one for Johnson. He ran into a series of disasters in this country and abroad that would have given a lesser man pause. He tried to smuggle in a diamond necklace from England which the Federal government confiscated and sold at auction for two thousand dollars. He had to pay damages to a lady theatregoer in Chicago when his punching bag came loose from its moorings and struck her in the face. (She asked for twenty-five thousand dollars but was awarded only a tenth of that.) Trouble continued abroad. He was arrested for swearing on a busy English street. He was fined for stopping traffic on another one by appearing in one of his gorgeous roadsters. Thought a bit much for a black man, he was greeted with boos when he appeared in a box at Eustice Music Hall in London. *The New York Times,* after examining the dispatches in London papers, called him "this sorry hero" in an editorial. (The Marquis of Queensberry, a relative of John Sholto Douglas, defended him in a letter to *The Daily Express,* asserting that it was all right for a black man to fight a white man or marry a white woman. He pleaded that "fair play" be shown Johnson.) He had financial problems in America: One of his autos, his safe and the fixtures of his Chicago café were seized by the sheriff to satisfy a judgment of $5,621 obtained against him by a brewery whose beer he had been dispensing without paying for it. He was banned from O'Connell's Gym in Chicago—the most popular place for pugilists to train—because of his carryings-on. The fighters did not want him there. He wept when he got the news. He caught pneumonia and nearly died. And Etta Duryea Johnson committed suicide.

The tale is one of horror. After a party at their home she suggested that Johnson drop off some of the guests at the depot. Jack rocketed down and back in his roadster and on his return was startled to see a crowd and police wagons outside his front door. Their faces, he saw in the lamplight, bore expressions of concern and shock. Police were threading their way through the crush. "For the love of God, what's happened?" he cried, knocking citizens to one side as he pushed his way to the door. He ran upstairs to the bedroom, wide-eyed and panting, full of premonition, terror on his face. There was a doctor by the bed, and policemen stood silent around the room. The pillows were drenched with blood. Etta's face—what remained of it—was a ghastly white.

Johnson staggered about, unable to absorb the new reality. The police, through respect or awe, left him to his own resources. Finally he sank into a chair, a defeated heavyweight. Etta had shot herself with a revolver. Part of her head was torn away—but she was still alive. An ambulance came to the front door, and attendants pushed their way through what seemed like half of Chicago to bring a stretcher up the stairs. Etta was taken to the hospital, and Jack sat by, head bowed in grief, tears streaming down his face, until the last flicker of life departed.

At the inquest he revealed that it was not only Etta who had entertained suicide; twice she had prevented her occasionally despondent husband from killing himself. Once he had tried to choke himself in a hotel room, but she had stopped him. Later he would write in his autobiography: "She was murdered by the world, by spiteful tongues, by my enemies, by race hatred. She paid the penalty of my being the heavyweight champion of the world."

Johnson's grief and shock over the tragedy did not prevent him from marrying Lucille Cameron of Minneapolis three months later, in spite of the violent objections of her mother, who came to Chicago to halt the marriage, and of a mulatto lady named Adah Banks, who shot Johnson in the foot out of pique over his attentions to Lucille. The girl had come to Chicago in a spirit of adventure. She saw Johnson in his saloon, touched his arm and asked him if he needed a secretary. Nothing loath, Johnson accepted, and the young lady lived at the nearby house of Jack Curley, the boxing and wrestling promoter, when she was not taking care of Johnson's correspondence.

Chicago's reformers had now focused their main attention on Johnson and his misdeeds. His wife's suicide, his preference for escorting white ladies, his flouting of rules and mores laid down by the white Establishment, his having beaten up and taunted Jim Jeffries—these wicked acts and others earned him a great deal of hatred. The Chicago *Inter-Ocean* stirred up a little trouble for him when it editorialized: "Popular indignation over the numerous outrages on public morals by Jack Johnson, the Negro prizefighter, has reached such a stage that it has become dangerous for him to walk the public streets." On the North Side a crowd hanged a dummy labeled "Johnson," and some members held up a large sign that said, "If only we had a real Negro." Even Booker T. Washington, the educator who was a recognized spokesman for blacks, put him down. "Jack Johnson has harmed rather than helped the race," he stated in a speech delivered at the Detroit Y.M.C.A. "I wish to state emphatically that his actions do not meet my approval, and I'm sure they do not meet the approval of the colored race."

Johnson continued to act up, and the country flexed its muscles and devised a legal solution. The Mann (White Slavery) Act of 1912 was not passed specifically to nail Johnson, but that was what laid him low.

In the first decade of the twentieth century, a vigorous campaign against prostitution was being waged by various civic groups, vice commissions, citizens' committees and the American Hygiene Association. U.S. Congressman James Robert Mann responded to their outcry by fostering a Federal law that placed severe penalties on persons involved in interstate or foreign transportation of ladies for immoral purposes. At the time, prostitutes frequently crossed borders from places of plentiful supply to places of urgent demand, generally in a westward direction. Mann was so zealous in his efforts to prohibit this traffic that in 1913 he publicly scolded President Wilson, the U.S. Attorney General and the Commissioner of Immigration for undercutting the Department of Justice by failing to prosecute a person of political influence on a white slavery charge.

On November 7, 1912, a Federal grand jury charged Johnson with violating the Mann Act, with Belle Schreiber of Pittsburgh as the victim (though God knows she was willing). Judge Kenesaw Mountain Landis, who was later to save baseball after the Black Sox scandal, set the wheels of justice in motion. He dispatched a posse of detectives to the Cafe de Champion, where, as Johnson wept, handcuffs were snapped on him. Taken into custody, he was freed on thirty thousand dollars bail. The next day, however, Judge Landis had second thoughts, and Johnson was taken back to the jailhouse, bond or no. Despite his shackles and attendants, he got in one good kick at the press and photographers who greeted him at the door. Placed all alone in a cell, he shouted defiantly for candles and wine, but was served up only candles.

His attorney, Benjamin Bachrach, went into action the next day. He demanded from Judge George A. Carpenter a writ of habeas corpus to spring Johnson, declaring that the Mann Act was unconstitutional and that Johnson was being detained in violation of the Fifth Amendment. Judge Carpenter told him in legal language to get lost. Johnson was to remain in jail. The charges in the indictment, after Federal agents conferred again with the obliging Belle, turned out to be ludicrous, though Chicago's reformers were properly outraged. There were eleven counts. Jack was charged with having brought her over the state line into Chicago on October 15, 1910, for purposes of—among other things—prostitution, debauchery, committing a crime against nature and unlawful sexual intercourse. After four days of languishing in jail he was released on a thirty-two-thousand-dollar bond.

The trial was held on May 13, 1913—ominous numbers for Johnson. Belle admitted to whoring for a livelihood, but her testimony was damaging. She had traveled, she said, around most of America and into Canada in Jack's flamboyant company. It took the jury an hour and forty-five minutes to reach a verdict: Guilty. Because prisons were then filled with Mann Act violators—Atlanta and Leavenworth were seriously overcrowded—sentences were generally relatively light. But Johnson drew big casino: A year and a day in the penitentiary at Joliet and a thousand-dollar fine. In pronouncing Johnson's doom, Judge Carpenter said in part: "The crime for which this defendant stands convicted is an aggravating one. The life of the defendant, by his own admission, had been such as to merit condemnation. . . . This defendant is one of the best known men of his race, and his example has been far-reaching, and the court is bound to consider the position he occupied among his people. In view of these facts, this is a case that calls for more than a fine."

It occurred to Federal agents that Johnson, who had been released for a period of fourteen days to settle his affairs, just might skip bail. Certainly it occurred to Johnson. Agents and detectives from the city force kept a close watch on him, and likewise on his wife and family. But now began one of the zaniest, best-timed and best-plotted escapes in history.

At a café, one of his black friends sidled over to him and asked, "Did you know that Foster's Giants were in town?" Johnson had never heard of them, but it seemed they were a colored team from Canada. Johnson soon learned that one of the players, Rube Foster, bore him a striking resemblance. Ever one for intrigue where white men were concerned, Johnson thought of a plan. He visited the ballfield where the team was playing and took his near-double to one side. The man was astonished. "You mean you want to change places with me when we go back to Canada?" Johnson nodded. "I ain't studyin' to go to no jail," said Rube. "What am I supposed to be doin' while you're pulling this?" "Just lay low in my restaurant." Rube was dubious, but Johnson convinced him. When he offered Rube money, it was turned down. "I'll do it because you're a black man in a jam." So it was arranged.

There remained the problem of avoiding the shadowers. Johnson outfoxed the police by outgunning them in his red touring car, then abandoned it and leapt into one driven by his nephew, Gus Rhodes, and raced to the railroad station. Both had a quantity of baseball equipment in their arms, and they mingled with the other ballplayers. The shadowers were fooled, thinking Jack was Rube, and the pair hopped onto the train as it was pulling out of the station, and so bade goodbye to Chicago. Johnson got off the train in Hamilton, Ontario, and was immediately arrested by Canadian police, who recognized him. But Johnson had anticipated this. He carried the names of two local lawyers, and they succeeded in convincing the justice of the peace that the Chicago police had not requested his return. His wife had already skipped out of Chicago with their luggage and had come to Montreal, where she had bought three steamship tickets to France.

Johnson entertained on the stage in France and in England, receiving mixed responses. But in England he cut up so much that he felt he was unwelcome. Besides, his money was running out. In some desperation he returned to France, where he wrestled a Russian named Al Spoul, a giant. Johnson became impatient with tussling after a while and knocked Spoul out with a punch. This feat over, he returned to London, where his unpopularity grew, partly because of the White Slavery conviction and partly because he kept defying the authorities and some of the common folk. Also, members of the press, who were generally poorly paid, resented his cigarette holders, white wife and powerful cars. When they could, they printed something unfavorable about him.

An event occurred in Paris in 1914 that hardened Johnson's heart even more against white promoters. Still needing money, he urged promoter Dan McKettrick to get him a fight. McKettrick produced Frank Moran of "Mary Ann" fame. Though tickets had been sold and percentages of the purse agreed on, no contract had been signed. At first suspicious, Moran told McKettrick he did not want a contract. The promoter became angry and shouted at him, "If that's the way you feel, you'll never see a dime of the purse!" He instructed his lawyer, Lucien Cerf, to tie up the money in the trickiest legal way possible. This Cerf did. Johnson knew about it but figured it was better to be owed money than have nothing to look forward to, so he agreed to fight, anyway. Twenty thousand Frenchmen stormed in to see the bout, which was refereed by Georges Carpentier, even then the idol of France. The gate receipts amounted to $36,000. Johnson would have received $14,000 and Moran $10,000. But the money was impounded, as McKettrick had threatened. Cerf, the only man with the key to the papers concerning the money, was called into the army, disappeared, and was later killed. When McKettrick tried to have the money released, the French bankers asked for some kind of paper to prove his claim to it. He had none, and none could be found in Cerf's effects. Presumably the money is still in the vault, accumulating interest and dust. Additionally, Moran landed Mary Ann a few times on the poorly conditioned Johnson's jaw, and the champion was lucky to earn a decision in twenty rounds.

The fight took place on June 27. The following day a political assassin shot the Austrian Archduke Francis Ferdinand in the town of Sarajevo.

The outlook seemed bleak for Johnson. If he dwelt in England, that austerity-minded land, he could not earn enough to pay his debts, much less amaze the natives with his life style, as of yore. In France, he might get drafted or accidentally shot by a Boche sniper. (Curiously enough, the French, out of respect for his punching power, called a German piece of artillery that could really hit *"le Jack Johnson."*) If he returned to America, it was weary nights of brooding in Joliet, whither he had been remanded before his escape from Chicago.

So at the end of 1914 he went to Buenos Aires, thence to Barbados and Havana. In that tempestuous city he conferred with Jack Curley, the promoter who had nearly gone broke trying to find a White Hope. Curley had finally found one worthy of Johnson's attention—Jess Willard, of Pottawatomie, Kansas. Johnson, low on funds, was agreeable, so long as he did not pass within the jurisdiction of Federal law. As to where to fight, Europe was preoccupied with a big war, Africa with many little ones and South America with bullfights and *futbol*. Havana was settled on as being close enough to draw American fans and out of reach of Federal agents.

Jess Willard, who was born on a ranch in Pottawatomie, was a homely, shy fellow who happened to grow to be six feet six inches tall and weigh 252 pounds, a great deal of it muscle. He had been a cowpuncher, had broken horses, had been a plains teamster and then, at the age of twenty-eight, had gone into boxing because it promised better pay. In some of his fights he showed a good left jab that, because of his immense reach, was difficult for an opponent to avoid. He had plenty of courage in the ring and great durability. His record was a spotty one and would have been even less impressive had he not had for a manager Tom Jones, a former Illinois barber. Jones, with his waspish tongue, could sometimes needle Willard into fighting hard.

Some time after the Johnson fight, Jess would write a friend:

"God made me a giant. I never received an education, never had any money. I knew that I was a big fellow and powerful strong. I just sat down and figured that a man as big as me ought to be able to cash in on his size and that was what started me on the road to boxing.

"So I got this boxing game in my head. I never liked it; in fact, I hated it as I never hated a thing previously, but there was money in it. I needed the money and decided to go after it.

"I never really knew how to fight. In the fights I engaged in I never could do anything to the other fellow in the way of damage. I simply couldn't do it. Harming the other fellow seemed to be cruel, and so long as the other fellow didn't harm me much I didn't see any reason why I should hurt him.

"I never hurt any of my opponents before the eighth round, and when they hurt me I got real mad and just swung on them and settled matters as quickly as I could. But even then I didn't like this boxing business. It was the dough I liked and I went after all I could get."

His fight record was far from impressive. He had been beaten by a sluggish veteran, Bearcat McMahon, and had fought no-decision bouts with Arthur Pelkey and Luther McCarty. In his fight with Gunboat Smith he had been heartily hooted at for his apathetic performance. Then Jones badgered him into worrying about his career. The press taunted him. As a result, Willard suddenly turned fierce and in a subsequent fight smashed Bull Young under the jaw with a terrific right uppercut. Young went down and stayed in a coma. After an emergency operation, he died. The gentle Willard was grief-stricken for weeks. He was arrested on a charge of manslaughter but was completely exonerated.

He was psyched out of his next fight, with Boer Rodel. Jimmy Johnston, Rodel's crafty manager, informed him that Rodel had a bad heart. "You better not hit him too hard," warned Johnston, "or you'll kill him." Willard held back, with occasional apprehensive looks at the nodding Johnston, and Rodel began to whale away at the giant, gaining confidence as the fight progressed. It was a no-decision affair, but spectators came away thinking that Rodel was Jess's master. Who could not beat a tree? Then Rodel hollered for a rematch. This time Jess, ears ringing from Jones's insults, knocked him out in the ninth.

Willard's temper—or instinct to survive—was evident in his fight with Sailor Kearns. Moving about in his leisurely, somewhat preoccupied way, he was smashed hard in the heart with a straight right. His "Oof!" as he bent over could be heard for three hundred yards. Bellowing with anger, he ran at Kearns and swung an uppercut like a windmill. Shattered, Kearns had to be dragged to his corner as Willard fumed.

After beating one Dan Daily, Willard, not yet rich, grew somewhat disenchanted with his profession and went loafing for several months. He considered quitting the ring. Then Jones got news to him that Curley wanted him to fight Jack Johnson, the exile, for the heavyweight championship. Willard, thinking of the land and stock he might own if he won, promptly went into hard training and got into the best shape of his life, pushing his weight down to 230 pounds.

There were several factors to account for Willard's victory over the great black fighter. The bout, held on April 15, 1915, took place under the broiling sun, with twenty thousand sweltering fans in attendance, most of whom—even though

Cuban—rooted for the Pottawatomie Giant. It was scheduled for forty-five rounds. Presumably Willard's durability over that distance would be telling, especially since it was known that Johnson was thirty-seven years old and hated to train. Johnson was also overconfident, aware of his own abilities and Jess's unimpressive record.

The fight went precisely as the Willard forces planned. In splendid condition, Jess fought defensively, making Johnson come to him—something Johnson never liked, at least in the early rounds. The first ten were clearly Jack's, from the standpoint of aggressiveness and damage done. Willard had a cut on his cheek, and his mouth was covered with blood. Johnson kept up the pace, and Willard stoically accepted his punishment until the twenty-first. Then it was apparent that Jack had run out of steam. Willard kept landing more often, and Johnson's punches no longer bothered him. Just before the bell for

Jess Willard, the last in a long line of "white hopes," is seen with his manager Tom Jones. The place: Havana, Cuba. The date: April 15, 1915. The rest is history.

the twenty-sixth, Johnson signaled for Curley to take his wife out of the arena. He did not want her to see him knocked out. At the bell, he arose on unsteady legs. Willard moved forward swiftly and smashed his left into Johnson's face. As Jack straightened up, Willard shot home a hard right to Jack's stomach. A left to the stomach brought down Jack's guard, and then came Willard's hardest punch of the fight, a right to the jaw that made Johnson's knees sag. He looked as though he were trying to tackle Willard before he hit the canvas. He took the full count. If the fight had gone for twenty rounds, Johnson would have been the winner; but it had been scheduled for forty-five. A white man's trick?

Johnson claimed verbally and wrote later that he had thrown the fight, ostensibly so that some of his past sins would be forgiven by Americans and the Federal authorities would mitigate his sentence. But the confession was false. The sun, his poor condition and Willard's strategic plan had been his undoing.

Well, the white man had his title back.

A defeated but temporarily solvent man, Johnson wrote his lawyers in Chicago to find out what would happen if he returned to the United States. He was assured he would be put in prison. He then went to England with films of the fight, hoping to reap a fortune but realizing only two thousand pounds. He put on his show at the Hippodrome in Preston for inattentive patrons, petulantly smacked his manager in the eye over a money squabble, was promptly sued and lost. This earned him disapproval from the English. He garnered more by uttering pro-German sentiments while drunk in a pub. He was often hauled into court for not paying his bills. English officialdom decided it did not want him, and he was presented with an expulsion order: He must leave by the first week of January, 1916. Reluctant to go, he was nearly killed by three professional thugs but was rescued by a bobby. He decided he was unwelcome and packed. Then followed a series of amazing adventures.

With Gus and Lucille he journeyed to Spain via South America and settled in Barcelona. There he starred in a Spanish movie called *False Nobility* and fought bulls under the tutelage of Joselito and Manolete. He also lent himself to wrestling and boxed a poet named Arthur Craven, who claimed to be related to Oscar Wilde. Mexico City beckoned in April, 1919. There he fought some more bulls and some inept heavyweights, earning the admiration of President Venustiano Carranza, who had been victorious in his feud with Pancho Villa.

Shortly afterwards he traveled as close to the U.S. as you can get—Tijuana—where he promoted fights. An old friend from Chicago, brick manufacturer and politician Tom Carey, visited him there and advised him to return to America and take the consequences. The idea had been on Jack's mind for some time, anyway. He was frankly homesick. Carey informed the Federal agents of Johnson's decision, and Johnson stepped over the border, journeyed up to San Diego and with an embarrassed smile gave himself up.

Despite the fact that the public attitude toward Johnson had changed and immorality was becoming acceptable again, Judge Carpenter refused to lessen the sentence. Johnson was sent to "The Walls," the penitentiary in Leavenworth, Kansas. But there he learned that the superintendent was ex-Governor Dickerson of the Reno fight. After a long chat, Johnson was given his choice of activities, and he elected to be head of physical training. Prison turned out not to be so bad after all. Johnson was king there, as everywhere.

And what about the fight game? Johnson was in jail, Willard was a ballooning circus performer and farm owner and the vast crop of White Hopes were getting old and cautious. With another kind of war going on, the game lacked excitement.

But a new order was coming. It was: Move ahead and keep swinging. Generalissimo Ferdinand Foch and chess champion Alexander Alekhine exemplified it in classic terms: *"L'attaque, toujours l'attaque."*

A hobo named Kid Blackie exemplified it best. ■

Young Jack Johnson shortly after the turn of the century. In frontier days boxing wasn't the noblest of professions, and being a fighter meant swift moves in and out of the ring, often in front of a shotgun barrel. Above, Johnson and Joe Choynski are seen in a prairie jail in 1903. Choynski taught Johnson the nuances of defense.

Rushcutter's Bay, Australia, at one o'clock in the afternoon. It is the day after Christmas, 1908, and it is hot, for the seasons are reversed below the equator. Jack Johnson and Tommy Burns are being introduced to 26,000 fans. For Johnson it is the end of a long pilgrimage in pursuit of the title. In 1905 James J. Jeffries had retired undefeated, naming Marvin Hart, who had beaten Jack Root, as his successor. Tommy Burns then won a decision from Hart and claimed the title. Burns, a Canadian whose real name was Noah Brusso, was a diminutive man by heavyweight standards. When he took his title on tour he selected his challengers carefully. He went to England, Ireland, France, and finally all the way down to Australia. And right behind him was the man who cast a giant shad-

ow—Jack Johnson! At each of Burns's title defenses Johnson would plant himself at ringside and challenge the champion: "Mistuh Tommy, what you got?" he would yell derisively. "You ain't got nothin'!" Though perturbed, Burns ignored the challenges. After all, being champion gives one the privileges of rank, such as choosing one's adversaries. Enter Hugh McIntosh, an Australian entrepreneur who specialized in generating wealth from unorthodox investments. McIntosh understood the line that separated black from white, and he had a Scotsman's respect for the power of money. He gained Tommy Burns's confidence and convinced him that Johnson was all talk: it was well known that black fighters quit under pressure. Anthropology aside, Hugh McIntosh clinched the

deal by guaranteeing Burns $35,000 for step-
ping into the ring with Jack Johnson. In 1908
$35,000 was an enormous sum, certainly more
than Burns had ever made before. And to
boost his ego, Burns received counsel from
aficionados like the novelist Jack London,
who couldn't abide the likes of Johnson. After
all, London argued, loudmouths like Johnson
usually have only words as weapons, and in
the ring fists not words tell the story. Bol-
stered by all this expert advice and secure in
the knowledge that he was on the road to
riches, Burns was a confident man when
he entered the ring. And so, at age thirty,
Jack Johnson finally got his chance.

Tommy Burns at 5 feet 7 inches and 175 pounds was the smallest heavyweight champion in history.

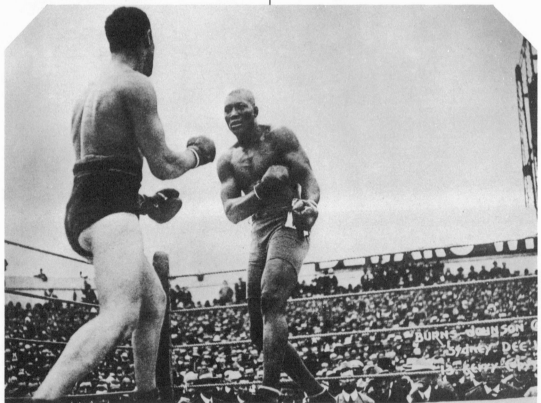

At the upper left, Johnson is young, proud, and determined. In 1908 Johnson met Burns in Australia and became the first black champion. Novelist Jack London, writing for the New York Herald *(opposite), was outraged by Johnson's mocking victory. And so began a long and passionate search for "the Great White Hope."*

Jack London Says Johnson Made a Noise Like a Lullaby with His Fists as He Tucked Burns in His Little Crib in Sleepy Hollow, with a Laugh

Plucky, but Absolutely Helpless, the White Man Seemed To Be the Victim of a Playful Ethiopian Who Did Just as He Would.

NEGRO'S GOLDEN SMILE A TAUNT FOR HIS OPPONENT ALL THE TIME

Smashed to the Floor in the First Round, the Canadian Fighter Was Going Uphill Ever After and Never Had the Ghost of a Chance for Victory.

SHOULD HAVE ENDED IN THIRTEENTH ROUND

Writer for the Herald Says in This Stage of the Fight Burns Ought To Have Been Knocked Out and Johnson Should Have Stopped Him Then.

WHITE MAN HITS NEGRO WHERE THE LATTER INDICATES

Burlesquing the English Accent of His Opponent, the Laughing Black Man Tells Him to Land Blows Here and There, and the Vanquished Man, Dazed, Does So.

By Jack London.

SYDNEY, Australia, Saturday.

JACK LONDON

THE FIGHT! There was no fight. No Armenian massacre could compare with the hopeless slaughter that took place in the Sydney Stadium to-day. It was not a case of "Too Much Johnson," but of all Johnson. A golden smile tells the story, and a golden smile was Johnson's.

The fight, if fight it might be called, was like unto that between a Colossus and a toy automaton. It had all the seeming of a playful Ethiopian at loggerheads with a small and futile white man—of a grown man cuffing a naughty child; of a monologue by one Johnson, who made a noise with his fists like a lullaby, tucking one Burns into his little crib in Sleepy Hollow; of a funeral with Burns for the late deceased, Johnson for undertaker, gravedigger and sexton.

START OF THE BATTLE.

Twenty thousand men were at the ringside and twice twenty thousand lingered outside. Johnson, first in the ring, showed magnificent condition. When he smiled a dazzling flash of gold filled the wide aperture between his open lips, and he smiled all the time. He had no trouble in the world.

When asked what he was going to do after the fight, he said he was going to the races. It was a happy prophecy. He was immediately followed into the ring by Burns, who had no smile whatever. He looked pale and sallow, as if he had not slept all night, or as if he had just pulled through a bout with fever. He received a heartier greeting than Johnson and seemed a favorite with the crowd.

It promised to be a bitter fight. There was no chivalry or good will in it, and Johnson, despite his carefree pose, had an eye to the instant need of things. He sent his seconds intently into Burns' corner to watch the putting on of the gloves for fear a casual horseshoe might stray in. He examined personally Burns' belt and announced flatly that he would not fight if Burns did not remove a tape from his skinned elbows.

TAPE IS REMOVED.

"Nothin' doin' till he takes 'em off," quoth Johnson.

The crowd hooted, but Johnson smiled his happy golden smile and dreamed with Ethiopian stolidity in his corner. Burns took off the offending tapes and was applauded uproariously. Johnson stood up and was booted. He merely smiled. That is the fight epitomized—Johnson's smile.

The gong sounded and the fight and the monologue began all right.

"Tahmy," said Johnson, with an exaggerated English accent, and thereafter he talked throughout the fight—when he was not smiling.

Scarcely had they mixed when he caught his antagonist with a fierce uppercut, turning him completely over in the air and landing him on his back.

the fierce, vicious, intent expression only apparently for the purpose of suddenly letting his teeth flash forth like the rise of a harvest moon, while his face beamed with all the happy carefree innocence of a little child.

PLAYING ALL THE TIME

Johnson play-acted all the time, and he played with Burns from the gong of the opening round to the finish of the fight. Burns was a toy in his hands. For Johnson it was a kindergarten romp.

"Hit here, Tahmy," he would say, exposing the right side of his unprotected stomach, and when Burns struck Johnson would neither wince nor cover up. Instead he would receive the blow with a happy, careless smile, directed at the spectators, turn the left side of his unprotected stomach and say, "Now here, Tahmy," and while Burns hit as directed Johnson would continue to grin and chuckle and smile his golden smile.

One criticism, and only one, can be passed upon Johnson. In the thirteenth round he made the mistake of his life. He should have put Burns out. He could have put him out. It would have been child's play. Instead of which he smiled and deliberately let Burns live until the gong sounded, and in the opening of the fourteenth round the police stopped the fight and Johnson lost the credit of a knockout.

But one thing remains, Jeffries must emerge from his alfalfa farm and remove that smile from Johnson's face. Jeff, it's up to you.

"NIX, NOTHING DOING," SAYS J. J. JEFFRIES

[SPECIAL DESPATCH TO THE HERALD.]
LOS ANGELES, Cal., Saturday.—"Nix, nothing doing; the alfalfa and this on the side for mine."

This was the reply of James J. Jeffries, the retired undefeated champion heavyweight of the world, to the suggestion of Jack London that he emerge from his alfalfa farm and remove the smile from Johnson's face.

Jeffries was contentedly watching six busy bartenders rustling in his drink emporium when seen by a reporter for the HERALD.

"It isn't the color. It is the same old story—the color line. I refused time and again to meet Johnson when I was in the ring and now I am out of it for good. I'll never fight again, no matter who holds the championship. Of course, I may spar for

"JOHN L." IS NOT SURPRISED

ST. PAUL, Minn., Saturday.—John L. Sullivan, who is here, was not surprised over the outcome of the Burns-Johnson fight in Australia.

"The fight came out very much as I had predicted," said Sullivan to-day. "Even with his victory over the so-called champion—though, in my opinion, Burns never was the champion prize fighter of the world—the negro can't assume that title, for the present day bouts cannot truly be styled prize fights. They are boxing matches, when padded mitts are used by the contestants.

"I can't see where Johnson will be given a high position in the opinion of the general American public. I am of the opinion that the American public is fast losing interest in the manly art of self-defence.

"Johnson will undoubtedly get two or three fights in this country after his return, and it will be only a question of time until he runs up against a better man, as is always the case unless a man pulls out

If one quality characterized Jack Johnson it was his constant need for an audience. First and last he was a performer who rarely failed to go on. Later fighters emulated his flamboyant style of living, but none performed with the éclat and ingratiating in-solence of Li'l Arthur. Above, he is seen posing with acrobats on one of his many trips to the Continent. Although the picture was taken long after he lost the title, he was as familiar as any French celebrity to habitués of bistros off the Champs-Élysées.

Below, Johnson with his first wife, Etta Terry Duryea. When she committed suicide, Chicago was thrown into an uproar over its most famous black citizen. Bottom, Johnson visits his mother before jumping bail and fleeing into exile.

In the circular picture at top, Johnson marries Lucille Cameron shortly after his indictment under the "White Slavery Act." Immediately above, he is shown with Clara Kerr, the only woman ever to leave him for another man.

Johnson's fight with Stanley Ketchel in 1909 in California remains a classic confrontation between two monumental egotists.

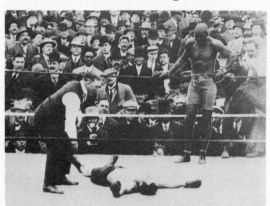

Middleweight Champion Ketchel after he was knocked out in the twelfth round. But before that he had floored Johnson.

James J. Jeffries, acclaimed as the first "Great White Hope," came out of retirement to reclaim the title from Johnson.

Promoter Tex Rickard, who served his apprenticeship as a professional gambler, staked his entire bankroll on the Johnson–Jeffries battle.

Johnson neutralizes Jim Flynn. Flynn, who later destroyed Jack Dempsey in one round, never laid a glove on Johnson.

This study of Jack Johnson just after he won the title suggests something of the complex personality of the man behind "that golden smile." He had traveled a long road before finally forcing a showdown in a society that reserved a separate status for the black athlete. It was a society groping to discover its true identity. Johnson had a profound understanding of what it took to reach the top. His is the story of America then and now.

Johnson is about to leave California in one of his high-powered cars in June, 1910. Beside him Tex Rickard, the promotional genius who conceived of pitting Johnson against Jim Jeffries, is explaining that the fight will be held in Reno rather than in California as originally planned. Rickard reasoned that a black and a white fighting for the Champion-

ship of the Universe and for the biggest purse ever known could not fail to make him boxing's first millionaire. Billed as the Battle of the Century, the match drew tremendous crowds and so aroused the passions of the nation that white America believed it would settle the issue of racial supremacy once and for all.

Champagne flows while the protagonists smile the smile of affluent victory. Never before had so much money been guaranteed two men to put on the gloves. For merely agreeing to sign a contract to fight each was given $10,000 in gold pieces. The purse was $101,000—60 per cent to be paid to the winner and 40 per cent to the loser. In addition, each fighter received $50,000 for the motion-picture rights.

Johnson dressed regally for his historic signing with Jeffries. He is flanked by a trainer (left) and by George Little, who acted as his manager. But Johnson was his own man and made his own deals.

In Reno, Johnson shakes hands with John L. Sullivan. The New York Times engaged Sullivan as its correspondent for the Jeffries fight.

Whether as a touring fighter, racing-car driver, or controversial champion, Jack Johnson was always stage center. His talent as the greatest defensive fighter of all time was exceeded only by his appetite for living to the fullest. Each and every moment had meaning: "I like life and I like it NOW!"

Downtown Reno on July 4, 1910. It was as if a desert town stranded in the West had become the pulse of a nation. From near and far, from baronial Newport to dust-blown frontier towns, the high, the low, and the notorious found their way to Nevada. It was more than another championship contest. What tragedy had meant to the Greeks the Johnson–Jeffries

fight meant to Americans. Color was the theme: being the wrong color limited a man's opportunities and fixed his social standing. In that simplistic era it was generally believed that two fighters struggling in the ring for forty-five rounds or less would settle a complex problem that has not even today been resolved.

As the crowd roars, Jim Jeffries makes his way to the ring. The fabled Jeffries, now thirty-five and showing the stress of having shed one hundred pounds of flab, is pre- sented. This is not, close observers can see, the indomitable stalker of old—not the man who in London's words would "wipe that golden smile off Johnson's face!"

In the early rounds the action is tentative and cautious. Both men jockey for position; both men fully respect their opponent's reputation; both men are aware that the eyes of *the world are on Reno. As the fight progresses, the balance decisively shifts to Johnson. OVERLEAF: Jeffries collapses under a barrage of blows.*

Above is the Café de Champion, which Johnson opened in Chicago in 1911. It was here that Etta Terry Duryea committed suicide.

Though he infuriated white America, Johnson had many admirers. Black friends in Chicago gave him their version of the Championship Belt, above.

'ACK JOHNSON HAS DONE NO DIFFERENT
FROM ANY OTHER BIG SPORT

or No Other Reason Than Whipping Jeffries and Being a Negro Is Jack Johnson Persecuted. Consorting With White Women No Cause. Jack Is One of That Host That John Couldn't Number.

By Dr. M. A. Majors.

Johnson is being persecuted ipping Jeffries. It is not cost- as much, however, as it cost ite race. Besides, he is get- of fun out of it. Of course viewed from the point of in- nce. His conduct is not up to tandard of the college man. rather it is in keeping with his upation as a fighter, which be- to the realm of sport—Mr. Jack ohnson, fighter, differs from all the others fighters in the white race solely by color.

Just Like White Men.

The grand escapade, wine, women and song, do not functionate scandal where there can be none, and no one the great fighters has ever boasted e wanted to teach a Sunday Fighters are fighters, and it be that they claim the bigger e of leading the life of convivi- and moral unconcernedness. As citizen in court it is highly oable that he could not get a trial. No white man who quali- as a juryman can conscientiously miss the fact that Jack conquered white race in the science of pugil- law. This is too big a crown for negro to wear acceptably to the te race from which he in every way took it by knocking it off the d of Jim Jeffries. What Jack has e, however wrong it may appear, never been so magnified when e white sport absorbs the spot- light with a woman to whom the preacher has never uttered a sacred njunction in a marriage ceremony.

Crucified for His Race.

At first it would never do to ex- ibit the moving pictures, letting white children see as conqueror in stic science a big black Sampson. That would make the white children row up with certain fear and dread f the colored boy. It is the negro oy that would have to fear the white oy. Jack did for his race what great ature did for him—reversed the lever f what the white man considered ight. Next they must discredit him. ince they failed to kill him at Reno. Jack Johnson has done no different rom any big rich sport, and he hasn't disgraced sport in any particular, un- ess it reproached him for marrying a pretty white woman who looks like any banker's wife robed in diamonds and dressed in the Parisian styles. Of course, no very sensible negro can envy him for suiting himself.

Exercised His Right as a Man.

To marry whom he pleases is a ight guaranteed by the statutes of Illinois and a quite a number of north- ern state. The peculiar sentiment at all times sickly when the Cauca- ian will and pleasure is frustrated, is one of the phenomena of the times. It is no harm for the country to be flooded with mulattoes—children with- out legal fathers ranging over a period of three centuries—but it is a crime against nature for a negro to marry a white woman by her own consent. Then Jack lives in a mansion fit- or any judge, governor or president. He rides in a $10,000 50-horsepower

low at Reno. All kinds of sharpers began to whet their wits—fight pro- moters, theatrical managers, crooks, and silly money-hunting women. He found himself suddenly rich, surround- ed by all the beauty of the gaudy gloss of earth in Paris, London, New York and Chicago. Surfeited by this pass- ing show of the gilded and the great, he was oblivious of pitfalls and cun- ning of the incarnate fiends of graft and double dealing. Coming suddenly into possession of more than $150,000, it would seem to us at such distance down the paths of exciting needs that everything and everybody in the world is most glorious when one is loaded down with hundred-dollar bills. Jack Johnson is no fool. He has never yet merited such amazing pity as some of his friends are frail enough to suppose. He has never yet slept with both eyes shut.

One Eye Always Open.

Let us admit that he has allowed some golden opportunities to go astray, and that much of his conduct seems to have created certain kinds of race strife. The writer knows that some good will result from Jack's championship. It has already whispered in the ears of every black boy that he can be the president of the United States fistic ring, and there is no congress or supreme court to impeach him. It has told every mem- ber of the fifteen millions of the negro race that the white people of the world, except France, China and Japan, don't like it. This will in time result in race unity. What if Jack Johnson must be crucified in order that his race may get sense enough to unite its forces in a thousand dif- ferent avenues and channels of trade? Mayhap it is this very crucible of strife that is forging the negro through the white heat of hate that is to make for him solidarity and everything needful in the family of nations.

Colored—What Nationality Are You?

Jack married one or two white women. He did not dishonor them. How many congressmen, governors, judges and clergymen of the white race have consorted with colored women? From the present day ap- pearance of four millions of negroes in America, hosts of whom God alone can only tell whether they are white or colored, there must be left very lit- tle loyalty among white men, and less confidence among white women in them.

It is all very easy to imagine, and jump at conclusions and find fault. The only crime Jack Johnson has committed is in doing little things like big men. He has invited the envy of his own race and pricked the ever- growing abscess of American preju- dice by spending his money like he had a plenty, and mixing somewhat with the big white sports, many of whom are sober, sensible, and possess but very little prejudice against a man for being what God made him.

The Dreaded Spotlight.

The spotlight is a fearful ordeal. It ran Roosevelt to Africa, Carnegie to Skibo castle, J. P. Morgan up and

Jess Willard poses before meeting Johnson. Below, Johnson's wife Lucille is seen at the Willard fight, where she allegedly received $50,000. Johnson later claimed that he threw the fight.

Long before Harlem, Chicago had the largest black community in the country. It was there that Johnson made his home. The Chicago Defender *boldly spoke out on matters of color. The cause of Jack Johnson gave black America the ammunition to attack the roots of racism.*

1915. Havana. Temperature: 105 degrees. Round 26! Jess Willard studies Johnson's eyes. For Johnson, age thirty-seven, time is running out. Willard launches an overhand

right that connects. As Johnson starts to fall
he instinctively clutches at Willard, forcing
him into the ropes. Willard dances free as
Johnson falls.

Johnson, arms above his head, lies motion-less. (The upper photo will lead to the biggest controversy in boxing history.) Below, Jess Willard is the new champion.

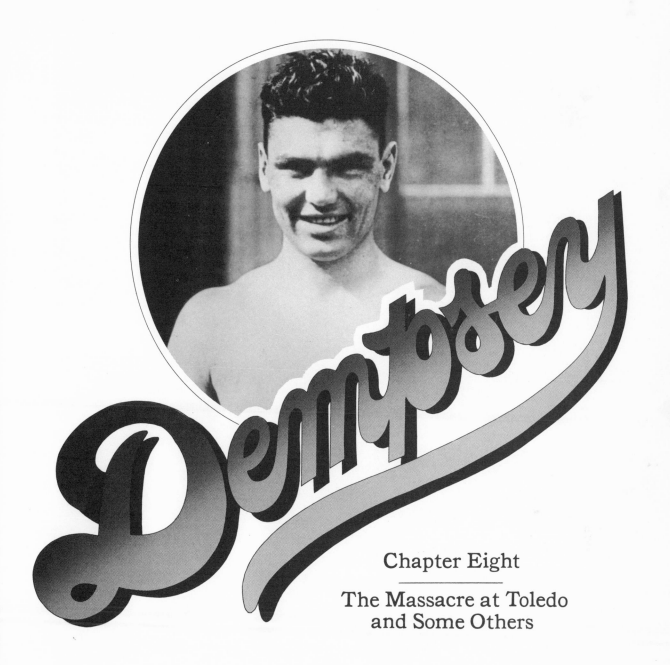

Chapter Eight

The Massacre at Toledo
and Some Others

J ack," said Tex Rickard, the promoter, to Jack Dempsey, the fighter, when they were alone in the locker room just before the Willard fight, "listen a minute." There was a look of concern on Rickard's usually bland face, and he took a paternal puff of his cigar. "This bozo is big and tough. He might kill you. You remember what a single punch of his did to Bull Young." The eyes of the two met, Dempsey's hardly focusing. "If he hits you a good shot and you go down, my advice is to stay down. That way," the wheeler-dealer misnamed "the Rube" concluded, "you won't get hurt." He appraised the copper-colored, shaven-haired, finely drawn challenger. After wishing Jack good luck, he left.

He did not know his man. If Jack "Doc" Kearns, Dempsey's manager, had heard the advice, he would have busted a gut trying to keep from laughing aloud. Kearns had bet ten thousand dollars to a hundred thousand dollars that Dempsey would flatten the champion in one round. Writer Damon Runyon had made a smaller wager but at even better odds.

As usual, Dempsey was working himself up into a prefight rage against his opponent. It lent impetus to the bull-like charge he generally made across the ring to assault bigger men. And Willard was bigger. Spectators and bettors who relied largely on the comparative measurements of fighters to determine the winner gasped at the disparity. The challenger was six feet one-half inch tall and weighed 188 pounds—though he was officially listed at 195. (In a weigh-in the week before, Kearns had fooled the public and the press into thinking Dempsey weighed two hundred pounds by a clever stratagem: He had had Dempsey forgo his morning workout, eat two hearty breakfasts and feed all morning on bananas and water. Of course, Dempsey felt waterlogged and slightly nauseous, but at least on seeing the scale—which cynics had checked for accuracy—townspeople, politicians and the press had stopped worrying about Dempsey's imminent death in the ring.) Willard outweighed him by fifty-seven pounds, was five

inches taller and outreached him by seven inches. But Dempsey's 188 pounds housed a rather remarkable starveling child.

He may not have been the greatest fighter who ever lived—though denying it will get you a stiff argument in any bar in the land—but he was certainly the most exciting, the most colorful, the most dynamic and the most savage. There was an immense fury coiled inside him waiting to be released.

He appealed to spectators because he was willing to take six blows to land one, because of his intense, pantherlike concentration on demolishing his enemy and because he carried explosive charges in both hands. A swift, accurate hitter, he could knock down or knock out his opponent with a blow that traveled no more than eight inches, and the blow might be unleashed at any moment.

Another characteristic that did not displease his fans was that sometimes, in his zeal to conquer, he would exceed the bounds of propriety. It was not unknown for him to hit a stubborn opponent below the belt. It was an extension of the prizefighter's dictum, "Kill the body and the head will fall." His opponent's hands would automatically come down or he would bend forward, losing concentration, and the deadly short left hook would collide with his unprotected jaw. Sometimes Dempsey hit after the bell. On at least one occasion, with the referee between him and his opponent, he threw a straight right over the referee's shoulder into his opponent's face. He rabbit punched. A few times he managed to maneuver his opponent's head between the top and middle strands of the ropes and belabored him artfully before the latter could free himself. He sometimes seized his opponent behind the neck with his left hand and flung him off-balance so he could nail him with his right. He won a very critical bout, which he had been losing badly for several rounds, by hitting low—and when his opponent turned his head to protest to the referee, smashing him in the jaw so hard that he was counted out. In this same fight, he hit his opponent on the left *leg* with a low right. His opponent later formally pro-

217

tested, but in prizefighting, *ex post facto* ranks with the snows of yesteryear as an instrument of justice.

His most pronounced instinct as a killer in the ring, however, was standing over a downed opponent, in defiance of the rules—teeth showing in a primordial grin and fists clenched—and clouting him just as he regained his feet. In one championship fight he clouted his opponent while the latter still had one hand on the floor—technically, he was still down. In the same fight he hovered over his opponent like the Angel of Death while the victim tried to avoid his fate by crawling all over the ring on his hands and knees. Dempsey should have been disqualified in several of his bouts, but referees were either too awed by him, too friendly toward him and toward Kearns, too inexperienced or too panic-stricken by the purposefulness of this machine of destruction to call a halt to the irregularities. On the other hand, one did not see Dempsey protesting about the other fellow's fouls. "Sure he hit low," mused another great fighter after his retirement. "But he never hollered if you hit *him* low."

After years of fighting literally to stay alive, he was so constituted psychologically that he could not pull punches in the ring, which made it tough on his sparring partners. When he was training for the Willard fight he knocked out at least one a day.

Part-Indian on both sides of his family, Dempsey had blue-black pompadoured hair, swarthy skin that did not cut easily, thick black eyebrows that could scowl fear into an opponent, intense black eyes above high cheekbones, a nose that made a poor target, a strong, rounded jaw and a beard that seemed to grow while you were looking at it. He developed good deltoids, good biceps, good forearms, springy if thin legs and a strong belly, which his crouching, weaving style of fighting demanded. He never had any trouble with his hands.

In his early years as a hobo fighter, he showed that pleasing arrogance of the young man who knows he will one day become champion. When Billy McCarney, the well-known manager, introduced him to looming Carl Morris in 1915, Dempsey appeared to be unimpressed, even though Morris was ranked number four among the country's heavyweights. Morris stuck out his hand in a friendly way, but Dempsey ignored it and pulled open Morris's bathrobe. Noting the roll of fat around the former Oklahoma oil worker's stomach, he grinned owlishly and made as if to bury his right fist in it. "I'd knock this bum flat in a round," he told the astonished McCarney, turned and, shoulders shaking with silent laughter, strolled out. Morris was stupefied with rage. "Who does that punk think he is?" he demanded of McCarney, who could do nothing but shrug. Three years later, in New Orleans, on December 16, Morris had a chance for revenge. He lasted until the first round. Fourteen seconds after the gong rang he was laid out, victim of a Dempsey assault.

There was immense drama and color about the fellow. He demonstrated a few times that he was the greatest *unconscious* fighter in the history of mankind. In his fights with Gunboat Smith and Luis Angel Firpo he was knocked out, yet his murderous instinct for self-preservation made him carry on. Kearns ballyhooed him as a "thrill fighter," and he was all of that. There were six million-dollar gates up to and including Dempsey's second fight with Gene Tunney; Dempsey was a principal in all six. Sometimes cast as a hero, sometimes as a villain, Dempsey launched what has been called the Golden Age of Boxing. Without him to capture the public imagination, it is unlikely that there would ever have been a million-dollar gate. He was the star performer in the craziest championship bout ever fought, a principal in the most ferocious single round ever fought and a participant in the most bizarre promotion for a fight the world has ever seen.

Dempsey's motto, from his saloon-fighting days, was "the quicker, the better"; hungry and tired, he could not afford to be outlasted by some miner or cowpuncher. As a result of this philosophy, in official bouts he scored more one-round knockouts than any other fighter in history—twenty-one up to the time of the Willard fight. Two of them were extremely important. If he had not scored them, Rickard probably would not have matched "the little feller" (his condescending term for Dempsey) with the Pottawatomie Giant.

On February 14, 1918, Dempsey scored the first, over Jim Flynn, "the Pueblo Fireman." On February 15, there was a squib about the fight in *The New York Times* sports section. Dempsey knocked Flynn out after two minutes "in what was to have been a 10-round fight here tonight." Willard, in the same story, announced he would meet the winner of the upcoming Dempsey–Fred Fulton battle.

The result of the fight between Dempsey and Fulton, "the Sepulpa Plasterer," was announced in the *Times* of July 28, 1918:

ONE PUNCH FLOORS
FULTON FOR COUNT
Dempsey Disposes of Rival
After Twenty-three
Seconds of Fighting
RIGHT SWING ENDS BATTLE
Californian Wastes No Time
Shoving Huge Opponent Into
Pugilistic Discard

The press was howling, Kearns was yowling and the public was hollering for Rickard, who had Willard under contract, to produce him. Most fans thought he could beat Dempsey, but a heavyweight champion should not remain invisible from the ring for great lengths of time. There had been enough absenteeism from Johnson. Finally Rickard consented to the blandishments of Kearns, who virtually implied that his man would fight for free. But when Rickard made the announcement to the press, thus committing himself, Kearns suddenly demanded fifty thousand dollars. Rickard was aghast and furious. Then, in a most curious way, a new figure was settled on. A group of newspapermen were called in to decide what the proper figure should be. They settled on $27,500, and that was that.

The site selected was Toledo, Ohio, hideout site for gangsters, a glassworks town and the biggest shipper of coal in the world. Toledo was picked because it was a railroad nexus, because it was near the country's population center

and because Ohio Governor James M. Cox said the fight could go on. With his usual deftness, Rickard found a copromoter, a Memphis cotton broker named Frank Flournoy, and the project was under way.

Willard's only boxing adventure since beating Johnson had been a treacly bout against Frank Moran, the redheaded, jolly, playboy ex-sailor who had once worked on J. P. Morgan's yacht, *The Corsair*. Among the ladies Moran was fond of escorting were Pearl White, the elastic and gutsy heroine of *The Perils of Pauline* serial, and Lillian Lorraine, a paragon among the Ziegfeld beauties.

Rickard had staged the fiasco in Madison Square Garden, and it was an especially eerie spectacle because the lights beaming down on the fighters and spectators were green—an experiment to see if the fight films could be made clearer. John L., an observer, was thoroughly disgusted by the inaction of the fight and said he could lick both fighters in the same ring in the same evening. One observer was most impressed by the visual aspects. The seventh round was the only exciting one of the fight, and he wrote: "Willard hooked a vicious left to Moran's head, sending his man back on his heels. Blood ran down Moran's head from the gash over the eyebrow. In the green Cooper-Hewitt lights put up by the movie men, that gave those at the ringside a deathlike pallor, the blood on Moran's face resembled corroded copper. . . ."

What the fight did, however, was to get boxing barred in New York. Even before the fight, William Randolph Hearst had launched a campaign in his papers to effect this action. He had gotten friendly clergymen to send his New York editors telegrams protesting the sport as being a brutal spectacle, animalistic, nothing but two men trying to beat each other's brains out in the ring for the amusement of fans, and so on. Perhaps the powerful publisher needed a crusade to boost paper sales, or perhaps he was genuinely appalled by the sport. On the day after the fight there were two contradictory versions of it in Hearst's paper. In an apparent crossing of signals, Thomas A. Dorgan, the great Hearst cartoonist, wrote on the sports page that the fight had been extremely slow and dull, while a front-page story considered the spectacle as though it had been Armageddon or the final battle between Loki and Thor. But the article on page one carried the field. A year later, so slowly do the wheels of justice move, boxing was prohibited in New York. It remained so up to the time that a state assemblyman and songwriter named Jimmy Walker pushed through the Walker Law in 1921, which got the boys back in business.

But the Willard-Moran fight did produce the largest indoor gate to date in prizefight history—$152,000 from disappointed customers. Rickard had the golden touch.

———————

William Harrison Dempsey, called Harry in his young years, was born in the tiny mining town of Manassa, Colorado, on June 24, 1895. Corbett was champion; he would lose his title two years later. Harry, the ninth of eleven children, enjoyed a gypsy childhood. His father, Hyrum, had been a teacher in Mud Fork, West Virginia, but hated struggling with inattentive, unscholarly boys and girls of all ages. He had converted himself into a Mormon and ridden West with his wife, Celia, and his brood. He had a wagon, provisions and three hundred dollars in his pocket, which he obtained by selling some forest acreage he had inherited. (Jack sometimes referred to him as a jack Mormon —one who did not abide by the strict rules of *The Book of Mormon*. He smoked and drank coffee and used bad words.)

As a youngster Jack was a good hunter and fisherman—not for sport, but to put food on the table for the voracious Dempsey clan. Hyrum, a small, tough individual, guided the family from town to town in that inhospitable land, he and the eldest boys trying to get work as miners or cowhands. When Jack was eleven he started to spend time under the ground as a miner, breathing the dank air while on his knees or bent in a crouch, smashing a pick against the unyielding walls. He loved it. He said many times that he did not have to become a boxer. He could have been a suc-

cessful miner.

On the other hand, he could hardly have escaped his destiny. His older brother Bernie had boxing ambitions, but he also had a glass jaw. But while taking his lickings for the small purses that then obtained, Bernie began to tutor young Harry and the other Dempseys in the fine art. He was a magnificent instructor. He showed them how to feint and slip punches and how to inject power into a blow. He fashioned for them heavy bags of sawdust and whatever else came to hand and taught the kids how to hammer them as though they were Jeffries. Originally the bags were painted white, then black, as the new champ took over. Some friend had given Celia a book on John L. Sullivan, which inspired her. "I want you to be the next John L.," she told her son, for whom she was the moon and the stars.

Bernie, who had memories of being set down with aching blows to his chin, sought to strengthen Jack's jaw by having him chew daily a very unappetizing gummy resin cajoled from pine trees. Jack did it without complaint. Bernie had Jack soak his face in foul-smelling beef brine, begged from a local store, to leatherize his already tough skin. Jack hated to smell the stuff and then thrust his face into it, but Bernie was his god. He soaked his hands in brine, too, as the famous prizefighters did. That was dull, but pleasanter than the first two rituals.

Because the family was almost always en route somewhere and there was mining or hunting or fishing to be done when the wagon stopped, Jack's formal education was inevitably skimpy. He did not take much to books anyway. One day one of his schoolmarms lost patience with what must have been her oldest, most preoccupied pupil. "Harry Dempsey!" she cried. "you're the biggest, dumbest kid in school! Maybe you'd better leave." So he struck out for a silver mine, in which milieu he was a great deal happier.

Jack, like his brothers, fled home at age sixteen, relieving the family of another mouth to feed. Probably he had an urge to go adventuring; perhaps his threshold of attending to dull farm chores had been far overreached. He hoboed for three years, risked his life on the rods and fought tough guys in saloons. To substitute for his lack of education, he developed what is called mother wit. He learned how to survive. His most profitable venture at the age of sixteen was the saloon bit. He would march into one of them and holler, John L. fashion, "I can lick any. . . ." Most times he would just get stared at. He was a hungry-looking, skinny kid, dark-complexioned (hence the name Kid Blackie), and he had, like many men of the ring, a high-pitched, scratchy voice.

In busy bars, no one paid much heed to the half-starved kid, no matter how irritating he made himself. Sometimes the bartender would chase him out. Occasionally somebody would oblige him—and, overconfident, would march into that devastating left hook, feel the floor or the bar on his back and think better of getting up, if he could get up at all. No man would ever get up *twice*. Then the hat was passed around, and Jack would head up the street, maybe, for another declamation and another fast KO. There was no shortage of saloons in that world of males.

He preferred another ploy, however. He would go into a saloon early and catch the bartender's ear. "Is there some kind of pest you've got here that every customer would like to see popped in the jaw?" "Only you," the bartender was thinking but had the grace not to say it. "Because," Jack would continue, "I can knock him out." Jack had this going for him: Not only would the pest be KO'd, but to be knocked upside down by this skinny kid would be so ignominious that he might stay away for days, and when he returned he might tone down a bit. So the arrangement would be made. The bartender was the promoter and would arrange to pass the hat after the event, keeping half.

But there was not always easy pickings in flattening huge, grizzled miners, cowpokes, railroad men, lumberjacks and pesky barflies in saloons. To stay alive, Jack shined shoes, plucked fruit, did menial labor in a hotel, cut firewood, scrubbed floors and returned to mining when a new lode begged for attention.

When no honest work was to be found, he hustled at pool and bowling. And all the time he was getting, if not much bigger, a lot stronger and tougher. Heredity as much as environment helped. Hyrum had been a descendant of Irish immigrants who had labored in the death-dealing coal mines of West Virginia; Hyrum's father had been a blacksmith; and Jack's mother was a woman of immense endurance and fortitude. Then there was the Indian strain from both parents, which came out stronger in Jack than in his brothers: Stoicism, purposefulness, the ability to meet Fate head on and survive.

Oddly enough, Jack developed the idea for a bobbing, weaving, cobralike style from tossing large beets off railroad cars into farmers' wagons. To keep his balance while surfing on the unsteady, rolling pile, he had to bend his knees and crouch, ready to shift his weight rapidly from one side to the other. When he began to fight professionally, he fell into the position naturally. It enabled him to present some kind of defense while leaving both arms free for punching purposes. Years later, when he had strong ambitions to become heavyweight champion of the world, he built a cage four feet high. He would shadowbox inside it even after back pains developed; and if he raised his head, he got a nasty bump.

Jack made his official ring start (as Kid Blackie) in Salt Lake City for Hardy K. Downey, the local promoter. The purse was $2.50. Pitted against a bruiser called One-Punch Hancock, Dempsey lunged from his corner and One-punch lived up to his name—in reverse style. A feint with the right and a left hook to the jaw did him in.

The audience, a pretty tough crew, howled its disappointment over the brevity of the fight, and Downey became furious at Dempsey for being so efficient. "Call up some bum from the crowd," Dempsey hollered over the furor, "and I'll fight him for another two-fifty."

A huge man stepped forth, snarled to Dempsey that he was a lucky puncher and whisked off to the dressing room, where he was outfitted with trunks, gloves and boxing shoes. It developed, when the ring announcement was made, that he was One-Punch's brother. His name might have been Two-Punch. Dempsey sprang forth, feinted with his right, then threw two rapid left hooks—a crusher to the ribs and a smasher to the chin. Hancock fell into a coma. It was an auspicious debut for Dempsey.

During this Kid Blackie period, Dempsey had good times and bad. Once he received the amazing sum of twenty dollars for a one-rounder. Another time the local sheriff strolled into his dressing room and mentioned that boxing was illegal thereabouts. Dempsey would either have to wrestle his opponent, which was legal, or he would have to go to jail. The sheriff neglected to mention that the opponent was a wrestling champion. Dempsey was no wrestler but he knew what the jail must be like, so he consented to grapple and took a terrible beating.

Since riding the freights was likewise illegal, he had many a brush with railroad yardmen. One time he was nearly killed. He was scaling a freight-car ladder of a moving train to enjoy the luxury of a ride atop rather than one below, when from above his head a voice bellowed down, "Get off, ya bum!" The railroad worker kneeled down, the better to reach Jack with his club. The train was picking up speed, and Jack did not want to let go. He would have been better off if he had. The brakeman kept hitting him on the top of the head until Jack was so groggy he could no longer hang onto the ladder. He fell off, hitting the cinders with terrific force, rolling over and over, skinning himself from top to toe. After about a half hour he could raise himself up without toppling over, and he limped forty miles to the next town, wondering how he was going to get a meal.

Harry Dempsey acquired the name "Jack" from his brother Bernie, who had borrowed it from Jack Dempsey, the Nonpareil. As Jack Dempsey, Bernie was boxing as a heavyweight around Salt Lake City and Ogden, Utah, when he was matched in Denver with George Copelin, a two-hundred-pounder. He was to receive two hundred dollars for the fight, win or lose, and he promised Harry five of this grandiose

sum if Harry would act as his cornerman. Then, the day before the fight, Bernie decided that, at the age of forty, he was too old to last in the thin mountain air. "I can't get my breath," he told Harry. "I'm going to call off the fight." Jack was sore about losing the five dollars and, to spur Bernie on, said, "He's just a bum. Hell, I could lick him myself." Bernie took his brother up on it, even though, with lead in his shoes, Harry weighed no more than 150.

The promoter, when he was told of the switch, acted gloomy. "The kid's only 140 pounds," he complained. "A hundred sixty," Dempsey corrected. "I'll fight under the name Jack Dempsey. The crowd'll never know."

Copelin was sent for. A hard, dogged puncher with a tough chin, he sneered at Harry. "I'll kill him," he said, and agreed to the substitution. It would be an easy payday.

Harry was introduced as Jack Dempsey, and the crowd booed and hooted when they noted his ravaged, skinny appearance. But the punk could hit, and he could take a punch. Copelin went down six times in the first round. In the second round he went down once. But the thin air was giving Jack (as we shall call him henceforth) trouble. In the third, he started to conserve his strength. By the end of the sixth, he could hardly gulp in air, and he was ready to quit. "Just one more round," Bernie urged. Across the way, Copelin was on his stool, chest heaving, his mouth wide open. Bernie propelled his brother forth and Jack, summoning his last reserves, landed a few hooks that Copelin did not bother to block. Afraid he would have a corpse on his hands, the referee stopped the bout, and Jack was awarded a TKO. Bernie and he split the purse.

Bernie went back to mining and told Jack to keep the name—it sounded good.

Jack resumed his old trade of saloon fighting and once in a while fought professionally. In Ely, Nevada, he fought a good heavyweight named Joe Bond, who was managed by Jack Kearns. He did not knock Bond out, but his aggressiveness and punching power impressed Kearns, who was to figure strongly in Dempsey's future. Neither could have reached the pinnacle he did without the other.

In 1916 Dempsey and his sometime manager, Jack Price, invaded New York. Both carried cardboard suitcases containing their other suit, and both talked funny, by Gotham standards. They lived in a fleabag hotel. To eat, like Jack Johnson in bygone days, they would invade a saloon, flourish a nickel glass of beer and raid the free-lunch counter, stuffing themselves and pocketing enough for the next meal. Finally, after pounding on many doors, Jack got a fight with a huge heavyweight named Andre Anderson. New York did not allow referees' decisions in those days, but the newspapermen agreed Dempsey had won. He received twenty dollars for his efforts. Price then had to return to Salt Lake City—his mother was ill—and he sold Jack's contract to "John the Barber" Reisler, who promptly overmatched Dempsey with John Lester Johnson. A sinewy black with a terrific punch, Johnson had beaten Gunboat Smith and even Sam Langford—though it is possible that Langford's mind had been on something else. Johnson gave Dempsey the worst beating of his life, in the second round hitting him with a right-hand hook that caved in three of Jack's ribs. The pain was agonizing, and for the rest of the fight Jack was fearful that a second blow there would drive bone splinters up into his heart and kill him.

As the fight wore on, however, Jack's recuperative powers asserted themselves, and he was able to land a few shots of his own. He managed to last the ten rounds, and a few newspapermen even gave him the decision. Dempsey himself would have awarded the bout to Johnson—easily. The thirty-five dollars he received, after Reisler took his cut, was hardly enough to pay for bandages, tape and iodine.

Taped up so tight he could hardly breathe, aching in most joints, virtually broke, Jack was disgusted with the fight business. Without bothering to thank John the Barber, he entrained belowdecks for Salt Lake City, where his mother had set up a home. After a spell of mining, he returned to New York and

John the Barber, who wanted to match him with Gunboat Smith or Frank Moran, one of Willard's challengers. Either Reisler had immense faith in Dempsey, or he wanted to see him killed. Jack said no to both propositions, departed and in Kansas City got a job as a seventy-five-cent-a-day sparring partner for Carl Morris, "the Sepulpa Giant." He took some punching around but realized happily that, if he wanted to, he could beat this top contender among the heavyweights. In Salt Lake City he fought Fireman Jim Flynn for the first time, and some have speculated that, for monetary reasons, he did not go all out. In any event, Flynn knocked him down in the first round. He got up, to be knocked down again. This continued for a while, and then his brother Bernie threw in the towel. After that, Jack found it hard to get fights in the area. He drifted off again to find other work.

Working in a shipyard in Oakland, Jack happened to pop into a saloon for a beer and noticed a brawl at the other end of the bar. Two big fellows were beating up a little one; indeed, the boots were about to be put to him. Jack was generally peaceful in saloons unless a purse was offered, but he felt sorry for the smaller man. He got the attention of one of the assailants and flattened him, then repeated the process. The little man was Jack Kearns. The two discussed Dempsey's engaging him as manager, but Dempsey at that time preferred the security of his job, and the two parted. However, the possibility of linking up with the skinny youngster who backed off from no one stayed with Kearns.

There was more serendipity for Dempsey in a saloon in Ely, Nevada. For there, playing ragtime piano, was petite brunette Maxine Cates, some years older than he. She was a lady of easy virtue, as she confessed to him—everybody knew it, anyway—but he fell in love with her and married her. (Later she was to become a deadly enemy.) Married life did not suit her particularly, and once in a while Jack would have to track her down in some saloon or other in the Far West. Then, to earn money to keep the household running, Jack went to Seattle to work in a lumberyard.

On learning that his brother Bruce had died, Jack hastened home. He was too late for the funeral, but waiting for him was a communication from Kearns, who wondered if he was still interested in prizefighting. Dempsey was. The partnership was formed.

A word about Kearns. Born John Leo McKernan in Michigan, he had as checkered a career as Tex Rickard. Though small, he had the courage of a lion, as proven by the fact that he was once a bouncer in a dive on the Barbary Coast. He also became, as the years passed, a gold weigher in a saloon, a taxi driver (in Seattle), a miner, a dealer in a gambling house, a ballplayer (temporarily, with Seattle, in the Pacific Coast League) and a welterweight fighter. He had the honor to be beaten by Honey Mellody and Mysterious Billy Smith, both of whom, at one time or another, held the welterweight title. When he was in the money he changed clothes three times a day, splashed himself with perfume and wore a big diamond ring. He was expert at ballyhoo and had the ethics of a shell-game operator. He hated Rickard because he felt Rickard had swindled him out of the management of a promising fighter from Australia, Les Darcy. But Rickard had merely outsmarted him, as he had a dozen other managers. Kearns had something of a double standard about this kind of thing. However, he was good for Dempsey.

The two had no contract, merely a handshake, and they were to split the money down the middle. Impressed by Kearns's splendor and glib talk, Dempsey let him make all the decisions. If a proposition was put to him, Dempsey would say, "Let Jack decide. He's the doctor." Hence Kearns's nickname of Doc.

Kearns launched his tiger on a whirlwind tour to promote his skills and gain a reputation. First came a bunch of nobodies, and then Gunboat Smith in San Francisco. In the second round Dempsey got careless and took a terrific clout on the chin. On the ferryboat returning to Oakland, Jack apologized for losing. "What do you mean?" asked Kearns, astonished. "You won by a knockout!" It seemed that Dempsey had no memory

of the fight after the punch in the second round, but he had fought on by sheer instinct and had battered Smith to pieces. Then came a victory over Carl Morris, in line for a Willard shot, and knockouts of Homer Smith, Fireman Jim Flynn, Bill Brennan, Bull Sadee and the eighteen-second KO of Fred Fulton. Rickard could ignore him no longer. "You've got to fight me," the redolent Kearns insisted. And so, though he was the youngest, smallest and least known of all the challengers, Dempsey got the nod.

More suspicion than is usual surrounded the arrangements for the Willard-Dempsey fight. Jess wanted the bandaging of hands done in the ring, and he got his way. Willard's rabbit punch, delivered from his great height to the back of the neck, was accepted by Kearns as a legal punch, so long as it was not delivered with the heel of the hand. Major Biddle and Rickard were to be the judges. Kearns insisted that they operate from opposite sides of the ring so they would be unable to confer with one another. Rickard had his way about a decision on possible fouls: All three officials were to discuss them before any binding decision was made. (Rickard's investment was such that he wanted to have a measure of control over decisions rather than leave them to the referee.)

Sparring did not go well for either fighter. Willard suffered a painful cut lip; the Jamaica Kid, a very tough sparring partner, gave Dempsey a hard smash over the eye that started the claret flowing. Dempsey soaked his face in brine to make his skin tougher, and Kearns threatened to kill anyone who hit the cut.

Toledo never had it so good. "The greatest stadium ever built"—a quote from a New York *Sun* reporter—was erected by Jim McDonald of San Francisco. Costing one hundred thousand dollars, it sat eighty thousand, and twenty thousand more, if they chose, could stand up.

Rickard was always one for style. He wanted to elevate boxing, fill the stalls with swells. And if swells, why not ladies? The stadium included a special section, fenced off by barbed wire, for members of the suffragette sex. Here they would be safe from attack by excited males, and it was hoped that their ears would not explode from the bad language they were certain to hear.

Hotels gouged their customers, as did restaurants. A cot in an overcrowded hotel just before the fight could cost as much as a bridal suite in less prosperous times. Battling Nelson, on assignment from the Chicago *Daily News,* slept in a pup tent next to the stadium and one night got so soused he thought the lemonade tank was a swimming pool and bathed in it. He finally took in a mouthful of the stuff and realized it had a lemony taste. He was swimming either in a concessionaire's prize or in the pool of the world's richest man. It served to cool him off, however.

A heat wave had descended, and it was *hot.* Concessionaires had their troubles. Ice cream melted before it could be served. Nobody wanted anything salty to eat because it only increased thirst. Two things sold well: Water at fifteen cents a cup, and seat cushions. The heat caused pitch to rise from the green planks used for seats, and many a fellow who didn't have a cushion found his pants ripped when he stood up. What saved people from barking in the streets, driven mad by all this discomfort, was booze. Prohibition had been thrust on a trembling nation on midnight of June 30, four days before the fight. Yet Toledoans managed to get liquor, and visitors could purchase it for a price. "John Barleycorn is everywhere available," a newspaperman reported.

The fight was the most bizarre in boxing history. Dempsey, who was formally presented to Willard by referee Ollie Pecord, was rough-bearded, tanned, intense, with his hair shaved over his ears so he could sweat better. Willard was huge, not so hard, not so finely trained, not so fierce—but huge. A couple of fans, seeing Dempsey eye Willard, nudged one another: "Look, the big guy's got him buffaloed already." But Dempsey, with his killer's eye, was appraising Willard not as a danger but as a target—that long body so easy to hit, that sizable jaw, those arms that could

not push you away once you got inside. Would the jab of a thirty-four-year-old man who did not relish fighting stave off a stalking, weaving, hungry, hooking challenger? Dempsey gave a final scowl, and the two parted to their corners.

At the gong, Dempsey did not charge, as was his wont. To confuse the giant, he stayed away, accepting a light jab or two, crouching, his jaw tucked behind his left shoulder. He bounded clear of a jab. Willard advanced, left foot forward, left arm outstretched. Dempsey was not unmindful of Kearns's bet. Suddenly he exploded. He charged forward, ignoring the jab, and shot a wilting right to the heart, then swung the left hook that poets should write about. It hit Willard in the jaw and broke it in seven places. Willard went down, got up and, with Dempsey standing over him, was smashed down again. The next time he got up, Dempsey bore in, hitting body, jaw, eye, mouth. Willard went down seven times, and the last time—four teeth missing, jaw broken, eye closed, bleeding from the nose—he could not get up.

Imagine yourself Willard in that first round. Here was the champion of the world, the man who had placed the white man back on his throne, now smashed and battered about the ring, feeling pain and unable to defend or escape beyond the twenty-four-foot ring. The blows from this engine of destruction kept coming. Dempsey moved in, crouched, uninjurable. He brushed off the famed Willard left jab like a man erasing gnats, and wham, wham, wham. Not the pretty one-two of Peter Jackson or the smart pecking of your eyes by Sayers or the discouraging slipping of blows by Corbett (who, like Johnson in his best days, simply could not be hit) or the single smashing belt to the liver of Jeffries, but the blows of a man who kept advancing and firing shots at your stomach and head and neck and temple. And when you fell, as fall you must, there he was standing over you while the referee counted. Now, from instinct, you are up at eight or nine. But here he comes again. When you are up, he smashes you down. And every time, you go down more easily. You are bloodied, broken, groggy, unable to see or hear distinctly, no longer anything but a tired old man. . . .

The crowd roared and kept roaring. Never had a champion taken such a thorough beating, and never had such a dynamic, merciless hitter been seen. The beauty of Dempsey was that he never let his man recover. He had fought too many miners, cowhands, wranglers, ramrods, brakemen, railroad guards and the like, in saloons and out, to give his man a chance to recover once he was vulnerable. The fans, Ethel Barrymore among them, were seeing just what 188 pounds, *used efficiently*, could do.

Ollie Pecord raised Dempsey's hand in victory. The ring was filled with fans eager to congratulate Dempsey. Willard, meanwhile, was sitting half-conscious in his corner. Kearns shooed Dempsey, along with Bill Tate, a second, and the Jamaica Kid, to the dressing room.

Then suddenly, as Dempsey pressed through the throng, he heard Kearns yelling at him and waving. He was screaming for Jack to return to the ring. Dempsey was about thirty yards away. He turned around with a great deal of difficulty and tried to plough his way back through the packed aisle. If someone was stubborn about blocking his passage, he gave him a short rap on the chin. Tate got in front of him to clear the way, and the Jamaica Kid brought up the rear. By the time he reached the ring, exhausted from his efforts, it had been cleared. Then Kearns explained. "The round was over before ten," he said over the din. "The son of a bitches are making me do it again!" (Most managers say "we" when they really mean "he"—their fighter. But Kearns's ego was such that he assumed all the credit. "I knocked out Fireman Flynn in one round," he would remark.)

This was the totally incredible situation: The crowd had been making so much noise that the gong, though struck seconds before the count of ten, had not been heard by either fighter, either corner or the referee. The official timekeeper, Warren Barbour (later to be a U.S. senator from New Jersey), was the only person in the shouting, screaming, sweltering dough of spectators to recognize that Willard had not been officially knocked out. Barbour finally convinced Pecord, who must have been the most confused referee in history, that the fight should continue. Curiously enough, Willard could have won the fight on a technicality at that point because Dempsey had been out of the ring for about four minutes, and the rules stated that he must be ready to resume the battle after one minute.

Kearns had lost his bet, but he knew he had the world's greatest meal ticket if Dempsey could take the title, so he told him to coast. Willard had had about five minutes to pull himself together instead of the usual minute, so he was not quite as debilitated as his appearance indicated. Dempsey, arm-weary from his assaults in the first round and the effort of fighting through the crowd, fought lackadaisically in the second. Suddenly, as if from nowhere, Willard unleashed his finest punch, the right uppercut. Dempsey's head nearly flew from his shoulders. He staggered back, and a roaring pounded against his ears. If he had not worked himself into splendid condition and if Willard had not been weary himself, the latter might have hung on to his championship. (When one considers what he managed against Dempsey, that preposterous victory over Johnson takes on an aura of reality.) Dempsey was discreet the rest of the round, recuperating his strength.

By round three Jack was resigned to the fact that he would have to pace himself to last out the fight. His battle plan was to stay on Willard's blind side (his right eye was swollen shut) and keep pumping punches to the body until Jess dropped his hands, then go for the head. Willard was a pitiable spectacle: blood all over his face, his jaw hanging loose, his body, ribs broken, bent forward from the hard smashes he had absorbed there, his legs tottering. Dempsey hit him a few blows in the stomach, staying out of reach of the uppercut. There were no knockdowns in the round.

When the bell rang for the fourth, Jess was still on his stool, a completely beaten man who simply could not fight another round. His chief second threw in the towel, and the world had a new champion—the first time the title had been won between rounds. Technically, it was a knockout for Dempsey in the third. An exultant crowd carried him off to the dressing room.

After the inevitable celebrating, with Kearns as the jolly master of ceremonies, Dempsey flung himself into bed, completely exhausted. He had a terrible nightmare—that the giant Willard was battering him all over the ring. He woke in a cold sweat, arose and anxiously turned on the lights. The mirror showed there was not a mark on his face. He threw on some clothes and strode downstairs and out onto the street. A newsboy was hawking papers on the corner. Dempsey hurried over to him.

"Listen," he said. "The fight this afternoon. Who won it?"

The newsboy leaned forward to look in Jack's face. "Say," he said, broadly smiling, "you're Jack Dempsey, ain't you?"

Dempsey nodded.

"You did, you dope!"

Relieved, Jack flipped him a dollar, returned to the hotel and sank into bed.

The wages of fame and affluence are good times. As champion, Jack was now under the public microscope, fighting off adulation wherever he went, and he had automatic entree into the hearts of the high born, the rich and the mighty. He drew crowds and posed for photos. He had to wear a necktie, which he detested, learn to use the right knife and fork, stumble around a dance floor and make small talk with celebrities at parties. He became at one with the greats of the time: Jimmy Walker, not yet mayor, Bugs Baer, Rube Goldberg, Bert Lahr, Paul Whitman, O. O. McIntyre, Fred and Adele Astaire. A single man (he had been divorced by Maxine before the Fulton fight), he was much in demand by matchmakers. He visited nightclubs and speakeasies like Texas Guinan's, Club Richman, Legs Diamond's Hotsy Totsy and the Cotton Club in Harlem, generally drinking beer, because wine made him sleepy. He was not completely metamorphosed. A practical joker, he delighted in giving hotfoots to celebrities.

Hollywood sent out its siren call, and Jack repaired there to make some short subjects and a serial called *Daredevil Jack*, which was no better and no worse than a dozen others assembly-lined by the thriving movie industry. He became good friends with kindred soul Douglas Fairbanks, erudite Charlie Chaplin and Wallace Reid, who had played Jeff the Blacksmith in *Birth of a Nation* and who later became a victim of the drug habit and committed suicide. He even sparred with Valentino. His comment was, "He has nice footwork, but he can't hit worth a damn."

While Jack was partying and making pictures, seemingly without a care, a terrible blow fell in February, 1920. He was indicted by a San Francisco grand jury for having evaded the draft. Specifically, he was charged with direct evasion of the selective draft, false statements in his questionnaire as to his dependents and false statements to the district draft board in San Francsico. The story behind the charge was that a San Francisco newspaperman had

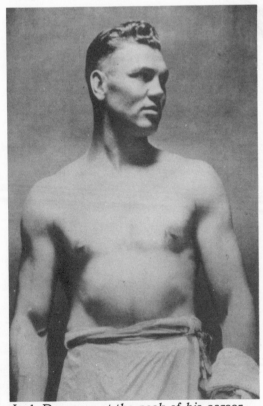

Jack Dempsey at the peak of his career

asked Jack as a favor to box an exhibition for some charity, and Jack had turned him down. Incensed over the refusal, the reporter had vindictively gone to the draft board files and dug out Jack's records. Then he had chased down Maxine, whom Jack had claimed as a dependent, and had gotten her to state that she had not been a dependent of Jack's at the time.

In June Maxine repeated her statement in Federal court. Indeed, she claimed she had been supporting *him*. She also admitted she was a lady of loose morals, "a woman of the underworld," which was where she got her money. Jack spent a good deal of time cringing, and the trial got immense play in the California press, though not so much nationally.

A few days after this testimony Maxine did a volte-face, her lawyer producing an affidavit stating that she had made these assertions about Dempsey out of "pique" and that they were false. A week later the indictment charging Jack with conspiracy to evade the draft was dismissed. The jury was out ten minutes and took only one ballot. However, the image of the heavyweight champion took a terrific walloping.

Dempsey's having been branded a slacker by many fans and the degrading draft-dodger trial were grist for Rickard's mill in the summer of 1921. Looking around for a worthy foe for the champion, he lit on Georges Carpentier, who had held every weight title in France while growing up. He was at the time heavyweight champion of France and light-heavyweight champion of Europe. He was a fast, game boxing artist with a powerful right-hand punch.

Dempsey was cast as the villain of the drama, and the Frenchman, a genuine war hero, took the sympathetic role. He had been decorated twice for flying his plane low over Boche lines on a reconnaissance mission and had been wounded in the hand and head. He was, in addition, a very nice-looking young man, educated, a philosopher of sorts and charming and courteous to all. He was reputed to be a skillful billiard player and as graceful on the ballroom floor as he was in the ring. As a consequence, he was a great favorite with the well born and the sophisticated. When he knocked out Joe Beckett, the British heavyweight champion, George Bernard Shaw covered the fight for a London paper. Shaw was much impressed by Carpentier's speed and right-hand power. (Later he would write that he thought Carpentier, more for spiritual reasons than physical, would defeat Dempsey.) Even Edward, Prince of Wales, (who was to become both king and the Duke of Windsor later on) was impressed. The Frenchman was invited to box an exhibition before King George and Queen Mary. As a boxer and a socialite, his qualifications were impeccable. The trouble was, he weighed only 170 pounds—about 25 pounds less than the champion.

After a great deal of haggling with Kearns and François Descamps, Carpentier's excitable manager, Rickard agreed to pay Dempsey three hundred thousand dollars and Carpentier two hundred thousand dollars. These were fantastic fees at the time, but Rickard never did anything on a small scale. Each was also to get a percentage of the movie rights. Rickard knew if everything came off as planned (which it nearly did not), he would make a handsome profit. Besides, there was always exhilaration in a wild gamble.

Tex ordered the construction of a huge stadium, seating about ninety thousand people, in a desolate lot near Jersey City called Boyle's Thirty Acres. (Boyle was a manufacturer of paper boxes.) The press played up the contrasting backgrounds and personal popularity of the two men (Americans loved the people of France at the time), and ticket orders came pouring in.

Their choice of camps reflected the different images of the battlers. The Dempsey-Kearns headquarters was in a second-rate hotel on the Atlantic City boardwalk, and Dempsey trained on a nearby deserted airfield. With the ebullient and indefatigable Kearns as impresario, nearly everything was permitted at the hotel. The lobby featured a dice game. All kinds of hangers-on, riffraff, marginal show-biz types and sportswriters poured liquor down their throats at Kearns's expense, and female companionship was always available.

Later on the company might go out and cut up in restaurants. A couple of the rowdier element got themselves arrested, embarrassing both Kearns and Dempsey.

The Frenchman's camp, or castle, was established on an estate in the Eastern social capital of Manhasset, L. I., which Jack Curley had arranged for the invaders to occupy. Carpentier's entourage included Descamps, reputed to be able to put the whammy on the Orchid Man's opponents with his hypnotic eye; Marco, his chef; Gus Williams, his masseur; Charles Ledoux, the bantamweight champion of France, and Carpentier's poodle, Flip.

For one of the rare times in pugilistic history, a boxer's camp was off limits to the press. Barbed-wire entanglements and state troopers discouraged reporters from watching the French Ambassador of Swat do his training. They had to climb trees to spy or mount a disguise to fool the guards at the entrance. A number of society folk were permitted in—Carpentier was lionized by society on those nights he stepped out—but that was all. Rickard's office let it be known that the reason for the strange interdiction against the press and the great unwashed was to prevent Carpentier's secret punch from being revealed. The real reason was to keep both press and public from realizing the truth about Carpentier's size. Charm was no defense against *Homo neanderthalensis,* and Rickard felt the gate might be hurt.

When the Prince of Wales showed up in the U.S., partied to the gills by wealthy matrons trying to outdo one another, the two kindred souls met at an affair, sneaked off and had themselves a plebeian good time at a roadside inn. They became so crocked that they slept on the floor in Carpentier's room.

On the day of the fight—July 2, 1921—Jersey City's Mayor Frank Hague, foreseeing all kinds of bottlenecks, riots and confusion, assigned eight hundred police to patrol the area, inside and out, along with 160 plainclothesmen. Tex supplemented these battalions with several of his own, paid for out of his personal pocket, along with an elite corps of ushers. Waterloo was not more carefully planned.

That morning limousines, private railway cars and even yachts disgorged more of society's finest than even Rickard could have hoped for. Their numbers included the Biddles of Philadelphia, John D. Rockefeller, Jr., Vincent Astor, Harry Payne Whitney, William H. Vanderbilt, Kermit Roosevelt, Alice Roosevelt Longworth, Harry A. Sinclair, George H. Gould; along with ambassadors and chargés d'affaires, special envoys, M.P.'s, princes, counts, countesses, baronets, ministers. Boxing was given an aura of respectability, nay, grandeur, that it had never enjoyed before. And in addition to these flocked the mighty of the show-biz and sports worlds, including Sam H. Harris, George M. Cohan, Blanche Bates and Colonel Jacob Ruppert, a baron of sorts himself and the owner of the Yankees. An American Association doubleheader was called off because the ballplayers wanted to go to the fight.

Standing at the top of the arena, outside the fighters' locker rooms, Rickard, brandishing a cigar, admired his clientele. "Did you ever see so many millionaires?" he demanded of every crony who passed.

When Dempsey arrived, Rickard halted him before he entered the locker room. "Listen, Jack" he said, "you saw that crowd down there. It's a million-dollar gate, maybe more. The biggest payday in boxing history. And there can be others as good."

"So?" said Dempsey, puzzled.

"So my advice is," said Rickard, staring at Jack, "don't spoil it. If you kill this Frenchman, you'll kill boxing."

Jack was nonplussed. He thought about it a second and then, expressionless, noncommittal, went into the dressing room. Rickard wondered what the decision would be. Well, at least he had done what he could to save a man's life.

There probably hadn't been a yell like it since the charge at Little Big Horn when the stirring "Marseillaise" was struck up and Carpentier, wearing a gray robe with black cuffs, a towel around his neck, appeared at the top of the aisle, ready to descend with his handlers and manager. The spectators leapt from their seats and howled and yowled and whistled and stamped their feet and hollered encouragement. But as Carpentier started to walk down, all that violent concerted movement caused the huge structure to sway back and forth, and those perched high up wondered if it was going to topple completely over, crushing them all to death. A few of them hollered in alarm. But other noises drowned them out, and those down front did not feel the swaying and paid no heed in the general excitement and anticipation. Even Rickard, at ringside, did not know about the potential disaster. Fortunately, there was no general panic, which would have been as bad as the collapse of the bowl, and then Dempsey appeared, wearing a raggedy red sweater and blue trunks. Mild cheers went up, intermingled with boos, and he marched down the aisle to a few cries of "Slacker!" and "Bum," which he had become used to. (No one ever remembers, or credits, exoneration.)

The ritual of celebrity introductions began—the mayor, the governor, Tex, some visiting fighters—and then Carpentier and Dempsey. Again the Frenchman's far greater popularity was noisily in evidence. Dempsey, who looked bearded and fierce and large compared to the jaunty, relatively frail-looking Frenchman, was stoic through it all. The weights were announced as 172 against 198. Then came the instructions from Harry Ertle, the perfunctory tap of gloves, Carpentier's wish of good luck to his opponent and the fight began.

On Kearns's advice, Dempsey did not rush the Frenchman, who was not one of these big, slow fighters who could not escape, but a clever boxer. As a result, Jack found himself looking clumsy for a while, dazzled, as they say, by footwork. His best move, to avoid Carpentier's stinging, peppery jabs, was clinching, trying to make use of his weight advantage. Then, stung by a jab that landed on his right eye, he hurled himself forward and hooked a left to Carpentier's body and threw a straight right at his nose. First blood for Dempsey.

In the second round Carpentier showed a desire to stand and slug with the champion, and the two traded punches without much regard for defense. Then, to the amazement of the crowd, a left jab by Carpentier was followed by a hard right. It caught Dempsey high on the jaw; a little lower and the fight might have ended then and there. Dempsey reeled backwards, stunned, and the crowd, rising to its feet, grew hysterical, shouting for the Frenchman to follow up his advantage. He did. Pinning Dempsey on the ropes, he shot seven or more hard punches at Dempsey's head. The champion, weaving and bobbing, his hands held in front of his face for protection, blocked some and slipped some and took some, but he managed to stay on his feet. The bell rang.

The applause was deafening for the Ambassador as he walked back to his corner. The arena buzzed with hope. Dempsey had been hurt. He turned out to be a sucker for a right. Maybe the championship would change hands. Up top, the spectators were less concerned with that than with their own limbs, for the upper reaches had started to sway again.

One of Dempsey's great strengths was his power of recuperation. Another was his instinct to fight hardest when hurt. He sprang at the Frenchman as hammer hit gong and, heedless of punishment, belabored the challenger with some of the hardest blows ever thrown in the ring. Carpentier tried to escape, but Dempsey pursued. Left hook to the body. Left hook to the head. Left and right hooks to the body. Left hook to the body, straight right to the head. Feint with the right, left hook to the body and head. The blows went through the Frenchman's guard as though it did not exist. Carpentier's body grew pink, and his eye swelled up. His nose and mouth grew red with blood. Two heavy shots to the stomach nearly tore him in half. The bell rang, and Carpentier's courage drew applause as he slowly made his way to his corner.

The gong, and once again the pursuit of a game but beaten fighter. Short lefts and rights and Carpentier went down for the count of nine. He desperately threw himself to his feet, only to be attacked with another flurry of punches.

He went down again.

On the radio, an excited J. Andrew White was yelling for his audience: "The Frenchman is down! The referee is counting—three, four . . . Carpentier makes no effort to rise . . . six, seven, he's sinking to the mat . . . nine, ten! . . . The fight is over! Jack Dempsey remains heavyweight champion of the world!"

There was no applause or cheering. Most men were glum and a few women were heard to sob. The villain of the piece bent down, raised his fallen foe and helped carry him to his corner.

Not many persons in that great arena paid much attention to a light-heavyweight boxer named Gene Tunney, who, in a preliminary, had knocked out Soldier Jones in the seventh round. After the fight Tunney had dressed and kneeled at ringside to study the champion's moves. He had ambitious, ridiculous plans.

Kearns gasped when the figures were announced: $1,553,422 had been taken in from 77,328 customers. "Damn it," he told Dempsey, "I should have held him up for more money."

Dempsey fought a few exhibition bouts in the remainder of 1921 and the beginning of 1922 just to keep his hand in and, as befitted his position, became something of a fashion plate. He got involved in a few business interests, including ownership of a racing stable. Then he journeyed to Europe with Kearns, a couple of raffish friends and writer Damon Runyon. There his popularity was unbounded. In England he hobnobbed with the Royal Family, generals and earls. At the Longchamps racetrack in France he was nearly smothered to death by adoring fans. He refereed a bout in Paris and was awarded a medal by the French government. In Berlin he made the mistake of telling reporters he was fond of German sheep dogs. The next morning sheep dogs belonging to a thousand owners invaded the lobby of the hotel, snarling and barking and tugging at leashes, causing a near-riot. After more touring and putting nightclubs to bed, the group was forced to return to America— money was running low. Kearns realized he must find Dempsey somebody important to fight.

Back in America, Dempsey casually knocked out nearly everybody who had the nerve to step in the ring with him, sometimes three in a single night. And he waited for Kearns to come up with a worthwhile opponent. Then came Shelby, Montana. If ever a town in peacetime could be said to have been raped by two people, that would be Shelby in the summer of 1923, the two people being Kearns and Dempsey.

Shelby was a town of five hundred, consisting mainly of farmers, cowboys and sheepherders. There were three rooming houses, a hotel, a railroad depot, a general store, a feed store and an army-navy store. But oil had suddenly been struck there, and the town's aristocracy, such as the mayor and the owner of the army-navy store, wanted to sell oil stock, in the fashion of a number of Texas oil-boom towns. But first they had to put the town on the map. In a saloon one evening, the suggestion was made to put on a championship fight. All were enthusiastic. Dempsey would be a good man to get, they reasoned. Through a Minnesota boxing-magazine publisher they contacted Kearns. He had never heard of the town, but Dempsey needed the work and money was always useful. The town fathers offered Dempsey $300,000—$100,000 to be paid on signing the contract, $100,000 payable on June 15 and $100,000 on July 2, two days before the fight. The papers were signed in Chicago in May, and the first payment was duly made. Dempsey's opponent was to be Tommy Gibbons of St. Paul, a good, brainy boxer, but not much of a hitter. So anxious was he to try his wares against the champion that Gibbons agreed to accept $7,500 for training expenses and then take 50 per cent of whatever profits accrued from the fight. It was an over-optimistic contract, it developed.

Dempsey did not take the fight too seriously. Training at Great Falls, he shared in practical jokes with his staff and played with a timber-wolf cub. Gibbons worked like a Trojan in Shelby. June 15 rolled around, and Kearns demanded the second payment. It did not seem to be available, so Kearns threatened to pull out. In desperation, the merchants and oil operators pooled their resources, including mortgaging their sheep, and came forth with it, mollifying Kearns.

Space was at a premium in the town. Some reporters and other visitors solved the problem of where to sleep by wandering through the town saloons and sawdust gambling palaces till dawn, then rousting a friend from his bed and sleeping in it most of the day. Liquor, brought down sub rosa from Canada in oil tank cars, flowed freely. Since Shelby had no paved streets, cloudbursts were disastrous. Dozens of reporters and tenderfoot visitors lost their boots in trying to get from one side of a street to the other. There was a store fire and the local constable, excitedly running toward it, shot himself in the foot. Around June 29 the mayor told Kearns he doubted if he could raise the third $100,000, and Kearns again threatened to pull out. The mayor offered to let Kearns take over the box office until the sum was reached, but Kearns refused. He kept saying there would be no fight, which discouraged a lot of fans from attending. On July 2, he declared, "The fight is off." Local citizens and those who had made a long trip to see the spectacle turned away in disappointment. That evening Kearns was visited in his Great Falls hotel room by a delegation of lynchers. One of them carried a rope. They insisted on there being a fight. Kearns had a change of heart and the next day told the mayor the fight was on. He agreed to take his $100,000 from the gate receipts.

The crowd of 7,202 in the bowl built to seat 50,000 included cowboys, millionaires, Blackfeet Indians, Grantland Rice, Westbrook Pegler, Mae Murray, One-Eyed Connolly, shepherds, cowpokes and sleepless local citizens. Kearns and Dan McKettrick had charge of the box office.

Gibbons outboxed Dempsey thoroughly in the early rounds, to the crowd's delight, and, frustrated, Dempsey began to play rough. He hit Gibbons so low so many times that the spectators almost rioted, and their howls were audible for miles. But the referee, Jim Dougherty, was a good friend of Jack's and had been Kearns's personal selection. He affected not to see any of this. Gibbons never went down and lasted the fifteen rounds, but Dempsey got the decision. In the countinghouse, Kearns picked up $68,000. This was less than $100,000, so he kept all of it. After the fight he and Dempsey and McKettrick and their entourage skipped out of town, having made $268,000 out of the fight. The city went bankrupt, the merchants went broke and four banks went bust. Gibbons got nothing. So much for Shelby, Montana.

Dempsey had been slow and out of shape when he fought Gibbons. He tried to rectify that condition during the summer, for Kearns had signed him to fight Luis Angel Firpo on September 14. Firpo was one of the strangest fighters who ever lived, and he was to involve Dempsey in the most vicious first round ever engaged in by two boxers.

Firpo was a large, savage-looking man with gigantic shoulders and chest and soulful brown eyes. He was an amazingly tough, if crude, fighter (he never had a boxing lesson) and an even better businessman. If he had not been such a good businessman, the outcome of the fight might have been different. He had the habit of coming out of his corner snorting and tossing his great head with its mane of black shaggy hair, which intimidated a great many opponents. Damon Runyon nicknamed him The Wild Bull of the Pampas. He was six feet three and weighed 220 pounds. He owned a clublike right hand that could fell an ox. Indeed, he did it once, thus earning comparison with the legendary Greek athlete Milo of Crotona, who performed the same feat, having gained strength from carrying a calf upstairs every day (the same one, which kept getting heavier as Milo got stronger).

Born in Junín in the province of Buenos Aires, Firpo worked as a butcher, a brickmaker and a drugstore clerk before turning to prizefighting in 1919. He was a year younger than Dempsey. He beat everyone he faced for two years, including transient fighters from the United States, and then decided to seek his fortune up north. Deemed the champion of South America, he came to New York with a couple of dollars in his pocket and a cardboard suitcase with his other suit in it. In his first fight, with Sailor Tom Maxted, he showed his business savvy. Without telling Maxted, at his own expense Firpo arranged to have pictures taken of the fight. (Maxted, who was KO'd in the seventh, later sued but got no satisfaction from Firpo.) Firpo fought two more optimists who thought his clumsiness was an index to his ability, and then, armed with traveling money, he returned to Buenos Aires. Suggesting that Maxted was a top contender for the heavyweight championship, he showed the films. Patriotic South Americans, happy to see one of their number whip a good *Nortamericano,* swarmed to theatres over most of the continent, and Firpo is said to have realized one hundred thousand dollars from the venture.

On his second trip to the United States in February, 1923, Firpo went to see Rickard and apparently reached some sort of understanding with him. He was matched with Bill Brennan, whom he knocked out, and Jack McAuliffe, whom he also knocked out, and then he was matched with the aging Willard, who was making a comeback. The fight with Jess at Boyle's Thirty Acres drew eighty-two thousand fans, despite the fact that not many thought the ex-champion had a chance. It was the largest prizefight crowd in history up to then. Because the prices were reasonable, however, the gate was only four hundred thousand dollars. Firpo got 25 per cent of it. The forty-one-year-old Willard did better than expected. He outboxed the South American for eight rounds, then sort of wilted away in the ninth. A KO was acknowledged for Firpo.

Now the Wild Bull was to face Dempsey. In his early training for the Dempsey fight, he picked up pin money by traveling around the country knocking out palookas. When he set up his camp under the careful eye of Jimmy DeForest, one of the most erudite trainers in the business, he found he did not like to do roadwork or be starved under the diet prescribed for him by Jimmy, and so he fired him. For two reasons this might have cost him the championship: De-Forest would have gotten him into even better shape than he was to withstand Dempsey's assaults; and DeForest knew his boxing rules. As substitute, Firpo imported two Argentinian friends with whom he was more compatible, and he ate what he liked. His sparring partners were a discontented lot because he paid them only half the going rate and made them pay their own hospital bills. He was a prudent man.

Some eighty-eight thousand fans stormed into the Polo Grounds that balmy night, some to see U.S. honor defended against the jungle creature from an exotic land; some to see Dempsey get his block knocked off (after the Shelby swindle he had lost some popularity); and some just to see a fight between two guys who could hit. The gate totaled $1,127,882, which was gratifying to Rickard; it showed he had not lost his ability as a stage director.

In his prefight ritual, Tex came into Dempsey's dressing room. Earlier, he had warned Dempsey not to be overconfident; though untutored, the Wild Bull was a helluva fighter. Now another fear beset him. "Jack," he said. "There's at least eighty thousand fans out there, swells among them. This guy is a clumsy bum. Take it easy. If you knock him out too fast, they won't think they got their money's worth."

Dempsey, who knew something about the might of Firpo's right hand, stared at Rickard a moment. His answer is unprintable. Then he lay down on the dressing table and allowed his back to be massaged by his trainer, Jerry Luvadis. Rickard left to count the house.

When referee Johnny Gallegher introduced the fighters, cheers for the South American, who outweighed Jack by twenty-five pounds and looked hairy and fierce, were loud. But those for Dempsey were louder. The fighters went back to their corners, awaiting the sharp clang of the bell. In Firpo's corner, his Argentinian friends encouraged him in excited voices. Dempsey scowled across the ring.

The gong rang.

Now began the greatest round in the history of prizefighting; the most exciting, the most suspenseful, the most confused, the most savage, the most memorable.

The spectators rose to their feet with a roar as the Dempsey of old sprang across the ring like a bolt of lightning and, gambling, flung a long left hook at Firpo's jaw. The blow fell short, and Dempsey was thrown off-balance, temporarily defenseless. Firpo's right chopped down at Dempsey's jaw. The fight would have ended then and there but for one thing. Dempsey fell forward, and Firpo was close enough to him so that he hit Firpo's chest with his head and instinctively held on, his knees not yet touching the mat. As Gallegher looked on in bewilderment, Dempsey clutched with the grip of death, and Firpo could not shake him off. Finally he did, but the respite had put strength into Dempsey's legs and he was able to function again—as a savage automaton. Suffused with a blinding rage, in a frenzy of self-preservation, hatred and fear, he tore at Firpo, his arms working like pistons. Firpo had never met such an assault. He backed off; then a left to the chin, cannily aimed, sent him rocketing to the canvas.

Now began Firpo's ordeal. He could not escape the demon hovering directly over him. Every time he got up, he was sent crashing down by one of those thunderous blows. Once he tried to escape by crawling on his hands and knees. The demon pursued. Meanwhile, the referee was counting, stopping, counting again. Once Dempsey had to step over Firpo to get into better position to fire his shot. Once Firpo could not even *rise* before the demon struck. The seconds in his corner were dumfounded at what was going on. There were five knockdowns in all.

But rise Firpo did. On unsteady legs, he brought his right around, hitting Dempsey in the side of the jaw. Dempsey fell forward on his hands and knees. But before Gallegher could start the count Dempsey had lunged forward and up, and a short right uppercut sent the South American down again. Then Firpo was up and rushing at Dempsey, who backed off, getting set to work inside the right with his left hook. Firpo's charge drove Dempsey to the ropes, where he was pinned by Firpo's weight, helpless to swing or escape. Six times

the famous right struck him about the head, but without its usual force because of the cramped position. In desperation, Dempsey tried to duck out from under. His head was below the top strand of the ropes when he was hit with another right. He spun and flew through the ropes in a kind of backward dive. The crowd, standing on chairs, leaping in the aisles, grew delirious. Where had Dempsey gone?

He had landed on a row of reporters in the front seats. Some claim he busted a typewriter when he fell. In any event, a great deal of confusion and consternation ensued. One would have thought a revival meeting was being held, from the sounds that exploded from the press section.

Dempsey was kicking and thrashing, trying to find some hold for his hands or knees, acting like some great fish, violent in its efforts to return to the water. The reporters were no less eager to get rid of him, but they were also interested in defending themselves from his flapping fists and feet. According to Frank G. Menke, who had a ringside seat, Dempsey did manage to catch one of the judges, Kid McCartland, with a shot in the eye, a shiner that the Kid proudly wore for ten days. The referee peered over the strands to watch the action, and Firpo exchanged glances and shrugs with his cornermen. The crowd, meanwhile, was in a state bordering hysteria, some imploring Dempsey to get up and some hollering for Gallegher to start counting. After about twenty seconds, Dempsey was pushed back onto the ring apron, and he crawled inside the ropes and knelt to recuperate his strength. (At this point DeForest would have claimed the fight for Firpo.) He was up before the fatal ten—but helpless, hardly able to stand, his jaw asag, his arms hanging by his sides. He presented a tempting target for the challenger. One punch and Dempsey would have gone down for good.

But Firpo did not attack! Perhaps he suspected a *Nortamericano* trick; and he got no advice from his corner. Finally he moved forward cautiously, pawed with his left and launched his right. But Dempsey, recovered somewhat, managed to duck under it. To the astonishment of everyone, he surged forward at the Argentinian, shot a desperate left to the chin and sent Firpo down once more. The challenger got up, and when Dempsey moved forward again, he did not give ground. The two traded punches at close range in the center of the ring until the bell rang.

But it did not ring for Dempsey. Driven by some primordial urge, he chased after Firpo, who was headed for his corner, and started the attack anew—on the back of Firpo's head and on his shoulder blades. Firpo turned with a snarl and struck back. For several seconds the blows flew, until Gallegher managed to step between the battlers, at great risk of life, and after tying up one arm of each as the gong made frantic sounds, convinced them the round was over.

So ended round one. Dempsey stood in mid-ring until Kearns hopped through the ropes and escorted him to his stool. He flung a bucket of water in Dempsey's face, and Dempsey began to realize where he was. "The smelling salts!" Kearns screamed at Luvadis over the shouting of the crowd, which was still reacting to the battle it had witnessed. "Where are the smelling salts?"

Luvadis tried to take the bottle from Kearns's shirt pocket. Kearns angrily hit him in the nose. Despite this, Luvadis managed to extract the bottle. Kearns snatched it and let Dempsey have some strong whiffs. The groggy champion shook his head to escape the fumes. Conscious for the first time since Firpo's initial right to the jaw, he asked through swollen lips, "What rounzit?"—thinking it must be at least the eighth and not knowing if the fight was over or if he had won or lost.

"The second!" Kearns shouted in his ear. "Stay away from him! Watch his right!" Dempsey shook his head in an attempt to clear it.

At the gong he moved out slowly to meet Firpo's bellowing charge, aware that he was on the verge of losing his title. Despite all caution, he took a right under the heart that sent him reeling backwards. The crowd increased its noise. Niagara Falls seemed to be roaring inside Dempsey's head. He saw the ominous face of the Argentinian moving in toward him. Reporters were typing furiously, handing copy to their telegraphers. They were thinking of leads: "In the most savage fight ever seen in modern history. . . ." "The sledgehammer blows of Luis Angel Firpo. . . ."

Firpo brought back his right for the finishing blow. Dempsey brought up his left inside it—a distance of about eight inches. It struck Firpo on the chin, and he toppled over like a giant oak. Reporters stood up in disbelief. Gallegher started the count. The fallen giant stirred, shook his head, cast a wary eye out for Dempsey and was up at the count of eight.

The champion moved in, throwing a flurry of punches as he advanced from which there was no escape. The killing left hook to the jaw that started Firpo on his way down was followed by a fierce right uppercut as a kind of lagniappe. The reporters started thinking of new leads as Dempsey leaned exhausted against the ropes and the referee's arm swept up and down. Firpo stirred at "Eight," but he could not push himself up from the floor. James Crusinberry wrote in the Chicago *Tribune* that it was "the greatest round of battling since the Silurian Age." At least.

It is thought that if Firpo had retained Jimmy DeForest as his trainer and had had him in his corner, Dempsey would have lost the fight on a foul on at least a half-dozen occasions. And Jack might well have been disqualified because of the newspapermen thrusting him back in the ring, though it is presumed they did it more out of a sense of self-preservation than for patriotic reasons. The refereeing was quite lax. Among other things, Dempsey should not have been allowed to chase a downed Firpo around the ring. To clarify things for the future, the New York State Athletic Commission made it clear that the referee must not start his count until the fighter scoring the knockdown went to a neutral corner.

The day following the fight, Rickard presented Dempsey with his half-million before Kearns could lay hands on it. At the time, the high-living Kearns owed Jack quite a bit, and Rickard, out of affection for the trusting Dempsey, did not want to see the debt increased.

After visiting Tex, Kearns showed up at Jack's hotel that day, all aboil, and was aghast to see Jack subtract the debt from Kearns's share of the money. Given Kearns's philosophy, it did not cement their relationship any.

Hollywood and Los Angeles promised good times, so Jack made that his headquarters. He bought his mother and sister Elsie a luxurious home there and moved in with them. His mother, however, found the atmosphere too rich for her bucolic tastes, so Jack bought her a twenty-two-acre farm near Salt Lake City.

His nose refashioned into something straighter and more streamlined, Jack cut up old touches with former friends and made some new ones. Director Mervin LeRoy introduced him to Estelle Taylor, witty, urbane and beautiful, an actress who had starred with Milton Sills in *The Alaskan*. Dempsey courted her successfully, and they were married in a small wedding in San Diego. When she was looked at peculiarly for marrying a boxer, Estelle replied, "I didn't marry a boxer, I married a champion!"

They honeymooned in Europe, Jack receiving his usual adulation. He showed a few ring hopefuls the hazards of the profession, and Estelle brought back with her a huge hound which they installed in their Hollywood home. Then, to the surprise of the fistic and theatrical world, Jack consented to star in a Broadway play. He was to take the role of Tiger in *The Big Fight,* directed by David Belasco. Jack was no actor and his voice did not carry the authority of that of, say, Edwin Booth, but then Sullivan and Corbett and Fitzsimmons and Jack Johnson and Kid McCoy were no actors, either, and they had pulled in crowds. For Jack's part the money was good, and he would be playing opposite Estelle. Few plays have been so devised to accommodate the peculiar talents of the leading man. The plot of the play had Jack rising from rags to riches with his fists and winning both the championship and the girl the same night. He was not onstage very often, and when he was on, he had very few sides. For this he got a thousand dollars a week; Estelle got three hundred.

Kearns was getting half of what Jack made, however, and handling the money, besides. One day, after Jack learned about a deal Kearns had pulled without consulting him, he got sore and the two had a confrontation.

"If you want to stay on as my manager," Jack told Doc, "you'll have to be satisfied with one-third. It's that or nothing."

Kearns was astounded. God had given him the right to swindle others, and who was this ex-hobo to challenge Him? "If that's the way you feel about it," he raged, "I'll see that you never fight again." And he stormed out.

There followed a series of annoying lawsuits which saw Kearns attach Dempsey's Rolls Royce (while Estelle was in it, forcing her to walk several miles to the nearest town); arrange for a sheriff to serve Jack with a subpoena, forcing Jack to smash through a clapboard wall to escape; and sue twice for a third of a million dollars and twice more for lesser sums. He realized only a fraction of these amounts, but the pressure played havoc with Jack's natural complacency.

The Broadway vehicle lasted six weeks, and then Jack and Estelle returned to Hollywood to pair up in a film called *Manhattan Madness*. This was also terrible. Then Jack became estranged from Estelle. Missing the old bunch, he decided he wanted another fight. Acting as his own manager, under the advisement of Rickard, he nearly signed a contract to fight Harry Wills, "The Black Menace," who seemed the only worthwhile gate attraction. However, the matchmaker could not meet the down payment Jack asked—three hundred thousand dollars—so the deal was never consummated. It sat just as well with Rickard, for he felt race riots like those of 1910 might ensue if Wills won. Dempsey, however, had no doubts. "These big, slow guys are meat for me," he declared.

Rickard kept looking around in some anxiety, since three years is about as long as a champion can stay away from a major fight and hope to recover his old skills. Finally he contacted Jack.

"I think I got somebody for you," he said. ■

Few fighters ever dominated an era as Jack Dempsey did. In the Roaring Twenties the name "Jack Dempsey" was on everyone's lips. In an age of the most flamboyant celebrities, the heavyweight champ was the greatest celebrity of all.

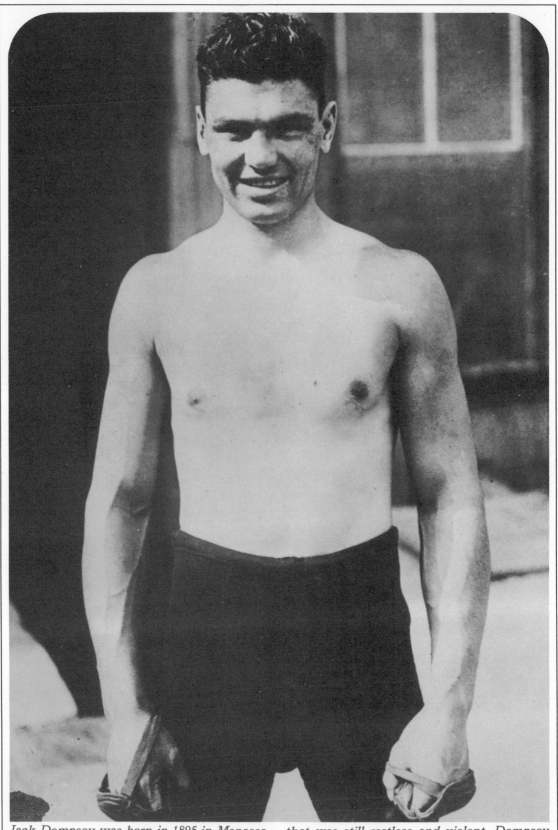

Jack Dempsey was born in 1895 in Manassa, Colorado, of Scotch-Irish parents, both of whom had some Indian blood. In an America that was still restless and violent, Dempsey battled his way to fame from the ranks of the itinerant fighters.

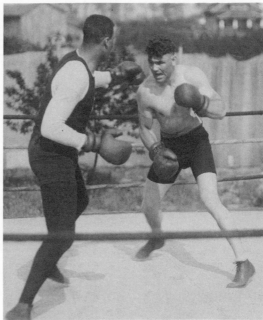

Balanced, relentless, ready to strike at the first opening, Dempsey shows his intense determination in a training match.

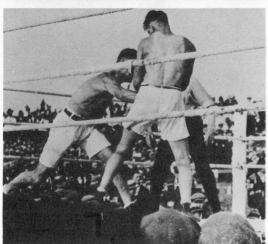

Challenger Tommy Gibbons stays out of range as he launches a left. Wisely, Gibbons avoids the champion's power.

As champion, Dempsey was devastating. In the sequence above, he shows his form by knocking out Billy Miske in Round 3.

In this 1924 exhibition with Sailor Burke, we see the cobralike Dempsey ready to spring into action.

On July 4, 1919, Jack Dempsey finally got his big chance in Toledo, Ohio. The years of slugging his way through saloon brawls, mining camps, and dreary prairie towns culminated in his title match with Jess Willard. Tex Rickard, the promotional

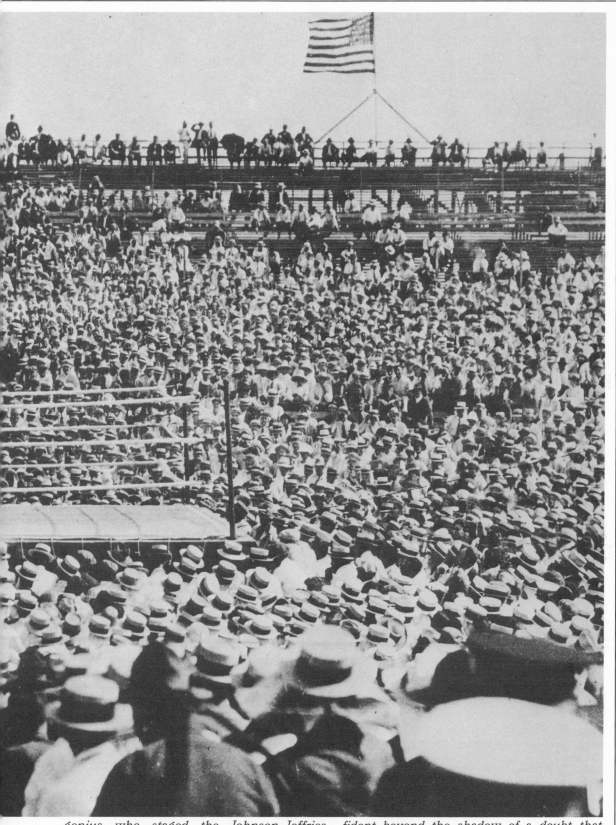

genius who staged the Johnson–Jeffries classic, again was in command. Lean, hard, and ferocious, Dempsey was confident beyond the shadow of a doubt that he could demolish the much heavier and older Willard in a single round.

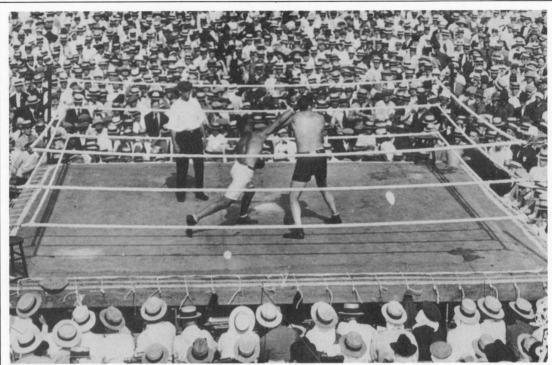

As forecast, Dempsey swiftly lunged at Willard in Round 1. Dempsey was not to be denied. His years of hunger, struggle, and poverty seemed to be packed in every punch. Brutality and anger surfaced; Dempsey's future was now.

Standing over the fallen champion, Dempsey ignores the ritual of the neutral corner. The Kansas Giant looks up, almost plaintively, as he tries to regain his strength after Dempsey's relentless advance. The crown is about to change hands.

Now—the Age of Dempsey! Above, Boyle's Thirty Acres in Jersey City, where on July 2, 1921, Dempsey knocked out Georges *Carpentier in four rounds. Nearly 80,000 fans paid more than $1,500,000. The big money had arrived.*

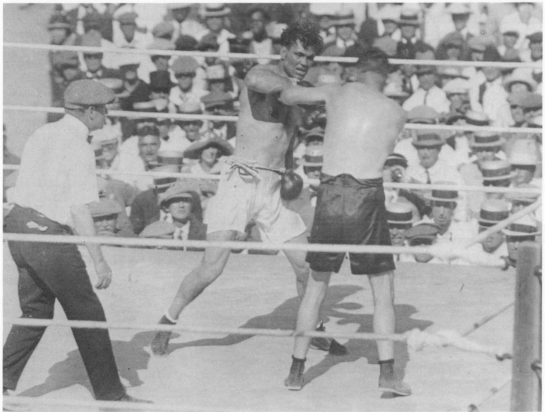

Controversy followed Dempsey and his manager Jack Kearns wherever they went. Above, Dempsey fights Tommy Gibbons *in Shelby, Montana, in 1923. Dempsey's $300,000 guarantee, demanded by Kearns, bankrupted the town of Shelby.*

In 1918 Dempsey knocked out Fred Fulton in twenty-three seconds of Round 1. One punch, a devastating right, catapulted Dempsey into contention for the crown.

In Hollywood Jack Dempsey became a celebrity's celebrity. Comedian Eddie Cantor, center, takes time from his shooting schedule to meet the champ.

In the middle twenties Dempsey made his home in Hollywood. Now famous and affluent, he was invited to all the glamorous parties. Film director Mervyn Le Roy introduced him to actress Estelle Taylor. In the photograph above, Dempsey is seen with the beautiful Miss Taylor after their wedding in San Diego.

At United Artists Studios, three of the most famous performers of all time get together. On the bottom, belying the fragility of his embattled tramp, is Charlie Chaplin. Above him stands the dashing Douglas Fairbanks. On top, physically and symbolically, sits Heavyweight Champion Jack Dempsey.

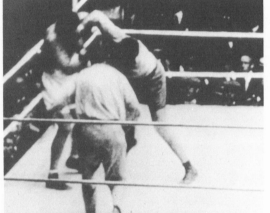

On September 14, 1923, Dempsey met Luis Firpo, who had been dubbed the Wild Bull of the Pampas. In Round 1 Firpo's furious attack forces Dempsey back against the ropes and then (below) completely out of the ring.

The crowd was hysterical. At least twenty seconds elapsed. Instinct and sheer determination brought Dempsey back into the ring. Miraculously, the round was completed. In Round 2, seen above, Firpo launches a wild right to finish Dempsey. Middle frame, Dempsey steps in with a short, perfect left and Firpo slumps to the canvas.

Top frame, Firpo tries desperately to rise and continue. The emotional exhaustion of Round 1 has taken its toll. Time begins to expire. Dempsey wisely disappears to a neutral corner. Middle frame, the courageous Argentinian is counted out. Bottom frame, in a final gesture of condolence, Dempsey helps Firpo to his feet.

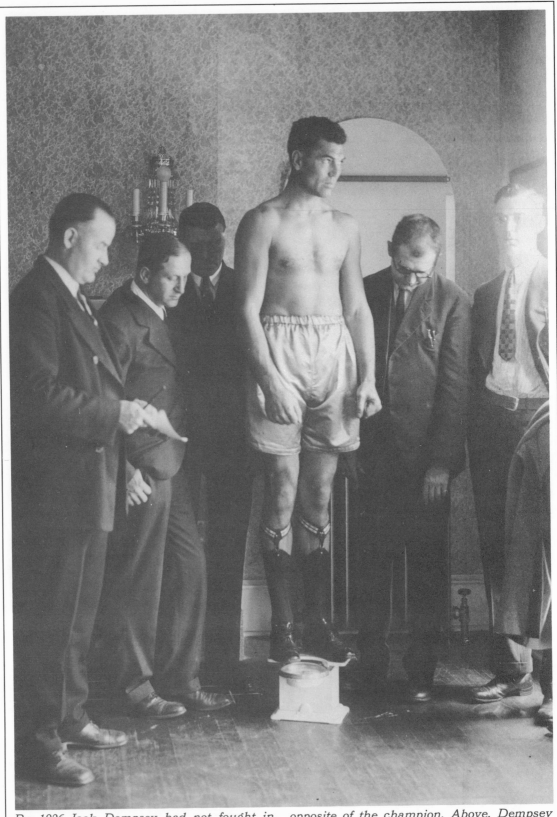

By 1926 Jack Dempsey had not fought in a single major contest for three years. New York suspended his license. Enter Tex Rickard! He had a challenger, the perfect opposite of the champion. Above, Dempsey weighs in for his first meeting with Gene Tunney, to be held in Philadelphia's Sesquicentennial Stadium on September 23.

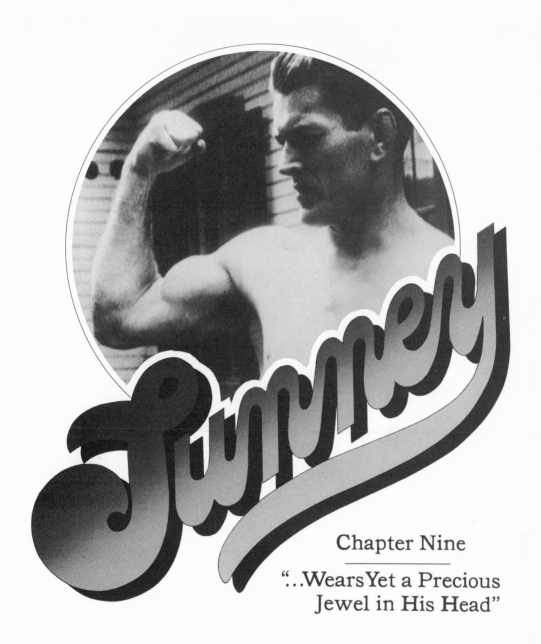

Tunney

Chapter Nine

"...WearsYet a Precious
Jewel in His Head"

If Jack Dempsey was smoldering iron, Gene Tunney was cold burnished steel. Dempsey was an instinctive fighter by training and temperament. When the cage door opened, he hastened out to destroy his opponent. Tunney was a synthetic fighter. He studied, analyzed, rehearsed, pondered. He saw his opponent as a case history, a specimen, an anatomical subject. He analyzed his foe's strengths and weaknesses and constantly analyzed his own —noting improvements—to determine how best to attack and defend. There has never been a fighter who strove so assiduously to correct flaws, physical, mental or spiritual. He was a kind of ascetic come to box. Tunney's ambition was to be an elitist, and he chose prizefighting as the quickest, surest means of realizing that ambition. His attitude toward the sport did not make him extraordinarily popular with prizefight fans or the press. He did not like to be called a prizefighter. "I'm a boxer," he would say, and with a touch of irony, Tex Rickard had his ushers at the second Tunney-Dempsey fight wear armbands proclaiming the encounter the "Tunney-Dempsey Boxing Exhibition."

Dempsey's pleasure was in hitting, Gene's in blocking or slipping blows. His idol, inevitably, was Corbett. Dempsey was merciless in the ring. Tunney showed at times a curious compassion for his opponent, which occasionally worked to his disadvantage. In the late rounds of one of his championship fights, his opponent kept clawing at his own eye with his glove, as though trying to remove an irritation. He paid little heed to Tunney, and the average fighter would have belted him soundly for his inattention. Tunney did not. He paused to ask the referee if his opponent was all right. The referee started to examine him, the eye suddenly got better and the fight resumed. Later his opponent was to claim, for God knows what reason, that Tunney was a dirty fighter. In the late rounds of another title bout, Tunney, after being butted and backhanded, was asked by his opponent to let him stay for the duration of the fight; he did not want to suffer the ignominy of a knockout. Tunney complied, though a knockout would have looked better on his record at a time when he was striving mightily to gain a reputation. In another fight, with a hometown boy whose friends were solidly behind him, Tunney received the same request. He backed off to let his opponent recover. The fans, incensed over his mercy, hollered for him to flatten their favorite—who was going to lose anyway—and many of them shouted "Fake!" and "Phony!" when Gene refused to move in for the kill.

In a battle for the American light-heavyweight championship, Tunney was handily thrashing the titleholder in the late rounds when he got a murmured request to take things easy. He did. Coming out for the next round, he was smashed in the face by two right-hand punches that sent him back on his heels and nearly knocked him out. He weathered the assault, however, and, filled with fury over the wile, cut his duplicitous opponent to pieces and took the decision. In another important fight, with his opponent out on his feet in a late round, Tunney stood stock still in the middle of the ring and looked pleadingly at the referee to call a halt. Seeing that Tunney was not going to hit the man any more, the referee stepped between the fighters and awarded Tunney a technical knockout.

Tunney believed in working to develop a powerful will. When he lived on the west side of Greenwich Village in Manhattan between the ages of fifteen and eighteen, he read a book on the subject, and he determined to strengthen his own. Thus obstacles that seemed insurmountable could be conquered and insoluble problems solved. He made it a habit to force himself to perform unpleasant or feckless tasks and to frustrate his hedonistic instincts. He would undress for bed at home, turn out the light, then stand on a chair in the dark and count up to five hundred. He would take a box of wooden matches and, to pique his patience and develop his powers of concentration, would neatly lay out five hundred of them, head to tail and tail to head. He would come home at night, tired from school or work, and instead of flopping right into bed, would walk around the block three times before turning in. He gazed at the sun, as Spartan babies did at the behest of their mothers, to increase his fortitude and mortify the demands of the flesh. (Tunney admitted later that this particular exercise was not especially salutary, and he did not continue it long.) He would refuse a helping of ice cream at home when he wanted it and it was readily available. He was a kind of interested arbiter in a daily battle between what he wanted to do and what he felt he must do to forge his body into an acquiescent tool of his psyche.

The program sounds immature, but it worked for Tunney. It became useful when his physical weaknesses interfered with his progress toward his goal and he set out—bursting with confidence and a sense of destiny—to correct them. He had very small, weak hands, and his knuckles had the habit of breaking and staying sore for months. To strengthen his fingers, he would push himself from a wall with each one five hundred times a day. Besides squeezing a rubber ball for hours on end to strengthen his fingers and wrists, he did fingertip push-ups and soaked his hands in brine. Later in his career he would add long hours of chopping down trees in Maine and Canada as corrective therapy.

If young Tunney had had a motto, it would have come from his favorite playwright, Shakespeare: "Sweet are the uses of adversity." Tunney found value in the fact that his hands were weak and subject to breaking; he was forced to become an excellent boxer because he did not dare hit hard, and an excellent marksman because he could not afford to waste punches. Even after his hands became tough and durable and he could smash a blow as hard as the majority of heavyweights, his boxing skills remained immensely valuable. Tunney seldom won by quick knockouts in his early fights. He pronounced this beneficial, pointing out that if he knocked out a man in two rounds, he was not learning anything. If he won by a decision in ten or fifteen he added to his store of knowledge about his own abilities, those of his opponent and the art of boxing generally.

His career, pursued with single-minded dedication, was unbelievable enough to have been rejected as a plot for a Horatio Alger pulp novel (*Pluck Makes Luck,* Or *The Manly Marine Manhandles the Mauler from Manassas*), but the facts cannot be denied: Poor boy becomes a boxer, wins the title after a hard struggle, makes a fortune with his fists, is befriended by the cultured and the mighty and marries a socialite heiress, after which he becomes a spectacularly successful businessman. He was John Gully and Gentleman Jackson reincarnate.

Often aloof, seemingly pompous, a prizefighter with a taste for the humanities, Tunney alienated many fans and most of the press during his climb to the heavyweight championship. To some, this tall, slender young man with the light brown hair, Mediterranean blue eyes and singularly open, trustworthy countenance was priggish, too All-American for the image of a gutsy ringman. He did not look as though he could sweat. Newspapermen liked to poke fun at him and deprecated his fighting skills; a prizefighter was somebody like Dempsey or Ketchel or good old Jeffries. They amused readers by reporting Tunney's speech of dismissal to a pest at his training camp: "You are full of self-approbation and deceit." He was dismissed as a sesquipedalian. The joke of the early twenties was his avowal that he would one day beat Dempsey.

However, Tunney did have that human failing, a temper. As we have seen, he was not especially tender toward the fighter who tried to cross him. Once, in Cuba, after he had won the heavyweight championship, Tunney was casually sparring without gloves with Ernest Hemingway and told the author about a dock fighter he had known who had an unusual move in a scrap. The man had lost the thumb of his left hand, but his fingers were like steel. He would throw an overhand right and, while his opponent was fending off that, would dig his left hand in to his foe's groin, ending the battle. Tunney demonstrated slowly for Hemingway. Proud of his knowledge of self-defense, Hemingway pondered a moment, then said, "Try that again." Tunney did so, at one-quarter speed, and Hemingway suddenly smashed his elbow against Tunney's mouth as hard as he could. If Tunney had not been gifted with strong teeth, he recalled later, several of them would have been lying on the ground. Tunney reacted immediately by hurling a lightning left at Hemingway's jaw—stopping short just before touching the skin—and a straight hard right to his jaw, pulling this in time, too. Hemingway blanched, acknowledging the message, and the incident was never mentioned again. After Jack Dempsey, who had been his idol, published something about Tunney before their second fight that the latter considered heinous, Tunney grew immensely bitter toward him. When the two faced one another in the ring, Gene went steaming after Dempsey with more abandon and fury than he would have evinced on one of his cooler days.

A measure of Tunney's immense self-confidence and his knack of seeing himself objectively was most dramatically shown in his first fight with Harry Greb, in May, 1922. Stanley Ketchel may have been a better fighter pound-for-pound than Greb (although this is arguable), but no fighter of any size ever gave his opponent a more confusing, frustrating battle. Nicknamed "the Pittsburgh Windmill," Greb fought as a middleweight and light-heavyweight. In the ring he resembled a man who had just burst loose from his strait jacket. Blows rained on his opponent from every angle and altitude and with such rapidity that his opponent could not block or evade even a small proportion of them. The *busiest* fighter in history, Greb would bend far down and unleash a dozen fast punches with either hand. He would rapidly circle an opponent and fire a dozen blows to the head and body before his opponent could retreat or retaliate. The blows were not especially hard, but they stung and cut, and Greb's pace increased as the bout progressed. Eventually his opponent would become so bewildered that he would surrender to the string of popping firecrackers that was Greb.

Greb had this going for him, too: He was perhaps the dirtiest Queensberry fighter who ever lived. He would knee, butt, hit with the heel of his glove, hit on emerging from a clinch, hit backhanded, hit after the bell, rabbit punch, scrape his opponent's face with his glove laces and use his thumb to pluck out an opponent's eye. The most illegal Queensberry bout ever fought was that between Greb and Kid Norfolk, a black from New England, in Boston. (Years before, Norfolk had swatted Greb in the right eye, blinding it; Greb was thereafter a one-eyed fighter.) In this bout, Greb became so angry at his inability to land effectively against Norfolk by conventional means that, during a clinch, he bent down and took a hard bite of Norfolk's shoulder. Norfolk hollered and retaliated with a bite of his own. The referee separated them and the various fouls continued, both fighters so evil and intense that the referee did not see his way clear to disqualifying either one of them. Eventually Greb lost the decision. His thumb needed two weeks to recuperate.

Greb did not bother to train for his fights. He partied most of the time he did not spend in the ring, and he dreaded going to sleep lest he miss something. He ate what he pleased and was fond of entertaining ladies in his hotel or dressing room just before a fight. It seemed to give him energy. These practices did not prevent him from winning both the middleweight and light-heavyweight titles. He was just as eager to fight outside the ring as in it. After successfully defending his middleweight title against welterweight champion Mickey Walker, the Pittsburgh Windmill and the Toy Bulldog met in a New York nightspot. The two had a few rounds of drinks, then Walker accused Greb of gouging and committing other fouls a few hours before. Greb offered to fight him then and there. As he began removing his jacket, Walker stepped over and belted him, and the fight continued in the speakeasy and out on the street. It was stopped before either party was knocked out, and subsequently the two became excellent friends.

When Dempsey was training for his fight with Billy Miske in Benton Harbor, Michigan, in 1920, Greb, then weighing 160 pounds, dropped by and asked Kearns if he could spar with the champion. Kearns agreed, and some fun-loving newspapermen captured Harry's ear and informed him gravely that Dempsey was going to cut him to pieces, then knock him out. Greb's normally explosive temper fragmented, and he could hardly wait to get into the ring. All unknowing, Dempsey was surprised at the violence of Greb's assault. Greb quickly pinned him in a corner and let loose a fusillade of unstoppable blows. Dempsey became enraged; the blows did not hurt, but the humiliation was annoying, as was the feeling of helplessness in the face of the assault— all in the purview of the amused press and puzzled Michiganders. As the crowd marveled at Greb's turning the champion into a scowling punching bag, Dempsey finally broke away. But before he could smash his pestiferous foe to the canvas, Greb was yards off, dancing about and taunting the Mauler. Then he attacked again, jockeying Dempsey into the ropes and flailing away. Noting Dempsey's discomfiture, Kearns called "Time," and the round ended with Dempsey completely befuddled, the crowd pulling for Greb and the newspapermen possessors of a lively story.

Not at all pleased, the next day Dempsey told Kearns to stick Greb in the ring with him again; this time the champion would be ready. At the gong he rushed Greb in his most terrifying style, only to be met by a flurry of blows coming from all directions that prevented him from getting set to launch his destructive hooks. Greb shepherded him into a corner, and the ignominy of the day before was repeated. Dempsey swung desperate blows that Greb avoided; the peppering continued for four more minutes. Kearns, seeing that Dempsey was not going to land effectively, again called "Time." Greb waited in his corner for the next round to begin, but Kearns figured that Dempsey had had a surfeit of Greb. He announced that the champion would now punch the light and heavy bags and dismissed Greb from the ring.

Tunney had won the light-heavyweight title—not worth much from the standpoint of financial return or prestige —from Battling Levinsky at the old Madison Square Garden in January, 1922. Greb planned to relieve him of it and delivered his challenge. In his acolyte stage, his eye on the main chance (that is, Dempsey), Tunney was willing to fight anyone, even so experienced and dangerous an opponent as Greb. He told his manager, Doc Bagley,

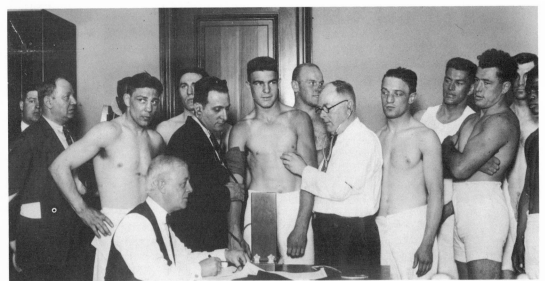

June, 1924, at Yankee Stadium. A group of fighters will do battle for the benefit of the Milk Fund. Among them is Harry Greb, seen at the extreme left with hands on hips. Fourth from right, in white shirt, is Gene Tunney, who had yet to reach legendary stature. Although only a middleweight, Greb inflicted on Tunney the only severe beating he ever sustained.

to arrange the bout.

The smart money was placed at 3 to 1 odds on Greb, who weighed 162 to Tunney's 174. Before a packed house at the Garden, Greb pleased his Pittsburgh followers by giving Tunney the worst beating of his life. Harry used every weapon in his arsenal and moved so rapidly in and out, up and down, landing his rapier-fast punches, that Gene was constantly off-balance and unable to get an attack going. A long left in the first round gave Gene a violent nosebleed, and Greb used the nose as a target thereafter. A butt from Greb's head broke Gene's nose in a later round, and another butt during a clinch caused a broad gash over Gene's left eye. Greb was soon covered with Tunney's blood, and by the fourth round so was the referee. On rare occasions Tunney would jar his opponent with a left or right to the ribs.

Yet all this time another Tunney, an objective, analyzing fighter, was studying the battle and figuring out how best to thwart his tormentor in a return match. He felt he knew how to solve the problem toward the end of the fight, but he was physically unable to do it. Toward the end Tunney was plied by his seconds with a rum-and-orange drink which did not mix well with the blood he had swallowed, and he became extremely nauseous. Now was not the time to launch a counterattack. Gene stood up under Greb's pounding for the entire fifteen rounds, proud that he was not knocked off his feet. After congratulating Greb—who was breathing hard but unmarked—on his victory, Tunney was taken to his dressing room, where he collapsed.

The second day following the fight, still showing the effects of his terrible beating, Tunney appeared at the Athletic Commission office in New York's Flatiron Building to post a challenger's bond of $2,500 for a return bout with Greb. "You're way out of your class," said Commissioner Muldoon, marveling that the young pugilist would return for more manhandling by the tricky, unsporting Greb. He did not know of Tunney's grand design—obsession, it might have been termed at the time—or he might have knocked the walls down with his laughter.

But Gene came back on four more occasions to confront Greb. He regained his title in a fifteen-round fight in which the decision was disputed, won a decisive victory the next time, and was conceded the victor in two no-decision bouts. In the last he gave Greb nearly as thorough a lacing as Greb had administered to him in the first fight. The Pittsburgher, thoroughly cut up, came to Tunney's dressing room afterwards and told Tunney he was through fighting him; Tunney was too big, too clever and too hard a hitter. When Greb died after an auto accident and an operation in 1926, Tunney was a pallbearer at his funeral and spoke highly of him as an adversary. He meant every word.

A curious sort of man to strive for honors in the prize ring, James Joseph Tunney was born on Bank Street in Greenwich Village on May 15, 1898. The section was a bit of the ould sod transplanted to a warren-filled portion of lower Manhattan and was a good breeding ground for young men interested in a prizefighting career—or one in politics or the saloon business. The sector could point with pride to such residents of Irish descent as John Morrissey and Bill Poole, along with the Hyers, father and son. It was also a coven (known as Little Bohemia) for persons in the arts. The Village featured saloons and coffee houses where revolutionary poets and writers expressed revolutionary thoughts and toiled in gloomy garrets. Walt Whitman held forth at Joe Pfaff's cellar cafe on Broadway, just off Bleecker Street (originally known as Herring Street). Other residents were William Dean Howells, Thomas Bailey Aldrich and Artemus Ward, the humorist; also Ada Clare, the bold poetess whose Muse was Erato, and Adah Isaacs Mencken, the celebrated actress and horsewoman, who probably wished she had never heard of prizefighting.

Other writers who derived inspiration from the narrow, twisting streets, the picturesque decrepitude of the area and the free exchange of ideas with persons of similar bent and comparable talent were Eugene O'Neill, Lafcadio Hearn, John Masefield (a bartender in Luke

O'Connell's saloon who was to become Poet Laureate of England), Lincoln Steffens, Stephen Crane and Frank Norris of *The Pit* and *The Octopus*. The outdoor headquarters was Washington Square and the indoor was the Lafayette Hotel, a structure that Roderick Usher might have found intriguing. The main street was MacDougall. Louisa May Alcott wrote *Little Women* there. Currier and Ives ran a lithograph shop there. Edna St. Vincent Millay was an actress with the Provincetown Players, that energetic Village troupe, before getting serious about melancholy poetry. Others whose dreams reached fruition were Sydney Porter, terrified of blackmailers who threatened to expose him as an embezzler; Theodore Dreiser and Willa Cather; Georges Clemenceau, later the Tiger of France, who was a physician in the Village. Washington Irving wrote *The Legend of Sleepy Hollow* while dwelling on Commerce Street.

What is an artists' colony without artists? Among their myriad number who strove for recognition in skylit garrets were Winslow Homer, George W. Bellows (whose favorite subject was lean prizefighters), William M. Chase, the dean of American painters during the Mauve Decade (Corbett's, Fitz's and Jeff's decade), John Turnbull, who painted "The Signing of the Declaration of Independence," and Daniel Chester French, the sculptor of Lincoln's statue in the Lincoln Memorial. Modernist painters of the clan had the honor of being condemned by outspoken President Theodore Roosevelt as lunatics. One can see how young Gene, raised in such a heady, freethinking atmosphere, came to be bitten by the literary and cultural bug.

Gene's father, John, had been a day laborer in Kiltimagh in County Mayo, that part of Ireland so afflicted by the great famine that few remained there, and had immigrated to America when he was eighteen. Shortly afterward came his sweetheart, Mary Lydon of nearby Gortgoriff. John got a job as a stevedore on the Hudson wharves, and he and Mary were married in the late 1880's. They had four children, two boys and two girls. Gene got his nickname

because of the way one of his sisters pronounced "Jim." John Tunney raised his family in reasonable comfort if not luxury, and Gene as a youngster lived a normal city boy's life. He threw rocks back when they were hurled at him, swam off the docks, attended parochial grammar school and high school. He became a good long-distance runner, baseball player and basketball player, and he liked to spar informally with his schoolmates. When he was ten his father bought him two pairs of boxing gloves, and Gene and his brother and other neighborhood kids pummeled one another after school in a vacant lot. Gene had a for-real fight with one Goo Goo Delaney, whom he beat up, and another with Goo Goo's older brother, who beat Gene up. Subsequently young Tunney learned how to defend himself so that the experience would not be repeated.

After graduation from high school Gene got a job as office boy in the office of a steamship company at five dollars a week; was promoted to mail clerk at eleven dollars per week; and then became a freight classifier at seventeen dollars per week. Sometimes, like Corbett in San Francisco, he sparred with his colleagues at work, with the boss's approval. Sometimes he boxed at night in local gyms. As his skill at boxing became known, Gene was asked to spar with a man named Green, a veteran who had retired to become a stock-company thespian but, falling on hard times, had decided to make a comeback. Green was merciless with the novice, slashing and stabbing him to pieces, and sometimes the timekeeper would let rounds run on for six minutes. Little by little, however, indomitable Gene mastered his difficult trade.

The war came, changing Gene's life and choice of a career. At the age of eighteen he joined the Marines, trained as a Parris Island boot and was shipped to France. Although Gene was later billed as "The Fighting Marine," his military career was hardly out of *What Price Glory?* His outfit, the Eleventh Regiment, in a brigade commanded by General Smedley D. Butler, was the sharpest and most gung ho of any in the Corps. When Ludendorff drove south from the channel ports, outflanked the French and nearly captured Paris, the Eleventh Regiment, having trained in France for nearly a year, was dispatched to Romorantin, six miles southwest of the capital. There Gene's company was put to work guarding sheds containing balloons. Other companies became involved with the Services of Supply. The Fighting Eleventh, to its frustration, learned about the progress of the war from soldiers on furlough and the wounded who passed through. Like everyone, Gene found guard duty extremely tedious and welcomed being allowed to attend occasional boxing bouts staged in the Y.M.C.A. hut by various companies to give a boost to morale.

With the middleweight championship of the camp about to be settled one evening, the officer-promoter was short a contestant. Gene's gunnery sergeant, who had seen Gene in action against instructors at Parris Island, offered to relieve him from guard duty the next night if he would substitute for the missing battler. Gene was amenable, though the conditions were unfavorable. His opponent wore boxing shoes, while Tunney pranced about on a slippery canvas in hobnailed boots. Tunney fought so intelligently, however, that his opponent quit on him. Later Gene won the camp heavyweight championship, despite taking a terrific battering.

Using his ingenuity, Tunney found a way to train while on guard duty. He would hold his rifle by the stock in his left hand and throw left jabs to develop his arms, shoulders and back muscles. Off duty he would skip rope and jog. Occasionally he found someone to spar with. Later he would contend that guard duty, unpleasant as it was, was excellent training for a boxer. It taught discipline and responsibility. From his endless tours, he also learned how to relax to conserve his energy—a useful quality for a boxer in the ring.

Reports came in of great bloody battles against the Germans at Belleau Wood. The Eleventh Marines were scheduled to join the Third French Army in the Metz Sector. The great fortress in Metz was the keystone of the entire German line, and it looked as

though there would be glory enough for all. Then two company cooks went A.W.O.L., sneaked into Romorantin and got drunk on cognac. The rest of the company, milling about hungrily, realized something was afoot. A little later the news blared forth: The Armistice had been signed, which was why the cooks were celebrating. Soon the entire company was in the village, drinking cognac, toasting the elderly and joyously pinching the girls. They paraded through the streets with their rifles and bottles, happy the war was over but disappointed that a crack regiment like theirs had not seen action.

The problem of maintaining morale while the troops passed time in France and Germany arose, and boxing bouts were part of the answer. The AEF organized a series of tournaments which were immensely popular, and Gene's company commander entered Gene as a light-heavyweight. Gene was assailed by doubts. Although he had put on seventeen pounds while in the Corps and was an inch taller than when he enlisted, his hands were not those of a boxer, and he suffered from chronic broken knuckles. "If you want to know what a complicated and breakable mechanism the human hand is," he said at one time, "just be a boxer with cracked knuckles."

After a bout with an Indian private his knuckles swelled alarmingly, and in the light-heavyweight final against a boxer named Ted Jamison he nearly met disaster. The spectators included General Pershing, Admiral Bensen, French generals, diplomats, prominent French citizens and Crown Prince Leopold of Belgium.

Jamison, more experienced than Tunney, knew about Gene's aching right hand. When Gene ventured to throw a straight right, Jamison merely ducked his head into it, and Gene's knuckles broke all over again. He was in agony as the hand threatened to burst through the glove, and he realized that he would have to depend entirely on his left. He defended with his right and occasionally feinted with it but piled up points and kept Jamison from pinning him in a corner by jabbing with his left. Despite his injured hand he won the decision, becoming the light-heavyweight champion of the AEF. As such, he qualified to tour France and Germany, sparring with other tournament winners to entertain the wounded.

An event of significance occurred one afternoon in 1919 when he was chugging down past the castles on the Rhine in the company of a corporal who had been a newspaperman in Joplin, Missouri. News of the terror from the West, Jack Dempsey, had reached the troops in Europe, and Gene was curious about him. It turned out that Corporal McReynolds was not only a boxing authority but had seen Dempsey in action. "What's he like?" Gene asked, planning ahead.

"He's a big Jack Dillon," McReynolds replied, and Tunney got the picture. Dillon was a husky, scrappy middleweight, nicknamed "the Giant Killer," who had been middleweight champion since 1908. His style was to move in in a crouch and throw hard, fast punches until his opponent crumpled to the canvas. However, Tunney knew that Dillon had been outpointed by Mike Gibbons, a superb boxer, and speculated that a superb boxer of Dempsey's size, which he proposed to be, could tame the raging Dempsey. "He'll murder Willard," McReynolds added by way of afterthought.

Back home Gene found his job with the steamship company filled, and the money he had saved quickly went for respectable garments to walk around New York in. Boxing seemed the only way to make a quick dollar, so he engaged a manager, Billy Roche. Tunney fought a satisfying no-decision bout against Dan O'Dowd and felt he was on his way. In his next fight he KO'd K.O. Sullivan under dim lights but broke his hand. After a six-month layoff, he concentrated on preserving his tender knuckles and scored a string of unspectacular victories. Around the gyms he was known as "The Fighter with the Brittle Hands."

Because he had fought in the war, he was put on the Dempsey-Carpentier card with Soldier Jones, chosen for the same patriotic reason. Hands aching, Tunney knocked his man out in pedestrian fashion in the seventh round.

Dismayed by his lack of progress and impressed by the show Dempsey put on before Rickard's society folk, Tunney began to prepare in earnest for his destiny. He studied the styles of Fitzsimmons, Corbett and Jeffries. He read about nerve centers and vulnerable organs in anatomy and kinesiology books. He sharpened his marksmanship in Stillman's gym in midtown Manhattan. He attended every New York fight Dempsey engaged in, boxed with and quizzed Dempsey's former sparring partners and studied films of Dempsey's bouts. It turned out to be a six-year seminar on the psychology, weapons and possible weaknesses of Dempsey. The problem was being allowed to take the examination.

A new string of victories followed. One fight was with Eddie O'Hare, a worthy ex-sparring partner of Dempsey's. Moving quickly about the ring and snapping a savage left into Gene's face, O'Hare had all the best of it in the early milling. The Fighting Marine finally solved O'Hare's style, however, and knocked him out with a right to the jaw in the sixth round.

Tunney was far from colorful, but he was consistent—he had won twenty-nine straight fights—and Roche managed to arrange a bout with Battling Levinsky, the curly-haired Philadelphian who held the American light-heavyweight title. Levinsky, a smart boxer, had taken the championship from Jack Dillon in 1916 by avoiding Dillon's heavy blows and jabbing him silly. Tunney saw a moral in this. Younger, stronger, a harder hitter than Levinsky, Gene beat him in twelve rounds and became the first New Yorker to hold the light-heavyweight title.

The vicious series with Greb followed. Then, having utterly disposed of this troublesome rival, Tunney sought the biggest game he could find. This turned out to be a fighter whose manager wanted him to have a second shot at Dempsey: Georges Carpentier, the pride of French *avion,* who had fallen on bad days in his native land and needed his reputation refurbished. He had been beaten by Tom Gibbons and Battling Siki, the Senegalese who later became overwhelmed by the sophistication he met in cities and his own susceptibility to powerful drink; he was found dead in a Manhattan gutter. Carpentier was not eligible to compete for the American light-heavyweight title and he had none of his own to place on the line, but the fight drew a great deal of interest; it was clear that America was eager to find out who would claw his way to the position of challenger for Dempsey's inviolate title. The loser, of course, would be in a fix. If Carpentier, then thirty, lost, he would never see Dempsey again except on visits of state. If Tunney lost, he would have to start the wearying task of building anew. Jimmy Johnston, of Boer Rodel fame, promoted the fight, a fifteen-rounder to be held at the Polo Grounds on July 4, 1924. What ensued that evening was one of the most thoroughly mixed up, discombobulated contests in boxing history. One is reminded of the Sayers-Heenan bareknuckler at Farnborough in 1860. If the fight had taken place in France, neither Tunney nor his manager nor his seconds nor some of his adherents would have emerged from the arena alive.

The Fighting Marine trained in Red Bank, N.J., and the idol of France worked out on the Great Neck, L.I., estate of Jack Curley. No reports of a secret punch were leaked to the press, but Georges did some of his sparring at night under arc lights to accustom himself to the real thing later. Tunney was two inches taller, at six feet one and a half inches; both came in two pounds under the light-heavyweight limit, at 173.

Society had not wooed the French gallant as it had in the summer of 1921, and on the night of the fight cheers for Tunney outdecibeled those for his opponent. War fervor was over, and the love affair with France had been replaced by one with sybaritic living—hip flasks, speakeasies, flesh-colored silk stockings, bobbed hair, cloche hats, Valentino pompadours, carefree shenanigans by high-ranking public officials, aerial circuses, solemnly impressive gangster funerals, bounding roadsters, jokes about anthropomorphic monkeys and giggling defiance of a totally insane law that induced more crime than Gaiseric's

orders to his Vandals. Peggy Hopkins Joyce was in attendance, as were One-Eyed Connolly and Tammany Young, gatecrashers supreme, as well as a smattering of Tunney's moneyed friends. But it was not a crowd that Rickard would have gloated over. Fans numbering 30,133 paid $136,681 to see the bout, and they garnered conversation enough to last them a decade.

Descamps had instructed Georges to start slowly, feeling out his man and saving himself for an explosive finish in the later rounds; he was not fearful of Tunney's punching power—though Carpentier may have been after taking those first terrible whacks in the body from a man noted primarily as a clever boxer. The pattern was that Carpentier would jab and dance away, Tunney advancing like Nemesis and throwing heavy punches. Occasionally he was tagged with the Carpentier right, but it was not the blow of 1921. In the tenth round, when Georges was about to be unleashed, Tunney moved in and threw a short left to the jaw that sent the Frenchman down for an eight-count. When he rose Tunney pursued him all over the ring, aiming mainly for the head, and knocked him down for a count of four. Descamps, by now hysterical, tried to throw in the sponge, but Carpentier took time to run over to him and cry *"Non! Non!"* and Descamps retired to the corner. At the end of the round the plucky Orchid Man went down for the third time. He was slow and dizzy coming out for the eleventh, and Tunney resumed the attack. Carpentier feebly tried to retaliate while soaking up a lambasting that would have felled nearly anyone else, and the crowd's greatest cheers were for his courage. (The next day *The New York Times* ran an editorial about it.)

In the twelfth, Descamps' hypnotic powers, having failed to work on Tunney, were devoted to Carpentier, and he emerged from his corner remarkably fresh. He leaped at Tunney—by now arm-weary and with both hands aching from the great number of punches he had thrown—and rocked the champion's head back with sharp left jabs and battled him head to head for the first time during the fight. The thirteenth saw him fatigued again, and Tunney did all the forcing in a relatively slow round. Carpentier seemed almost out on his feet as he repaired to his corner.

The fourteenth round brought a number of surprises. Carpentier came roaring out, leaped at Tunney in a last-gasp effort and pounded his face with lefts and rights. Tunney backed up but landed a number of blows to Carpentier's stomach and ribs. Carpentier, moving forward, had Tunney against the ropes, with Gene's head out over them as he tried to avoid face punches. Tunney raised his bent right knee and Carpentier, half-falling forward, half-driving toward Tunney, was struck hard and squarely in the groin. With an involuntary cry of pain he doubled up and fell, writhing in the resin beside the ropes. Tunney moved away and stared at his opponent, shaking his head in bewilderment and disavowal of having delivered a low blow. Descamps was screaming in French, the gist being that Tunney had committed a most Mephistophelean foul and that Georges should be awarded the decision. The referee, Andy Griffith, paid no attention to him, did not start a count and kept gazing at the twisting, squirming man on the canvas. Some of the crowd rushed down to ringside to get a closer look at the tableau. The entire arena was in an uproar, some urging Carpentier to get up, some yelling foul and some urging the referee to toll off the seconds before Carpentier should rise. Very few spectators, if any, saw a low blow from Tunney's hand or knee, but Francophiles and Carpentier backers were willing to take Descamps' word for it. After fully a minute and a half of riotous conjecture and indecisive action in the ring, Carpentier's seconds came in, dragged him to his corner and sat him, in a kind of stupor, on his stool. Finally aroused by their ministrations, he indicated by motions that he wanted to resume the attack. The gong for the end of the round then sounded, entitling both fighters to a minute's rest.

At the beginning of the fifteenth, Carpentier was pushed to his feet and his handlers escorted him to the center of the ring. There he adopted the classic fighter's stance and awaited Götterdämmerung. Tunney, halfway toward him, backed away. Descamps shrilly demanded that the fight continue. Tunney was reluctant to hit the totally helpless man and suggested that the referee stop the bout. Fourteen seconds passed in discussion and argument, and finally Griffith stepped between the two, dispatching Tunney to his corner. Announcer Joe Humphries entered the ring and held up Tunney's hand in token of victory as a perplexed shout went up. Humphries was followed by a number of uniformed policemen who sprang into the ring just in time to keep Descamps, also inside, from ripping off Carpentier's trunks to show the howling, hooting, booing crowd that Carpentier had been fouled. Carpentier fought him in this. It was not one of boxing's most edifying moments.

Carpentier was then borne away to his locker room—the swan song of the Orchid Man. There a feverish Descamps claimed to all that Carpentier had been struck in the groin by Tunney's right hand, and even though it might have been accidental, his fighter was legally the victor. Carpentier was in bad shape. He was spitting blood and gasping for breath, his face was crimson and the right side of his body was red and raw from Tunney's left hooks. Carpentier insisted he had been fouled but declared the blow to have been unintentional. Descamps produced a protective cup that had a dent in it. Dr. William Walker, a State Athletic Commission physician, examined Carpentier and said he found no trace of a foul. (But, as one always adds in those circumstances, he pointed out that the evidence did not always manifest itself immediately after the alleged blow.) Carpentier, asked if he was through with boxing, angrily declared he was not; for one thing, he wanted revenge on Tunney.

Tunney and Tunney's flock denied the foul. Tunney said he was unaware of his knee ever having struck Carpentier, and he certainly did not fire a single low punch. Carpentier the next day asserted that it had been Tunney's knee that had done the mischief but that he was sure it had been inadvertant. The referee claimed to have seen no foul and added that it was a terrific right hook to the body by Tunney that had settled the Frenchie's hash. Tunney said Carpentier's hardest blow had been a left to the head in the thirteenth round. The motion pictures did not reveal anything, Tunney's back having been to the camera.

Tunney's victory over Carpentier left only Tom Gibbons in his path to big casino, and the Greenwich Village favorite demanded that his manager get him the fight. Dempsey was vacationing in Europe at the time, cheerily responding to the "Hoch! Hoch! Hoch!" of adulatory Germans. He explained that he was engaging in a week-long series of four-round bouts with Germany's best heavyweights because he needed the money to pay for the dresses his wife had bought in Paris. Estelle also bought a dog collar with bells.

On hearing of the upcoming Tunney-Gibbons encounter, the papers predicted that the winner would probably fight Dempsey. Dempsey sent a cable from Berlin corroborating this.

Tunney had studied Gibbons only half as long as he had studied Dempsey, but he felt he had worked out an effective battle plan. As a boxer, Gene would be expected to duel with the artistic Minnesotan at long range, accepting minor punishment in the early rounds but relying on his youth and stamina to change the pattern of the fight in the later ones. However, after a thorough analysis of Gibbons's strengths and weaknesses, Tunney decided he would press, crowd, rush, harry and tie up Gibbons, forcing him to fight in close, pummeling him hard and frequently. The object was to go Dempsey a step better and knock Gibbons out, something no fighter had accomplished. It was the style Dempsey should have followed at Shelby. Gibbons had shown he had enough experience and guile to weather a boxer's polite assault. Unexpected aggressiveness, Tunney felt, would carry the day.

At the opening bell Tunney marched into Gibbons, ignoring fists, and began pounding him around the body. He gave Gibbons little room to prance and flick out his snakelike left jab. Because Tunney kept on top of him except on those rare intervals when Gibbons was able to clinch, Gibbons's jab-hook combinations either carried no steam or wound around Tunney's back. The relatively small crowd—about forty thousand—was enchanted to see the metamorphosis in Gentleman Gene. Tunney battered, punished, slashed and bulldogged Gibbons for the first four rounds, and it was clear, from the way Tom staggered to his corner on shaky legs, that a knockout was imminent.

In the following rounds, Gibbons showed brief spurts of offensive activity, but mainly he backed away and covered up. In the ninth Tunney hit Gibbons low, was warned and apologized. He then ripped a vicious left hook to Gibbons's stomach and drove a right straight at Gibbons's heart. Gibbons recoiled and Tunney moved on top of him, attacking his face and head, striving for the knockout.

Gibbons gamely lasted the round, but his nose was bleeding, his left eye was puffed up, blood flowed from a cut above it and his body was bright red from the punches he had received. A combination of ring generalship and Tunney's becoming arm-weary enabled him to last through the tenth and eleventh. In the twelfth, after an exchange of jabs that allowed Tunney to time his final assault, Gene moved in, was short with a right cross to the jaw, then landed a left hook to the body that set Gibbons up for a crisp right uppercut. The Minnesotan went down, and the crowd rose and hollered its approval. At seven Gibbons was up, to be felled by a right to the jaw. This time he could not rise. One minute and twenty-three seconds of the round had passed.

In the hubbub of his dressing room Tunney was ecstatic over his accomplishment as he accepted congratulations and adulation from his supporters. No one—no newspaperman, no fan, no promoter—could fail to see what he had done. He had delivered a terrible beating to, and knocked out, a fighter who had given the invincible Dempsey a worrisome battle. "They've got to see I've improved," he boldly asserted. "Now I want Dempsey!" Most of his friends admired his gumption, because of course Gibbons was not Dempsey. The next day Tunney had lunch with Governor James Cox of Ohio, a staunch admirer, and spoke about his plans for cornering Dempsey. Then he repaired to the State Athletic Commission office in the Flatiron Building and posted a challenger's bond to fight the heavyweight champion.

Because of a brouhaha over Dempsey's failure to fight Harry Wills, the New York State Athletic Commission had revoked Dempsey's boxing license. Promoter Tex Rickard therefore chose Philadelphia as the site for the Tunney bout, the event to be held on September 23, 1926, in Sesquicentennial Stadium, a horseshoe-shaped structure large enough to contain the crowd he expected to collect.

Dempsey set up training quarters in Atlantic City; Tunney in Stroudsberg, Pennsylvania. In his spare time Dempsey played poker with the fourth estate; Tunney read Samuel Butler's *The Way of All Flesh*. Dempsey got a chuckle when he heard about it. Dempsey smashed his sparring partners to bits, while Tunney practiced particular punches and counterpunches. He had noticed that Dempsey could be hit with a right: Carpentier had managed it, and so had Firpo. Tunney set out to develop one of the most accurate and powerful straight rights in prizefighting. He realized that he had the reputation of being a weak hitter because of the care he was forced to lavish on his hands and knuckles. They were now impregnable, he felt, and the blow might come as something of a shock to the champion—a secret weapon, as it were.

All was not smiles in the Dempsey camp. Jack was finding it hard to round into shape after his long layoff, and Jack Kearns's process servers were everywhere. "These lawsuits, injunctions, restraining orders and attachments are annoying when they come at you from all sides," he complained. On another occasion he mentioned ruefully that every time he punched the heavy bag he expected one of Kearns's process servers to fall out. He had the distinct impression that his enemies were trying to *worry* him out of the title.

A new suit was instituted by Kearns for $250,000—in addition to the one pending for $333,333,333 as his share of Dempsey's earnings in various enterprises and ventures up to August 3, when their contract expired. Kearns sued him in New York and Pennsylvania for various monies, and Dempsey had to post a bond of $600,000 to enable him to leave the state of New Jersey. An attachment was obtained by Kearns in Philadelphia against Dempsey to compel him to make an accounting of all his earnings. Others beleaguered Dempsey with litigation. An injunction was issued in Indiana enjoining Dempsey from meeting any other boxer before he fought Wills. It was not recognized in Philadelphia, however.

Dempsey struck back. He charged that Kearns was an ex-convict and had defrauded him out of $500,000. Kearns countered by obtaining an attachment against Dempsey naming Rickard as garnishee and fixing bond at $600,000 to cover Dempsey's end of the fight receipts. Dempsey found the deluge of legal attacks bewildering. It affected his concentration on working himself into shape.

The crème de la crème of every field, from bankers and politicians to gamblers and pickpockets, planned to attend the fight. They included Samuel Vauclain, head of the Baldwin Locomotive Works, who spent $27,000 on tickets for distribution among the loyal officers of that industry; Charles M. Schwab of the Bethlehem Steel Co.; E. T. Stotesbury of J. P. Morgan and Co.; Percy Rockefeller, Vincent Astor, George M. Pynchon; Samuel T. Bodine, chairman of the board of the United Gas Improvement Co.; producer Morris Gest; Bobby Jones, the golf king, and George von Elm, his usurper; James M. Cox, Democratic nominee for president against Harding; three cabinet members, six governors and Mayors Walker, Hague and Kendrick. Private railroad cars disgorged such nabobs as Harry Payne Whitney, W. Averell Harriman, Vincent Astor and George H. Walker, donator of the Walker golf cup. The Victor Talking Machine Co. and the Parkard Motor Co. each ordered a block of one hundred seats. W. Harry Baker, secretary of the Republican State Committee, sat with Republican politicians. Joseph E. Widener, the horse-racing tycoon, would be there, and Robert E. Strawbridge, the polo player, bought a block of thirty seats for his polo-playing friends. Johnny Broderick, New York City police lieutenant, was engaged to keep bomb throwers away from the arena.

Others present were members of the diplomatic corps and military brass; Barney Oldfield and Peggy Hopkins Joyce; John McGraw, Wilbert Robinson and Jacob Ruppert, representing New York's powerful baseball clubs; the Roosevelts, Theodore, Kermit and Archie; Gertrude Ederle, who was escorted by Dudley Field Malone. Writers present, cussing the downpour that rendered their typing paper soggy, included Paul Gallico, James Dawson, Elmer Davis, Damon Runyon, John Kieran, W. O. McGeehan, Grantland Rice and Westbrook Pegler.

The city was jammed to the hilt. No taxis were to be had, restaurants were impossible to squeeze into, cots were set up in hotel ballrooms and visitors crowded the lobbies waiting for some lucky room occupant to drop dead so they could grab a place to sleep. Inevitably, crooks of all persuasions swarmed down on Philadelphia like locusts on Olan's rice fields. The city detective bureau issued ominous warnings: Don't leave articles of value in hotel rooms; check them at the hotel desk. Don't expose your money in public. Be careful in elevators. Don't carry your purse loosely on your arm. Don't leave valuables in your parked car. Don't make friends with strangers, male or female. Don't carry money in your hip pocket. However, the expected crime wave did not develop.

Not many fans took Tunney's chances seriously. The odds ranged from 5 to 1 to 3 to 2 on Dempsey, with little Tunney money in evidence. It was suspected, however, that Tunney backers were waiting to see if they could get better odds and would do their most serious plunging on the day of the fight. Dempsey backers were as optimistic as the champion. Ethel Barrymore stated that no one could beat the man she saw beat Firpo. Firpo, in South America, picked Dempsey. Jack Kearns was reported to have wagered fifty thousand dollars on Dempsey to win by a decision. From France, François Descamps telegraphed Dempsey, "Bonne chance, Jack." Jerry the Greek, whose preference always had the effect of pushing the odds up, came out for Dempsey. Bill Tate, a Dempsey sparring partner, predicted a Dempsey knockout unless Tunney stopped at a crucial point to read a stanza of Tennyson and Jack paused in his assault to listen to the strophes. The Thirtieth Corps Area of the U.S. Army telegraphed its support of Dempsey.

Tunney had a few adherents, many from the cognoscenti. Governor Pinchot picked him, as did Bernard Gimbel, the department-store executive who sometimes sparred with Gene. Bill Wandergrift, a star football player and boxer at Yale who had also sparred with Tunney, pronounced Tunney's left jab followed by a right cross deadly and predicted a Tunney decision. Abe Attell, prominent in the Black Sox scandal of 1919, picked Tunney. Arnold Rothstein, the noted New York gambling figure, picked Tunney. Harry Greb told all his friends to bet their shirts on Tunney. His buddies of the AEF were behind Gene to a man. King Leopold of Belgium, the former crown prince, rooted for Tunney. Benny Leonard had faith in Tunney. And Tunney picked himself: "The heavyweight championship is the target at which I have aimed the shafts of my ambitions for the last five years. I am glad to get the chance to win the championship, and I am going to make the best of my opportunity. . . . I want to thank the newspaper boys for their kindness to me and I want to thank all my friends who have helped me reach the threshold of the throne room."

The fight itself developed precisely as Tunney had stage-managed it in his mind and was therefore kind of anticlimactic. At the gong the two moved around each other discreetly, shooting out jabs that were short and feinting. Dempsey was short with a left hook. Tunney studied his man and awaited the next one. When it came he stepped in and lashed out with his secret punch, the hardest blow he ever threw. It struck Dempsey high on the cheek—lower and it might have knocked him down. Its effect was immediately apparent. Dempsey was staggered; his knees sagged. He fell forward into a desperate clinch and for most of the remainder of the round simply hung on to Tunney to allow himself time to recover. Aware that Dempsey was dazed and that his ability to hit accurately and hard was markedly reduced, Tunney pranced back to his corner at the gong and elatedly told his new manager, Billy Gibson, "I hit him hard enough to knock down a horse and my hand feels great. I know I've got the title. I know I've got it!" Gibson muttered something about watching out for Dempsey's left, wiped rain and sweat from Tunney's face and body and sent him forth again. For his part, Dempsey was aware he had been hit a surprisingly vicious blow, and he tried not to show that he was slightly groggy. Jerry the Greek administered smelling salts, but Dempsey felt the punch more in his legs than anywhere else. Round two was coming up and already he felt weary.

With Dempsey's effectiveness impaired, Tunney now began to tantalize him with jabs at the nose and the eyes at long range, slipping, blocking and moving out of reach of punches and occasionally shooting his straight right inside Dempsey's left hook. The champion looked slow and clumsy in the face of Tunney's superb boxing skill and his adroitness in firing straight punches to counter Dempsey's more circuitous ones. Occasionally Dempsey would rush pell-mell at the challenger, fling a desperate hook or two and retire to avoid Gene's incessant and troublesome jabs.

In the fourth round, on instructions from his corner, Dempsey sprang across the ring at the bell and surprised Gene with a left hook and a right hook to the head. Tunney was sent reeling back against the ropes, but he retreated to the center of the ring before Dempsey could pin him in a corner. The rain was now coming down harder, making splattering sounds on thousands of raincoats, droplets glinting brightly in the arc lights of the ring. Footing was becoming perilous for both the boxer and the slugger. Dempsey charged again, landing a long right to the jaw. But Tunney was full of tricks. Instead of backing off, he countered with a hard right to Dempsey's head and a right uppercut that stopped the champion in his tracks. Breathing hard but aware of what he must do, Dempsey lunged forward, wildly swinging, and nearly slipped to the canvas as Gene ducked out of the way. Now Jack began to bleed from a gash over his eye caused by repeated Tunney jabs. He seemed weary, and Gene pressed the attack, with Dempsey bobbing and blocking with his forearms.

Between rounds, Mickey Walker, Jack's good friend, was upset enough about the lacing Jack was taking to say to Kearns, who was sitting near him at ringside, "Doc, go up there and tell Wilson [Gus Wilson, Dempsey's new manager] that Jack has got to keep swinging that left hook. He's bound to land one of them." He found Dempsey's passivity disturbing. Kearns shook his head with a wry smile, so Walker marched to Dempsey's corner himself and talked with Wilson. The manager was too busy trying to restore circulation and strength to Dempsey's legs to pay much heed.

Tunney easily blunted Dempsey's brief flurry in the sixth, but in the seventh Dempsey began rushing again and butted Gene in the head, forming a long cut over the challenger's right eye. Dempsey fans roared approval. Undaunted, Tunney attacked the champion with accurate shots to the nose and eyes, forcing Dempsey to cover up. Before the eighth round started, a nervous Gus Wilson gave Dempsey a swig of something strong that he carried in a flask in his pocket. Dempsey grimaced and spat it out. By the tenth and final round the champion was covered with wounds, and no one in the vast crowd expected a spectacular reversal, though, to be sure, Dempsey was throwing as many desperate rabbit punches as was humanly possible against a stolidly upright opponent. He was warned, but he was not especially pleased at having the referee stick his nose in. When the bout was over, Dempsey clearly was a beaten fighter; his left eye was swollen shut, there was a cut over his right eye, his nose was bleeding, his face was bruised and he felt weary and sick to his stomach.

The police who swarmed into the ring at the final gong surrounded Tunney; it was clear to everyone who the champion was. Back in Dempsey's hotel room, after all had gone but Jerry the Greek, the ex-champion began to realize what he had lost, and wracking sobs shook his body. The next morning, however, he had recovered his spirits and was willing to talk to the press. Estelle came in the room, shattered that he had lost but putting a good face on it. "What happened, Ginsberg?" she asked, calling him by a pet name. "Honey," replied Dempsey with a rueful smile, "I just forgot to duck." A newspaperman overheard the remark and ran it in his column. For some mysterious psychological reason it endeared Dempsey to the American public as nothing ever had before. From that time forward he took on a heroic dimension.

Rickard was not too crazy about Kearns and his battery of lawyers, and he was fond of Dempsey. To thwart the manipulations of Dempsey's ex-manager, he drew out Dempsey's purse— $740,000—presented it to Dempsey and advised him to send it to his brother in California. This Dempsey did, and it was hidden away in a bank where Kearns would have a devil of a time trying to lay hands on it. It was the brightest spot in Dempsey's day.

For his part, Tunney was accorded a tumultuous welcome by Mayor Walker in New York City. Later he capitalized on his new fame by making vaudeville appearances and a Hollywood movie called *The Fighting Marine*. He lectured, at the request of William Lyon Phelps, on Shakespeare for the edification of a large group of Yale students. He visited Europe and had lengthy chats with George Bernard Shaw. Prizefighting was a rewarding business.

Rickard now began to cast about for a worthy challenger for Tunney. Several names suggested themselves: Jack Delaney, Jim Maloney, Jack Sharkey, Bud Gorman, the Basque Paolino Uzcudun, Paul Berlenbach, Harry Wills, the European heavyweight champion Harry Persson. None of the names sent Rickard into fits of ecstasy as a gate attraction. Of course there was always the dark-visaged fellow from whose head Tunney had whisked the crown. Dempsey indicated he was willing to make a comeback if the price was right, and Tunney said he didn't care whom he fought, so long as the opponent would pull in the fans. Jack Sharkey of Boston, known as "the Garrulous Gob," had been enjoying a lively streak and seemed to be a natural for a bout with Dempsey, the winner to get a crack at Tunney. Sharkey's reputation would be enhanced by a victory over Dempsey, and Dempsey's stock would rise if he should whip the ex-sailor. The arrangements were made.

Dempsey went into training in Saratoga under the tutelage of his new manager, Leo P. Flynn, who insisted on altering the fighter's style. Instead of crouching and weaving, Dempsey was metamorphosed into a stand-up fighter and practiced blocking left jabs and hooks, Sharkey specialties. To reporters Jack looked uncomfortable and awkward, but he meekly acceded to Flynn's edicts as though convinced he had been doing something wrong all these years. Sharkey, on the other hand, training on the skating rink atop Madison Square Garden on Forty-ninth Street, paid little heed to the advices of his manager, Johnny Buckley.

Shortly before the bout, Flynn requested that the State Boxing Commission order both fighters to have painted on their waists a black line that would show clearly if a punch was above or below the belt. The inference was that Sharkey, if he should find himself in desperate straits, would go down claiming to have been fouled. He had already won three fights in this manner, though few doubted that he actually *was* fouled. Flynn's request was turned down.

Sharkey, who liked to clown about in the ring, sometimes imitating a medal-laden Irish jigger, was extremely confident. Born Josef Zukauskas of Lithuanian parents, he had boxed in the Navy and had been a professional for three years. He picked the name Sharkey from Sailor Tom and the name Jack from Jack Dempsey, his idol as a young man, whose style he used to emulate in front of a mirror. In the past year he had defeated Mike McTigue, Jim Maloney, Harry Wills and Homer Smith. He was fast on his feet and had an extremely rapid, powerful left jab. "Dempsey is a dynamo that has burned out," he stated for the press.

His words seemed to be borne out when the two met on July 22, 1927, at Yankee Stadium in a fight that provoked more controversy than any previous fight. Dempsey, still harried by Kearns and newly by Ted Hayes, his former confidant and secretary, was not in the best of shape, and his new, classic stand-up style was made to order for Sharkey. The latter landed so hard and so frequently that his confidence burgeoned, and he strove mightily for a quick knockout. This would have been suicide against the Dempsey of 1922, but little damage was inflicted on Sharkey in the early rounds. Dempsey, on the other hand, was cut and jarred and smashed in the jaw so frequently that spectators wondered how he managed to stay upright. Once in a while Dempsey would make an awkward, floundering lunge, which Sharkey easily avoided. Dempsey's nose was bleeding, one eye was closed and the weariness in his legs was apparent even to witnesses in the bleachers. If Dempsey had a strategy it seemed to be to take everything Sharkey could dish out and then, hopeful that Sharkey would grow tired, launch a counterattack. It was the Jeffries strategy as promulgated by Tommy Ryan, but it did not seem to be working for Dempsey, who was eight years older than his opponent.

At the end of the sixth Dempsey recovered enough to hit Sharkey twice in the face. The bell had already rung, ending the round, and Sharkey angrily retaliated with a right to the face. He was soundly booed for his lack of sportsmanship. Then in the seventh, with Sharkey battering the ex-champion all over the ring, Dempsey fell into a desperate clinch. Sharkey immobilized his left arm, but Dempsey's right arm was free and he swung mighty blows at Sharkey's body. Sharkey, his face a little green, released the arm, stepped back and turned to the referee, making

a loud protest about Dempsey's marksmanship and indicating where the blows had landed. So Dempsey stepped forward and threw his hardest left hook at Sharkey's unprotected jaw. Sharkey sank to the canvas. Part of the crowd was screaming "Foul! Foul!" and part of it was castigating the writhing Sharkey as a quitter. Dempsey moved to a neutral corner and watched while the referee counted out his glassy-eyed opponent. Apoplectic Johnny Buckley, having seen victory snatched from his fighter, rushed to the referee and screamed that Sharkey should have won on a foul. The referee shrugged. He had seen some body blows, but they were not below the belt. Sharkey, shaking his head, was led away to his dressing room in obvious distress.

Joe Humphries, the fight announcer, over waves of roaring, booing and individual shouts of disapproval from the aroused crowd, cried out: "Time: Forty-five seconds of the seventh round. The winner: Dempsey by a knockout."

The last bit of information helped straighten things out for those spectators who thought Sharkey was to be awarded the decision on a foul.

In the dressing room Sharkey and his manager loudly proclaimed that he had been hit below the belt. In *his* locker room an overjoyed if thoroughly battered Dempsey was receiving the congratulations of his friends, basking in the adulation that derives from an unexpected knockout and answering questions about the alleged low blow. What he might have replied was, "Aah, the Goddam Polack is a Goddam crybaby." But instead of that the press quoted him as saying, "The right-hand blows I drove home were fair and square to Sharkey's body."

The next day there was a semiofficial roll call on the alleged foul. These personages at the fight did not see a foul committed by Dempsey: Tex Rickard, Tommy Loughran, Jim Corbett, Ed Sullivan of the *Graphic,* Westbrook Pegler of the Hearst press, Bob Edgren of the *Evening World,* Paul Gallico of the *Daily News,* Hype Igoe of the *Morning World* and a number of other sportswriters. Leo P. Flynn, Dempsey's manager, saw no foul.

These personages present *did* see one: Charles F. Mathison, one of the two boxing judges, Benny Leonard, James P. Dawson of *The New York Times*, W. O. McGeehan of the *Herald Tribune*, Damon Runyon of the N. Y. *American*, Bill Corum of the N.Y. *Journal*, Joe Williams of the *Telegram*, E. H. Gavreau of the *Graphic* and John Kieran of the *Times*. Johnny Buckley saw it clearly. Dawson of the *Times*, a long-time Dempsey adherent, saw not one but four low blows, all delivered from a tight clinch and in rapid succession. He claimed to have been in a perfect position to witness them. Sharkey, he said, had withstood three, but the fourth had so weakened him that he had begun his protest.

The following day Rickard and Buckley went to see movies of the fight. The camera had not been placed where it had a clear shot of the alleged foul or fouls. Rickard came away certain none had been committed, and Buckley was convinced that he saw his fighter illegally struck. Most fans at the fight who saw the films later found themselves supported in their original judgment—whichever way they had seen it at Yankee Stadium.

James A. Farley, chairman of the State Boxing Commission, had seen no foul and refused to alter the outcome of the bout. "If we made a habit of overruling the referee," he said, "we'd have two winners in every fight." Despite the malodorousness of the affair—*both* judges later said they had seen a foul— Rickard was satisfied. The gate was $1,083,529, a record for a nontitle bout. He had not lost his touch. And he had an opponent for Tunney in September.

The second Tunney-Dempsey fight, held at Soldier Field Stadium in Chicago on September 22, 1927, was the crowning achievement of Rickard's career, from the standpoint of gate receipts, international interest, money wagered, the paralysis of a city, the influx of the celebrated and the mighty as avid witnesses of the spectacle, the purses received by champion and challenger and the amount of excitement engendered. The crowd that assembled was the greatest ever to see a sports event up to that time. The radio hookup was the largest ever. And it also was the most controversial fight in all history.

Not everything went smoothly, of course. Some clergymen, among them the Reverend Elmer Williams, petitioned Federal court to have the fight stopped on the grounds that such exhibitions were vulgar and brutal. Judge George A. Carpenter (of Mann Act fame) threw the petition out of court. "If 150,000 people are coming to see it," said His Honor, "it can't be all that evil."

There was some heated discussion about the rules. While Dempsey trained hard at Lincoln Fields Racetrack outside of Chicago and Tunney at Lake Villa, the respective brain trusts met with the Illinois State Boxing Commission, and regulations were agreed on. A twenty-foot ring would be used (not one eighteen feet square as the Dempsey forces wished). Hands were to be taped in the locker rooms just prior to the bout, before an inspector from the commission and two representatives of the principal's opponent. Three handlers were allowed in each corner. Having memories of the Dempsey-Firpo fight in New York and the howls about that, the commission was insistent that the boxer who had floored his opponent move to a neutral corner. The count, both sides were warned, would not officially start until this stipulation had been observed. The decision would be rendered by the two judges; in case of disagreement the referee would decide.

A carnival spirit prevailed in Chicago. Crowds were so dense in the Loop that it was impossible to make any headway on the sidewalks. Hotel lobbies and rooms were jammed. Special trains rolled in from every large city in the country, with section after section added as the cars neared their destination. The Twentieth Century Limited Pullman Co. reported that for the first time in the railroad's existence, every private car in the service had been placed in rolling operation. Daredevils flew in by plane from Michigan and New York. Thomas Cook and Sons, the travel agents, chartered thirty planes to whisk fans in and out of Chicago. Hour after hour, celebrities detrained at the heavily thronged depot, from the Madison Square Garden Special, the Clicquot

Club Special, the Harris-Turner Special, the William Duffy Special. In attendance were Sam Rosoff, the subway builder; State Senator Abraham Greenberg; former and current boxers Jim Jeffries, Jim Corbett, Jack Johnson, Benny Leonard, Battling Nelson, Jack Sharkey, Packy McFarland, Tom Sharkey, Johnny Dundee and Paolino Uzcudun; Hollywood folk Rudolf Valentino and Mary Pickford; Harry N. Frazee, the theatrical magnate beloved by New Yorkers because when he had owned the Red Sox, he had peddled Babe Ruth to the Yankees; and Admiral Richard E. Byrd.

A few days before the fight, Dempsey unleashed a blockbuster that caused the heads of boxing fans to swim. In a copyrighted and syndicated "open letter" which local residents (and the Tunney camp) saw in the Chicago *Herald Examiner,* Dempsey reported that he had learned from someone in political power that the Tunney forces had planned to "steal" the title from him in Philadelphia. He intimated that the only way he could have avoided being disqualified for hitting below the belt would have been to hit Tunney on the top of the head. According to Dempsey, if both had been standing at the end of the bout, Tunney would have been awarded the decision. He accused Tunney of having had secret conferences with Abe Attell, and Attell of having seen Max "Boo Boo" Hoff, a Philadelphia beer baron who had a subtle hand in politics and the fight business. Further, he accused Tunney and Gibson of having seen Hoff on the day of the fight—after which the "wise money" people suddenly started placing bets on the challenger. He called Attell a "tool for the gambling clique." Specifically he accused Gibson of borrowing twenty thousand dollars from Hoff, and Tunney of promising Hoff 20 per cent of all his earnings as champion should he beat Dempsey. Gibson was reported to have needed twenty thousand dollars to put through a real estate deal in New York. "Can't we have a little explanation of this?" Dempsey's letter concluded wistfully. The country rocked with conjecture.

Dempsey likewise accused Jimmy Bronson, Tunney's chief second, of hav-ing inspired the charges hurled at him in 1919 of having been a slacker, "of picking me out of about 20,000,000 American men who were exempt from war duty and trying to wreck and ruin me in the public opinion." According to Dempsey, Bronson wanted to have his own fighter take on Carpentier and figured out this means of short-circuiting Dempsey's bid. (Bronson was innocent of the charge, incidentally.)

Bronson replied, "This is a pretty late date for Dempsey to prove that he was back in the shipyards during the war." Gibson countered with the irrelevancy that Dempsey had deliberately tried to foul Sharkey at Yankee Stadium and had sought to drag a red herring across the trail with all this talk about painting black lines on his body and that of his victim. Tunney wrote a brief formal reply which was reprinted on page one of most papers:

AN OPEN LETTER TO JACK DEMPSEY
My Dear Dempsey:
Your open letter to me has been brought to my attention.
My reaction is to ignore it and its evident trash completely.
However, I cannot resist saying that I consider it a cheap appeal for public sympathy.
Do you think this is sportsman-like?

Gene Tunney

Gene did not call Dempsey "mister" and he did not finish with a complimentary close. A cynic might reply, in answer to Tunney's query at the end: "Hell, no. Otherwise he wouldn't have done it."

Apart from throwing Tunney into a cold rage, the accusations made in Dempsey's letter were largely ignored. Proving any misfeasance or conspiracy a year later would have been difficult, and all authorities felt it advisable to pretend the letter had never been written. However, a closer watch was kept on the manipulations and machinations in Chicago.

The sinister Al Brown, sometimes known as Al Capone, made no secret of his wagering on Dempsey. Mayor Walker, from Paris, where he was studying French governmental systems, bet on Dempsey. Broadway figure Walter Kingsley supported Dempsey. Three miners from Scranton pooled their money and bet fifteen hundred dollars on Dempsey. Capetown, South Africa, rooted for Dempsey. "I'll flatten that bookworm," was Jack's prediction. It was the old Dempsey talking.

Arnold Rothstein, who had backed Tunney the year before, took all he could get on Tunney at six to five. The Marines in Shanghai were for Tunney. Friends of Tunney showed up from Shanghai and Mangalore, India, setting a record for distance traveled to see a heavyweight fight. The Earl of Clydesdale was strong for Tunney.

Eighty-two broadcasting stations were to carry the fight—a new record for any kind of event. Fans in the upper reaches carried binoculars, opera glasses and telescopes. Some even carried portable radios, unable to trust what their eyes might see at a distance of seven hundred feet.

On fight night, electricity was everywhere in the arena. Camera flashlights kept popping, and the knowledgeable jumped every time, thinking another gang war had commenced. Reporters, who had been jammed close together so that more seats would be available for paying customers, made angry analogies to sardines. Celebrities in all fields walked by unnoticed, so intent were the spectators on spotting the principals. Outside, expert engravers were posted at the turnstiles to check for counterfeit tickets. Burns Agency operatives were on hand to keep out crashers. A light drizzle fell. Nobody seemed to notice it. The gate was an all-time record of $2,658,660. The paying crowd was 104,943; when everyone in the arena was counted, there were over 140,000.

Finally Dempsey appeared, wearing a white sweater around his shoulders and black trunks. He looked tan, fit and confident. A huge cheer went up as he marched down the aisle. He had become beloved in defeat. The yells for Tunney, clad in his Marine robe, were less noisy. Fans had forgiven Dempsey for losing, but they had not forgiven Tunney for dethroning the champion.

In the ring, referee Dave Barry care-fully explained the neutral-corner rule to both fighters and their chief seconds. All four nodded understanding of it. Dempsey and Tunney both wanted to get the fight underway. Tunney, the open letter much on his mind, did not act very kindly toward the challenger.

The fighters started out cautiously, feinting, shuffling about, gauging distance by flicking out long jabs. In the second round Tunney jabbed hard at Dempsey's head as the latter tried to close in. His jabs carried a lot of power; one might say they were vindictive. In the third round Dempsey, accepting a beating around his eyes and nose, got in a good hard right to the side of Tunney's head which rocked the champion back a step. Tunney was all aggression in the fourth, moving around Dempsey swiftly and scoring with jabs and straight rights. Dempsey nearly went down when struck by a left hook to the body. In the fifth, radio announcer Graham McNamee said that Tunney was out-Dempseying Dempsey—that is, aggressively rushing and throwing hard blows. Dempsey landed a hard right to the head and followed with a left to the body. Was it low? Tunney remonstrated to the referee. In the sixth Dempsey, his nose stung by smelling salts, sprang out and accepted a series of jabs to land his hooks. He threw a series of fast punches, most of which Gene caught on his elbow. "Some of the blows Dempsey hits," said McNamee to his millions of listeners, "make this ring tremble and the microphone down below it."

Then, in the seventh, came history's most debated decision. Gene threw a straight right at Dempsey's chin and kept his left in Dempsey's face. As though annoyed beyond patience by this treatment, Dempsey charged fiercely at Tunney and slammed home a left to the jaw. Tunney went backward and down. He lay awkwardly against the ropes, supporting himself on the middle strand. Dempsey moved to his own corner—not the farthest neutral corner—and tried to circle around behind Gene so he could clobber him when he got up. Referee Barry, however, did not start the count but ordered Dempsey to a neutral corner. "I stay here," Dempsey growled, forgetting previous instructions in his desire to crush Tunney to the canvas if he should rise. Barry said he would not start the count till Dempsey moved. Gene Normile, Jack's business manager, and Dempsey's seconds screamed at him to go to the neutral corner. Finally he complied, and Barry —after some five seconds had passed —started the count at "one." Tunney's eyes, at first glazed, began to clear, and he appeared to be recuperating rapidly, the strength returning to his legs. At the count of eight he was ready to rise, and at nine he was up. "My God!" exclaimed Battling Nelson from the press section, where he had held a stopwatch on Gene, "He was down for sixteen seconds!"

While waiting for the count of nine, Gene's mind had been racing. He had three choices after rising. He could try to clinch; he could try to surprise Dempsey with a sneak punch; or he could retreat. If he clinched, Dempsey might land some devastating body blows. If he tried to counterattack, Dempsey might land the harder blows. Clearly the thing to do was to run. It was something Tunney had prepared for in training—running miles and miles backwards for just such a contingency. He found his legs were sound and, as they say, got on his bicycle. Dempsey pursued, frustrated and overanxious. His own legs could not propel him that fast, and he was the picture of dejection as Tunney, wraithlike, skipped out of his path. Tunney began to attack with jabs as his strength and coordination returned. Dempsey accepted most of the blows, intent on landing the finisher. Then Tunney paused to throw a hard right at Jack's mouth before resuming his retreat. So disgusted did Dempsey become at Tunney's eminently sensible tactics that at one point he stood in the middle of the ring and beckoned Tunney to stop running and fight. Tunney did not pick up the gauntlet. He appeared to have recovered completely, so

Jack Dempsey meets Gene Tunney, facing camera, in their second battle in Chicago. It dwarfed all others for drama, controversy, and size of gate receipts.

finely was he conditioned, at the bell.

From that point on, as the chronicles record, it was all downhill for Dempsey. Tunney was the aggressor in the eighth, ninth and tenth rounds, flooring Dempsey in the eighth and landing when he pleased in the last two rounds. Dempsey was woefully weary at the end of the fight. Both eyes were cut, there was a dark, bluish lump under his right eye, his left ear was cut and swollen and he was bleeding around the mouth. Tunney was comparatively unmarked, though his cheek bore a red splotch where Dempsey's hook had tagged it.

In Dempsey's dressing room the challenger, all aches, was commiserated with to the counterpoint of Leo P. Flynn raging and shouting that he would protest the decision because of the length of time Gene had been on the floor. All was jubilation in Gene's quarters. He was asked the inevitable question and replied that he could have gotten up at the count of nine—though some reporters doubted it. (Seeing the films in Ireland, George Bernard Shaw was sure he could have.) But if he could have gotten up, would he have been able to backpedal as efficiently? Tunney shrugged. One thing was clear to all: Dempsey had no one but himself to blame. The rules had been explained to him several times—but instinct overpowered judgment. Tunney had to be given credit for making the best of a disastrous situation; it was an example of superb ring generalship and the power of the will. He had planned for the emergency and stayed cool throughout, unruffled by taunts from the crowd or Dempsey's pawing gesture for him to come on and fight. "It was what Dempsey would have done," Paul Gallico wrote later.

True to his word, the following day Flynn submitted a formal protest and notice of appeal to the State Athletic Commission. It was summarily rejected. "We have never reversed a decision," Chairman John Righeimer asserted. In New York, Commissioner James A. Farley maintained the situation never could have come up in New York State: After backing the standing fighter away to a neutral corner, the referee there would have picked up the count from the timekeeper. Asked a couple of days later if he could have gotten up within ten seconds, Tunney replied, "It was a new experience for me, being on the floor. But I was in possession of my faculties all the time. I felt myself hit the floor and whether it was that fall or not, I was counting with the referee all the way."

Tunney felt that an injustice would have been done had the commission reversed the decision. He maintained he had been fouled three times in the third round by low blows, and he showed reporters the black-and-blue spot five inches in diameter, five inches below the groin—eight inches below the belt—inflicted by Dempsey's punches. He also said that Dempsey had clubbed him over the back of the head countless times with illegal rabbit punches.

For his pains Tunney received a little over $990,000, the highest sum ever paid a fighter, and Dempsey received $425,000, the highest ever paid a challenger. In a fit of whimsy, when Gene went to collect the money in Rickard's office, he gave Rickard a check for a little under $10,000 so that he could hold a check for one million dollars in his hand. He had a photostat of the check framed and hung it on a wall of the garage at his home in Connecticut.

The long-count argument was the main topic of conversation for weeks, and the consensus was that Dempsey actually had won the fight. The fight was so exciting that five fans died listening to the seventh round, while five more died at other times during the fight. Estelle Taylor Dempsey locked herself in the bathroom of her Edgewater Hotel suite and refused to come out till the fight was over. A man in Dubuque paid off his bet to a Dempsey supporter, saying that Tunney had been down for fourteen seconds.

Tunney departed for Cleveland with Eddie Egan, a Rhodes Scholar and amateur boxer, then relaxed among the greenery of the Maine woods. Then he went to Europe to chat with the Prince of Wales and his old friend Shaw. Curiously, Shaw discussed Shakespeare and Tunney discussed boxing.

Nearly a year had passed since Tunney had defended his title against Dempsey. He was now independently wealthy, a country squire, the boon companion of literary, musical and artistic people, on a first-name basis with the great and near-great in two dozen fields of endeavor, admired and respected by all. He had made wholesomeness fashionable. Rickard fretted. Dempsey did not want to fight Tunney again—he was worried about the battering his eyes might take—and Rickard wanted to make a payday for his Madison Square Garden Corporation and keep the public's interest in heavyweights whetted. Who could furnish opposition? Tom Heeney of New Zealand had beaten Risko and knocked out Maloney in half a round. He had fought a draw with Jack Sharkey. It was a choice between Heeney and Sharkey. Rickard the showman preferred Sharkey. Tunney preferred Heeney, and that settled it.

Heeney was a dogged, plodding fighter whose main attribute was his ability to absorb large amounts of punishment. Called "the Hard Rock from Down Under," he lived up to his name against Tunney. In a one-sided bout fought at the Polo Grounds on July 26, 1928, Tunney demonstrated that he could be aggressive if he wished and could throw a series of hard punches when he put his mind to it. Heeney was battered all around the ring and bled over Tunney and referee Eddie Forbes before the bout was finally stopped by Forbes in the eleventh round, after it was clear that both Heeney and Tunney had had enough. The Madison Square Garden Corporation lost two hundred thousand dollars. Rickard's instinct had been correct.

Shortly afterward Tunney announced his retirement from the ring, and an elimination tournament was begun to find a successor. Wise enough to quit at his peak as a fighter, Tunney married Polly Lauder, an heiress related to the Carnegies and a member of the Social Register. Wed in Rome, they honeymooned in Europe. The former champion was immensely popular wherever he went. Back in America he became a director of several companies, showing a remarkable acumen for business. He wrote his memoirs and raised a family; his son John was elected a Congressman from California. His old foe Dempsey, involved in several business enterprises, including a popular restaurant in New York, campaigned for young Tunney. During World War II both made valuable contributions to the Armed Forces. Commander Tunney had charge of the Navy's physical fitness program, and Lt. Commander Dempsey instructed in athletics in the Coast Guard. Dempsey captured a Japanese soldier on Iwo Jima—a feat he does not take too seriously.

They will mainly be remembered, though, for their fights in the ring—Dempsey against Willard, Firpo, Carpentier and Sharkey; Tunney against Carpentier, Gibbons and Greb. And mainly, of course, for the two classic bouts they fought against each other; bouts that raised American sports fans to a peak of excitement that will probably never be equaled.

The two left the sport when boxing was at its zenith. Rickard had made attendance at fights respectable and had infused the sport with a sense of drama that a large part of the public found irresistible. He captured the public's imagination by building huge stadiums for the spectacles. He obtained large purses for the fighters, elevating their status as athletes and attracting strong young men into the profession. In his efforts Rickard had the tacit help of those fighters who had fought for small rewards in ruder times, yet had showed that courage is not limited to the battlefield—fighters such as Mendoza, Tom Hyer, Jem Mace, Jake Kilrain, Tom Cribb, Peter Jackson, Tom Molineaux and many others. And he had, in addition, the public's memory of the charisma of such heavyweights as Corbett, Jeffries, Johnson, Sullivan and Fitzsimmons. The accounts of the great triumphs and noble defeats of all of these, recorded in print, in sound, in art, in verse, by the still camera, the kinetoscope and the modern motion-picture camera, furnish the sports fan with a vivid picture of athletes who, in their own time and after, seemed larger than life. ■

Gene Tunney brought a new look to boxing. The passage of the crown to Tunney reflects a turning point in American culture. Dempsey's determination and brute force were frontier virtues. Tunney was a disciplined student whose aspirations went beyond the ring.

Harry Greb, on the left, beat Tunney in 1922. This loss spurred Tunney to analyze his mistakes and become a consummate craftsman in the ring.

Tunney beat Georges Carpentier, the courageous Frenchman, in 1924. It was an important step on Tunney's road toward his meeting with Dempsey.

In 1925 Tunney knocked out Tommy Gibbons, another boxer whom Dempsey had faced. This defeat, and Tunney's skilled defense and big punch, proved to skeptics that Tunney was a fighter who could put a man away.

Controversy is the lot of contenders, and Tunney was no exception. His match with Carpentier resulted in a claim of foul from the Frenchman's corner. This sequence from the film The Legendary Champions *shows Carpentier as he is hit and goes down.*

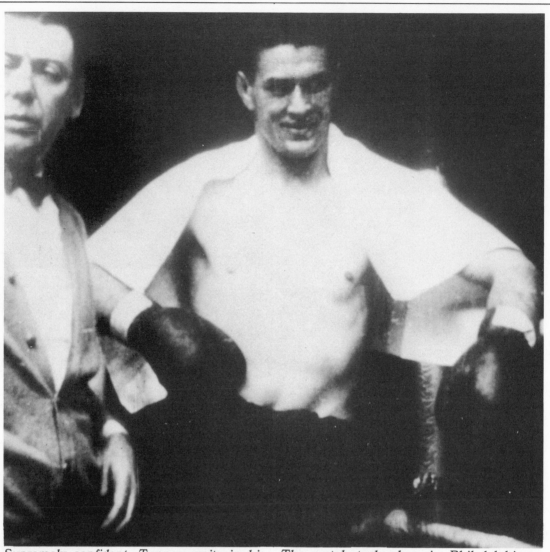

Supremely confident, Tunney waits in his corner to face Dempsey for the first time.

The match took place in Philadelphia on September 23, 1926.

The climactic moment in Tunney's career. He is cautious, mindful of Dempsey's reputation. Distance and speed are the rules he

has drilled into himself. Careful study of Dempsey pays off handsomely, and Tunney's swift lefts find their mark.

Dempsey, who hadn't defended since 1923, shows his years of inactivity. What his brain knows his body cannot deliver. Tun- ney shrewdly exploits this. Below, Demp- sey watches as Tunney's arm is raised in the gesture of triumph.

Boxing gained a new image. Discipline and constant study were the elements of Tun-ney's talent. Strength of mind became as important as strength of body.

With Tunney, boxing gained a new kind of social acceptance. Above, the fighter meets the celebrated author George Bernard Shaw.

Gene Tunney is given a hero's welcome by New Yorkers as he rides slowly down Broadway in the city's grand gesture of welcome, a ticker-tape parade.

A native New Yorker receives the highest honor: the key to the city. Mayor Jimmy Walker, right foreground, pays homage to the new champion.

Dempsey and Tunney met again on September 22, 1927, in Chicago, before the largest crowd ever to watch a sports event to that time. In Round 7, center, Dempsey connects with a left and Tunney falls. Bottom, a superimposed clock shows the seconds to elapse.

In the upper frame, Tunney is prostrate on the canvas as one second ticks off. In the middle frame, Dempsey wants to move in for the kill. But in the bottom frame, Referee Dave Barry points to a neutral corner. Only three seconds have elapsed.

Finally, four seconds after Tunney has gone down, Dempsey heeds the referee and moves off. At the fifth second (middle frame) Barry begins the count. In the bottom frame, with nine seconds showing on the clock, Tunney still appears to be dazed.

As the clock in the top frame shows, fourteen seconds have elapsed. Only then does Gene Tunney begin to rise from the canvas. In the middle frame, the referee motions to Dempsey to leave the neutral corner, and finally, bottom, they resume fighting.

INDEX

Numbers in italics refer to pages on which illustrations occur.